Inequality
and Heterogeneity

PETER M. BLAU received his A.B. from Elmhurst College and his Ph.D. from Columbia University. He taught at the University of Chicago before moving to his present position as Quetelet Professor of Sociology at Columbia. This is Blau's tenth book; he is the author of *The Dynamics of Bureaucracy* and *Exchange and Power in Social Life;* the co-author of *The American Occupational Structure* and *The Structure of Organization;* and the editor of *Approaches to the Study of Social Structure.*

Inequality
and Heterogeneity

A PRIMITIVE THEORY OF SOCIAL STRUCTURE

Peter M. Blau

THE FREE PRESS
A Division of Macmillan Publishing Co., Inc.
NEW YORK

Collier Macmillan Publishers
LONDON

The Free Press
A Division of Macmillan Publishing Co., Inc.,
866 Third Avenue, New York, N.Y. 10022

Collier Macmillan Canada, Ltd.

Library of Congress Catalog Card Number: 77-70272

Printed in the United States of America

printing number

1 2 3 4 5 6 7 8 9 10

Library of Congress Cataloging in Publication Data

Blau, Peter Michael.
    Inequality and heterogeneity.

    Bibliography: p.
    Includes index.
    1. Social structure.   2. Social status.
3. Social interaction. I. Title.
HM131.B5916   301.4   77-70272
ISBN 0-02-903660-7

TO THE MEMORY OF

PETER MICHAEL LEHMANN

1949–1976

Contents

vii

Preface

A MACROSOCIOLOGICAL THEORY OF SOCIAL STRUCTURE IS DEVELOPED IN this book. Its foundation is a quantitative conception of social structure in terms of the distributions of people among social positions that affect their social relations. Simmel's insights about the significance of numbers for social life, which have been used largely in studies of small groups, are applied to the analysis of entire societies. The concept of social structure is construed narrowly, stripped of its broader cultural and functional connotations to its core properties, its primitive meaning. Whatever else the term as used by various social theorists may encompass, social structure nearly always includes social positions, patterns of social relations, and a nexus between the positions of people and their social relations. Social structure is conceptualized in terms of these elemental properties: different social positions, the numbers of their incumbents, and the implications of differentiation among positions for social relations.

Of major substantive concern are the influences of social differentiation on social integration. Social differentiation is defined by the distributions of a population among social positions. Inequality and heterogeneity are the two generic forms differentiation assumes, depending on whether the positions among which people are distributed constitute a rank order, as socioeconomic status and power do, or are unordered categories, like religion and sex. A fundamental characteristic of social structures is the degree to which various forms of inequality and heterogeneity intersect or the extent to which social differences along various lines are correlated. Variations in this structural condition govern largely the strength of the integration of the different segments of society.

The endeavor is to construct a deductive theory of social structure. Theorems are deduced, directly or indirectly, from two kinds of primitive proposition: analytic propositions that define structural properties, such as inequality or penetrating differentiation; and synthetic propositions assumed to be true on logical or empirical grounds, for example, that social associations depend on opportunities for contact. Some theorems are tautological, entailed by the definition of terms, but others deducible from them are neither tautological nor obvious. Although empirical findings are often cited that support, and sometimes qualify, the theoretical implications drawn, only future research that fails to falsify its predictions can corroborate the theory and establish the pragmatic utility of the conceptual scheme on which it rests.

The nature of a social theory depends not only on the axioms explicitly introduced to deduce theorems but also on the theorist's view of the social world—on what Gouldner (1970) calls domain assumptions, which direct attention selectively to some problems of inquiry and not to others. Let me mention some domain assumptions underlying my theoretical orientations, though there may be others of which I am unaware. I am a structural determinist, who believes that the structures of objective social positions among which people are distributed exert more fundamental influences on social life than do cultural values and norms, including ultimately the prevailing values and norms. As a social theorist, my primary interest is in the formal, quantitative properties of social structure, notably those indicated by differences in size and size distributions. This interest is reflected in the deductive theory presented, and it has characterized my previous research on organizations and the theory inductively built on the basis of its findings. The greater significance of some kinds of position than of others tends to be ignored by this focus on the frequency distributions among positions, whatever their substantive content. Since I consider the division of labor and inequality in power of distinctive significance, however, I have singled them out for special attention. I also believe that the integration of various segments of society depends on actual associations among their members, on social intercourse between persons in different groups and hierarchical strata, not merely on common values or functional interdependence. Strong ingroup bonds do not appeal to me personally, inasmuch as I think of them as expressions of ethnocentrism, which may have colored my judgment that they are detrimental for the integration of large and complex societies, which depends on extensive intergroup relations. Finally, my bias with respect to the two generic forms of differentiation is that there is too much inequality but that there cannot be too much heterogeneity.

I am indebted to the Netherlands Institute for Advanced Studies for giving me an opportunity to write this book by inviting me to be a fellow in 1975–76, and to its staff and the other fellows in that year for making the time spent among them in Wassenaar so pleasant and intellectually rewarding. Although the present theory is not based on my research on organizations during the preceding twelve years, this research has greatly influenced my thinking and indirectly contributed to the theory, and its support by the National Science Foundation is gratefully acknowledged. I have greatly benefited from the advice on statistical and other problems generously furnished by J. P. van de Geer, Mark Granovetter, John L. Hammond, Herbert A. Simon, Arthur L. Stinchcombe, and Werner H. Tack. My inadequate mathematical knowledge undoubtedly prevented me from taking as much advantage of their counsel as it deserved. I am deeply grateful to several colleagues and graduate students for reading the entire manuscript and making many helpful criticisms and suggestions: Judith R. Blau, Ralph Bulle, Herbert Gans, Bruce Mayhew, and Hilary Silver. I am also obliged to Charles E. Smith for his aid in preparing the manuscript. My bibliographical research was greatly facilitated by the innumerable references to research findings on 25,000 propositions in William J. Goode et al., *Social Systems and Family Patterns: A Propositional Inventory* (1971). Finally, I am thankful for the bibliographical and typing assistance rendered by Sean Courtney, Katherine Murphy, and Cassandra Trimble.

CHAPTER ONE

Structures of
Social Association

THE FUNDAMENTAL FACT OF SOCIAL LIFE IS PRECISELY THAT IT IS social—that human beings do not live in isolation but associate with other human beings. The associations of people—their recurrent social interaction and communication—exhibit regularities that differentiate their role relations and social positions. Frequent and intimate social contacts, for example, establish close social relations between persons; the tendency of one person to defer to another establishes a superordinate-subordinate role relation. Social positions can be distinguished on the basis of the prevailing associations and role relations of their incumbents. To state that people belong to different groups or that they differ in status implicitly asserts that they have distinctive patterns of role relations and social associations.

The study of social structure, as conceived in this book, centers attention on the distribution of people among different positions and their social associations. People occupy different positions either because they are members of different groups or because they differ in hierarchical status. The distinct social positions themselves as well as the relations among them are manifest in observable patterns of social associations. The concept of social structure is an abstraction from these observable patterns, which are the empirical foundation of the abstracted structures of differentiated social positions and role relations.

Structure and Process

A structure is usually defined in dictionaries as something made up of more or less interdependent elements or parts. According to this definition,

1

a social structure comprises different parts (not a homogeneous mass of individuals) and the parts are interrelated (not a disconnected aggregate). There is no general agreement among social theorists, however, on how to conceptualize the component parts of social structure and their relations. One fundamental difference is whether the concept of structure refers to a structure of *social* relations among subunits in a society or a structure of *logical* relations of propositions in a theoretical model. Radcliffe-Brown (1940) and Lévi-Strauss (1963) represent these contrasting conceptualizations of social structure.[1] In the latter view, social structure refers to a theoretical system constructed by the analyst to explain social reality—to a deep structure, in Lévi-Strauss's terms, that explains the superstructure, in Marx's. It does not refer to certain aspects of social reality, as Lévi-Strauss (1963, p. 279) emphasizes: "The term social structure has nothing to do with empirical reality but with models built after it."

The alternative view, adopted here, is that social structures are observable aspects of social life, not theories about it. To be sure, social structures are not empirical phenomena in the raw but abstractions from them in terms of a conceptual scheme. However, the structures of social positions and role relations abstracted from observable social associations are not a theory that explains these associations; they are merely a basis for building such a theory. Lévi-Strauss fails to make explicit this distinction between the concepts used in a theory of social structure and the propositions in which they are used and which constitute the theory.

Another important distinction between conceptions of social structure is in their substantive focus: whether the primary concern is the microsociological analysis of interpersonal relations in groups or the macrosociological analysis of the relations among various parts of society (Laumann 1973). Microsociological theory seeks to explain human relations in terms of the psychological and social processes underlying them, such as processes of symbolic communication, of competition and cooperation, of social exchange. Its focus is on the social processes that shape the interpersonal relations of individuals in a social structure, which is conceptualized as a configuration or network of social relations among individuals. Homans's (1961) exchange theory illustrates one version of this approach; Merton's (1968, 1972) analysis of status sets and role sets another; graph theory (Harary et al. 1965) and network analysis (Barnes 1954; Mitchell 1969) still others. Macrosociological theory, on the other hand, seeks to explain the relations among various parts of entire societies in terms of the differentiation of these parts. Its focus is on differentiation and its implications for the interrelations of parts in a social structure, which is conceptualized in terms of differentiation. The substantive content of macrosociological theories de-

---

1. For a discussion of the two contrasting views of social structure, see Nadel (1957, pp. 149–51), Boudon (1971), and Lévi-Strauss (1963, pp. 299–309) himself.

pends on how society's parts and their interrelations are defined. In Parsons's scheme, the parts are institutional systems, and they are functionally interdependent. In Marx's scheme, the parts are social classes, and they are in conflict.

The microsociological and the macrosociological approaches to the study of social structure are complementary, not contradictory. The difference is one of perspective, and both are valid. Only theories that focus on the same problems have contradictory implications that can be investigated to furnish empirical grounds for rejecting one theory in favor of another. A choice between perspectives can only be made on pragmatic grounds: which one is more useful for clarifying given problems. The microsociological perspective gives priority to the analysis of human relations in depth on the basis of the underlying sociopsychological and interaction processes, which restricts the range of vision to interpersonal relations and their configurations in fairly small groups. The macrosociological perspective gives priority to the analysis of patterns of social relations in entire societies, sacrificing depth for a wider scope. There is more emphasis on social processes and their influences on social relations in microsociological studies (for example, social relations within families), more on social structures and their effects on social relations in macrosociological inquiries (for example, relations between social classes).

The approach in this book is macrosociological. The component parts of social structure are conceptualized as groups or classes of people, such as men and women, ethnic groups, or socioeconomic strata. More precisely, the parts are the positions of people in different groups or strata. The interrelations among the parts are the social relations of people that find expression in their social interaction—specifically, the associations between persons who belong to different groups or strata. Thus, social structure refers to population distributions among social positions along various lines—positions that reflect and affect people's role relations and social associations.

To speak of social structure is to speak of social differentiation among people, for social structure, as conceptualized, is rooted in the social distinctions people make in their role relations and associations with one another. These social distinctions give rise to differences in roles and positions, which in turn influence subsequent social intercourse. What is meant here by social structures is simply the population distributions among these differentiated positions. Attention centers on the quantitative properties of social structure, indicated by the frequency distributions among social positions. Of course, persons occupy several social positions, not just one. They have occupations, belong to religious groups, live in communities, work in establishments, are more or less educated, and occupy a socioeconomic status. A population distribution exists for any of these types of position, and society's social structure comprises all of them. This is why Nadel (1957, p. 97), a pioneer in the structural approach adopted in this book, notes that "it seems impossible to speak of social structure in the singular." Even a simple tribe has at least an age structure, a kinship structure, an ecological structure, and a power structure, and the complex structures of industrial societies have many dimensions.

A social structure can be defined as a multidimensional space of different social positions among which a population is distributed. The social associations of people provide both the criterion for distinguishing social positions and the connections among them that make them elements of a single social structure. The defining criterion of a distinction in social positions is that the role relations among incumbents of the same position differ, on the average, from those between incumbents of different positions. For instance, the former may be more intimate, or the latter may involve more superordination and subordination. If no differences in social relations can be discovered, positions cannot be considered to be socially distinct. This is a very broad criterion, and a narrower one will be introduced later as a substantive assumption of the theory, namely, that the likelihood of face-to-face associations among incumbents of the same or proximate positions exceeds that between incumbents of distant positions.

Of central concern in the inquiry to be presented is the analysis of the various forms structural differentiation assumes, changes in them, and their implications for social associations. The focus is on structures of differentiated positions and their influences on the relations of human beings, not on the intensive analysis of the sociopsychological processes involved in human relations. But this does not mean that the significance of social processes for understanding social structures is ignored. Two social processes of great importance in the analysis are processes of social association and processes of social mobility; some others, such as processes of social exchange, will also be examined.

Structure and process are complementary. Processes of social interaction and communication reflect existing structures of differentiated social positions, and may well have generated these structures originally. The differentiation of role relations and social positions that emerges in processes of social interaction often becomes crystallized by having labels attached to the positions—working class, college educated, vegetarian. But people also discriminate in their social associations between positions that do not have explicit labels, for example, between persons in their fifties and those in their thirties, not only between "old" and "young." This original etiology in which processes of social associations produce differences in social positions can only be observed in newly formed groups, because once distinct social positions have become established they channel further role relations and associations. Appropriately, therefore, microsociological studies of interpersonal relations and small groups focus on the influences of social processes on the emergent differences in roles and positions, whereas macrosociological studies of established social positions in societies focus on the influences the structures of these positions exert on processes of associations.

Social structures consist of social positions that are not only differentiated but also interrelated, because unrelated positions do not compose a coherent social structure. One assumption, already noted, is that the face-to-face associations among persons in the same position exceed those between persons in different positions, reflecting the social distinctions among positions. Another assumption is that different groups and strata in a society are connected by some face-to-face associations between their members, since otherwise they can hardly be considered to constitute a single society. These intergroup relations, though less extensive than ingroup relations (according to the first assumption), are what interrelates and integrates the various parts of a social structure. To be sure, not all social associations are integrative. Social relations may entail domination, exploitation, and conflict, as well as reciprocal regard, mutual support, and cooperation. What is assumed is, not that any kind of social association is sufficient for integration, but that some kind of social association is necessary for integration. The assumption is that the integration of various groups and strata in society cannot rest solely on their functional interdependence; it requires some actual social interaction among their members.

Processes of social mobility are an essential element in most forms of structural change, whatever the conditions that precipitate the change. Social mobility is defined broadly to encompass all movements of persons between social positions, including not only occupational mobility and migration but also religious conversion, marriage, rising income, unemployment, and changes in political affiliation. Excess mobility in one direction alters the population's distribution among social positions and thereby changes the social structure. Other forms of structural change are also furthered by high rates of social mobility, as will be shown, and extensive mobility in opposite directions that does not alter the population distribution nevertheless contributes to social change.

Both processes of social association and processes of social mobility connect social positions by providing conduits of transmission among them, though the nature of the transmission is quite different. Social associations involve the transmission of messages which convey communications of various kinds, such as approval, information, advice, respect, demand, and disagreement. The communications in both directions may be equivalent, as in the mutual support peers supply each other, or different, as when a superior commands a subordinate's compliance. Social mobility involves the transfer of persons from one group or stratum to another. The extent of these transfers or movements may be the same in both directions, which leaves the population distribution the same, or different, which changes that distribution. Extensive social mobility as well as extensive social associations strengthen intergroup relations, and equivalent transfers of either kind do so particularly. Mutual exchanges in social associations cement intergroup relations, and so does exchange mobility, that is, the exchange of persons in both directions between two groups, whether through marriage, migration, or other kinds of moves.

Parameters

A social structure is delineated by its parameters. Structural parameters are the axes in the multidimensional space of social positions in terms of which social structures have been defined. They are the criteria implicit in the social distinctions people make in their associations with one another. Age, race, education, and socioeconomic status illustrate structural parameters, on the assumption that differences in these respects affect people's role relations. In other words, parameters are attributes of people that influence their role relations and thereby differentiate their social positions. Whether an attribute is inborn, like sex, or acquired, like occupation, what is crucial is that it has a discernible effect on social associations. If no such effect can be discovered for an attribute, the initial assumption that it has relevance for social life must be rejected, and the attribute cannot be considered to be a structural parameter in the society under consideration. Even if the attribute refers to a biological or psychological trait that seems very conspicuous and that influences social life in other societies, it apparently does not do so in this one (though this conclusion may later have to be retracted if some such influences, initially overlooked, are subsequently discovered). Thus, the assumption that an attribute is a structural parameter and serves as a base for making social distinctions is subject to empirical testing. The finding that a certain attribute influences social relations in some societies and not in others is of course of substantive interest.

Two kinds of variable that can be derived from parameters must be distinguished. First, the attributes to which parameters refer are variables that characterize individuals, such as their occupation, religion, income, and wealth. These attributes and their influences on human conduct are not of direct concern in structural analysis. Second, the distributions of these attributes yield new variables that characterize the social structure, for example, the shape of the occupational distribution and of the income distribution in society. Structural analysis centers attention on these variables characterizing structural conditions and on their influences on social associations. Thus, concern is not with the implications of occupational performance but with those of the division of labor; not with the significance of religious dogmas but with that of religious heterogeneity; not with the consequences of poverty and wealth but with those of income inequality and the concentration of wealth.

The most distinctive task of sociology is the structural analysis of various forms of differentiation, their interrelations, the conditions producing them and changes in them, and their implications for social relations. Of course, structural conditions are not the only factors that influence human conduct and relations. Psychological, economic, ideological, biological, and physical conditions do so as well. Whether two persons establish a social relation, for instance, depends on their psychological preferences and dispositions as well as on structural conditions that provide them with opportunities for social intercourse. But this does not mean that the influences of structural conditions on social associations are contingent on the influences of psychological factors and that sociological theories dealing with structural influences rest ultimately on psychological assumptions, as Homans (1961) claims. Deterministic theorems about intergroup relations can be derived from purely structural assumptions, without any psychological assumptions, or in conjunction with psychological assumptions that alone imply the very opposite, as will be seen. To be sure, these theorems are deterministic only for groups, not for individuals, for whom they are only probabilistic. They state that the rate of intergroup relations is higher for group A than for group B, which makes it more probable that A members than that B members have such relations, but which does not indicate which individuals do. Which individuals in either group have established intergroup relations depends largely on psychological factors, but the influences of these psychological factors must operate within the limits set by structural conditions. By the same token, physical, biological, and psychological conditions limit the ways conditions in the social structure can influence social associations.

There are two basic types of structural parameter: *nominal* and *graduated*. A nominal parameter divides the population into subgroups with distinct boundaries. There is no inherent rank-order among these groups, though empirically group membership may be related to differences in hierarchical status. Sex, religion, race, and occupation are nominal parameters. A graduated parameter differentiates people in terms of a status rank-order. In principle, the status gradation is continuous, which means that the parameter itself does not draw boundaries between strata. But the empirical distribution may reveal discontinuities that indicate class boundaries. Income, wealth, education, and power are graduated parameters. (Figure 1 illustrates the two types of parameter.)

Two kinds of social position are distinguished by these two types of parameter: membership in a group and status. All characteristics of people that influence their role relations are designated either as group membership or as status; if such characteristics classify people categorically, the nominal categories are defined as groups; if they classify them in rank order, they are defined as status. Hence, group and status are defined very broadly. The term *group* is not confined to primary groups all of whose members have direct relations with all others but includes any category of people who share an attribute that influences their role relations, typically in ways that make ingroup relations more prevalent and closer than outgroup relations. This

FIGURE 1.   BASIC TYPES OF STRUCTURAL
PARAMETER

Nominal Parameters	Graduated Parameters
Sex	Education
Race	Income
Religion	Wealth
Ethnic Affiliation	Prestige
Clan	Power
Occupation	Socioeconomic Origin
Place of Work	Age
Place of Residence	Administrative Authority
Industry	Intelligence
Marital Status	
Political Affiliation	
National Origin	
Language	

criterion unequivocally distinguishes groups from arbitrary categories of un-connected aggregates, for which ingroup relations do not differ from out-group relations. *Status* refers to all attributes of people that exhibit gradations, not only those associated with prestige or power. For example, age is a status, as the term has been defined. Not all forms of status superior-ity are manifest in superordination in social relations, though many are, including undoubtedly age, at least for much of the age range.

The theoretical concept of status refers to a continuous gradation, what-ever the nature of the empirical measures. For many forms of status, ratio scales exist; for some forms, only ordinal scales may be available, but this is treated as a lack of accuracy in the measurement of the underlying status gradation. Only a conception of status as a gradation, whatever its empirical measure, makes it meaningful to speak of variations in inequality. For in-stance, one might consider employers and employees an ordinal status rank-ing. But unless one is willing to assume that there is no variation in status among employers (or among employees), one implicitly assumes that the dichotomy is merely a crude indication of an underlying status continuum, for example, the power employers have over employees, or the wealth they must own to employ many workers. A hierarchy of authority is another ordinal status ranking. However, to be able to say that authority is more centralized in the army than in a research institute, or that the difference in authority between a general and a colonel is greater than that between a sergeant and a corporal, one must assume an independent gradation of au-thority that is only roughly reflected in the official ranks.

The two generic forms of differentiation, under which the variety of its specific forms can be subsumed, are heterogeneity and inequality.

Heterogeneity or horizontal differentiation refers to the distribution of a population among groups in terms of a nominal parameter. Inequality or vertical differentiation refers to the status distribution in terms of a graduated parameter. The operational criterion of the degree of heterogeneity in a population is that two randomly chosen persons do not belong to the same group.[2] For any nominal parameter, the larger the number of groups and the more evenly the population is divided among them, the greater is the heterogeneity. Thus, there is more ethnic heterogeneity if there are many ethnic groups than if there are few; but if nine-tenths of the population belong to the same ethnic group and merely one-tenth to others, ethnic heterogeneity is less than if the population is more evenly distributed among ethnic groups. The operational criterion takes both components of heterogeneity into account.

The meaning of inequality is not unequivocal, since much inequality in one sense implies little inequality in another, even if a single and easily measured aspect of status is under consideration, such as wealth. If most of the wealth in a town is concentrated in the hands of a few persons, inequality is more pronounced than if the wealth were more widely distributed. However, when wealth is so highly concentrated, it implies that most people are equally poor, whereas a greater dispersion of wealth would reduce the number of persons who are equal in their lack of wealth and in this sense increase the inequality in wealth. The paradox of inequality is that much concentration of power or wealth or some other status resource implies widespread equality. Simmel (1950, p. 198) refers to this in his discussion of despots who fortify their positions by leveling status distinctions among their subjects and "equalizing hierarchical differences."

· Inequality must be distinguished from status diversity. When a few people are very rich and most are equally poor, or when a few are very powerful and most are equally powerless, inequality is more pronounced than when wealth or power is more widely distributed. The widespread equality that accompanies extreme concentration of wealth or power indicates low status diversity, not low inequality. To say that such extreme concentration of wealth or power means little inequality would be contrary to common sense. It would also contradict the criterion of inequality that makes this concept meaningful and that is implicit in the most widely used empirical measures of it (see chapter 3). This criterion is that the greater the

2. The measure of heterogeneity is

$$1 - \frac{\Sigma x_i{}^2}{(\Sigma x_i)^2} ,$$

where x_i is the number of persons in each group and the sum is taken over all groups. The formula simplifies to $1 - \Sigma p_i{}^2$ if the number of persons in each group is expressed as a fraction of the total population. If all persons are in one group, there is no heterogeneity ($1 - 1.00 = 0$); if all groups have the same size, heterogeneity approximates unity with increasing numbers of groups.

average status distance between all pairs of persons relative to their average status, the greater is the inequality. Much concentration of wealth or power increases the average difference in wealth or power and therefore inequality. The criterion applies to all status attributes, including those for which it is not meaningful to speak of concentration, such as education. In a society where there is a small university-educated elite and most people have only a few years of schooling, the average difference in education is pronounced, and so is educational inequality.

Status diversity is the graduated-parameter equivalent of heterogeneity. Its theoretical minimum is that all persons have exactly the same status; its theoretical maximum, that no two persons have exactly the same status. The theoretical minimum of inequality is also that all persons have the same status, whereas its theoretical maximum is that all status resources are concentrated in one person and all others have none, for instance, no wealth or no power. Minimum inequality is identical with minimum status diversity, therefore, but maximum inequality entails near-minimum status diversity, which is the reason for the inequality paradox. Within the limits imposed by these extremes, inequality and status diversity can vary independently of each other and occur in various combinations. The operational criterion of status diversity is the probability that two randomly chosen persons do not have the same status or do not belong to the same stratum, with stratum being defined by any equidistant status interval, for example, equal income intervals, or equal intervals of years of schooling, or equal intervals on a power score that represents, or is assumed to represent, an equal-interval scale.[3]

Both heterogeneity and inequality create barriers to social intercourse, on the assumption that common group membership and proximate status promote social associations. This assumption implies that the greater the differentiation of either kind, the more extensive are the barriers to sociable intercourse, although more extensive barriers are not necessarily stronger barriers, as we shall see. These barriers cannot be absolute and prevent any social associations; if they were, the various groups and strata would not constitute a single social structure. As has been stressed above, social struc-

---

3. The measure of heterogeneity can be adapted to yield a measure of status diversity. The population is divided into equal status intervals, for example, equal income intervals, not equal population percentages. The formula shown in the preceding note is applied to the number of persons, or fraction of the total population, in each category, possibly weighted to correct for the arbitrary number of categories by multiplying it with $c/(c - 1)$, where c is the number of categories. For highly skewed distributions, an approximate indication of low status diversity is the proportion of the population whose status score is zero or very low. For instance, low diversity in wealth is indicated by the proportion of the population who have no wealth, or by the proportion whose assets are below a certain small amount that is considered to constitute personal savings for an emergency rather than wealth available for investments. The corresponding approximate indication for inequality in wealth, which is often used, is the proportion of the total wealth owned by the top 1 percent or other small fraction of the population.

tures are conceptualized as being composed of different parts that are inter-related through the direct associations between persons positioned in the different parts.

Differentiation and integration are complementary opposites, and the definition of integration takes this into account. Differentiation implies barriers to face-to-face associations among the various parts in the social structure, and integration is defined in terms of the face-to-face associations among the various parts. The integration of individuals in their groups rests on the ingroup bonds established in the direct associations among persons in the same group, as Cooley (1902) has stressed, and the integration of the various groups in society rests correspondingly on the intergroup bonds established in the direct associations between persons belonging to different groups. Salient parameters which entail strong barriers to intergroup relations promote ingroup relations and integration. For example, when religion is of great importance to people, religious solidarity will be strong and religious intermarriage rare. But the prevalence of strong ingroup integration does not contribute to society's integration. On the contrary, it fragments society into groups with few connections and therefore impedes society's integration, as defined. Two distinctive implications of this conception of macrosocial integration should be emphasized: First, it rests on extensive intergroup relations, not on strong ingroup bonds. Second, it rests on the face-to-face associations between individuals from different groups and strata, not on their common values or sentiments, nor on the functional interdependence among different parts, though common values and interdependence may contribute to society's integration by fostering social intercourse between members of different groups and strata.

Theoretical Scheme

An attempt is made in this book to construct a deductive theory of social structure based on the conceptual framework outlined. The focus is on structural differentiation, conceptualized as the distributions of a population in terms of parameters, and comprising two generic types, heterogeneity and inequality, both of which assume a variety of specific forms. The substantive content of people's social attributes and positions is ignored, as attention centers on their distribution. For example, not the significance of race but that of racial heterogeneity is a subject of structural inquiry; not the significance of the nature of occupations but that of the division of labor; not the significance of leadership but that of inequality in power.

The major questions the theory seeks to answer are: How is the influence of given psychological tendencies (such as ingroup preferences) on social relations modified by structural conditions? What are the implications for social associations of the distributions of people among social positions? How do heterogeneity and inequality affect intergroup and interstratum relations? What are the implications of social mobility for social associations and structural change? How do multiple parameters and the degree of their correlations influence macrosocial integration? How does the significance for social life of heterogeneity and of inequality within communities compare with that of heterogeneity and inequality among communities? What is the comparative significance of the division of labor within and among work organizations? What implications does the concentration of power have for social conflict?

These and a variety of related questions are answered by theorems that are derived from primitive assumptions and definitions. I call it a primitive theory not only because theorems are derived from primitive propositions, in the technical sense of the term, but also because the axioms, the concepts used in them, and the initial theorems deduced from them are simple, so that these propositions are primitive in the colloquial meaning of the word. Indeed, some of the theorems are tautological, already contained in the axioms or definitions from which they are derived. But such a tautological theorem sometimes furnishes unexpected insights, and it is often needed to derive other theorems that are not tautological. An inherent danger in chains of deduction that involve probabilistic propositions is that the probability of the conclusion, which is the product of the probabilities of all preceding propositions, is very low. To minimize this danger, the theorems most often used as premises in deduction are deterministic ones.

The theory is abstract in one sense and not in another. Two properties of abstract theoretical concepts are that they are general—powerful official, not Franklin D. Roosevelt—and that they are not empirically observable but used in explaining empirical observations—electric-field vector, anomie (Braithwaite 1953, pp. 50–87). In the social sciences, abstractions in the latter sense often involve what Blumer (1954) calls "sensitizing concepts," which are complex and rich in connotations, provide subtle insights, but defy precise definition and measurement. Weber's ideal types are abstract in this sense; so are Parsons's theoretical concepts; but the theory to be presented is not. The concepts used are straightforward rather than profound, can be precisely defined, and are readily translatable into operational measures. However, these concepts refer to very general and formal analytical elements abstracted from concrete empirical realities, which makes them abstract in the first sense.[4] An illustration is the concept of group size, defined by the number of members of a group. This is clearly not a profound theoretical concept, and it is easily observed and measured. At the same time, group size is a very general abstraction which singles out for theoretical

4. Parsons (1937, pp. 34–36, 603–24, 748–53) stresses the importance of abstracting analytical elements for theorizing and contrasts this method to Weber's ideal-type approach.

attention one universal property by which all groups can be characterized, ignoring all their distinctive properties.[5]

Starting with propositions that employ such simple analytical terms as *size* and *number*, the theory progressively moves to employ more complex terms which are constructed on the basis of the simpler ones. From the size distribution among groups, the concept of heterogeneity is derived; from the status distribution of a population, the concept of inequality. Since the distributions of people among social positions do not remain constant, the significance of social mobility and structural change are examined. The earlier inquiry is confined to people's distribution in terms of any one parameter, but people are differentiated on the basis of numerous parameters. The analysis of the relationships of parameters yields new structural concepts, such as multiform heterogeneity and consolidated status inequalities.

The components of complex social structures are themselves social structures. Communities, for example, have social structures which constitute substructures of society's structure. The various forms of differentiation in society can be partitioned into the differentiation within and that among its substructures. Increasingly abstract theorems are derived from this analysis, culminating in one concerning the implications of penetrating differentiation for macrosocial integration.

The theory is built by moving from simple concepts and propositions to complex ones, but it does not progress from less general to more general propositions. Some of the simple theorems introduced early are completely general, whereas some of the complex ones discussed later are not. For example, the theorem about intergroup relations derived first is a universal proposition, applying to all groups anywhere. Some less general theorems are advanced later in the book, in order to take into account distinctive properties of certain forms of differentiation that are of special interest. Thus, the division of labor is a form of heterogeneity, and the general theorems about heterogeneity apply to it. But the great significance of the division of labor for society makes it of interest to analyze it in its own right and to try to derive theorems that apply specifically to it. Similarly, the great importance of power in social life prompted the decision to consider the theorems about inequality insufficient for clarifying power and to devote a chapter to the analysis of the concentration of power and its implications for group conflict.

Theories can be developed inductively or deductively: either by starting with less general empirical observations and subsuming them under more general theoretical propositions, which go beyond the empirical generalizations and logically imply them; or by starting with more general axioms and

5. The use of universal concepts in propositions—all men are mortal—makes them abstract in both senses, since universal propositions necessarily go beyond empirical observations (see Braithwaite 1953, pp. 82–87).

theorems that logically imply empirical predictions, which make the theory falsifiable. In either case, the theory constitutes ideally a deductive system, and the more general propositions explain the less general ones (Braithwaite 1953). The deductive procedure is used in this book, but I consider both procedures legitimate—and have used the inductive one elsewhere (Blau 1974, pp. 297–348)—although some philosophers of science, like Popper (1959, pp. 27–48), reject the inductive method. To be sure, truly universal propositions cannot be derived purely by induction, as Popper stresses. Generality is a matter of degree, however, and not all theoretical generalizations are universal propositions, surely not in the social sciences.

Description involves particular statements. Structural analysis can be used to make descriptive comparisons between societies, or between communities in one society, or between some other collectivities. For instance, one might compare income inequality in the United States and the United Kingdom; or ethnic heterogeneity in Chicago and New York; or the extent to which prestige differences influence social relations among business managers and among academics. If the number of collectivities being compared is large, the need arises to summarize the large number of descriptions in some way, which can be done by making a generalization. This requires that the particular labels used in the descriptions—United Kingdom, Chicago, the academic profession—be replaced by some analytical property of these collectivities in terms of which they can be ordered (Przeworski and Teune 1970).

To arrive at a generalization, it is necessary to classify the particular objects under consideration on the basis of two or more analytical properties that order them and thereby make it possible to establish how these properties are related. Particular labels or names cannot be related to anything, because they describe unique objects. Such objects can be compared in terms of some of their analytical properties, as in the above statements comparing two particular societies, communities, or occupations. But generalizing about the structure of societies requires ignoring the unique combinations of characteristics that their names represent and abstracting from these complex wholes merely a few analytical elements the ordering of which can be related to one another. For example, a generalization about the implications of heterogeneity for intergroup relations ignores everything about the United Kingdom and Chicago, ignores even that one is a nation and the other a city, and merely treats them as two instances of all kinds of collectivities that can be classified by these two analytical properties or variables.

In the study of social structure, however, the unique names of societies are simultaneously general categories for classifying the communities and individuals in them (by nationality), and the unique labels of communities, occupations, and other collectivities are similarly general categories of their subunits. Consequently, the same statement can be a descriptive comparison about some social structures and a generalization about their subunits or the individuals in them. The statement that British cities have less ethnic heterogeneity than American cities is a descriptive comparison about the two countries, but it is a generalization, albeit a limited one, about cities which ignores the unique characteristics of cities and simply relates two of their properties: to which nation they belong and how ethnically heterogeneous they are. Similarly, the statement that prestige differences influence social relations among business managers more (or less) than among academics is a descriptive comparison of two particular occupations, but it is a limited generalization about their individual members which relates three of their characteristics.

To formulate generalizations about social structure requires that collectivities, not just their individual members, be classified on the basis of analytical properties. As long as countries or cities are designated by their names, the only statements that can be made about them are descriptions of the differences among them, for example, that average incomes are higher in certain named cities than in other named ones. To go beyond description, cities must be reclassified by substituting for their unique labels some property of cities that distinguishes them, such as their regional location. This makes it possible to state that northern American cities have higher average incomes than southern ones, which is a rather limited generalization. The question immediately arises: What is it that produces the higher incomes in northern cities? The answer that suggests itself is likely to involve a further reclassification of cities on the basis of a property that rank-orders them, for instance, degree of industrialization. The hypothesis that incomes rise with increasing industrialization is a broader generalization which is not restricted to American cities, and which might explain the regional differences among American cities.

Analytical properties of social structures that rank-order them apparently permit broader generalizations than properties that divide them into nominal categories, and unique labels preclude any generalizations. Accordingly, social structure is conceptualized in terms of its quantitative properties, which entails transforming unordered classifications of collectivities and of their members into ordered classifications that describe properties of social structure. One kind of transformation is to categorize communities and groups of all sorts by their size in theorems dealing with the implications of size for social associations. Another type of transformation is illustrated by the concept of heterogeneity, which translates nominal categories into a continuous variable that refers to population distributions and represents a property of social structure. Graduated parameters are similarly translated into distributions indicative of inequality, in this case not to effect an ordering of categories, since status gradations are already ordered, but to combine information about positions into a concept that refers to the structure of positions.

Nominal as well as graduated parameters are thus used to abstract ordered properties of social structures that can be employed in general theorems. This is the case for various forms of differentiation and also for more complex concepts, such as structural consolidation, indicated by the positive correlations of parameters. The analysis of differentiation within and among substructures entails still another type of transformation of nominal categories. Substructures are defined by a nominal parameter, since only nominal parameters delineate subunits with distinct boundaries. The nominal parameter of place of work divides the labor force into discrete categories, for instance, but the graduated parameter of income does not. The particular establishments where people work are of no interest, however. The nominal categories are simply used to circumscribe components of social structure in order to be able to decompose differentiation in terms of other parameters into that within and that among these components, for example, into the division of labor within and among work organizations, or into inequality within and among communities. A further abstraction involves ignoring the nature of the subunits—whether they are communities, organizations, or any other groups—in theorems about the implications of differentiation within and among structural components of any kind.

In sum, the approach to theorizing is deductive, and social structure is conceptualized in quantitative terms. This conception is inspired by Simmel, the father of quantitative sociology. To be sure, Simmel did not employ quantitative methods in his work, nor did he use deductive procedures. But by quantitative sociology I mean a subject, not the techniques used in studying it. Quantitative procedures can be used to investigate entirely qualitative aspects of social life, such as the influence of social background on attitudes. Quantitative sociology is the conceptual and theoretical analysis of the quantitative dimension of social life—of size, numbers, distributions—and in this Simmel was a pioneer.

Another source of my conception of social structure is that of the British structuralists in anthropology, notably Radcliffe-Brown (1940), Evans-Pritchard (1940), Fortes (1945), and Nadel (1957), whose concepts pertaining to the structure of small tribes are adapted to make them applicable to the study of large societies. The French structuralism of Lévi-Strauss rests on a broader conception of social structure that encompasses and centers attention on cultural values and symbols, rules and myths. I consider my focus on group structures and status structures, and explicitly not on culture, to be in the tradition of Marx, with his emphasis on class structure, notwithstanding the substantial difference in content as well as form between the theory advanced and Marx's. The central concern with differentiation is, of course, in the tradition of Spencer, but without his emphasis on linear evolutionary progress.

An important model has been Durkheim's systematic focus on social structure, notably in his theories of division of labor and suicide, though not so much in his later theory of forms of religious life, which deals largely with cultural values, as Parsons (1937) stresses. Value orientations also play the predominant role in Weber's major work on religion and economy, but his analyses of bureaucracy and of power are largely structural and have influenced my approach. A more direct influence has been Merton's conception of structural constraints, which pervades his theoretical analyses. Finally, the approach in this book may be distinguished from the contrasting ones of two other contemporary social theorists, Parsons and Homans. Although I share Parsons's aim of explaining macrosociological phenomena in structural terms, our conceptions of social structure differ sharply, his being the functional integration of institutions rooted in cultural values on which there is consensus. Homans and I have in common the objective of developing deductive theory, but he seeks to explain social relations on the basis of psychological assumptions and theorems, whereas I seek to explain them in terms of structural ones.[6]

Two convictions have prompted me to write this book: my belief in the importance of the quantitative dimension of social life and my belief in the need for conceptual clarification of this dimension before it can receive mathematical treatment. Were it not for the second conviction, my meager mathematical knowledge would have prevented me from venturing into an analysis in which numbers and distributions play such a crucial part. A theory is no better than the theoretical terms it employs, for these concepts provide the insights that the theory systematizes. A systematic theory of social structure cannot be developed without first clarifying the concepts describing social structure and translating them into precise terms. Thorough conceptual analysis of such terms as *inequality* and *heterogeneity*, and the more complex structural properties derived from them, is required to elucidate these terms and their implications before they can be employed in a rigorous theory that is not sterile. That is what I have attempted in this book. What is not attempted is to formulate the propositions mathematically, or to supply empirical evidence to corroborate the theory, although some research findings are cited to illustrate implications and limitations of theorems. Meaningful corroboration of a theory depends on unsuccessful endeavors to falsify the empirical predictions it implies (Popper 1959, pp. 93–111), and persons other than a theory's author are best qualified to furnish such corroboration.

Organization of the Volume

The building of the theory starts in the next chapter with the simplest structural terms—differences in group size or in the number of incumbents of positions. Chapter 2 is concerned with the implications of size for social

6. Three contemporary sociologists whose structural focus is somewhat akin to mine are Mayhew (1973), Laumann (1973), and White (et al., 1976).

associations and for conditioning other influences on social associations, such as those of discrimination. The consequences of processes of mobility for processes of associations, which are partly mediated by changes in size, are then analyzed.

The following two chapters deal with the two generic forms of differentiation—inequality and heterogeneity. The concepts of status and inequality are dissected in chapter 3, theorems about the implications of inequality for associations and about the conditions affecting inequality are formulated, and Marx's thesis of the impoverishment of the masses with the growing concentration of wealth is scrutinized. In chapter 4 an analysis of heterogeneity in terms of a single parameter is followed by one of multiform heterogeneity in terms of several parameters. Chapter 5 presents a fuller discussion of the significance of multiple parameters and their correlations for social associations, conflict, integration, and structural change.

The analysis then turns to substructures and the relationship between substructures and the social structure that encompasses them. Whereas the preceding inquiry centered on intergroup relations, that in chapter 6 focuses on ingroup relations, the processes of social exchange that promote them, and how these processes reinforce the effects of structural conditions on them, which elucidates the concept of structural effects. The ecological distribution of a population among different communities is the subject of chapter 7. After a discussion of urbanization, the implications for society's integration of various forms of differentiation within and among communities are examined, and the theorems derived are subsumed under more general ones about the implications of differentiation within and among any substructures. Chapter 8 is devoted to an analysis of the division of labor, a form of heterogeneity that itself assumes the contrasting forms of routinization and expert specialization. Main topics discussed are conditions that promote the division of labor, the division of labor within and among work organizations, and the implications of the division of labor for inequalities. Conceptual distinctions among three facets of power are made in chapter 9, followed by an analysis of the concentration and consolidation of powers and their implications for group and class conflict. All the theorems derived are presented together in the last chapter.

CHAPTER TWO

Size and Number

VARIATIONS IN THE SIZE OF GROUPS AND THE NUMBER OF INCUMBENTS of social positions constitute basic structural conditions in a society or any other large collectivity. These conditions do not remain constant but continually change, partly as the result of social mobility. Structural conditions influence processes of social association, and so do processes of social mobility, both directly and indirectly by effecting changes in the social structure. These influences are the subject of the present chapter.

An initial assumption is that *people associate not only with members of their own groups but also with members of other groups.* Social association refers to actual direct interaction between persons, whatever the nature of their relation. It is not assumed that every member of each group has associates in every other group, just as it is not assumed that every member of a group associates with all its other members. The latter assumption would be untenable for large groups, and the former would be untenable for many groups, whereas the assumption applies to groups regardless of their size and number. What is assumed is that every group in society is related to other groups through direct associations between group members. The principle that all groups maintain some intergroup associations is introduced as a primitive assumption, for the derivation of theorems about groups defined by a single parameter, but subsequent analysis that takes multiple parameters into account will reveal that this principle itself can be derived from other primitive axioms, which means that it does not remain a primitive assumption of the theory.[1]

---

1. For the derivation from other propositions of the principle that people have intergroup relations, see the analysis of multiform heterogeneity in chapter 4. Once intersecting parameters in complex structures are taken into consideration, this principle is no longer a primitive

19

Intergroup Relations

Why do some groups have more extensive intergroup relations than others? Given the significance attached to intergroup relations, this is an important question. Various kinds of social associations must be considered. One of special significance is marriage: Is racial intermarriage more prevalent among blacks or among whites? Mutual friendships are another form of association: Do Jews have more Christian friends or do Christians have more Jewish friends? Associates spend more or less time together: How does the average amount of time blacks spend in social interaction with whites compare with that whites spend with blacks? The specific nature of the social interaction may be taken into consideration: Are Jews or are Christians more likely to engage in premarital sexual intercourse with members of the other religious group?

Such specific questions could be answered on the basis of empirical research, though it would not be easy to obtain the information necessary for answering some of them, such as amount of time spent and frequency of premarital sex relations. In any case, a hypothesis is needed to guide the research, or at least to interpret its findings, concerning what properties of groups account for differences in extent of intergroup relations. Thus, one study tested the cultural hypothesis that extent of intermarriage among denominations depends on their similarity in religious dogma or value orientation (Bealer, Willits, and Bender 1963); but the evidence negated the hypothesis. Another study found negative evidence for a structural hypothesis, namely, that extent of racial intermarriage depends on the sex ratio (Burma 1963). Other hypotheses may be inferred from the literature on the properties of various types of groups. Discrimination against minorities is often held to strengthen their ingroup solidarity, which suggests that Jews and blacks have lower rates of intermarriage and intergroup friendships than their counterparts, which are majority groups. On the other hand, research has shown that Jews are generally less religious than Christians (Lazerwitz 1961), which leads to the opposite expectation that Jews, being less restrained by their faith, are more likely than Christians to enter into religious intermarriages. Might the weaker religious convictions of Jews make them also particularly inclined to engage in premarital sex relations with the religious outgroup? Might the lesser sexual inhibitions frequently attributed to blacks make them similarly more inclined than others to engage in interracial premarital sex relations?

Jews are indeed more likely than Christian to have sex relations with

---

proposition, but it is one before the introduction of other assumptions and for the analysis of single parameters. Laumann's (1973, p. 81) research on friendships among religious, ethnic, and occupational groups shows, as here assumed, that "all groups manifest more or less strong tendencies to have some intimate intercourse with members of the most disparate groups."

members of the other religious group, and blacks are more likely to engage in interracial sex relations than whites, in the United States and in virtually all Western countries. The reason is not that Jews are less religious or that blacks are less inhibited sexually, nor is it that either group is less moral. It is simply that there are fewer of them than of their counterparts. If society is divided into two groups that differ in size, and if there are any social associations between members of the two groups (which is assumed to be the case), it logically follows that *the rate of intergroup associations of the smaller group must exceed that of the larger.* This is the first theorem (designated T-1).

Any small group is more involved than a large one in the intergroup relations between the two, unless the two groups have no social contacts. The theorem applies to all forms of *actual dyadic associations* between members of any two groups, which are necessarily symmetrical. It does not apply to sociometric preferences or sentiments, which are often asymmetric, and neither does it apply to relations between a speaker and audience or between a leader and followers, which are also asymmetric. The number of intermarriages necessarily involves the same number of persons in each of two groups, so that the rate of intermarriage, that number divided by the number of persons in a group, is an inverse function of group size. The same is the case for mean number of other intergroup associations—be they premarital sex relations, mutual friendships, or any other dyadic associations. The principle applies to intergroup contacts that entail conflict, as Stinchcombe (1975, p. 607) notes, as well as to friendly and cooperative ones.

To be sure, the number of persons participating in intergroup associations must only be the same for exclusive associates, like spouses; it need not be the same for nonexclusive intergroup associates, because one person can have many such associates. However, the total number of dyadic intergroup links or associations must be identical for two groups, which makes the mean number of these associations an inverse function of group size. The average amount of time spent in dyadic intergroup associations is also an inverse function of group size, since the total time must be the same for the two groups. A small group must be more involved than a large in the intergroup relations between the two, either because a larger proportion of the small group's members than of the large group's have intergroup associates and spend time with them, or because those that do have more intergroup associates and spend more time with them, or as the result of a combination of the two.

Accordingly, the first theorem and the arithmetic properties of groups imply three more specific theorems, which together stipulate what is meant by differences in intergroup involvement. *For any dichotomy of groups, the proportion of group members intermarried is an inverse function of group size* (T-1.11). *For any dichotomy of groups, the mean number of intergroup associates is an inverse function of group size* (T-1.12). *For any dichotomy of groups, the mean amount of time spent in intergroup associations is an inverse function of group size* (T-1.13).[2] These four theorems—T-1 and the three derived from it—are deterministic propositions about group differences in rates of intergroup associations, not probabilistic ones, though the implications of such rates for individuals are naturally probabilistic. They are also virtually tautological, entailed by the definitions from which they derive. Tautological theorems are not useless, however. They may furnish insights that are not apparent in their premises, and other theorems that are not tautological can be derived from them.

All minority groups, singly or in combination, are more involved in intergroup relations with a group constituting a majority than the majority group is with them. This theorem (T-1.2) is implied by the first (T-1), and so are its three specific versions: that *the proportion intermarried in the minorities exceed that in the majority* (T-1.21); that *the same is the case for the mean number of intergroup associates* (T-1.22); and *also for the mean amount of time spent in intergroup associations* (T-1.23).

Extensive associations with persons who have different backgrounds and experiences are likely to make people more tolerant, broaden their horizons, and provide intellectual stimulation (Simmel 1908, pp. 685–87; Veblen 1919; Lewin 1948, pp. 186–200; Seeman 1956). If intergroup relations have these psychological consequences, the theorems imply that structural conditions promote tolerance, widen perspectives, and stimulate intellectual activities among members of small minorities, while having the opposite influences on members of large majorities. Not all minorities have larger proportions of members who are successful in intellectual endeavors, of course, because such success is contingent on a variety of other conditions, such as lack of discrimination and sufficient resources to acquire the necessary education. The conjecture is not implausible, however, that independent of such counteracting conditions the more stimulating social experiences of small minorities, owing to structural constraints, are expected to make a greater percentage of a minority than of a large majority excel in intellectual pursuits. One might even speculate that American blacks, once they no longer suffer from severe discrimination and poverty, will have disproportionate numbers who are successful in intellectual work, as disproportionate numbers of other minorities, such as Jews (McClelland 1961, pp. 364–67), apparently are. That this speculation is not entirely groundless is indicated by

2. The numbering of theorems is somewhat arbitrary, using the sequence in which they are discussed. A rough rule followed is to designate closely related theorems by the same first digit (e.g., T-1.1, T-1.2), and to use the same first two digits (e.g., T-1.11, T-1.12) for propositions that are virtually identical, using either different operational criteria for the same concept, as here, or substituting a theoretical term for an operational criterion. But the distinction is not clear-cut. T-1.11, T-1.12, and T-1.13 could be considered to refer to three conceptually distinct forms of association, and designated by two digits, instead of as criteria of the broader concept of intergroup relations.

recent research that finds that the educational attainments of blacks, when their initial handicaps are controlled, exceed those of whites (Portes and Wilson 1976).

Most members of a group that constitutes a large majority have no close associate in small minority groups (T-1.3). Most white Americans have no black friend, no Chicano friend, no Japanese friend. This would be the case if there were absolutely no prejudice, simply because there are not enough members of the minorities for all or most members of the majority to have one of them as a friend. Liberal whites who are convinced that they have no antiblack prejudice sometimes wonder why they have so few or no black friends. Structural conditions explain why. Although any one white can have black friends, most of them cannot. T-1.3 follows from T-1, but it follows strictly only for fairly close associates and not for entirely superficial contacts (that is, it follows from T-1 and the definition of close associate). The reason is that one person can have superficial contacts with a large number of different others but close relations only with a much more limited number. Close associates are defined as those of which one person can have only a limited number. All whites could have superficial contacts with blacks in the United States, but only if the average black has contacts with many more whites—ten times as many—than the average white has with blacks, and such a difference cannot exist for close associates. Actually, empirical data indicate that most whites are also insulated from superficial contacts with the black minority. Williams (1964, p. 245) finds that none of the blacks in Elmira, but 67 percent of the whites (who constitute the large majority), report no social contacts with the other group.

The larger the difference in size between two groups, the greater is the discrepancy in the rates of intergroup associations between them (T-1.4). The discrepancy in intergroup relations is an inverse function of differences in group size, whether percent intermarried, mean number of intergroup associates, or mean time spent in these associations is considered. The smaller a minority, the greater is the discrepancy between its members' greater role involvement with majority members and the majority's lesser one with its members. This is another deterministic and virtually tautological proposition. But all the theorems derived about dichotomous groups imply probabilistic theorems about all groups in a society.

The probability is that the rate of intergroup associations increases with declining group size for the groups distinguished by a given nominal parameter (T-1.5). If in every dichotomy of groups the rate of intergroup associations of the smaller exceeds that of the larger (T-1), it follows that the average rate of associations of all small groups must exceed that of all large ones, wherever an array of groups by their size is divided into smaller and larger ones. Although this does not preclude that some small groups have lower rates of intergroup associations than some large ones, it does imply the probability that any small group has higher rates of intergroup relations, with any specific other group and with all others combined, than does any larger one. Corresponding probability theorems can be derived about the consequences of variations in group size for intermarriage, mean number of intergroup associates, and mean time spent in intergroup associations, and so can probability theorems about discrepancies in rates of intergroup associations. A simpler equivalent formulation of T-1.5 is that the size of the groups distinguished by a given parameter is inversely related to the extent of their intergroup relations.

Parameters differ in salience: Some nominal parameters restrict intergroup relations more than others. A survey of research on intermarriage (Barron 1951) concludes that racial differences inhibit marriage more than religious ones, whereas other ethnic differences inhibit marriage less than religious ones. Such differences in salience make the implications for intergroup relations of structural conditions defined by different parameters not directly comparable, which is the reason why T-1.5 refers to variations in group size delineated by a single parameter (as do the other theorems implicitly, since a dichotomy can only pertain to a single parameter). One would hardly expect the proportion of blacks who are married to whites to be greater than the proportion of blue-eyed married to brown-eyed persons, although there are undoubtedly fewer blacks than blue-eyed persons in the United States, because so-called skin color is much more salient in American social life than eye color.[3] The salience of a given parameter may also differ for various groups. For example, religion is likely to have more salience for religious groups whose members are very devout than for other denominations. But this kind of cultural factor is deliberately not taken into account by the theory, which is explicitly confined to the significance of structural conditions, narrowly conceived, for social life. This means that some conditions known to influence social relations are intentionally ignored, and it raises the question of whether the theory neglects so much that its structural propositions fail to receive empirical support.

Research on intermarriage and other intergroup relations indicates that this is not the case, though it does reveal some limits of T-1.5. Thus, Barnett's (1962) survey of research on religious intermarriage lists as one of the most often observed group attributes that influence intermarriage a group's relative size in its community. Thomas (1951, p. 489) also concludes from his analysis of diocese records that one of the "main factors influencing the rate of intermarriage [of Catholics is] the percentage of Catholics in the total population." Locke and colleagues (1957) observed a perfect inverse rank-order correlation between percent of Catholics in a Canadian province and

3. I used to think that eye color is an example of a biological trait that has no relevance for social relations, but I recently came across a reference (Berelson and Steiner 1964, p. 309) that cites an old study by Pearson (1907) indicating that people with the same eye color marry disproportionately often.

percent of them who are intermarried. The two studies mentioned earlier, which initially tested different hypotheses, both discovered a strong negative influence of group size on intermarriage. In Burma's (1963, p. 160) research on interracial marriage in Los Angeles, the data on seven racial groups reveal a perfect inverse rank-order for males and a nearly perfect one for females between group size and rate of intermarriage. Bealer and colleagues (1963) find that not closeness of religious dogma but size largely governs rates of intermarriage among thirteen religious groups, and their data indicate an inverse rank-order correlation of − .79 between size and rate of intermarriage (computed from their table III). A deviant case are the Mennonites, who have the lowest rate of intermarriage although their size is below average, which may well reflect the inhibiting effect on intermarriage of strong religious convictions, reinforced by geographical segregation.

The negative consequences of group size for intergroup relations are not confined to marriage, nor are they confined to Western culture. For example, the size of ethnic groups has been found to be inversely related to sociable interethnic associations in several American communities. This is the case even when opportunities for establishing these fairly close social relations are controlled. Williams (1964, p. 162) observes: "In general, minority-group members were more likely to report interacting with majority-group individuals on all opportunity levels."

Studies of marriage in other cultures also support the theorem (T-1.5). Barnes (1949) concludes from his research in simple societies that the smaller the residential, ethnic, or religious group, the higher its rate of outmarriage. Indeed, even the incest taboo and conformity with it appear to reflect the structural constraints exerted by group size. Small kin groups are more likely than large ones to be exogamous (Mayer 1953–54; Goode 1964); exogamy rules tend to be more strictly enforced in small kin groups (Ardener 1954); and they are less likely to be violated there than in large kin groups (Loeb 1933). These findings suggest that even basic cultural norms and practices, like exogamy, develop and become modified in response to existing and changing structural conditions, inasmuch as the size of kin groups is not constant but changes owing to exogeneous circumstances, such as droughts and epidemics. On the other hand, the influence of structural constraints on social relations is modified by cultural factors, for example, by the salience race has for people.

Race does not assume the same significance for social relations in all societies. Racial differences inhibit intimate social relations more in some countries than in others, and more in some parts than in others of a large and diverse country like the United States. Heer's (1966) analysis of black-white marriages in five nonsouthern states discloses this difference in racial salience, notably between Hawaii and Michigan. Race has much less salience in Hawaii, as indicated by the greater prevalence of interracial marriages there than in Michigan. If black-white marriages are more prevalent in Hawaii, it naturally means that both the proportion of blacks married to whites and the proportion of whites married to blacks is greater there than in Michigan. The proportion of blacks in the population is much smaller in Hawaii (1 percent), where many are married to whites (12 percent), than in Michigan (11 percent), where few are married to whites (1 percent), which conforms to the negative relationship theoretically expected. However, the proportion of whites is smaller in Hawaii than in Michigan, and so is the proportion of them who are married to blacks, which does not accord with T-1.5. Differences in a parameter's salience among societies or their segments that affect various groups in parallel ways neither corroborate nor contradict the theory, though they indicate limits of the predictions it can make. Some structural conditions that influence salience will be analyzed presently.

A parameter does not necessarily have the same salience for all groups distinguished by it. Religion has special salience in denominations whose members are devout, which may account for the low intermarriage rates of Mennonites, a negative case for T-1.5 already noted. Another negative case is the intermarriage rate of Jews, which numerous studies have shown to be lower than those of Protestants or Catholics (for example, Kennedy 1944; Glick 1960; Yinger 1968), although Jews constitute a much smaller proportion of the American population than either Catholics or Protestants. The reason is that marriages between Catholics and Protestants are much more likely than marriages between either and Jews, undoubtedly because both Catholics and Protestants are Christians. As a matter of fact, it is not correct to consider the difference between Christians and Jews to be on the same analytical level as that between Catholics and Protestants, just as it is not correct to treat the difference between two cities as equivalent to that between neighborhoods of one. Some nominal parameters make both broader and finer distinctions among groups. Thus, religion draws broad distinctions among Christians, Jews, Muslims, and other major faiths, narrower ones between Catholics and Protestants, and still finer ones among specific denominations. The marriage rates of Jews with Catholics and with Protestants exceed those of Catholics and of Protestants with Jews, but this is very weak empirical support for T-1.5, as it is virtually, though not quite, a mathematical necessity.[4] Although the distinction between a parameter's major and secondary subdivisions supplies a reason for the observed differences in intermarriage when Protestants, Catholics, and Jews are treated as equivalent categories, these differences must be considered negative evidence for T-1.5. As a probability theorem, T-1.5 is not refuted by exceptional negative cases, but it would be, of course, if many were to be discovered.

---

4. It would be a mathematical necessity for two groups, as T-1 is; it is not quite mathematically inevitable for three.

Facets of Social Associations

A theoretical analysis need not be concerned with the details of measurement techniques and other research procedures. However, the clarification and precise delineation of the concepts employed in a systematic theory often require taking into account the nature of the measures that serve as operational criteria of these concepts. This is especially important for a theory of social structure that conceptualizes it in quantitative terms. The line between empirical techniques and operational criteria of concepts is not sharp. It is roughly drawn for the purpose of this inquiry by not dealing with problems of collecting reliable information about individuals in research but analyzing to some extent how to combine data about individuals into measures that reflect theoretically relevant properties of social structure.

The terms employed in the preceding analysis make implicit distinctions among social associations that need to be explicated. Three facets of intergroup relations can be differentiated on the basis of two dimensions of a social association: first, whether it involves exclusive associates, of whom a person can have only one, or nonexclusive associates; second, whether number of associates or amount of time spent with them is considered. Spouses are the main type of exclusive associates; mutual best friends are another. The two dimensions yield the three facets of a group's intergroup relations employed as terms in the theorems presented: percent intermarried, mean number of intergroup associates, and mean amount of time spent in intergroup associations. These three facets do not exhaust the logical possibilities of the analytical dimensions. Thus, one could distinguish amount of time spent with nonexclusive associates only and with exclusive associates only, as well as the time spent with both combined. Ingroup relations can be conceptualized in a parallel manner. Exclusive intergroup (or ingroup) associates, though a dichotomy for individuals, is a variable with a range from zero to 100 percent for groups. The number of intergroup (or ingroup) nonexclusive associates of an individual can vary within a narrow range for close and a wider range for superficial social relations, and the mean in a group must be positive and has a very high theoretical upper limit. The amount of time spent with certain associates can vary for both individuals and groups between zero and a very high theoretical upper limit.

Further distinctions can be made for mean number of associates and mean amount of association time. The theorems apply not only to the total number of associates (per person in a group) and to the total number of minutes spent with them, but also to any subset of either number, that is, to the number of associates of any particular kind; the number of associations of any particular kind; the time spent with a given kind of associates; and the time spent in a given kind of associations. For example, the theorems apply to the number of mutual friends, the number of acquaintances who have regular contact, the number of business associates, the number of colleagues or fellow workers in mutual interaction. They do not apply to such asymmetric relations as number of employees or number of subordinates, which need to be treated separately. Moreover, the theorems can be confined to any particular kind of symmetric, dyadic, social association, be it sexual intercourse, talking about a specific subject, kissing, playing cards, or boxing.

Not all forms of social associations cement social relations and strengthen social integration, of course. Conflict involves social interaction that is not integrative, and it will be considered separately (in chapters 5 and 9). Many theorems are concerned with the integrative implications of social association, and in these the term is restricted to social intercourse between persons in which both engage voluntarily because they are interested, excluding pure conflicts, such as holdups; social contacts under compulsion, such as arrests; and perhaps also purely instrumental contacts, such as those between supermarket cashier and customer. To make these distinctions in empirical research may be quite difficult, inasmuch as many social relations are mixed games comprising both conflicting and integrative elements. But this is a technical problem of research procedures. From the theoretical standpoint, it suffices to note that the theorems are applicable to those subsets of social associations that strengthen social relations, whatever the problems of reliable measurement of these subsets.

A fourth facet of intergroup relations, which is complementary to the other three, is a group's relative insulation from intergroup contacts, as indicated by the proportion of group members without any such contacts. For individuals, insulation is simply the absolute minimum number of intergroup associates or time spent with intergroup associates, zero, which is naturally the same for both number and time. This dichotomous classification of individuals into those with no and those with some intergroup associations supplies new information for groups, supplementing that indicated by the other facets of intergroup relations. The average extent of intergroup relations does not reveal whether most group members have some intergroup associations or most have none and a few have many. For example, native-born Americans may average 1.5 foreign-born associates either because most associate with one or two foreign-born persons or because most associate with none but a few associate with many. The concept of insulation pertains to this difference. The proportion of a group without any or that without a close associate in another group is a meaningful concept, but the proportion without an *exclusive* associate there is not, and does not provide additional information, since it simply is one minus (the mathematical complement of) the proportion with an exclusive associate there.[5] Insulation as

5. The rates of change in a measure and those in its mathematical complement are not the same, however. For example, as the proportion of group members who are intermarried increases from 10 to 20 percent, or at a rate of 1:2, the proportion who are not intermarried decreases from 90 to 80 percent, or at a rate of 9:8.

well as the three other facets can refer to a group's relation with a specified other group—for instance, the majority group—or to its relations with all other groups in the larger collectivity.

The degree of insulation of groups from other groups is determined by four conditions. The first is the parameter's salience. A very salient nominal parameter is one that entails strong group barriers to social intercourse, which implies that large proportions in all or most groups are insulated from intergroup contacts. The proportion of group members without associates in other groups also depends on the group's size, just as the proportion with extensive intergroup relations does. A group's large size is a second condition that makes prevalent insulation likely. The rates of intergroup associations of small groups tend to exceed those of large ones (T-1.5), but this does not necessarily mean that the proportions insulated from intergroup contacts are lower in small than in large groups. Whether this is the case depends on the degree of variability among group members in extent of intergroup associations, which is a third condition affecting insulation.

A group can have a high rate of intergroup associations and nevertheless a high proportion of members who are insulated from intergroup contacts, but only if there is disproportionately great variability in intergroup associations among its members, many of whom must have very extensive intergroup relations for many others to have none and yet the group average to be high. The possible range of variation among individuals in the number of their associates depends on the nature of the social relation under consideration. The maximum range is less for close than for superficial role relations. A person cannot have more than one legal spouse at a time and no more than a few good friends but a large number of casual acquaintances. Since a wider range of individual variation makes a group's insulation (percent without intergroup associates) more independent of its intergroup involvement (mean number of intergroup associates), insulation from intergroup relations is more independent of involvement in them for less close than for close role relations. The closeness of the role relations studied is thus a fourth factor that affects insulation—specifically, how much it can vary independently of differences in extent of intergroup relations and in the conditions governing them.

This analysis of the group properties on which insulation is contingent makes it possible to derive theorems about it. *If the small group in a dichotomy has a higher proportion than the large who are insulated from intergroup contacts, the variations in extent of intergroup associations are greater within the small than within the large group* (T-1.6). This follows from T-1, that the smaller group in a dichotomy has a higher rate of intergroup relations, and the arithmetic property that a group can have higher rates of both insulation from and relations with another only if the variability in intergroup associations among its members is higher. A small group, so defined for purpose of the analysis, may consist of several still smaller ones.

In accordance with this conception, another theorem is deducible from T-1.6. *If some minorities are more insulated from the majority than the majority is from them, other minorities have particularly extensive intergroup relations with the majority* (T-1.7). A corresponding theorem about extent of intergroup associations of minorities can be derived from T-1.2, that the rate of intergroup associations of a minority in a dichotomy exceeds the majority's. *If some minorities have lower rates of intergroup associations with the majority than the majority has with them, other minorities have particularly high rates of intergroup associations with the majority* (T-1.71).

These two deterministic theorems, which are essentially equivalent, help clarify the negative empirical cases for the probabilistic theorem that the likelihood of extensive intergroup relations increases with decreasing group size (T-1.5). Some small groups are more insulated than large ones from the rest of society, for a variety of reasons. For example, a small group may be physically isolated from other groups; its members may be committed to a distinctive ideology; other people may have a strong prejudice against this particular group; a parameter may have special salience for it. But such exogeneous factors can only inhibit the intergroup relations of particular small groups, not of most of them. They cannot contravene the fundamental principle embodying compelling structural constraints that any combination of smaller groups that constitutes a minority of the population must have more extensive intergroup relations with the majority than the majority has. For every small group that is particularly insulated from society, thereby constituting negative evidence for T-1.5, there must be other small groups with particularly extensive intergroup relations, in accordance with T-1.7, compensating for the negative evidence in a sense. It would be false, however, to infer from T-1.71 that an *increase* in the rates of association of some minorities with the majority must be accompanied by a decrease in the rates of association of other minorities with the majority. The extent of intergroup relations of all groups can increase, or decrease, because the parameter delineating the groups under consideration has become less, or more, salient. For example, if the salience of ethnic background for social life declines, it is reflected in an increase in the intergroup associations of most or all ethnic minorities, and simultaneously in an increase in the associations of the majority with them. But after this change, as well as before and during it, the rates of intergroup associations of most minorities must exceed the majority's, and for any deviant case of a minority that has a lower rate than the majority there must be at least one other minority that has an exceptionally high rate.

Group size affects the proportion of group members who are insulated from close intergroup relations more than the proportion insulated from casual intergroup contacts. The reason is that the maximum number of close associates an individual can have is much less than the maximum number of casual contacts she or he can have. If a person cannot have more than one associate (as in the case for current spouse), the proportion of a group without such an outgroup associate is completely determined by its proportion with one (because the two sum to one); hence the former, just as the latter, depends on the group's relative size. In contrast, if the possible number of a person's associates were infinite, the proportion of a group without such an outgroup associate would be completely independent of the proportion with one and hence also independent of its relative size. The more a role relation limits the theoretical maximum of number of associates for individuals, consequently, the more does a group's insulation from these associates depend on its size. In accordance with these considerations, a probability theorem about close associates can be deduced from T-1 and the arithmetic properties of groups: *The closer the role relation under consideration, the greater the probability is that the proportion of group members insulated from intergroup associates declines with the decreasing size of the groups delineated by a given nominal parameter* (T-1.8).

Salience and Discrimination

The salience of a nominal parameter is defined as the preponderance of ingroup relations. The more ingroup associations prevail over intergroup associations, the more salient is the parameter. Thus, salience refers to the significance group membership has for people's actual association, not to individuals' psychological attachment to, sentiments about, or valuation of groups, except insofar as these find expression in their associations. The measure of preponderance is the extent to which actual ingroup associations, however defined, exceed those expected on the assumption of statistical independence. The expected frequency of ingroup associations is derived from the population distribution among groups, by squaring the number of persons, or the fraction of the population, in each group and then summing the values for all groups. For example, if society is divided into two groups comprising one-tenth and nine-tenths of all members, respectively, the statistically expected proportion of ingroup associations is 82 percent ($.90^2$ + $.10^2$ = .82, or 82 percent). If the two groups are the same size, 50 percent of ingroup associations are expected by chance. Unless actual exceed expected ingroup associations, the parameter has no salience for the extent of ingroup bonds under investigation, though it may influence role relations otherwise and hence be a parameter as defined.[6]

6. Sexual intercourse obviously is an association that is not more frequent between members of the same sex than between those of opposite sex; so is marriage. But sex differences do govern these role relations, and other associations—at clubs, sports, work—tend to be more prevalent among members of the same sex than between men and women, as empirical research cited below indicates. It should also be noted that the formula for expected ingroup associations (Σp_i^2) ignores that people cannot associate with themselves, but this has a negligible effect on expected rates except for very small groups.

Whereas salience is operationally defined by the rate of ingroup associations standardized by the size distribution among groups, a group's extent of intergroup associations is operationally defined by the rate of intergroup associations without standardizing for the size distribution among groups in the population. There is a theoretical, a substantive, and a methodological reason for this difference. The theoretical focus is on the implications of variations in group size, which requires that these variations in the size of groups not be statistically suppressed by holding size constant, so that influences of size on associations can become manifest. Substantively, people's associations with one another are basic social experiences of central concern to the theory. For instance, if 80 percent of a black's friends were whites, or if the majority of all black men were married to white wives, it would be experienced as very extensive intergroup relations, but a standardized index would define either as a low rate of intergroup associations in the United States, since the statistically expected proportion is 89 percent.

These two reasons for not standardizing the extent of intergroup relations of various groups are closely related. An underlying assumption of the theory is that population distributions shape social experience. Testing the implications of this assumption requires that the terms used in the theorems do not ignore population distributions but, on the contrary, center attention on them to trace their consequences for such social experiences as people's intergroup and ingroup associations. There are also methodological grounds for not defining a group's extent of association by the ratio of observed frequencies to those expected on the assumption of independence. This ratio is misleading, since it seems to control for differences in group size without effectively doing so (Yasuda 1964; Blau and Duncan 1967, pp. 90–97). This can be illustrated most easily with ingroup associations. For a group that is 1 percent of the population, the ratio of actual to expected ingroup associations would be 20 if only 20 percent of all its members' associations are ingroup associations ($20/1 = 20$). But for a group that is 10 percent of the population, the ingroup ratio cannot possibly be 20, because this would require that 200 percent of its members' associations be ingroup associations ($200/10 = 20$). The case for intergroup associations is parallel though less extreme.

The effects of changes in salience on intergroup relations depend on a group's size. For example, if the salience of national origins in American social life declines with assimilation, the interethnic relations of small nationality groups tend to increase more than those of large ones. Similarly, if the salience of education for social life increases, the extent of association of college graduates with less educated persons decreases more than the extent of people without college education with college graduates. What accounts for this difference is the same arithmetic property of groups that is responsible for the higher rates of intergroup relations of smaller than of larger groups. Dividing the same numerator by a smaller denominator produces a higher value than dividing it by a large denominator. The number of associations or links between two groups must be the same, which implies that the mean number in the small must exceed that in the large groups, and any change in the number of associations or links must also be the same, which implies that this change alters the mean more in the small than in the large group.

Theorems about changes in intergroup relations can be deduced from these group properties and the principle embodied in T-1. *Changes in a parameter's salience change the extent of intergroup relations of a minority with the majority more than the majority's* (T-2). The theorem is deterministic and applies to proportion intermarried, mean number of associates, and mean association time, though to insulation only probabilistically for close role relations. Direction of change is specified simultaneously with transforming the proposition into probabilistic theorems about variations in groups size generally, which rest on the considerations explicated with reference to T-1.5. *The probability is that reductions in a parameter's salience increase the rates of intergroup associations of small groups more than those of large ones* (T-2.11). *The probability is that intensified salience of a parameter decreases the rates of intergroup associations of small groups more than those of large ones* (T-2.12).

These theorems have paradoxical implications for discrimination by a majority against a minority. Discrimination refers here to refraining from social intercourse with the members of a group, not to any other bias in making decisions about them, and the case considered is that in which the majority's discrimination largely accounts for the rate of associations between it and the majority and for changes in that rate. *The more a majority discriminates in social intercourse against a minority, the smaller is the discrepancy between the majority's lower and the minority's higher rate of intergroup associations* (T-3). If the purpose of majority discrimination against minorities is to control the majority's own members' tendencies to socialize with members of the minority, whether by enacting laws or through informal pressures, it serves its purpose well. But if the objective is to prevent minorities from having social access to the majority without infringing on its members' freedom of social choice, majority discrimination defeats its own purpose. For majority discrimination restricts the social access of its own members to minority members much more than the opportunity of minority members to associate with members of the majority, the more so the more severe the discrimination. This applies to the most intimate and the most casual associations, and it applies if concern is confined to completely mutual pair relations, leaving aside such well-known cases of minority exploitation as sweatshops and the sexual exploitation of minority women by majority men.

The complementary theorem is equally paradoxical: *As a majority's discrimination against a minority in social intercourse subsides, the discrepancy between the majority's lower intergroup involvement and the minority's higher one becomes greater* (T-3.1). Thus, by discriminating less against a minority, a majority increases the difference between the lower proportion of its own members and the higher proportion of the minority's members who are intermarried; between the fewer mutual friends its own members and the greater number the minority's members have on the average in the other group; and between the average amount of time its own members and those of the minority spend socializing with members of the other group. All this happens purely as the result of an increase in intergroup links, regardless of other conditions. To be sure, reduced discrimination by the majority increases the rate of association of its members with members of the minority, but not so much as it increases the rate of association of minority members with majority members.

Discrimination against minorities in education, employment, and other areas has undoubtedly declined in recent decades in the United States. This has reduced their handicaps and improved their life chances. Concomitantly, and partly as a result, discrimination in social intercourse against minorities has also declined. Whereas there is some backlash, it probably does not outweigh the declining trend. The decline in discrimination, assuming it has occurred, has increased the proportion of minority members who have majority friends and the extent of social intercourse of many minority members with members of the majority group, and it has thereby integrated minorities more into the mainstream of American social life. At the same time, however, the decline in discrimination has enlarged the difference between minorities and the majority in the extent to which they know each other, socialize with each other, associate sufficiently to understand and sympathize with each other, and have a close enough relation to trust each other. In short, a decline in discrimination, although it helps to integrate minorities in society, moves the social experiences involved in intergroup life of minority members and majority members further apart.

Reduced discrimination by a majority against a minority in social intercourse enlarges the probable difference between the majority's higher and the minority's lower proportion of members who are insulated from close intergroup relations (T-3.2). This theorem follows from T-2, that a change in salience affects the intergroup relations of the smaller of two groups more, and T-1.8, that group size is inversely related to insulation for close role relations. If the minority is very small, the theorem applies to superficial as well as close relations. Indeed, the difference in the proportions insulated from associations with the other group increases relatively as well as absolutely with reductions in discrimination, while that in extent of intergroup relations increases only absolutely. This can be illustrated with an imaginary case of the influence of reductions in majority discrimination on intergroup friendships. To simplify the illustration and make it clearer, it assumes that nobody has more than one close intergroup friend, which obviates the need to take into account variations in number of associates, except, of course, the difference between one and zero. Without this simplifying assumption, the analysis is more complicated but the pattern of change is essentially the same.

If there are one million pairs of mutual close friends between a majority of 100 and a minority of 10 million, 1 percent of the majority and 10 percent of the minority have an intergroup friend, and 99 and 90 percent, respectively, do not, a difference of 9 percent (table 1). We imagine that a decline in discrimination by the majority increases the number of intergroup friendships from one to three million. This reduces the majority members without an intergroup friend 2 percent, from 99 to 97, but it reduces the minority members without an intergroup friend much more, 20 percent, from 90 to 70. Consequently, the difference in the percent insulated from intergroup friendships increases from 9 to 27. This increase in the absolute difference in insulation is accompanied by an increase in its relative difference, as indicated by the ratio of the proportions insulated in the two groups, whereas there is no such relative change in the proportions with intergroup friends. The ratio of the proportions with intergroup friends in the majority and in the minority remains the same as discrimination declines and intergroup friendships increase, 1:10, because this ratio, as that of other rates of intergroup associations, is simply the inverse function of the ratio in group size. In contrast, the ratio of the proportion insulated in the majority and in the minority increases with declines in discrimination and in insulation, from 11:10 to 14:10, though there is no change in group size.

The paradox is that a decrease in discrimination by a majority against a minority increases the inequality in intergroup involvement between the two groups, most dramatically for the proportion insulated from intergroup associates. For the difference between majority and minority in the proportion insulated increases, both relatively and absolutely, as the proportions themselves decrease. If the trend of subsiding discrimination continues, all members of the minority will eventually have close associates in the majority group, while most members of the majority will still have no close minority associate. Ultimately, minority members may be as likely to marry and to be

TABLE 1.   CLOSE FRIENDS BETWEEN A MAJORITY AND A MINORITY

	Majority	Minority	Difference	Ratio
ONE MILLION INTERGROUP PAIRS				
1. Number of Persons (millions)	100	10		
2. Proportion with Intergroup Friend	1%	10%	9%	1:10
3. Proportion without Intergroup Friend	99%	90%	9%	11:10
REDUCED DISCRIMINATION: THREE MILLION INTERGROUP PAIRS				
4. Proportion with Intergroup Friend	3%	30%	27%	1:10
5. Proportion without Intergroup Friend	97%	70%	27%	14:10

intimate with members of the majority as with members of their own group, which would mean that the minority has become fully assimilated and has ceased to exist as a group governing social distinctions. The process of assimilation enhances some differences in the social experiences of a minority and a majority—those resting on intergroup involvement—before finally obliterating most or all of them.

What structural conditions foster reductions in the salience of parameters and thus in discrimination? One is social mobility, which is discussed next. Others are heterogeneity, particularly multiform heterogeneity, and intersecting parameters, which will be analyzed in subsequent chapters.

Mobility

Two assumptions of the theory are that people associate with others in different groups as well as their own and that they associate disproportionately with others in their own group or social stratum. The former assumption, introduced at the beginning of this chapter, will not remain a primitive proposition but will be derived from others later (in chapter 4). The latter assumption is explicitly introduced as the first basic axiom now, though it has been mentioned before and is implicit in the discussion of salience. People in similar social positions share social experiences and roles, and have similar attributes and attitudes, which promote social intercourse among them. This is the reasoning underlying the first axiom, on which numerous theorems rest.

Social associations are more prevalent among persons in proximate than between those in distant social positions (A-1). Reference is not to the absolute number of associates or associations but to the excess of this number over that expected from the population distribution on the assumption of independence, as in the definition of salience. Otherwise the assumption could not be met for a very small group with so few members that it is virtually inevitable that they have more associates outside their own group than in it. For a nominal parameter, proximate and distant are a dichotomy: same group or other group. For a graduated parameter, they vary in degree: proximity decreases with increasing status distance. This distinction can be explicated in two subsidiary assumptions entailed by A-1 that specify the parameter under consideration: *Ingroup associations are more prevalent than outgroup associations* (A-1.1); *the prevalence of associations declines with increasing status distance* (A-1.2).[7]

---

7. These two propositions are not, strictly speaking, primitive propositions, since A-1 implies them. But A-1 was deliberately worded to use a general term that entails the more precise ones used in the two specifications of it, which is the reason that they are designated as subsidiary axioms rather than theorems.

There is much empirical evidence in support of the assumption that associations between persons in similar social positions predominate. Thus, the prevalence of homogamy has been observed with respect to a variety of social attributes. For example, disproportionate numbers of marriages involve spouses of the same religion (Kennedy 1944; Hollingshead 1950; Willits, Bealer, and Bender 1963); community and residential area (Schapera 1946; Murdock 1949); education (Blau and Duncan 1967); occupation and socioeconomic status (Centers 1949; Hollingshead 1950; Blau and Duncan 1967). Such ingroup tendencies have been observed not only in American society but also in simple societies. Murdock (1949) concludes from his analysis of data on many cultures that some form of ethnic and class endogamy exists in nearly all societies.[8]

Friendship as well as marriage has been found to be influenced by common attributes. There is considerably less research on friendship than on marriage, however, and most of it comprises studies of children or teenagers which tend to focus on psychological traits (summarized in Hare 1976, pp. 163–66). The finding most frequently reported is that children and teenagers form friendships primarily with others of the same sex and age (for instance, Parten 1933; Smith 1944; Faunce and Beegle 1948). Adult friendships also usually involve persons of the same sex, as well as those of the same race (Merton, West, and Jahoda 1951; Maisonneuve 1966, pp. 260–64). Two other attributes that friends tend to have in common are religion and class background (Smith 1944; Hollingshead 1949; Goodnow and Tagiuri 1952). Dating, too, takes place mostly between boys and girls who share the same class background (Hollingshead 1949).

In terms of a single parameter, to which attention is still restricted, people can occupy only one social position at a time, and this position is assumed to influence their associations with others. But people who have moved from one social position to another tend to be influenced by both, though possibly less by either than those who have remained all their life in the same position. They cannot simply discard their old role attributes and role relations, and they cannot adjust to their new position without adopting new role attributes and forming new role relations. The social life of farmers who have moved to cities is undoubtedly influenced by both their rural background and their urban environment. A Catholic who has converted to Protestantism in all probability maintains some social relations with Catholics and has established some with Protestants. Professionals with working-class origins are unlikely to have cut all social ties with their families and relatives in the working class and are most likely to have some social ties with other professionals. The mobile are in some sense marginal men and women who have social roots, albeit perhaps less deep ones, in two places.

8. The possibility that complementary needs may also influence marriage (Winch 1958) cannot gainsay the overwhelming evidence for homogamy with respect to many social attributes.

Various associates of a person often—though not always, of course—become associates themselves. This occurs naturally in the process of sociability, as a person brings together friends and acquaintances to give a party, play games, join a club, go to a political rally, or participate in any other joint activity. Newcomb's (1961, pp. 4–23, 160–65) ABX theory, a version of balance theory, also implies that positive relations of two persons to a third tend to lead to a positive relation between them. Mobile individuals are especially apt to bring together people from different groups, because they are more likely than others to have many associates in different groups. Accordingly, mobile persons not only constitute channels of communication among various groups but may also be instrumental in establishing other, direct channels of communication among them. It is provisionally assumed that this is the case—provisionally because the two specific assumptions made are required solely for a few theorems about the influences of mobility on social life and not for the rest of the theory.[9] The two assumptions are that *established role relations are resistant to disruption* (PA-2) and that *strangers who have a common associate become associates themselves more often than strangers who do not* (PA-3).[10]

Social mobility promotes intergroup relations (T-4).[11] This theorem does not necessarily depend on PA-3, only on A-1 and PA-2. If people associate disproportionately with others in their own groups, and if mobile persons associate disproportionately with others in their former groups, it follows that high rates of mobility raise rates of intergroup associations. However, the higher average rates of intergroup associations so implied would be produced only by exceptionally high rates of association of the mobile persons with members of their former groups, without there being any change

9. A distinction is made between axioms (designated by A) and provisional assumptions (designated by PA). Axioms are assumed to be true, and numerous theorems are derived from them. Provisional assumptions are more tenuous, are required for only very few theorems, and have the purpose of indicating what additional theorems can be derived from the theoretical framework if specified assumptions are satisfied.

10. Numerous assumptions of the theory, like these, are sociopsychological principles. The theory treats such primitive sociopsychological propositions as givens to formulate theorems about variations in structural conditions and social processes, for example, about the consequences of structural conditions for processes of associations and about those of processes of mobility for structural conditions.

11. Given the assumptions made, social mobility must influence intergroup associations, but it is not the only condition that does. Terms like *promotes* and *reduces* are employed to indicate that a theorem is not deterministic but refers to an influence that may be modified or counteracted by other influences. Such terms indicate that the predictions of a proposition require that other conditions are the same. The term *ceteris paribus* is explicitly used only if the wording would otherwise imply that the theorem is deterministic (but in the synopsis of theorems in chapter 10, *ceteris paribus* is made explicit in every theorem that requires it). Probabilistic theorems differ from those referring to one of several influences as well as from deterministic ones. A probabilistic theorem does make definite predictions, not subject to counteracting other influences, for the average of all units, though not for every specific one.

in the extent of intergroup relations of persons who have not been mobile themselves and have no mobile associates. PA-3 implies that mobility has wider repercussions for intergroup relations that do affect these persons: *Much mobility between two groups promotes extensive associations between their nonmobile as well as mobile members* (T-4.1).

Increasing rates of social mobility among groups reduce a parameter's salience (T-4.2). This theorem simply extends T-4.1 from two groups to many and from differences in mobility to changes in it. Increasing rates of mobility among various groups imply increasing rates of intergroup associations among them, thereby reducing the preponderance of ingroup associations, which is the defining criterion of salience. When residential mobility increases, for example, the salience of neighborhoods in social life tends to decline. If growing numbers of people change their church affiliation, the salience of religion for social relations tends to diminish. Between purely ascribed social positions, such as sex and race, there is no or practically no social mobility, since ascription means that individuals are socially prohibited from moving out of one position into another. (Conformity with this social proscription, as with others, is not perfect: there are cases of transvestism and of passing as a member of a race different from that ascribed at birth.)

Ceteris paribus, parameters that delineate ascribed positions are more salient than other parameters (T-4.3). T-4.2 and the definition of ascription imply this theorem (the wording of which requires making explicit its being contingent on equal other conditions). The theorem can explain the salience of race for social relations without making any assumption that biological traits directly affect human conduct and relations. Whether and which biological traits influence social associations depends on social definitions, which single out some and not others as salient, and which typically distort biological differences, as indicated by the social definition as blacks of persons most of whose ancestors are whites. But the visibility of such biological traits as sex and skin color may have some bearing on their persisting significance for social life. Religion is close to an ascribed position, though not so close as ethnic affiliation, inasmuch as individuals can change their religion. The conclusion from empirical research that religious differences inhibit marriage more than differences among white ethnic groups (Kennedy 1944) therefore conflicts with T-4.3. The ceteris paribus clause takes account of such negative cases. A possible interpretation in terms of the theory, though admittedly ad hoc, is that over the generations there probably has been more mobility out of white ethnic groups through assimilation than out of religious groups through conversion.

Since changes in salience affect the intergroup relations of small groups more than those of large ones (T-2), so do changes in rates of mobility, which modify the salience of group distinctions (T-4.2). *An increase in intergroup motility in a dichotomy of groups increases the minority's rate of intergroup associations more than the majority's* (T-4.4). The term *motility* is used to refer to equal amounts of mobility (the same number of persons moving) in both directions, to specify that the theorem does not depend on a change in the size of the groups that may have been produced by mobility between them.[12] The deterministic theorem for two groups can be transformed into a probabilistic one for numerous groups varying in size: *Increases in motility among groups probably increase the rates of intergroup associations of small groups more than those of large ones* (T-4.5). Decreases in motility, which intensify salience, at least in the long run, correspondingly tend to decrease the rates of intergroup associations of small groups more than those of large ones.

The number of persons who move between two groups in opposite directions is rarely exactly the same, and the difference alters the relative size of groups. The direct influences of mobility on intergroup relations examined are supplemented by indirect influences owing to the changes in group size usually effected by mobility. *Net outmobility increases a group's intergroup relations more than net inmobility* (T-4.6). The reason is that the positive direct effect of mobility on intergroup relations (T-4.1) is reinforced by excess outmobility but counteracted by excess inmobility, as the result of their opposite effects on group size (T-1). For example, rural-urban migration, which is predominantly in one direction, increases the rate of associations of farmers with people in cities more than that of the urban with the rural population. Television is not the only reason, nor probably the main one, that farmers nowadays are familiar with city ways and have become urbanized in several respects. Most farmers have relatives and friends in cities (Lipset and Bendix 1959, p. 216) with whom they are likely to associate, while most people in cities have few if any associates who are farmers, owing to the great difference in size between the rural and urban population that has been produced by high rates of migration from farms to cities for many decades.

Social mobility not only influences intergroup relations but is undoubtedly in turn influenced by them. Such an influence of intergroup relations on mobility is implied by the assumption that *associates in other groups or strata encourage and facilitate mobility into them* (PA-4). Associates in another group are virtually a prerequisite for some forms of mobility, broadly defined as any change in social position. It is hardly conceivable that a person changes his or her religion without having first had associations with members of the new denomination. For other forms of mobility, such as migration

12. Studies of occupational mobility also distinguish excess mobility in one direction, usually termed *structural mobility*, from what is here called motility, for which a variety of terms have been used, such as social-distance mobility, exchange mobility, process mobility, and circulation mobility.

and occupational mobility, having associates in the new group is not essential, but it is a great help. To move to a new place is more inviting and less threatening when one has friends or relatives there. Knowing persons in an occupation enables young people to learn about it and the opportunities in it, provides them with role models, and furnishes them with realistic information on how to acquire the training needed for it, all of which improve their chances of moving into that occupation.

High rates of intergroup associations promote high rates of intergroup mobility (T-4.7). This theorem follows from PA-4, and it implies that the rate of association between groups at time one is related to the rate of mobility at time two, controlling other conditions that affect mobility, such as changes in occupational demand. To test this theorem empirically and distinguish it from T-4.1, time sequence needs to be taken into account in both of them. The same is the case for all implications of PA-4. For example, it is the case for the theorem that *a parameter's pronounced salience inhibits social mobility* (T-4.71). If hometown relations with one's family and neighbors are very salient, people are not inclined to leave and migrate to other towns where economic opportunities are better. Social as well as geographical mobility is likely to be inhibited by salient ingroup ties, since mobility tends to attenuate these social ties (Burgess and Locke 1953).

If intergroup relations and mobility mutually influence each other, as the assumptions made imply, an initial change in either, whatever conditions produce it, sets off a chain reaction of mutually reinforcing changes in both, until some structural or exogenous condition limits the process of mutual reinforcement. The size of a group sets limits on increasing rates of out-mobility and on increasing rates of intergroup associations of other groups with its members. Ingroup attachments limit increases in rates of intergroup associations, and so does ultimately the fact that association time is not infinitely expandable. The economic interdependence of groups counteracts continuing decreases in intergroup relations, which would eventually fragment society. The amount of mobility into an occupation or into a city has both upper and lower limits, governed by such conditions as the economic demand for various kinds of labor and differential fertility. These limits are very wide ones, however, and social processes engender structural change within them. Indeed, processes of change may alter the framework of structural parameters itself, though this occurs rarely. Increases in intergroup relations can proceed to the point when a parameter and the group distinctions it makes become obliterated, which can happen even for ascribed positions, as illustrated by ethnic assimilation and the absorption of ethnic groups into the generation population. Growing conflict occasionally leads to the cessation of social relations between parts of a society and splits it in two, as examplified by the American Revolution, the Civil War, and the separation of Bangladesh from Pakistan.

Compendium

In conclusion, the theorems derived in this chapter are presented in concise form, as are the axioms and provisional assumptions employed in deriving them. The definitions used in deducing the theorems are not included in this compendium. In the parentheses after each theorem, two pieces of information are supplied: first, the proposition or propositions, excluding definitions, from which it has been deduced; second, the primitive axioms and provisional assumptions, if any, underlying these propositions. Possible intervening theorems are not shown in these parentheses, but they can be easily found in the listing. A similar compendium will be presented at the end of every chapter.

A-0   The members of a society associate with others not only in their own but also in different groups.

T-1   For any dichotomy of society, the small group has more extensive intergroup relations than the large. (From A-0.)

T-1.11   For any dichotomy of society, the proportion of group members intermarried is an inverse function of group size. (From A-0.)

T-1.12   For any dichotomy of society, the mean number of intergroup associates is an inverse function of group size. (From A-0.)

T-1.13   For any dichotomy of society, the mean amount of time spent in intergroup associations is an inverse function of group size. (From A-0.)

T-1.2   Minority groups are more involved in intergroup relations with the majority than the majority is with them. (From T-1; based on A-0.)

T-1.21   The proportion of a minority group who are married to members of the majority exceeds the proportion of the majority who are married to members of the minority. (From T-1; based on A-0.)

T-1.22   The mean number of majority-group associates of a minority exceeds the mean number of associates in that minority of the majority. (From T-1; based on A-0.)

T-1.23   The mean amount of time minority members spend associating with members of the majority exceeds that majority members spend associating with members of that minority. (From T-1; based on A-0.)

T-1.3   Most members of a group that constitutes a large majority have no close associate in small minority groups. (From T-1; based on A-0.)

T-1.4   The larger the difference in size between two groups, the greater is the discrepancy in the rates of intergroup associations between them. (From T-1; based on A-0.)

T-1.5   The probability of extensive intergroup relations increases as the size of groups distinguished by a given nominal parameter decreases. (From T-1; based on A-0.)

T-1.6   If the small group in a dichotomy of the population has proportionately more members who are insulated from intergroup contacts than the large one, the variability in extent of intergroup associations is greater within the small than within the large group. (From T-1; based on A-0.)

T-1.7   If some minorities are more insulated from the majority than the majority is from them, other minorities have particularly extensive intergroup relations with the majority. (From T-1.6; based on A-0.)

T-1.71   If some minorities have lower rates of intergroup associations with the majority than the majority has with them, other minorities have particularly high rates of intergroup associations with the majority. (From T-1.2; based on A-0.)

T-1.8   The closer the role relation, the greater the probability that the proportion of group members insulated from intergroup associates declines with decreasing size of the groups delineated by a nominal parameter. (From T-1; based on A-0.)

T-2   Changes in a parameter's salience change the extent of intergroup relations of a minority with the majority more than the majority's with that minority. (From T-1; based on A-0.)

T-2.11   The probability is that reductions in a parameter's salience increase the rates of intergroup associations of small groups more than those of large groups. (From T-2; based on A-0.)

T-2.12   The probability is that intensified salience of a parameter decreases the rates of intergroup associations of small groups more than those of large groups. (From T-2; based on A-0.)

T-3   The more a majority discriminates in social intercourse against a minority, the smaller is the discrepancy between the majority's lower and the minority's higher rate of intergroup associations. (From T-2; based on A-0.)

T-3.1   As a majority's discrimination in social intercourse against a minority subsides, the discrepancy between the majority's lower and the minority's higher intergroup involvement becomes greater. (From T-2; based on A-0.)

T-3.2   Reduced discrimination by a majority in social intercourse against a minority enlarges the probable difference between the majority's higher and the minority's lower proportion of members who are insulated from close intergroup relations. (From T-2, T-1.8; based on A-0.)

A-1   Social associations are more prevalent among persons in proximate than between those in distant social positions.

A-1.1   Ingroup associations are more prevalent than outgroup associations.

A-1.2   The prevalence of associations declines with increasing status distance.

PA-2   Established role relations are resistant to disruption.

PA-3   Strangers who have a common associate become associates themselves more often than strangers who do not.

T-4   Social mobility promotes intergroup relations. (From A-1, PA-2.)

T-4.1   High rates of mobility between groups promote high rates of association between their nonmobile as well as their mobile members. (From T-4, PA-3; based on A-1, PA-2.)

T-4.2   Increasing rates of mobility among groups reduce a parameter's salience. (From T-4.1; based on A-1, PA-2, PA-3.)

T-4.3   Ceteris paribus, parameters that delineate ascribed positions are more salient than other parameters. (From T-4.2; based on A-1, PA-2, PA-3.)

T-4.4   An increase in motility between a minority and the majority increases the minority's rate of intergroup associations more than the majority's. (From T-2, T-4.2; based on A-0, A-1, PA-2, PA-3.)

T-4.5   The probability is that increases in motility among groups increase the rates of intergroup associations of small groups more than those of large ones. (From T-2, T-4.2; based on A-0, A-1, PA-2, PA-3.)

T-4.6   Net outmobility increases a group's intergroup relations more than net inmobility. (From T-1, T-4.1; based on A-0, A-1, PA-2, PA-3.)

PA-4   Associates in other groups and strata encourage and facilitate mobility into them.

T-4.7   High rates of intergroup associations promote high rates of intergroup mobility. (From PA-4.)

T-4.71 A parameter's pronounced salience inhibits social mobility. (From PA-4.)

CHAPTER THREE

Inequality

INEQUALITY REFERS TO THE DISTRIBUTION OF PEOPLE IN TERMS OF A status dimension—how widely they differ in power or wealth, education or income. Social status assumes a variety of forms, and so does inequality, since every analytical dimension of status is also one of inequality, though empirically various status distributions are often correlated. But the analysis in this chapter is confined to generic characteristics of status distributions in terms of a single parameter, whatever the form of status, so long as graded differences in it find expression in people's role relations and social associations. After examining consequences of the distribution of status for social associations, the concept of inequality is dissected, followed by an analysis of conditions that produce changes in inequality and of their implications for the hypothesis that the poor get poorer as the rich get richer. The significance of combinations of various status differences and that of specific forms of inequality, such as concentration of power, are subjects reserved for discussion in subsequent chapters.

Population distributions distinguish groups or strata of varying size, reflect varying degrees of social differentiation, and may be more or less correlated with each other. The implications of these three aspects of population distributions are discussed in sequence in chapters 2 to 5, separately for nominal and graduated parameters. The previous chapter was concerned with size differences in terms of a nominal parameter. The present one deals first with size differences in terms of a graduated parameter and then with the degree of differentiation delineated by the entire status distribution in terms of a graduated parameter, that is, with inequality. In the next chapter attention centers initially on the degree of differentiation in terms of a nomi-

45

nal parameter, that is, on heterogeneity, and the discussion then proceeds to take into account multiform heterogeneity and thus, for the first time, combinations of several parameters. A fuller analysis of the interrelations of both graduated and nominal parameters is in chapter 5, after which various forms of differentiation within and among substructures are investigated.

Status Distance and Associations

All social positions that vary by gradation rather than constituting nominal categories are defined as *status*. Hence, status differences pertain to those social distinctions people make in their associations with one another that differentiate role relations, not dichotomously into ingroup and outgroup ones, but by degree that reflects social distance of some kind. This broad definition of status encompasses all social attributes that vary by degree, although of primary substantive interest are status differences that reveal differences in social resources of general significance, such as power, prestige, wealth, income, and education. But all graded differences in human attributes that produce graded differences in people's role relations reflect variations in some social resource, limited as the resource's significance may be. For example, physical prowess has no relevance for the social life of most adults, nor does expert knowledge of poetry. If variations in either do affect role relations, however, it indicates that they are social resources of significance in these social circles, as physical strength is among boys and expertness in poetry among literature scholars. Whereas such special cases are not of concern here, the point the illustrations are intended to make is that the theory applies to all variations among people that affect their social associations.

The theorem that a group's size governs the extent of its intergroup relations with another (T-1) implies that the frequency distribution of a population by status exerts corresponding influences on the extent of social relations between different strata. To be sure, status gradations do not have natural boundaries, as groups do, so that divisions of the population into strata are arbitrary. But T-1 does not depend on natural boundaries; it applies to any two segments of the population that differ in size, whether natural groups or arbitrary strata, provided that there are some social associations between their members. The proposition that the members of every group associate with some members of other groups has been initially introduced as a primitive assumption, though it will be derived from other propositions in the next chapter. The theorems formulated below about differences in rates of associations among strata are similarly contingent on the existence of some associations between these strata, since zero associations between groups or strata clearly imply that any predicted difference in their rates of association must also be zero.

For any division of status above the median, the upper stratum has more extensive relations with the lower than the lower has with the upper (T-5). The size difference makes this inevitable, in accordance with T-1, unless there are no associations between the two strata. Specifically, the proportion of the upper stratum who are intermarried exceeds that of the lower; the mean number of associates in the other stratum is larger for the upper than the lower stratum; and so is the mean amount of time spend in social intercourse with members of the other stratum. The higher above the median the population is dichotomized into two strata, the more pronounced are these differences in their rates of social association. For example, the proportion of rich people who marry poor ones is far greater than the proportion of poor people who succeed in getting a rich husband or wife. Old people are more familiar with youth than young people are with old age, not merely because they were young themselves, but also because their number of young friends substantially exceeds the number of old friends of young people, on the average. College graduates tend to spend more time socializing with persons who have not gone to college than the latter spend with the former. If the difference in size is great, most members of the large stratum have no social contacts with any members of the small one (T-1.3).

Most people are insulated from social contacts with the elite (T-5.1). The definition of *elite* is the top stratum on any status dimension that constitutes a small fraction of the population—usually much less than 1 percent. Thus, most people have no face-to-face contact with persons in positions of great political authority, such as governors, senators, and mayors, not even the proverbial handshake during political campaigns, regardless of how extensive are the associations of these elected officials with their constituents. A person cannot maintain social contacts with millions of others. Although any one constituent may have direct access to his or her elected representative, most constituents cannot have such access in a large democracy (neither can most people have access to political leaders in totalitarian countries, of course). Similarly, few physicists, and still fewer persons in other fields, have ever talked to Nobel laureates in physics, despite the fact that these Nobel laureates associate extensively with other physicists and with persons who are not in physics.

The tendency of higher positions in a status hierarchy to have fewer incumbents than lower ones is not confined to elite positions. The elite is merely the polar case of the comparatively small size of higher strata generally. Status distributions are nearly always positively skewed, with a majority of the population occupying less than average status and small numbers occupying status that is far above average. With increasing status, be it prestige, income, or power, frequencies may first increase but they then decrease more or less regularly. Hence, status structures resemble either pyramids or pyramids with their two lower corners cut off. A pyramidal structure is illustrated by the liquid assets of American families, 30 percent of whom owned less than $200 in 1971, and increasingly smaller numbers of whom owned increasingly larger amounts of money (U.S. Bureau of the Census 1973, p. 341, table 561). The six prestige classes Warner and Lunt (1941, p. 88) distinguish in Yankee City compose a pyramid without corners, or a truncated diamond: the lower-lower class is smaller (25 percent) than the upper-lower (33 percent), but thereafter class size declines with increasing status (the four other percentages are 28, 10, 2, and 1). The income distribution of American families also exemplifies a truncated diamond: 18 percent of all families had income of less than $5,000 in 1971, 30 percent incomes of $5,000–10,000, with the proportions declining subsequently; other years and narrower income intervals reveal distributions of essentially the same shape (U.S. Bureau of the Census 1973, p. 328, table 531).

The status distribution is positively skewed so that the mean is above the median and the single mode is below it (A-5).[1] This is another basic axiom of the theory. Although square status distributions are conceivable, in which every hierarchical position has the same number of incumbents, empirically high status is rarely, if ever, either as prevalent or as close to the average as low status. Nor is it likely that empirical status distributions have more than one mode with maximum frequencies or one above the median, unless extremely narrow status intervals are used. The theorems deduced from A-5 do not apply to such exceptional cases. They apply to all status structures that are truncated diamonds—pyramids without corners—and, *a fortiori*, to all full pyramids. Strata are defined as equal status intervals, not equal population percentages, and the *lowest* strata are defined as those below the modal stratum with the highest proportion of the population.

Except for the lowest strata, the probability of social associations with status-distant persons increases with increasing status, ceteris paribus (T-5.2).[2] If population frequencies, except for the lowest strata, decrease with

1. The mode is employed here as a criterion of a theoretical concept, although it is rarely used in statistical operations owing to its instability and other undesirable properties. This requires a comment. Reference is to the highest point in a *smoothed* frequency distribution that ignores minor fluctuations among very narrow status intervals. These fluctuations are what makes the mode unstable. The assumption is that in a smoothed status distribution frequencies may first increase but then decrease over a considerably wider range of status.

2. The operational measures required for empirical tests of theorems about the relationship between status and social associations would be based on the average differences in status, ignoring sign, between persons and their associates, either all their associates or those in specified other strata. For marriage, the absolute differences in status between persons and their spouses are divided by the number of couples. For number of nonexclusive associates or association time, the mean absolute status distance between every person's own status and his or her associates' (for time, weighted by time) is computed first, and the mean of these means is then calculated, ignoring sign throughout. For insulation, the measure is the proportion of persons in one stratum without any social contacts with those in another, multiplied by the status distance between the two strata.

increasing status (A-5); and if the rate of associations with outsiders is inversely related to the size of a group or stratum (T-1.5); it follows that the rate of association with status-distant persons in smaller higher strata exceeds that in larger lower ones, wherever the strata are divided, unless there is no association between their members. But the proposition that status-distant associations are inversely related to status requires three qualifications: (1) it does not apply to the lowest strata whose size does not decrease with increasing status; (2) it is only a probabilistic proposition for numerous strata, corresponding to T-1.5; and (3) it necessitates a ceteris paribus, because status salience also influences the extent of status-distant associations. Another implication of A-5 and T-1 is a deterministic theorem: *Except for the lowest strata, the greater the social distance between two strata, the greater is the discrepancy between their rates of association with each other, specifically, between the higher rate of the upper and the lower rate of the lower stratum* (T-5.3).

It has been observed that marriages to persons outside one's own socioeconomic stratum are more prevalent in higher than lower socioeconomic strata (Centers 1949). Boys and girls from higher social classes have also been found to be more likely than those from lower classes to have dates with partners whose social class differs from their own (Hollingshead 1949, p. 231). Despite the qualified nature of T-5.2, it can explain these research findings without resort to interpretations that assume class differences to have less psychological significance for persons in the middle class than those in the working class, indeed, without assuming that class differences as such affect the associations of anybody. For the structural condition of the sheer size difference among social classes alone explains the marriage and dating patterns observed. The smaller size of higher strata makes cross-class associations more prevalent there than in lower strata.

These differences in social experiences may well color the ways different

Correlations can be used directly to ascertain the overall relationship between status distance and social associations in a population, which reflects the salience of a status as indicated by a given graduated parameter. For marriage, the correlation is simply that between ego's status and spouse's, for example, between their socioeconomic origins, education, or income. For number of nonexclusive associates and for association time, however, it is not the correlation between ego's status and mean status of associates, as this would cancel associations with both higher and lower strata. Rather, it is the correlation between ego's status and his or her mean absolute status distance from associates (for time, weighted by time), so that associations with both higher and lower strata do not cancel each other. Insulation is not suitable for deriving indications of the overall influence of status on associations.

Theorems about inequality, status diversity, or heterogeneity are not meaningful for the analysis of a single social structure, only for the comparison of several. Different societies may be compared, or different communities or other collectivities within one society, but in the latter case these collectivities are treated as independent units of analysis, not as structural components of societies that are the units of analysis. The correlations just described which indicate the influence of status distance on associations are used as variables describing every social structure in comparative studies of the implications of variations in inequality for social associations and for conditioning the influence of status on social associations.

social strata perceive and view the class structure. Class lines may appear to be less rigid to persons in upper than those in lower strata, because the social reality experienced by the latter actually restricts interpersonal relations more by class lines than that experienced by the former. But such differences in views and attitudes that may make class distinctions less significant in the thinking of upper strata are the consequences of the more prevalent associations across class lines among upper than lower strata, not their cause, which is accounted for by the structural variation in stratum size.

Status distance inhibits social associations, which is an axiom (A-1.2) introduced in the preceding chapter. This effect of status distance itself on social relations has not yet been considered; only the effects of size differences among strata have been. The influences of status distance and size difference on rates of social associations combine and modify each other. A simplified illustration of the resulting pattern for five strata is shown in table 2. The rate of association of every stratum with others below it (reading down from the major diagonal) is arbitrarily set to decrease, in accordance with A-1.2, at the same rate (.50, .40, .30, .20). From these association rates and the size distribution among strata, which is positively skewed to accord with A-5, the precise association rates of every stratum with others above it (above the diagonal) are deducible, in accordance with T-1. It can be seen that a stratum's rate of association decreases faster with increasing status distance as one goes up (from the diagonal) than as one goes down. This general pattern does not depend on the specific numerical assumptions initially made about rate and size differences, as long as the assumptions conform to A-1.2 and A-5, although particular rates may deviate from the overall pattern owing to irregular shifts in status salience or in the frequency distribution.

TABLE 2.   RATES OF ASSOCIATION AMONG FIVE STRATA

Rate with Stratum	Mean Status Score	Rate of Stratum				
		A	B	C	D	E
A : Highest	5	1.00	.25	.10	.04	.03
B	4	.50	1.00	.25	.10	.10
C	3	.40	.50	1.00	.25	.27
D	2	.30	.40	.50	1.00	.67
E : Lowest	1	.20	.30	.40	.50	1.00
Number (millions)		10	20	40	80	60
Total Rates						
Up		—	.25	.35	.39	1.07
Down		1.4	1.20	.90	.50	—
Both		1.4	1.45	1.25	.89	1.07

The rates of association with persons of lower status probably decline less with increasing status distance than do the rates of association with persons of higher status (T-5.4). The reason is that size differences counter the influence of status distance on the former rates but reinforce its influence on the latter rates. The combined influences of great social distances and large size differences strongly depress the rates of social association of low strata, including the lowest, with high strata, not merely the elite but also others whose status is substantially above the average. This double effect insulates most persons of low status from sociable contacts with persons of high status.

The imaginary five-stratum society in table 2 reveals why T-5.2 must be qualified by ceteris paribus. The rate of status-distant associations—the total rate with all other strata in the illustration—is not highest for the top stratum, as the last row of table 2 incidates (neither is it lowest for the bottom stratum, owing to its relatively small size). The reason is that status distance inhibits social associations, a proposition that has not yet been taken into account in T-5.2 and that modifies the influence of size it predicates. The status distance of A from three strata (B, C, D) is the same as that of B from three strata (C, D, E), which is reflected in the identical rates of associations of A and of B with the three strata equidistant from them (.50, .40, .30). But A's remaining stratum (E) is a distant one, whereas B's remaining stratum (A) is not so distant, which raises B's rate over A's rate with the respective remaining stratum (.25 v. .20) and consequently B's total rate with other strata over A's.

Decreasing frequencies with increasing status imply that in the relation between any two strata the rate of association of the higher exceeds that of the lower stratum. Size differences make this inevitable (T-1) for the relation between all strata except the lowest, and for its relations with high, smaller strata as well, though not for its relation with intermediate strata that are larger. (The prevailing difference, and the deviant, opposite pattern for the relations between stratum D and E, can be observed in table 2 by comparing the rates in two corresponding cells on both sides of the major diagonal; the left entry is always the larger, except for the two D-E cells.) If in the relation between any two strata downward associations are more prevalent than upward associations, chances are that all strata have higher rates of downward than upward association, though only in the part of the status structure that is pyramidal, where frequencies decrease as status increases.

Except for the lowest strata, the probability of people's associating with others below them in status is greater than the probability of their associating with others equidistant above them (T-5.5). There are more equidistant potential associates below than above all persons in a pyramid except those in the lowest strata, so that available associates make downward associations for most more likely. But the theorem can be derived without taking availability of associates into account, as can be exemplified by an administrative hierarchy, which is a pyramidal structure. Every administrative rank except the nonsupervisory employees at the bottom of the hierarchy associates more with subordinates than with superiors. The reason is not that more subordinates are available as associates, nor is it solely that supervising subordinates is an administrative responsibility. It is that the sheer difference in number of incumbents make this highly probable.

Persons in every administrative rank must associate more frequently with subordinates than the more numerous subordinates associate with them (T-1), though not necessarily more frequently than they themselves associate with superiors. But if first-line supervisors were to associate as often with their superiors as with their subordinates, and these superiors were to associate as often with their superiors as with first-line supervisors, and the same were the case for successive ranks, managers on the fifth level (above the bottom) would have to associate with those on the fourth 1,000 times as frequently as first-line supervisors associate with their subordinates (assuming a rather narrow superior-subordinate ratio of 1:4), which is not feasible. To illustrate: If first-line supervisors spend on the average only one minute a day talking individually with each of four subordinates, and thus four minutes with subordinates, for them to spend as much time with their superiors as with their subordinates requires that each second-level manager spend four minutes with each, and thus 16 (4^2) minutes with all four subordinates (first-line supervisors); repeating the computation for higher ranks indicates that fifth-level managers must spend 4^5 or 1,024 minutes a day with their immediate subordinates on the fourth level, which is more time than there is in a working day.

The same principle applies to status differences in society, which are not formal hierarchies of official positions. To be sure, most status distributions in society, such as those in income and in prestige, are less highly skewed than the distributions of formal authority in organizations (indicated by the superior-subordinate ratio), though some, such as the distributions of wealth and of power in society, may well be no less skewed. For highly uneven status distributions, which generally reflect great inequality, compelling structural constraints make it inevitable that most people above the lowest strata associate much more with others in lower than those in higher strata, because equal (or nearly equal) rates of association with both would require impossibly high rates of association between the highest strata, as has been illustrated. For less uneven status distribution, parallel structural constraints exist but they are not so strong, which makes it probable, though not inevitable, that persons who are not in the lowest strata associate somewhat more with others below than with others above them in status.

Differences in socioeconomic status, power, or prestige tend to find expression in social interaction. Individuals are likely to be respectful and deferential toward others who status is superior to their own, thereby providing social support and validation of the superior social standing that money, influence, or prominence command. Since persons in middle as well as upper strata associate disproportionately with others whose status is lower than theirs, many people whose status is not particularly high receive such supportive and gratifying social acknowledgment of superior standing in most of their social associations. If we assume provisionally that *superior status is manifest in superordinate roles in social associations* (PA-6), T-5.5 has a further paradoxical implication: *The probability is that most people above the lowest strata have the superordinate role in most of their social associations* (T-5.6).

But how is it possible for most people to be superordinate in most of their associations, inasmuch as the number of superordinate roles must be the same as that of subordinate ones for all associations? Indeed, how is it possible for most people to associate more with inferiors than with superiors, as T-5.5 implies, since the number of inferiors and of superiors must be the same for all associations? It is possible for the members of every middle stratum to provide most associates for the stratum above and yet associate mostly with the stratum below, because their number is greater than that in the stratum above and smaller than that in the stratum below. This is clearly not possible for the lowest stratum, however, whatever the shape of the pyramid. All the associations of the members of the lowest stratum are with persons in the same or in a higher stratum, so that none of their associations enables them to take the superordinate role and many require them to assume the subordinate role. The majority of people above the lowest strata are able to enjoy superordinate roles in most associations because persons in the lowest stratum must play subordinate roles in all their associations that cross status lines. The qualification "excluding the lowest strata" is required in T-5.5 and T-5.6 even for a pyramidal structure where the lowest strata are most numerous.

The social connections in a status structure are affected by vertical mobility, just as intergroup relations are affected by mobility (T-4.1). *The higher the rates of vertical mobility between two social strata, the more prevalent are the associations between their members* (T-6). If many professionals have working-class parents, or if many laborers once owned a farm themselves, more extensive social relations exist between these occupational strata than if there is less upward or downward mobility between them. This is deducible from two assumptions: that role relations resist disruption (PA-2), which implies that mobile persons have associates in their former as well as in their present social position, and that some of the different associates of the mobile become associates themselves (PA-3).[3] As a matter of fact, the

3. The application of these assumptions to vertical mobility is subject to the criticism that various psychological processes that affect human relations are ignored. For example, ambivalence, or plain snobbery, may motivate upwardly mobile individuals to avoid their former friends and relatives who have remained in the lower strata where they originated. The assumption made (PA-2) is that the positive influence of common background and established role relations on social associations exceeds, on the average, the negative influences of such more subtle psychological forces.

former assumption suffices to derive the theorem, and the latter simply broadens its implications. Mobility between distant strata is rare, and so are the associations between them, two conditions that undoubtedly reinforce each other (as implied by PA-2 and PA-4). Once again, the deterministic proposition for two strata (T-6) can be transformed into a probabilistic proposition for all strata defined by a given parameter.

Increasing vertical mobility in a society increases the probability of social associations among various strata (T-6.1). By the same token, a decrease in vertical mobility strengthens status barriers to social associations. Mobility in either direction—upward or downward—promotes social relations between members of different strata. Regardless of direction, therefore, *increasing rates of vertical mobility reduce the salience of status for social intercourse* (T-6.11), in accordance with T-4.2. The circulation of the elite is a form of motility, or mobility in both directions, which raises rates of cross-class associations. But it does not raise them equally, since the same change in amount of association alters the rate of association of a small group more than that of a large one (T-2). *Rapid circulation of the elite increases the rate of social contact of elite members with others substantially but reduces the insulation of most others from the elite little* (T-6.2).

Excess mobility in one direction changes the rates of associations between strata indirectly, by affecting their relative size, as well as directly, by affecting the amount of social interaction between them. *Ceteris paribus, predominant upward mobility increases the rates of association of lower with higher strata more than the rates of association of higher with lower strata* (T-6.3). The change in size distribution that excess upward mobility effects is responsible for the difference, in accordance with T-4.6. For example, changes in technology and economic demand have led to much mobility from manual origins to white-collar occupational status and from lower white-collar origins to professional status. This upward mobility is predicted to have raised the likelihood of upward more than that of downward associations in terms of occupational status, though only independent of other conditions affecting this likelihood. There are primarily two other conditions that have effects opposite from those of upward mobility on these associations. First, disproportionately high rates of net fertility of lower strata and net immigration into them increase their relative size, thereby counteracting the effect of outmobility on size, Second, increasing amounts of association increase the rates of association of the larger lower strata less than those of the smaller higher ones, thereby counteracting the effect of outmobility on rates. Since the influences of these two conditions are likely to be pronounced for the social relations between strata that are considerably apart, T-6.3 is expected only to reduce the differences between the lower rates of upward and the higher rates of downward associations that these other conditions would otherwise produce. When mobility is predominantly downward—as the result of unemployment or of inflation that shrinks mid-

dle incomes most, for instance—it increases the rates of association of higher
with lower strata more than those of lower with higher strata, which often
parallels and reinforces the effects of other conditions.

Changes in the population distribution alter the extent of social associations through which the various parts of the status structure are related.
Social mobility effects such changes in the status structure, and inequality
reflects them. *Ceteris paribus, a decline in inequality reduces the impact of
status on social associations* (T-7). This theorem follows from the axiom that
social associations decrease with increasing status distance (A-1.2), since a
decline in inequality entails a decrease in average status distance relative to
average status. The qualification by ceteris paribus is needed to take account
of the influences of changes in salience on social associations, particularly
whether decreases in absolute or in relative status distance are most salient
for social intercourse. A difference in income of $8,000, for example, is less of
a relative difference in a society where the average income is $16,000 than in
one where it is $4,000. Inequality defined in relative terms declines not only
when the average difference in income decreases but also when it remains
the same while average income rises, inasmuch as the latter reduces relative
income differences. Although reductions in absolute and in relative status
distance tend to be concomitant, the question left open in T-7 is which of the
two, if they do not coincide, predominates in influencing social associations.

When many people are very poor or powerless or uneducated and just a
few are very rich or have great power or are highly educated, inequality is
most pronounced. Generally, extreme inequality entails extreme differences
in size among strata. Although reductions in inequality depend not only on
the status frequency distribution, they usually do entail lesser size differences among strata. Hence, reductions in inequality often diminish the
discrepancies in the rates of association between strata, as these discrepancies are a function of the differences in stratum size.[4] When inequality in
status declines, inequality in the opportunities for social contacts with different strata frequently declines as well.

Great reductions in inequality may even raise the status of the social
strata whose members are most likely to be insulated from close relations
with other strata, as it pushes the mode of the frequency distribution from
the lowest toward the middle strata. At the end of the last century, the
majority of American adults had less than eight years of schooling, and these
least-educated strata were, owing to their large size, most insulated from
contacts with other educational strata. Now only a minority of the population
has never gone to high school, the majority has some or all four years of
high-school education, and another minority is college educated. The mean
number of associations of the high-school educated majority with both the

---

4. This is not formulated as a theorem because not all reductions in inequality diminish
differences in stratum size and thereby discrepancies in rates of association.

less- and the more-educated group must be less than the mean number of associations of these groups with high-school educated persons only, which makes it, *a fortiori*, less than the means of these groups when their associations with each other are added. It follows (in accordance with T-1.8, that insulation from close intergroup relations is inversely related to group size) that the persons most likely to be insulated from close relations with different educational strata are those with intermediate educational status, whereas at the turn of the century they were those with low educational status.

Shapes of Status Distributions

To examine the conditions under which inequality diminishes or becomes more pronounced, it is necessary to clarify the concept of inequality by analyzing its connection with the status distribution, which in turn requires a precise understanding of the variable that is distributed—social status. Since social status is a relational attribute of persons that characterizes them relative to other persons, it is sometimes defined directly by relational properties, for instance, sociometric choices received or social interaction initiated. The procedure employed here for defining status is somewhat different, involving two steps: After initially distinguishing persons on the basis of variable properties that describe them, not relations among them, the defining criterion of status is that variations in these properties are manifest in differences in social relations. The reason is that the status differences most relevant for macrosociological analysis are not those resting on interpersonal relations. Income and political power are important dimensions of status in society, not popularity among friends or power over associates. A sergeant may wield more personal power over larger numbers than a general, which hardly reflects the difference in their power in society. Although income, power, or any other attribute of persons would not be defined as status if it were not reflected in some role relations, it need not be reflected in superordination in social associations by definition. The provisional assumption that it is so related (PA-6) can then be empirically tested, and its implications follow only for status attributes that meet the assumption.

Three facets of status need to be distinguished for every form of status, be it wealth, education, seniority, or any other graduated characteristic of persons that influences their role relations. The first is absolute status, which refers to the variate itself and describes the quantity of the social resource available to various persons. Examples are the amount of wealth possessed or income earned, the years of experience accumulated or education attained—or, to refine the latter, breadth of knowledge. How many more dollars one person earns annually than another or than the average person in the labor force indicates absolute status distance. Second, proportionate status refers to people's position in the percentile distribution of a variate, without taking into consideration the actual value of the variate, such as median years of education, lowest income quartile, or greater wealth than that of 99 percent of the population. Proportionate status distance from the average is implicit in proportionate status.

Relative status, the third facet, defines each person's hierarchical position or social resources relative to those of all other persons. This concept, which is implicit in what is usually meant by hierarchical status, requires taking into account not merely the absolute distribution or the percentage distribution, but both. The operational criterion of relative status is the ratio of a person's social resources or absolute status variate to those of others. We speak of relative status when we say that one person's income is 10 percent less than another's, that her years of schooling are one-and-one-half times the average education in the population, or that his IQ is one standard deviation below the mean. In contrast to absolute status, which is not zero-sum, proportionate status is, and so is relative status. All persons' income can rise. But for some persons' standing in the income distribution and share of all incomes to rise, those of other persons must fall.

Inequality has been distinguished from status diversity and conceptualized in terms of average status distance in chapter 1. A further conceptual distinction can be made, depending on the facet of status under consideration. Absolute inequality is defined by absolute status distance. If one person's annual income exceeds another's by $1,000, the two are less unequal than if the difference is $10,000. Correspondingly, if the average income difference in society is $1,000 there is less inequality than if it is $10,000. This is a meaningful definition of inequality. A question that immediately arises, however, is whether a difference between $5,000 and $6,000 should not be considered to indicate more inequality than one between $25,000 and $26,000, though both are $1,000. To do this, inequality can be redefined on the basis of relative status as the ratio of the average status distance in a population to the average status. This conception of inequality is equivalent to the Gini index, the most widely used empirical measure of inequality, except that the ratio is divided by two, which makes it vary between zero and one, and empirically mean status distance between all possible pairs is not actually computed but estimated from grouped data.[5] (Average distance in proportionate status is a constant and thus not a meaningful criterion of inequality.)

5. Autobiographical note: I started to conceptualize inequality precisely in these terms. Since two individuals are more unequal the greater the difference in prestige, power, or income between them, I thought that inequality in a society should be defined as the average difference in status. Then I wondered about using absolute status differences and whether average status should not be taken into account. Only later did I discover, thanks to Professor van de Geer at Leyden University, that the Gini index represents mean status distance relative to mean status,

A variety of measures of inequality have been used in research (Alker and Russett 1966). A rough measure of relative inequality that often suffices is the share of the total resource concentrated in a given small fraction of the population, for instance, the proportion of all incomes earned or all wealth owned by the richest 1 percent. An evident shortcoming of this measure is that it ignores variations in relative status in the rest of the population, for example, whether two societies with equally small proportions of university-educated persons differ in the proportion who have completed secondary school. The Gini index takes this into account and has the further advantage of being equivalent to the theoretical conception of relative inequality advanced. Absolute inequality should not be completely ignored, however, since it calls attention to distinctive aspects of the status distribution that are neglected by relative measures. A measure of absolute inequality can be directly derived from the Gini coefficient by multiplying it with twice the mean status. Thus, a Gini coefficient of income inequality of .33 implies that the average income difference between all pairs is two-thirds of the average income, and one of .50 implies that the average status distance is the same as the average status. This information helps clarify the meaning of an observed Gini coefficient. What is more important, absolute measures of inequality furnish information about it that is not revealed by relative measures, because the two have opposite limitations.

Generally, relative inequality is a more meaningful concept than absolute inequality, which can be very misleading. A regressive tax that requires poor people to pay 20 percent and rich ones only 10 percent of their incomes reduces measures of absolute inequality, since the absolute income differences after taxes are less than before taxes. If everybody's income increases by exactly the same proportion, leaving the distribution unaltered, measured absolute inequality increases. One more illustration: The owner of a sweatshop earns ten times the $2,000 wage of the 50 workers, while the administrator of a research institute earns only twice the $18,000 salary of the 50 other employees; yet absolute inequality would be the same, as the absolute difference is the same. The serious limitation of absolute measures of inequality is that they are completely governed by absolute differences

---

which is not apparent in the formula generally used in calculating it (Alker and Russett 1966, p. 364). An alternative formula for the Gini index suggested by van de Geer (though using my own simplified symbols) is

$$\frac{2\Sigma s_i f_i\left(P_{b_i} - P_{a_i}\right)}{2\Sigma s_i p_i}$$

where s_i is mean status in a category, p_i is the fraction of the population in that category, and p_{b_i} and p_{a_i} are the fractions of the population whose status is below and above that category, respectively. (Thus, for every category, $p_i + p_{a_i} + p_{b_i} = 1.00$.) The sum is taken over all categories. The numerator is mean status distance, or absolute inequality; the denominator is twice mean status. The ratio of the two is relative inequality.

and ignore whether the rich have 1,000 times or merely twice the wealth of the poor.

The concept of relative inequality centers attention precisely on these proportionate differences, but exclusive focus on them can also give the wrong impression. Were a government to give a bonus to all families ranging from $20,000 for the richest to $2,000 for the poorest, one would hardly call this a program to alleviate inequality, yet it would reduce measured relative inequality, as the proportionate increase in affluence is less for the rich than for the poor. When rich and poor countries that have the same average income differences are compared, measures of relative inequality, which divide mean income differences by mean income, record less inequality in the rich ones. This seems quite appropriate, inasmuch as a difference between $2,000 and $3,000 is undoubtedly experienced as entailing more inequality than one between $12,000 and $13,000. Still, it is well to remember that the empirical finding that income inequality in Western nations is less pronounced than in less industrialized countries (Kravis 1973) is largely the result of the difference in income level between the two.

Whereas these limitations should be kept in mind when interpreting differences in relative inequality, another limitation is so serious that it requires not using the concept at all in certain cases or supplementing it with an analysis of absolute inequality. If the concentration of wealth or power is very great, the conception of relative inequality loses its meaning. When most people have no wealth or power and all of it is concentrated in a small elite, measured relative inequality is the same whether the elite has little or very great wealth, whether it has only moderate influence over the rest of the population or the power to enslave it. The reason for this failure to discriminate is both conceptual and methodological. The concept of relative inequality answers the question of how great are the differences in resources among people relative to the average amount they have, which is not a meaningful question if most people do not have any. Methodologically, it does not make sense to standardize the average difference in resources by dividing by the average amount of resources when the latter average is entirely or largely determined by the very resources of the elite it is supposed to standardize. Conceptually, it is meaningless to ask how much of a resource is concentrated in the elite when all of it is. The important question in this case is how much of the resource the elite has, which is answered by the absolute and not by the relative concept of inequality. Most forms of inequality are not so extreme that the majority of people have zero status, which makes the relative concept of inequality the most appropriate. But some resources are so concentrated that most people have hardly any or none; political power, administrative authority, and stock ownership are examples; in these cases an analysis of absolute inequality must supplement that of relative inequality.

The problem posed at the beginning of this section is how changes in inequality are reflected in the shape of the status distribution. On a graph with status—income or education or a power score—on the horizontal and frequencies on the vertical axis, the theoretical minimum, equality, is a vertical line at the point of the horizontal axis indicating the common status of all—say, an income of $10,000 or 12 years of education—with the length of the line representing the total population. The theoretical maximum of inequality would be a vertical line nearly as long at zero and a single point on the horizontal axis to the right. The distance of this point from zero reveals the amount of absolute inequality, which can vary from nearly zero to a very high though not infinite value while relative inequality is at the theoretical maximum. (Equality is, of course, the theoretical minimum for absolute as well as relative inequality.) Very great inequality is a hyperbola that is nearly rectangular, representing a large majority with zero or low status, few persons with intermediate, and still fewer with high status. (See figure 2.)

Inequality diminishes as the (horizontal) status distances decline for growing numbers, which implies that frequencies decrease at the extremes and increase closer to the middle. This can be symbolized by a force that pushes the left part of the curve toward the northeast (figure 2): The concave curve is transformed into a convex one, except at the right, and both intercepts move toward the intersection of the axes. With continuing de-

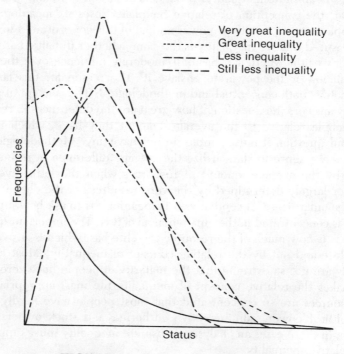

FIGURE 2.   STATUS DISTRIBUTIONS

creases in inequality the apex of the curve moves farther up and right and the two intercepts move closer to zero, so that the shape of the distribution increasingly approximates a normal curve, except for being positively skewed. These changes make the status distribution less skewed, reduce its standard deviation, and ultimately make it more leptokurtic, which represents many persons whose status is the same and few whose status differs much.

To visualize a status hierarchy, the coordinates are turned 90 degrees and the curve is duplicated by its mirror image, so that now status is on the vertical axis and frequencies are on both sides of the horizontal one. Very great inequality on this graph resembles a tent with very sagging sides (figure 3). Decreasing inequality acts like a wind that pushes against the sides from the inside to make them bulge, simultaneously reducing the height and narrowing the base of the structure. Continuing decreases in inequality further reduce the height and narrow the base, often though not always with the result that the base is no longer the widest part and the triangle becomes a truncated diamond. Ultimately, the figure approaches a straight horizontal line as the diamond becomes broader and flatter and inequality approaches equality.

Changes in inequality occur when the status distribution changes, often as the result of people's mobility that alters their relative status, including changes in relative income and power as well as occupational and educational

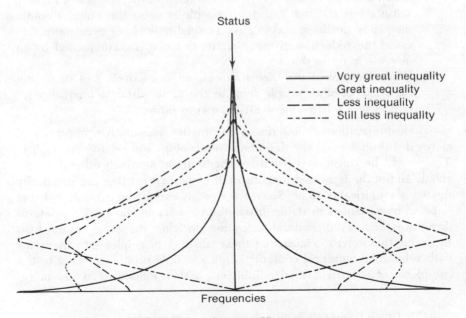

FIGURE 3.   STATUS HIERARCHIES

mobility. Some general principles about the effects of certain changes in status on inequalities implied by the foregoing analysis are the following:

1. If everybody's status (for instance, income) changes by the same absolute amount (same number of dollars), absolute inequality remains the same, and relative inequality changes in the opposite direction, because an increase in mean status reduces and a decrease raises inequality relative to (as a ratio of) mean status.

2. If everybody's status changes by the same proportion, absolute inequality changes in the same direction, because the absolute change is greater for higher than lower strata, and relative inequality remains the same.

3. If everybody's status changes toward the mean, both absolute and relative inequality decline.

4. If everybody's status changes away from the mean, both absolute and relative inequality increase.

5. Changes in some people's status that affect absolute inequality (mean status distance) and mean status in parallel ways have effects on relative inequality (defined by the ratio of the two) that are indeterminate, depending on the precise change in either.

6. Changes in some people's status that affect absolute inequality and mean status in opposite ways have determinate effects on relative inequality parallel to those on absolute inequality.

7. When some persons in low (below-median) strata experience a rise in status while the status of other people remains the same, absolute inequality declines, and relative inequality declines even more, because the reduction in mean status distance is accompanied by an increase in mean status.

8. When some persons in low strata experience a decline in status and the status of other people remains the same, absolute inequality increases and relative inequality increases more.

These propositions follow directly from the quantitative properties of status distributions and the definitions of absolute and relative inequality. They might be considered primitive theorems from which others are derived. All but the last two are so abstract, however, that they are practically devoid of empirical content. Since the first six essentially explicate what is entailed by variations in status distributions, it seems more appropriate to designate them as procedural rules for deriving theorems rather than theorems themselves. Translating these abstract principles into theorems with substantial empirical content[6] is not a simple problem, owing to the complexity of patterns of social mobility and of their influences on inequality.

6. The term is Popper's (1959, pp. 112–35).

Changes in Inequality

Attention centers on relative inequality, which is the relevant concept for most forms of status differences, and which poses more serious analytical problems than absolute inequality because it is affected in opposite ways by changes in absolute inequality and in average status. The problems involved in the analysis of inequality (which from now on always refers to relative inequality, unless otherwise indicated) can be illustrated by suggesting some more specific hypotheses based on the abstract propositions listed above. Thus, the last two, which are less abstract than the others, lead one to expect the following: If the average status of all the persons in lower (below-median) strata rises and that of all the persons in higher strata remains the same, inequality declines; if the average status of all the persons in lower strata declines and that of all the persons in higher strata remains the same, inequality increases. But both of these statements are false as worded, that is, not necessarily true, although propositions 7 and 8, from which they seem to derive, are correct. The reason that they are false is that a given status change of extreme strata influences mean status distance and inequality more than the same status change of less extreme strata, which means that the status changes of various strata must not be averaged when ascertaining their influence on inequality.

The greater dependence of inequality on the status of extreme strata suggests that one should restrict oneself to these strata to derive unequivocal propositions. For example, if all lowest strata experience status improvements, inequality diminishes; if all highest strata experience status declines, inequality diminishes. These propositions are also incorrect, however, because the effects on inequality of these status changes of extreme strata can be outweighed by the effects of opposite changes of other strata that involve larger distances or greater numbers. What makes it so difficult to specify how inequality changes is that the changes of different strata can nullify one another but must not be averaged. Note that these difficulties arise without worrying about changes within strata, which are often ignored, and in the simple case when only a single dimension of status is being considered.

We cannot even say that inequality remains the same when there is no difference at all in status change and every individual, not merely every stratum, experiences the same change in status. For the first principle above reveals that the same absolute status change for every person alters inequality, and the first two together show that any kind of status change that is the same for everybody alters either absolute or relative inequality. Hence, we seem to be reduced to the simple principle that inequality remains the same only if nobody in the society moves either up or down in status. Yet this apparent tautological truism is false, too. A society's population is not a closed system. New members are born, and others move into it from abroad;

some die, and others emigrate. Unless these net movements into or out of various strata are exactly proportionate to their size, they alter the status distribution, and with it inequality.

Ceteris paribus, if the net fertility of lower strata exceeds that of higher strata, inequality increases (T-8). Net fertility refers to birth rates minus death rates. Lower and higher strata, here and throughout, are those below and above median status, respectively. *Ceteris paribus, if the net immigration from abroad into lower strata exceeds that into higher strata, inequality increases* (T-8.1). Net immigration is the rate of immigration minus emigration. The two theorems apply to all forms of status, independent of any intrinsic difference in prestige between foreign-born and natives, provided that the status distribution is positively skewed (A-5). Only two conditions other than those stipulated in each theorem influence inequality (requiring the ceteris paribus), the one stated in the other theorem and internal mobility. These theorems call attention to conditions affecting inequality that are frequently ignored.[7]

When poor strata grow disproportionately owing to larger families and larger numbers of immigrants, as has been the case in the United States for generations, inequality increases. But this is not what is usually emphasized in discussions of class differences in fertility and immigration, including this author's (Blau and Duncan 1967, pp. 425–26). What is focused upon is that the differences in birth rates and the large streams of immigrants into poorer strata have improved poor people's opportunities for upward mobility to fill the ranks of higher strata that have become relatively depleted as the result of their much slower growth. Indeed, these two conditions that have expanded the lower strata disproportionately probably have enhanced their chances of upward mobility, but only after first increasing inequality. This can explain why high rates of upward mobility have prevailed in the United States for many decades, yet economic inequality has declined little if at all.

For upward social mobility to reduce inequality, it must first overcome the increases in inequality engendered by the larger families typically found in lower strata and the larger influx of immigrants into them typically observed in advanced industrial countries. For example, income inequality declines only if the incomes of the poor increase not merely proportionately more than those of other strata but, in addition, sufficiently more to outweigh the changes produced in the status distribution by class differences in net fertility and net immigration. To formulate theorems about the influences of social mobility on inequality, it is necessary to take these two other

7. Some economists have noted that the higher fertility of lower strata, which is typically not taken into account in empirical studies, would increase measured inequality (Kuznets 1966, p. 201; Champernowne 1973, p. 159). As a matter of fact, ignoring variations in family size depresses the generally used measures of inequality in family income doubly: by not counting the larger number of lower-status individuals in the frequency distribution, and by not weighting the family income to take into account differences in the number of persons it supports.

conditions that influence it into account. One procedure for doing so is to qualify the theorems accordingly; another is to make certain assumptions about variations in net fertility and net immigration which permit deriving unqualified or less qualified theorems. The latter procedure yields more elegant theorems, not hedged in by extensive qualifications, but unless the assumptions are made in disregard of known empirical data, they determine what unqualified propositions can be derived from them and which ones cannot be. (Although another possibility would be to ignore these other influences and simply treat them as subsumed under ceteris paribus, this is not satisfactory when these other influences are known. Disregarding information for the sake of pseudosimplicity is not a good procedure.)

Two provisional assumptions are made, on the basis of which it is possible to specify patterns of mobility that increase inequality. *The rates of net fertility of lower strata are no less than those of higher strata* (PA-7). This is a conservative assumption, since fertility generally declines with increasing status, and while the general decline in the United States is followed by some rise for the highest stratum, its rate of fertility is still substantially less than those of lower strata (Blau and Duncan 1967, p. 373). *The net rates of immigration from outside the social structure into lower strata are no less than those into higher strata* (PA-8). This is nearly always true for countries with high rates of immigrants, most of whom are generally poor. It may not be true for countries with high rates of emigration of lower strata, or for countries with many immigrants who are professionals. For such cases the assumption must be altered, and the propositions derived from it must be altered correspondingly.

Under these assumptions, net fertility and immigration can only increase inequality or leave it unchanged, but cannot decrease it, as indicated by T-8 and T-8.1. Consequently, when a given pattern of social mobility increases inequality, this is a sufficient condition for it to increase, as the only two other factors influencing inequality also increase it. However, if a given pattern of social mobility reduces inequality, this is not sufficient for concluding that inequality diminishes, since the opposite effects of the two other factors may outweigh that of mobility. On the other hand, it is possible to state what mobility patterns are necessary for reductions in inequality to occur, because such a reduction requires mobility that counteracts the opposite effects of the two other factors.

For inequality to diminish it is necessary that some low or middle strata experience upward mobility or that some highest strata experience downward mobility (T-9). To repeat the definitions and mention a new one: Inequality is relative inequality; mobility refers to any change in status; low strata are those below median status; and the line between highest and middle strata depends on the degree of inequality, as indicated below. The theorem is deterministic, provided the assumptions (A-5, PA-7, PA-8) are met, but it does not have much empirical content. It does not indicate from what conditions reductions in inequality follow. Inequality may increase despite improvements in the status of lower strata or declines in the status of highest strata, because their effects may be more than offset by differences in fertility or in immigration or by opposite status changes of strata other than those that experienced the stipulated change. The two pieces of information that the theorem does supply are: When inequality has declined, one of the two stipulated status changes must have occured; and any program that seeks to reduce inequality must effect one of the two stipulated status changes.

Propositions about status changes that are sufficient to alter inequality must be qualified in varying degrees. Whether the mobility of lower or higher strata is considered and whether its direction is downward or upward yields four basic patterns of status change: down of low, up of high, up of low, and down of high. The assumptions made about fertility and immigration differences (PA-7, PA-8) permit formulating propositions about increases in inequality, which cannot be counteracted by these differences, but not propositions about decreases in it, which can be, and which must be explicitly qualified accordingly. Besides, all propositions are qualified by statements about the effects of other mobility patterns, which obviate the need for ceteris paribus and make the theorems deterministic. For theorems about mobility above median status, moreover, a new line distinguishing the highest from other above-median strata must be drawn. The reason is implied by principles 3–6 listed above. A status change of a low stratum has opposite consequences for mean status distance and mean status, which makes its consequence for inequality, the ratio of the two, unequivocal. However, a status change of a high stratum has parallel consequences for mean status distance and mean status, which makes its consequence for inequality, their ratio, dependent on the difference in effects on numerator and denominator, and that difference is not the same for all high strata. This can be clarified with an illustration.

Any rise in income of a low stratum reduces the mean income difference and raises the mean income, thus necessarily reducing income inequality, defined by the ratio of the two. But any rise in income of a high stratum raises both mean income differences and mean income, so that the effect on their ratio depends on how much the higher incomes of that stratum have raised the mean income difference and how much they have raised the mean income for the entire population. (The same applies, reversing signs, for reductions in incomes of low and high strata.) The existing degree of inequality governs whether a certain rise in income of various high strata increases inequality (and a given decline reduces inequality), or whether it has no effect or the opposite effect on inequality, the latter paralleling the effect of a rise in income of a low stratum. The greater inequality is, the higher is the boundary line above which a rise in income raises and below which a rise in income reduces inequality. The operational criterion of highest stratum includes all those above this line whose rising income (or other status) increases and whose declining income reduces inequality. Mobility that crosses this line has an equivocal effect on inequality and is for this reason excluded from consideration in the theorems. For example, the highest strata are the upper two quintiles when there is little inequality (with a Gini index of .20) and the upper one quintile when inequality is pronounced (.60).[8]

Downward mobility of a low or middle stratum increases inequality in the absence of upward mobility of other low or middle or downward mobility of highest strata (T-9.1). *Upward mobility of a highest stratum increases inequality in the absence of downward mobility of other highest or upward mobility of low or middle strata* (T-9.2). These two theorems depend on PA-7 and PA-8; the next two do not, but instead must incorporate qualifications about fertility and immigration. A positively skewed status distribution (A-5) is assumed in all four theorems. *Upward mobility of a low or middle stratum diminishes inequality unless its effect on the status distribution is outweighed by those of downward mobility of other low or middle, upward mobility of highest strata, differences in net fertility, or in net immigration* (T-9.3). *Downward mobility of a highest stratum diminishes inequality, unless its effect on the status distribution is outweighed by those of upward mobility of other highest, downward mobility of low or middle strata, differences in net fertility, or in net immigration* (T-9.4). The extensive qualifications of these theorems, which limit their significance for making empirical predictions, are nevertheless of substantive interest.

There are only two conditions that can diminish inequality: increases in the relative status of the lower strata—the incomes of the poor, the power of the powerless—and reductions in the relative status of the highest strata—the affluence of the rich, the power of the powerful. This is clearly not a new insight, and no complicated analysis of status distributions is required to arrive at it. But this analysis discloses the many social forces that perpetuate

---

8. The precise criterion a high stratum must meet to be included as one of the highest is that the difference in the fractions of the population below and above this stratum is greater than the Gini coefficient of inequality. Thus, when the Gini coefficient is .60, the highest strata include the top 20 percent because the difference in the fractions below and above the twentieth income percentile is .61 (.80 − .19). The reasoning is as follows: Inequality is defined as mean status distance divided by twice mean status, which is

$$G = \frac{2\Sigma s_i p_i \left(p_{b_i} - p_{a_i}\right)}{2\Sigma s_i p_i}$$

(for symbols, see note 5). A positive change in status of a high category adds $2d_c p_c(p_b - p_a)$ to the mean status distance and $2d_c p_c$ to twice the mean status of the entire population (where d_c is the status change in that category, p_c the fraction of the population in it, and p_b and p_a the fractions of the population below and above it, respectively). For such a positive change to increase G, the ratio of these two numbers must be greater than the ratio of numerator to denominator in G. Dividing $2dp_c(p_b - p_a)$ by $2d_c p_c$ gives $(p_b - p_a)$, which must be greater than G for a stratum to be included as one of the highest because its rising status increases inequality and its status decline decreases it.

inequalities even when these conditions are met. It may thus help to explain the persistence of social inequalities, without assuming that these inequalities are inevitable and an intrinsic part of human nature. On the contrary, the assumption made is that programs to reduce any form of social inequality can be effectively implemented, which may also be unrealistic, but which is designed to bring into stark relief how counteracting forces can neutralize the effects of such programs and perpetuate inequalities.

Assume the wages of the poor have been raised substantially, which in and of itself reduces income inequality. But high rates of unemployment accompanying this change can nullify its effect on inequality. So can inflation, if it shrinks the real wages of the poorest while the better-organized strata of the working class are able to keep up with inflation through collective bargaining. The reason in both cases in that the status of extreme strata affects inequality more than that of less extreme ones, so that deteriorating positions of the lowest strata counteract status improvements of other low strata. When the earnings of all low strata rise, income inequality will still not diminish if the earnings of high strata rise disproportionately, as has happened in the 1950s and 1960s in the United States (Miller 1966; Gans 1973; Rainwater 1974). Even when lower incomes rise proportionately more than higher ones, economic inequality may well not diminish, because lower strata tend to have larger families and poor migrants from other places often swell their ranks. Cities illustrate this dramatically. The better wages for workers and lower rates of unemployment that reduce economic inequality may well attract poor migrants from other places whose influx increases inequality again. In a capitalist economy, finally, the greater demand resulting from higher incomes of lower strata may raise prices and profits enough to neutralize the initial reduction in inequality. As the result of the combination of these factors, programs that succeed in raising the standard of living of poorer strata often do not diminish economic inequality.

Policies that improve the economic conditions of poorer strata contribute to the alleviation of poverty, but they probably cannot reduce economic inequality, owing to the numerous counteracting forces, without being supplemented by policies that curtail the resources of the rich. However, policies that reduce the incomes of affluent strata do not necessarily thereby diminish income inequality, since counteracting forces often nullify their effect, too. A steeply progressive tax on earned incomes may not reduce inequality if a lower tax on the unearned incomes of the most affluent enables their aftertax income to continue to rise while only that of the less affluent is effectively reduced. For when economic inequality is pronounced, it can be diminished only by reductions in the affluence of the richest, not of the fairly affluent (who are those defined by the criterion in note 8 as not being in the highest strata). If the incomes of the richest do decline, it may not reduce income inequality because the income of other wealthy persons rises correspondingly. Even when the incomes of all affluent strata decline, inequality does not diminish if the incomes of poorer strata decline proportionately. In a capitalist society, heavy taxes that reduce the incomes of the very rich and thereby inequality may prompt many rich persons and wealthy corporations to withdraw their capital and invest it in another country, and the resulting loss of jobs and incomes of workers increases inequality again. These considerations are not intended to suggest that it is impossible to reduce income inequality, or other social inequalities, for that matter. They are designed to indicate that effecting reductions in inequalities is a complex task that is unlikely to suceed without clear understanding, concerted effort, and overcoming much opposition by those whom such reductions inevitably will deprive.[9]

Elite and Masses

Absolute status is not zero-sum, but relative status is. Most or even all people's education or income can increase without decreasing that of others. But most people cannot have a superior education, if superior means greater than the majority's, or superior income, prestige, wealth, or power. Moreover, for the relative social standing of some persons to rise, that of others must fall. Having graduated from high school used to mean that a person has a superior education, but it does no longer, since most Americans have graduated from high school. If powerless people achieve some power, the relative power of others declines. However, these statements apply only to a closed social system, inasmuch as the influx of people into various strata from outside also alters relative standings.

Disproportionately high rates of net fertility and net immigration of the lowest strata increase inequality, as has been noted. But this expansion of the lowest strata simultaneously raises the relative standing of other strata, whose members are now superior to larger numbers than they were in the preceding generation, when the lowest strata constituted a smaller proportion of the population. Paradoxically, therefore, many poor experience improvements in their relative standing while economic inequality increases. Such improvements are experienced not alone by those poor who benefit from the opportunities for upward mobility the expansion of the lowest strata tends to stimulate, but also by others whose relative standing is raised without their being upwardly mobile themselves by the influx of still poorer people. This paradox may help explain why in the United States, where large

9. Although I consider it desirable to reduce economic and other social inequalities, this is a value judgment, and the theory does not address the question of whether it is desirable or functional. My value judgment is reflected in the greater attention paid in the discussion to the implication of the theory for reducing inequalities than to its implications for increasing them, but it does not affect the formulation of the theorems—at least I hope not.

streams of poor immigrants have raised the relative standing of the somewhat less poor for more than a century, no major socialist movement has
developed, in contrast to most other industrial societies.

Variations in the rate of growth among social strata alter relative
standings gradually, and they make it possible for substantial numbers to
improve their relative standing more rapidly by being upwardly mobile
without anybody's relative standing having to drop. Although a rise in relative status of some persons entails a fall in relative status of others, the latter
is offset by the rise in relative status produced by the disproportionate
growth of lower strata. These status advantages of middle strata rest on the
disadvantageous position of the many offspring of poor families and the many
poor immigrants and their descendants who remain at the bottom of the
status hierarchy.

The circulation of the elite, however, is essentially governed by the basic
principle that the upward mobility of some requires the downward mobility
of others with respect to relative status. The operational criterion of elite is a
constant small fraction of the population, and the larger the number of
persons who move up into that fraction, the larger is the number whom they
displace by now outranking them. Defining the economic elite broadly as the
wealthiest 1 percent, for example, the growth in the wealth of others that
makes theirs now among the top 1 percent results in the wealth of some
former elite members being no longer among the highest 1 percent, although their wealth has not declined and may well have increased. Correspondingly, when some of the richest families lose their wealth others become part of the richest 1 percent without any increase in their wealth. The
number of persons who move up into an elite is not exactly the same as the
number whom they displace, because population growth slowly enlarges the
number in a given fraction, which reduces the number displaced below the
number entering, though typically not much.

The chances of upward mobility into the elite are very small, while the
risks of downward mobility from the elite are great. Elites are usually
thought of as being composed of a few thousand persons, not two million,
which would be 1 percent of the American population. The upward mobility
of a certain fraction of Americans into such a small elite displaces several
thousand times that fraction from the elite, notwithstanding rapid population
growth; for the movement of relatively few persons into a small elite displaces a substantial proportion of that elite. Accordingly, minute chances of
upward mobility into a small elite of the rest of the population, or even of the
upper quartile of the population, entail great risks of downward mobility of
elite members. The only way elite members can protect themselves against
these risks is by making elite status invulnerable and essentially ascribed,
which creates great temptations to use their extensive resources for this
purpose. The development of aristocracies is not the only example. Hereditary wealth is another. So are political leaders who abolish elections and

install their sons in high offices; nepotism of all sorts; and using as criterion of élite status that a family is "old," which makes elite status hereditary.

An elite's status is not a proportionate but a relative status defined by its status distance from the average person, by the extent to which power or wealth or knowledge are concentrated in a small proportion of the population and more or less monopolized by this elite. Great concentration of resources, which involves much inequality, has been distinguished from great status diversity, which involves a distribution of resources so that there is much variability or heterogeneity in status among a population. The theoretical minima of inequality and status diversity are the same: equal status of all persons. In contrast, the theoretical maximum of inequality, the concentration of all of a resource in the hands of one person, implies near-minimum status diversity, as all but one person have the same status, zero. The theoretical maximum of status diversity is that no two persons have exactly the same status. The question raised now is how changes in inequality are related to changes in status diversity.

A central thesis of Marx's is that the growing concentration of wealth among a few owners of the means of production is accompanied by the impoverishment of the masses and the atrophy of class differences, transforming most people into a large proletariat. In the terms used here, increasing inequality is postulated by Marx to reduce status diversity. Under which conditions is this assumption correct? To answer this question, the ways in which various changes in the status distribution affect inequality and status diversity are compared.

Ceteris paribus, if the net fertility of lowest strata exceeds that of higher strata, status diversity declines (T-10). The theorem follows from the skewed status distribution assumed to exist (A-5) and the definition of diversity, which makes diversity an inverse function of variations in stratum size. Higher fertility of lower than of upper strata enlarges the differences in stratum size and thus reduces diversity. *Ceteris paribus, if the net immigration from abroad into lowest strata exceeds that into higher strata, status diversity declines* (T-10.1). The theorem follows from A-5 and the definition of diversity, in corresponding manner. Hence, the prevailing differences in fertility and immigration in industrial societies increase inequality (T-8, T-8.1) and reduce status diversity, in conformity with Marx's thesis that the two change in opposite directions. The crucial question is, however, how internal changes in the status distribution affect inequality and status diversity.

Ceteris paribus, downward mobility from higher toward modal status reduces status diversity (T-10.2). This theorem depends on the assumptions that the status structure is positively skewed (A-5) and that both the rates of net fertility and of net immigration of lower exceed those of higher strata (PA-7, PA-8), which imply that differences in fertility and immigration can only decrease and not increase status diversity. The mobility stipulated is from smaller to larger strata and consequently reduces diversity by increasing size differences among strata. The only other conditions that can influence status diversity, requiring the ceteris paribus, are other patterns of social mobility. But one of these other patterns has the same effect. *Ceteris paribus, upward mobility from lower toward modal status reduces status diversity* (T-10.3). Since such mobility also increases size differences among strata, the theorem is implied by the assumptions A-5, PA-7, and PA-8, just as the preceding one.

Theorems about the two remaining patterns of mobility must include qualifications about fertility and immigration differences, since the plausible assumptions made about such differences (PA-7, PA-8) have counteracting effects and cannot be used in formulating these theorems. *Ceteris paribus, upward mobility from modal status increases status diversity, unless its effect on the status distribution is outweighed by those of differences in net fertility or net immigration* (T-10.4). This theorem and the next follow from A-5 and the definition of diversity, which imply that the stipulated mobility reduces variations in size among strata. The ceteris paribus in both cases refers only to other patterns of mobility, the influences of which are indicated by other theorems. *Ceteris paribus, downward mobility from modal status increases status diversity, unless its effect on the status distribution is outweighed by those of differences in net fertility or net immigration* (T-10.5).

A comparison of these theorems with those about inequality discloses that most changes in status distributions have parallel consequences for changes in inequality and in status diversity, whereas Marx's thesis implies that the two change in opposite directions. Downward mobility of the lowest strata (below modal status) increases status diversity as well as inequality (T-10.5, T-9.1); so does upward mobility of the highest strata (T-10.4, T-9.2). Similarly, upward mobility of the lowest and downward mobility of the highest strata reduce both status diversity and inequality (T-10.3, T-10.2, T-9.3, T-9.4). Thus, only changes in the economic status of the intermediate strata have opposite effects on inequality and status diversity. Improvements in the economic status of persons in the highest strata and deterioration of the economic status of persons in the lowest strata entail increases in status diversity as well as in inequality, and opposite status changes in these strata also have parallel effects on inequality and status diversity. The inference from these theorems, unless they are not well formulated, apparently is that most increases in inequality necessarily also involve increases in status diversity, which seems to make it improbable that the growing concentration of economic resources is accompanied by reductions in economic differences among classes, as predicted by Marx.

This conclusion is not warranted, however, although the theorems are well formulated, to the best of my knowledge. The error lies in the implicit assumptions of the inference that the influences of status changes in the intermediate strata on the status distribution are overshadowed by those of the more extreme strata on either side—which is generally the case, but not if the numbers involved differ greatly—and that increasing inequality does not depress the modal status itself and thereby lessen status diversity. Very great inequality implies a modal status close to or at zero and a contraction of the size of the highest strata, so that the majority of the population is included in the "middle" strata ranging from modal status, which is low, to just below the highest strata, which are small. In this situation, most status changes that increase inequality further diminish status diversity.

For some status distributions, extreme inequality with a mode close to zero is improbable if not impossible. Income is not distributed this way and cannot be if it is accurately defined, because people without any income would not survive. For other forms of status, modal status is in fact close to zero. Age is an example; wealth is another; power a third. Rising *incomes* of the elite are likely to be accompanied by greater income diversity, not by impoverishment of the masses and reduced income differences among them, which conflicts with Marx's prediction. But the growing concentration of *wealth* and, particularly, of *power* may well reduce diversity by depriving increasing numbers of virtually any wealth and any power, in accordance with Marx's prediction.

Compendium

T-5   For any division of status above the median, the upper stratum has more extensive relations with the lower than the lower has with the upper. (From T-1.)

T-5.1   Most people are insulated from social contacts with the elite. (From T-1.)

A-5   The status distribution is positively skewed so that the mean is above the median and the single mode is below it.

T-5.2   Ceteris paribus and except for the lowest strata, the probability of social associations with status-distant persons increases with increasing status. (From T-1, A-5.)

T-5.3   Except for the lowest strata, the greater the social distance between two strata, the greater is the discrepancy between their rates of association with each other, specifically, between the higher rate of the upper and the lower rate of the lower stratum. (From T-1, A-5.)

T-5.4   The rates of association with persons of lower status probably decline less with increasing status distance than do the rates of association with persons of higher status. (From T-1, A-1.2, A-5.)

T-5.5   Except for the lowest strata, the probability of people's associating with others below them in status is greater than the probability of their associating with others equidistant above them. (From T-1, A-5.)

PA-6   Superior status is manifest in superordinate roles in social associations.

T-5.6   The probability is that most people above the lowest strata have the superordinate role in most of their social associations. (From PA-6, T-5.5; based on A-5.)

T-6   The higher the rates of vertical mobility between two social strata, the more prevalent are the associations between their members. (From T-4.1; based on A-1, PA-2, PA-3.)

T-6.1   Increasing vertical mobility in a society increases the probability of social associations among various strata. (From T-4.1; based on A-1, PA-2, PA-3.)

T-6.11   Increasing rates of vertical mobility reduce the salience of status for social intercourse. (From T-4.2; based on A-1, PA-2, PA-3.)

T-6.2   Rapid circulation of the elite increases the rate of social contacts of elite members with others substantially but reduces the insulation of most others from the elite only little. (From T-2, T-4.2; based on A-1, PA-2, PA-3.)

T-6.3   Ceteris paribus, predominant upward mobility increases the rates of association of lower with higher strata more than the rates of association of higher with lower strata. (From T-1, A-5.)

T-7   Ceteris paribus, a decline in inequality reduces the impact of status on social associations. (From A-1.2.)

T-8   Ceteris paribus, if the net fertility of lower strata exceeds that of higher strata, inequality increases. (From A-5.)

T-8.1   Ceteris paribus, if the net immigration from abroad into lower strata exceeds that into higher strata, inequality increases. (From A-5.)

PA-7   The rates of net fertility of lower strata are no less than those of higher strata.

PA-8   The rates of net immigration from outside the social structure into lower strata are no less than those into higher strata.

T-9   For inequality to diminish it is necessary that some low or middle strata experience upward mobility or that some highest strata experience downward mobility. (From A-5, PA-7, PA-8.)

T-9.1   Downward mobility of any low or middle stratum increases inequality in the absence of upward mobility of other low or middle strata or downward mobility of highest strata. (From A-5, PA-7, PA-8.)

T-9.2   Upward mobility of any highest stratum increases inequality in the absence of downward mobility of other highest strata or upward mobility of low or middle strata. (From A-5, PA-7, PA-8.)

T-9.3   Upward mobility of any low or middle stratum diminishes inequality, unless its effect on the status distribution is outweighed by those of downward mobility of other low or middle, upward mobility of highest strata, differences in net fertility, or in net immigration. (From A-5.)

T-9.4   Downward mobility of any highest stratum diminishes inequality, unless its effect on the status distribution is outweighed by those of upward mobility of other highest, downward mobility of low or middle strata, differences in net fertility, or in net immigration. (From A-5.)

T-10   Ceteris paribus, if the net fertility of low strata exceeds that of high strata, status diversity declines. (From A-5.)

T-10.1 Ceteris paribus, if the net immigration from abroad into low strata exceeds that into high strata, status diversity declines. (From A-5.)

T-10.2 Ceteris paribus, downward mobility from higher toward modal status reduces status diversity. (From A-5, PA-7, PA-8.)

T-10.3 Ceteris paribus, upward mobility from lower toward modal status reduces status diversity. (From A-5, PA-7, PA-8.)

T-10.4 Ceteris paribus, upward mobility from modal status increases status diversity, unless its effect on the status distribution is outweighed by those of differences in net fertility or net immigration. (From A-5.)

T-10.5 Ceteris paribus, downward mobility from modal status increases status diversity, unless its effect on the status distribution is outweighed by those of differences in net fertility or net immigration. (From A-5.)

CHAPTER FOUR

Heterogeneity

ALL FORMS OF DIFFERENTIATION AMONG PEOPLE CAN BE SUBSUMED under two generic forms on the basis of whether or not they entail hierarchical distinctions of status—inequality and heterogeneity. In contrast to graduated differences in status, nominal differences among groups are inherently unranked. Although most members of some groups may actually be higher in status than those of other groups, this does not annul the analytical distinction between group membership as such and the status differences with which it is correlated, for example, between sex and sex differences in power, between race and race differences in income.

Heterogeneity refers to the distribution of people among different groups. The larger the number of groups and the smaller the proportion of the population that belongs to one or a few, the greater the heterogeneity is in terms of a given nominal parameter, such as the ethnic heterogeneity of a community or the religious heterogeneity of a society. Cross-cutting group memberships enhance heterogeneity further by making it multiform, as indicated by various combinations of ethnic and religious background— Italian and Irish Catholics, black and white Protestants, Russian and German Jews.

After examining the implications of simple heterogeneity in terms of a single parameter for social associations, this chapter analyzes those of multiform heterogeneity in terms of several parameters. Thus, the transition is made from the analysis of single to that of multiple parameters of social structure. A discussion of the macrosocial integration of various groups in society is included. Two social conditions that interact with heterogeneity in influencing social associations are also discussed: the spatial distribution of the population and the size differences among groups.

A Paradox

The two conditions that determine the degree of heterogeneity in terms of a given nominal parameter are the number of groups into which the population is divided and the distribution of persons among them. A community's industrial heterogeneity depends on the number of different industries located there and the distribution of the labor force among them; its occupational heterogeneity is greater if people work in a large variety of occupations than if most of them are concentrated in a few; its political heterogeneity is greater if there are numerous parties and voters do not largely support one or two. For some nominal parameters, the number of groups depends on the classification system employed, as in the case of occupations, which can be classified into major groups, detailed occupations, or narrow specialties. This naturally requires using the same category system for comparisons. The operational criterion of heterogeneity is the chance expectation that two randomly chosen persons do not belong to the same group, which takes both number of groups and the distribution of the population among them into account.

A concrete illustration of the influences of number of groups and population distribution among them on heterogeneity may be helpful. The operational measure of heterogeneity is one minus the sum of the squared fractions of the population in each group ($1 - \Sigma p_i^2$, where p_i is the fraction of the population in each group). Heterogeneity is at a maximum for a given number of groups when the population is evenly divided among them, and it increases with the number of groups. Thus, with ten groups, each consisting of 10 percent of the population, the measure of heterogeneity is .90 ($1 - 10 \times .10^2$), but with two groups, each consisting of one half of the population, it is only .50 ($1 - 2 \times .50^2$). Even with two groups, however, heterogeneity can vary greatly, depending on the population distribution between them. Examples on the effect on heterogeneity of shifts in the population balance between two groups follow:

Population Ratio	Heterogeneity
50:50	.50
60:40	.48
70:30	.42
80:20	.32
90:10	.18

Although heterogeneity is defined by two conditions, changes in it depend on four, the two endogenous ones defining it and two exogenous ones that also alter the population distribution. The first condition is a change in the number of groups. The formation of new political parties increases political heterogeneity; the development of new specialties increases occupational heterogeneity; the merger of denominations reduces religious heterogeneity; conglomerates that buy up firms reduce the heterogeneity of the economy. Second, social mobility among groups changes the degree of heterogeneity by altering the size distribution, unless mobility in both directions is the same in all cases. Migration from farms to cities increases the heterogeneity of a predominantly rural population, but it reduces the heterogeneity of a population that is already predominantly urban. Increasing marriage rates lessen the heterogeneity in marital status among adults; increasing divorce rates enhance it. The growth of small firms contributes to economic heterogeneity; that of large firms impedes it.

Third, group differences in net migration from outside are an exogeneous condition that changes a society's or community's heterogeneity. What has made the United States a melting pot of heterogeneous nationalities is that more immigrants enlarged the ethnic groups that were originally smaller than those that were originally large. Black migrants from predominantly black southern towns to predominantly white northern cities increase the racial heterogeneity of both, as they reduce the proportion of the majority in either. A final condition changing heterogeneity is the variation in net fertility among groups. The higher birth rates of Catholics than of Protestants increase religious heterogeneity in countries where Catholics are the minority but decrease it in places where they are the majority. The higher fertility of blacks than whites would have increased racial heterogeneity in the United States but did not because it was offset by the high rates of white immigrants. Generally, heterogeneity increases when the net fertility of small groups exceeds that of large ones.

Whatever the conditions that produce variations in heterogeneity among communities, these variations have paradoxical consequences for intergroup relations. The axiom that ingroup relations are more prevalent than intergroup relations (A-1.1) implies that homogeneous associations among members of the same group are more likely than heterogeneous associations between members of different groups. The greater heterogeneity is, the more pervasive are group barriers to social associations. One would therefore expect increasing heterogeneity to increase barriers to social associations. Surprisingly, however, this is not the case.

Whereas heterogeneity creates barriers to social intercourse, much heterogeneity weakens these barriers. This paradoxical conclusion follows from the definition of heterogeneity and a simple assumption, namely, that *social associations depend on opportunities for social contacts* (A-9). Lack of any opportunities for social contact precludes the establishment of social relations, of course. The greater these opportunities are, the greater the likelihood that people have casual associations and that some of these develop into regular associations and close social relations. Williams (1964, p. 162) shows that even friendships with minorities who are generally discriminated against depend greatly on contact opportunities. For example, the proportion of whites who have black friends is less than 10 percent when contact opportunities are low and 25 percent or more when they are high. The greater the heterogeneity, the greater are the chances that fortuitous social contacts involve members of different groups, by definition. These greater opportunities increase the probabilities not only of casual intergroup relations but also of intergroup friendships and marriages, as implied by the above axiom (A-9), because many casual associations make it likely that some develop into intimate relations.

Increasing heterogeneity increases the probability of intergroup relations (T-11).[1] In relatively homogeneous communities there are few group barriers to social associations, but those that do exist, and there are always some, tend to inhibit social associations more than the more prevalent group barriers in heterogeneous communities. Prevalent group barriers are not so great barriers to sociable intercourse. When social differences are rare, they stand out against the prevailing homogeneity of the community, but when they are pervasive they recede into the heterogeneous background, analogous to the way a bright color is more conspicuous on a white background than as part of a polychromic design. Heterogeneity makes minorities, be they Jews or homosexuals, less conspicuous, because there is a greater variety of them, and it simultaneously makes intergroup relations with them more likely. By enhancing the probability of intergroup relations in terms of a nominal parameter, heterogeneity lessens that parameter's salience and the tendencies to discriminate against outgroups. For example, K. Davis (1941) notes that racial intermarriage is more prevalent in societies with more than two races.

When group differences are conspicuous and intergroup relations are rare, group pressures are likely to arise that further discourage the deviant practice of associating with members of the outgroup. More frequent intergroup relations indicate that associating with members of other groups is more widely accepted and thus less deviant from prevailing customs, which makes it likely that group pressures discouraging relations with outsiders are weaker. Besides, the extent to which ingroup relations predominate over intergroup relations reflects the salience of the group distinctions made by a parameter, and deviation from salient social practices is most likely to meet with social disapproval, which discourages such departures from group standards. These considerations suggest that rare intergroup relations, and social practices generally, not merely reflect but further promote group pressures that discourage them, and that wider acceptance of the practice weakens the pressure. The assumption that this is the case is made an axiom of the theory: *As social practices in a group increase in frequency, group pressures that*

1. The probability of intergroup relations in a total collectivity that has become more heterogeneous increases, though the specific rates of association between some particular groups may decrease.

discourage them subside (A-10). The social processes generating these group pressures will be discussed in chapter 6, as will be procedures for testing the distinctive effects such group pressures are postulated to have. Concern now is with implications of the assumption.

It implies that increases in heterogeneity, by making intergroup relations less rare, weaken ingroup pressures that inhibit sociable interaction with members of outgroups and thus lessen discrimination against outgroups. Thus, A-10 reinforces the effect of A-9 on T-11. An increase in heterogeneity expands intergroup relations (T-11) initially, owing to the improved opportunities for them (A-9), and it thereby modifies ingroup pressures in ways (A-10) that lead to further expansions of them. Since discrimination is largely rooted in ingroup pressures that penalize associating with outgroup members, informally and sometimes formally, increases in heterogeneity are a structural force reducing discrimination against outgroups. However, heterogeneity does not have the same consequences for all groups' discrimination against outgroups.

A group may have few interpersonal relations with another, not because its members discriminate against associating with those of the other group, but because the other group's members discriminate against its members. The axiom about group pressures helps to answer the question of which one of two groups is most likely to discriminate against the other and thus is primarily responsible for the fact that intergroup relations are no more extensive than they are. *Ceteris paribus, the larger of two groups discriminates more than the smaller against associating with members of the other group* (T-11.1). If intergroup relations are rarer in the large than in the small group (T-1), and if rare intergroup relations strengthen group pressures that further inhibit them (A-10), it follows that such discriminatory group pressures and practices are more prevalent in the large than in the small group. It is not generally the clannishness of small groups that accounts for discrimination in social intercourse, though it sometimes is. The more typical case is that discrimination in social relations emanates from the majority or the larger group, because outgroup relations are most deviant and most apt to be discouraged there. Under special conditions, however, a minority may exert particularly strong ingroup pressures to discriminate against other groups. One such condition is that of a small elite, which may seek to protect its members against the high risk of downward mobility by discriminating against lower strata in order to inject an ascribed element into elite status, as noted in the preceding chapter. Another illustration of such a condition is that of a small sect with firm commitments to a distinctive ideology, which generates strong ingroup pressures, as will be seen in chapter 6.

Increasing heterogeneity not only makes intergroup relations more prevalent but also reduces the likelihood that only some groups are much involved in them while most members of other groups are insulated from intergroup relations. Hence, *increasing* horizontal *differentiation—*

heterogeneity—often *decreases* the *differences* in intergroup involvement among groups, which is another heterogeneity paradox. The reason is that discrepancies in intergroup relations are a function of differences in group size (T-1.4), and nearly all increases in heterogeneity reduce the size differences among groups. This is necessarily the case for three of the four conditions on which increases in heterogeneity depend—internal mobility, net migration from outside, and net fertility—and it is frequently the case also for the fourth—an increase in the number of groups. The latter tends to reduce size differences when large groups subdivide into smaller, but not when small groups subdivide or when small groups split off from large ones. *Increases in heterogeneity probably reduce the discrepancies in intergroup relations among groups* (T-11.2). By reducing these discrepancies, which are a major source of discrimination (T-11.1), increases in heterogeneity further diminish tendencies to discriminate in intergroup relations.

Status diversity is the graduated-parameter equivalent of heterogeneity among nominal groups. It is therefore subject to the same influences as heterogeneity, except that these influences are modified by those of status differences. *Increasing status diversity increases the probabilities of associations among persons whose status differs* (T-11.3). Status diversity increases the chances that two persons who differ in status meet and have an opportunity to establish a social relation (A-9), though the likelihood of their taking advantage of this opportunity decreases with increasing status distance (A-1.2). Owing to this inhibiting effect of status distance on social associations, status diversity is expected to promote associations primarily between persons whose status differs somewhat but not very greatly. As this effect of status diversity is reinforced by reductions in social pressures that discourage associating with persons in different strata (A-10), the salience of status for social relations is likely to decline, which may well diminish discrimination along status lines generally.

Increases in status diversity reduce the discrepancies in the rates of social associations between strata (T-11.4). Since the number of different strata considered is an artifact of the classification system and not an empirical phenomenon, only three empirical conditions can increase status diversity—internal mobility, net migration from outside, and fertility—and all three do so by reducing the variations in the frequency distribution with varying status. These lesser variations in the frequencies diminish the discrepancies in the rates of association between two strata (T-1.4), no matter where the division between them is drawn. Whereas status diversity is expected to have less impact than heterogeneity on the *extent* of relations between persons whose social position differs (T-11, T-11.3), owing to the counteracting influence of status distance (A-1.2), it is expected to have more impact on reducing *differences* among positions in the likelihood of role relations with other positions (T-11.2, T-11.4), because increasing diversity always lessens variations in frequencies and increasing heterogeneity does so only most of the time. Many status differences, though not great status differences, reduce the difference in the chances of persons of having associates whose status differs considerably from theirs.[2]

Multiform Heterogeneity

The simple heterogeneity in terms of a single parameter so far considered is an abstraction from empirical reality. Actual social structures are characterized by multiform heterogeneity in terms of several, and sometimes many, intersecting nominal parameters. Differences in sex, race, national background, religion, and occupation do not coincide, although some are correlated. Multiform heterogeneity refers to the overlapping groups and numerous subgroups generated by such differences. The structural constraints exerted by simple heterogeneity on intergroup relations are limited by the large size of a community or society. Whereas great heterogeneity in terms of a single parameter implies much opportunity to form friendships with persons in different groups, this heterogeneity infringes only a little on the opportunity of having ingroup friends when groups are large, as they are in a large community or in the entire society. Given the assumed propensity for associating with members of one's own group (A-1.2), people in this situation are likely to take only limited advantage of opportunities for intergroup friendships, so that great heterogeneity probably increases intergroup relations some but not much.

While simple heterogeneity affects the chances of intergroup relations, its structural constraints on them are not compelling, except in small communities. In contrast, multiform heterogeneity exerts compelling constraints on intergroup relations, even in the largest societies. Multiple nominal parameters that intersect increase heterogeneity exponentially, and thereby reduce the size of perfectly homogeneous subgroups to the vanishing point.[3] The large groups composing society make it easy to satisfy ingroup preferences in terms of any one parameter and confine sociable relations to the ingroup if one wishes, despite pronounced heterogeneity. But the multitude

2. T-11.1, that the larger of two groups is more likely to discriminate in the relation between the two, is not applied to status distributions (as T-11 and T-11.2 have been), because a stratum's size is not independent of its status (A-5), and the influence of an elite's interests (and resources) on discrimination may counteract that of size differences, as has been mentioned.

3. For ten orthogonal nominal parameters each of which divides the population into ten groups, the number of perfectly homogeneous subgroups is 10^{10}, or ten billion. Parameters are not perfectly orthogonal, of course, but there are more than ten, and some divide the population into a very large number of groups (e.g., detailed occupation), though some divide it into fewer than ten (e.g., sex). Graduated parameters further increase the multiplicity of homogeneous subgroups, despite their frequent substantial correlations, as they divide the population into many strata among which social distinctions are made.

of overlapping subgroups make it impossible to do so in terms of most parameters, regardless of one's wishes, when multiform heterogeneity is pronounced. Cross-cutting lines of differentiation reinstate the structural constraints to participate in intergroup relations that society's large size would otherwise nullify.

Multiform heterogeneity compels people to have associates outside their own group, because it implies that ingroup relations are simultaneously intergroup relations in terms of different parameters. We cannot help engaging in social intercourse with outsiders, because our ingroup associates in one dimension are, in several others, members of groups other than our own (Merton 1972, pp. 22–25). For individuals to satisfy their ingroup preferences that are most salient in a situation, they must set aside other ingroup preferences and enter into intergroup relations along other lines. This is by no means a minor constraint. In complex social structures, so many roles are important that people often must suppress strong group prejudices for the sake of other roles. The common interests of automobile workers constrain whites and blacks to join in a union and engage in social interaction, and the common interests of blacks constrain professionals and unskilled workers to join in common endeavors and associate with each other.

Multiform heterogeneity does not eradicate all prejudice, of course. It is a compelling force for the aggregate of the population, not for every individual. Bigots can maintain their ingrained prejudices and refuse to have anything to do with members of one group or another, though not without sacrifice. They may have to abstain from concerted social action that would serve their interests, and they must disregard other ingroup preferences more than most people in order to sustain their adamant refusal to associate with some groups, which narrows their other choices. Persons who rigidly restrict their friends to a narrow ingroup must put up with friends who do not share most of their other attributes and interests. Although discrimination in social relations on the basis of the most salient group differences can persist under conditions of pronounced multiform heterogeneity, this very persistence promotes more intergroup relations along other lines. Besides, different group affiliations tend to be most salient for different persons and in different situations, and the resulting variable ingroup preferences undermine most particular lines of discrimination. Once intergroup relations become more prevalent as the result of structural constraints, their wider acceptance reduces group pressures against them (A-10), which further stimulates the expansion of intergroup relations. All ingroup preferences entail some discrimination against outgroups, and the most salient group distinctions entail substantial discrimination, but discrimination along most lines, if not all, inevitably subsides with increasing multiform heterogeneity.

The multiple roles and group affiliations in complex social structures weaken the hold of ingroup bonds and alter the form of social integration. People have wider circles of less intimate associates than in simple societies.

The attenuation of profound social bonds that firmly integrate individuals in their communities is often deplored. But strong ingroup bonds restrain individual freedom and mobility, and they sustain rigidity and bigotry. Diverse intergroup relations, though not intimate, foster tolerance, improve opportunities, and are essential for the integration of a large society. Intimate relations, like those in the conjugal family and between good friends, are the main source of social support for individuals. Since intimate relations tend to be confined to closed social circles, however, they fragment society. The integration of the various groups in society depends on people's weak bonds, not their strong ones, because weak social ties extend beyond closed social circles and establish social connections among groups (Granovetter 1973).

The loss of extensive strong bonds in a community of kin and neighbors undoubtedly has robbed individuals of a deep sense of belonging and having roots, of profound feelings of security and lack of anxiety. This is the price we pay for the greater tolerance and opportunities that distinguish modern societies, with all their grievous faults, from primitive tribes and feudal orders. The social integration of individuals in modern society rests no longer exclusively on strong bonds with particular ingroups but in good part on multiple supports from wider networks of weaker social ties, supplemented by a few intimate bonds.[4] To use an analogy, a Norman structure with a uniform solid foundation has been replaced by a Gothic structure supported by multiple counterbalancing buttresses.

A Gothic structure can support a larger and more complex edifice than a Norman one. The integration of large societies depends on the weak social ties of individuals which extend beyond particular ingroups and thereby integrate the various groups into a coherent social structure. Large nations without any social connections among various parts have undoubtedly existed in the past, but they can hardly be considered single societies, and surely not single social structures. Interdependence among groups may promote their social integration, and so may social values they share, but only if they give rise to social associations among their members. For various groups to be integrated in a larger social unit requires direct associations among their members, just as the integration of individuals in a group requires direct associations among them. Individuals do not belong to a group with whose members they share values or on whose members they depend if they never associate with any of them, and groups are not part of a society unless their members associate with other members of the society. In short, the definition of macrosocial integration in terms of intergroup relations is not entirely arbitrary.

4. Simmel (1955, p. 163) notes that the individual in modern society "is deprived of many supports and advantages associated with the tightly-knit, primary group. [But] the creation of groups and associations in which any number of people can come together on the basis of their interest in a common purpose, compensates for the isolation of the personality which develops out of breaking away from the narrow confines of earlier circumstances."

Not insufficient ingroup bonds but excessive ones are what endanger society's integration most by threatening to fragment it. In simple tribes, where such strong ingroup bonds prevail, firm incest taboos extending far beyond a few close relatives are required to overcome this danger. In modern society exogamy norms cannot breach group barriers, because clans and lineages do not constitute the major group barriers. Here the integration of groups depends on the structural constraints on intergroup relations exerted by multiform heterogeneity. Many lines of differentiation create a multitude of group barriers and simultaneously weaken these barriers to social intercourse, though only provided that the various lines of differentiation do not largely coincide but cross-cut one another. The need for integrative intergroup relations does not assure that this need is met, and it is unlikely to be met equally well in all societies. Some are better integrated than others, and variations in heterogeneity largely account for the difference. When parameters are highly correlated—for example, when ethnic differences nearly coincide with differences in religion, occupation, and politics—they do not further intergroup relations, as cross-cutting parameters do, but on the contrary inhibit them. Only intersecting parameters constrain people to enter into some intergroup relations in the course of engaging in ingroup associations. Coinciding parameters have the opposite effect of making group barriers cumulative, which reinforces their inhibiting effects on intergroup relations. The lower the correlations of parameters, the more extensive are the intergroup relations that strengthen macrosocial integration.

However, the fact that *two* parameters are weakly correlated or completely orthogonal does not exert much constraint on people to establish intergroup relations. They may simply confine their sociable companions to others who share both social attributes, for example, to black women, black men, white women, or white men. But when many parameters each of which distinguishes many groups, not just two, are weakly correlated, virtually all people differ in some group memberships, which makes it inevitable that nearly all social relations are intergroup relations in some respects. Although the defining properties of parameters with extensive subdivisions imply these constraints when many are weakly correlated, an assumption is introduced that implies them regardless of the number of parameters under consideration and their degree of subdivision. The axiom is: *The influences of various parameters on social associations are partly additive, not entirely contingent on one another* (A-11). The assumption made is *not* that parameters do not have interaction or joint effects on social associations. As a matter of fact, such interaction effects will be examined later. The assumption only stipulates that the influences of a given parameter on social associations do not entirely depend on variations in other parameters that can completely suppress them. Thus, it is assumed that shared social positions increase rates of associations (A-1) even when other positions (in terms of other parameters) are not shared; in other words, persons who share several positions are more likely to associate than those who share only one. Since some suppressor effects may occur, the axiom is a restrictive assumption for two particular parameters, but it is assumed to be valid for most parameters in a social structure.

The lower the positive correlations between parameters, the more extensive are intergroup relations (T-12). The theorem follows from A-1 and A-11: Low correlations between parameters imply that many persons who have different positions in one respect share other social positions; the associations engendered by the latter common positions (A-1) produce some intergroup relations with regard to the former positions if the influences of the parameters are partly independent (A-11). The relationships of nominal parameters cannot be negative, but those of graduated parameters can be. This general theorem applying to parameters of both kinds specifies positive correlations, because negative ones of graduated parameters have a distinctive significance for social associations, as will be discussed in the next chapter. The important conceptual difference is whether and to which degree parameters are intersecting, as indicated by their low correlations, or consolidated, as indicated by their high positive ones. To focus on this conceptual distinction rather than its operational criterion, separate theorems about intersecting and consolidated nominal parameters are formulated, though the two are complementary.

Intersecting nominal parameters improve the integration of various groups by raising the rates of association between their members (T-12.1). *Consolidated nominal parameters strengthen ingroup bonds and attenuate intergroup relations that integrate various groups* (T-12.11). As the correlations of nominal parameters increase, their positive effect on intergroup relations turns into a negative one. Whereas the tendencies to associate with ingroups (A-1.1) promote intergroup relations in terms of other intersecting parameters, they inhibit intergroup relations in terms of other consolidated parameters, owing to the cumulative influences of the parameters on associations (A-11). Group barriers to social intercourse are breached by cross-cutting but reinforced by consolidated lines of differentiation. The consolidation of parameters transforms a multitude of subgroups that differ in some ways yet have something in common into relatively few larger subgroups that differ in many ways and have little in common. Conversely, as various lines of differentiation become themselves differentiated and their correlations decrease, their cumulative negative effect on intergroup relations turns, at some tipping point, into a positive one which promotes the integration of the different segments of society.

Multiform heterogeneity varies by degree, depending not merely on the number of nominal parameters that can be analytically distinguished but particularly on low correlations between them that indicate that they are intersecting. Highly correlated parameters are in effect virtually a single parameter that is especially salient owing to the combined influences. The intersection of nominal parameters is what generates multiform heterogeneity and the consequent structural constraints on intergroup relations. Numerous nominal parameters that intersect to a considerable extent characterize complex societies, although the degree to which they intersect and thus the degree of multiform heterogeneity vary. In complex societies, therefore, the proposition that people associate with persons in other groups as well as their own is dispensable as a primitive assumption (A-0), since it is implicit in T-12.1, that intersecting parameters promote intergroup relations, and thus is derivable from A-1.1 and A-11.

Whereas the theorems are couched in abstract terms, they have implications that make them empirically testable. Thus, the proposition that intergroup relations are fostered by intersecting nominal parameters (T-12.1) rests on the assumption that members of different groups are prompted to associate by their common group memberships along intersecting lines, which implies that persons who have established intergroup relations have other group memberships in common. This implication is supported by research on intermarriage. For example, ethnic intermarriages in our society tend to involve couples with the same religion (Kennedy 1944) and similar cultural background (Barron 1951). Intermarriage among simple tribes is also reported typically to involve couples whose culture and language are the same (Lessa 1950) and who live in the same area (Mercier 1951). The secular trends of increasing rates of racial (Heer 1966; Burma 1963) and other ethnic intermarriages (Kennedy 1944) may be attributable to the concomitant increases in heterogeneity, in accordance with another implication of the theory (T-11.1, T-12.1). T-12.11 implies that the new intersecting parameters resulting from industrialization and the greater heterogeneity resulting from urbanization weaken established kinship bonds, as has been often noted (for instance, Theodorson 1953; Barnes 1957; Anderson 1957; Little 1957).

Not all empirical evidence supports the theory. Angell's (1951) study of the moral integration of American cities in 1940 found it to be inversely related to ethnic heterogeneity, an index most heavily weighted by percent blacks (the other component is percent foreign-born). To be sure, his concept of moral integration is fundamentally different from the concept of integration in terms of interpersonal relations among groups here employed, as he himself stresses with respect to a similar conceptual distinction. The two components of the index of moral integration are low crime rates and contributions to community chests. Extensive intergroup relations are not expected to be reflected in low crime rates (indeed, the opposite is expected, as will be presently explicated). But one would expect the integrative force of extensive intergroup relations to find expression in voluntary contributions to community welfare. The 1940 study contradicts this expectation; but the 1970 replication (Angell 1974) supports it slightly, since the negative correlation between heterogeneity and welfare contributions has turned into a weak positive one (.21). Why is this correlation so low, and why was that 30 years earlier negative? A possible reason is that the strong correlations of race with status differences counteracted the effect of heterogeneity and inhibited integrative intergroup relations earlier, and that these correlations became sufficiently weaker after World War II so that the adverse effect of consolidation no longer overwhelmed the positive effect of heterogeneity. It should be said again that such ad hoc interpretations cannot corroborate a theory, nor can illustrative research findings that support its prediction. It may also be mentioned, however, that the hypothesis advanced that consolidation of race with status is what counteracts the effect of heterogeneity on integration is empirically testable.

Multiform heterogeneity and macrosocial integration are unmeasured theoretical terms, which are reflected in measurable characteristics of societies (or other collectivities), namely, the correlations of nominal parameters and the rates of intergroup relations with respect to these parameters in each society. The principle that multiform heterogeneity enhances macrosocial integration, which is implicit in T-12.1, is therefore tested, not directly, but indirectly through the predictions it makes about various specific parameters. This testing requires a comparative study of many societies. The correlations of parameters within each society are treated as variables describing variations in consolidation-intersection among societies. The predictions are that, with societies as units of analysis, the strength of correlation between any two parameters is inversely related to the prevalence of intergroup relations in terms of either parameter. The analysis need not be confined to simple correlations of parameters, however. To encompass in a single measure more of the theoretical concept of multiform heterogeneity, one could use multiple correlations for a number of parameters (the same ones for every society), or procedures that supply underlying dimensions of their correlations, such as factor analysis. Low multiple correlations or many orthogonal dimensions would be indicative of multiple heterogeneity and expected to be positively related to the prevalence of intergroup relations for the various intersecting parameters. It may also be possible to devise overall measures of the extent of intergroup relations or macrosocial integration in a society, to ascertain whether the indicators of multiform heterogeneity are, as expected, positively related to these measures.[5] But even in the absence of overall empirical indicators of multiform

5. A clue for such a measure is provided by "Small World" research (Travers and Milgram 1969; Korte and Milgram 1970), which shows how few steps are needed to connect any two individuals in a large society. A random sample is given a message with a specified target person and asked to send it to the person they know who is most likely to have some direct or indirect connection with the target persons, and the intermediate links are asked to do the same. By using target persons stratified by various social positions and employing such a procedure, the results could be used to construct a measure of extent of intergroup relations or macrosocial integration, based on the reciprocal of the properly weighted average number of steps needed to reach the various targets. Another possibility is to select a few parameters that are very salient in most societies, ascertain actual divided by expected frequencies of intergroup relations for each (based on a sample), and use the average of these least prevalent intergroup relations as a crude measure of the degree of overall integration, on the assumption that integration depends most on bridging the strongest group barriers.

heterogeneity and macrosocial integration, the principle that they are positively related can be tested through the many specific predictions it makes.

Segregation

The very axiom that implies that heterogeneity promotes intergroup relations also implies limits of this influence of heterogeneity. Intergroup relations, like all associations between people, depend on opportunities for social contacts (A-9). Heterogeneity fosters intergroup relations because it increases the chances of contacts between members of different groups. But if intergroup relations depend on opportunities for social contacts, heterogeneity cannot produce them when such opportunities are lacking because other conditions preclude contacts, and its influence on intergroup relations is diminished when other conditions restrict such opportunities.

Physical barriers—be they prison bars or oceans or long distances—naturally impede social associations. Groups that are located far apart have few opportunities for social contacts. Regardless of the great heterogeneity of a society, the chances that persons from different groups meet are small if different groups live and work in different places. The spatial segregation of groups limits the influence of heterogeneity on intergroup relations. It does not completely obliterate this influence, however, particularly in contemporary societies, where modern means of transportation and extensive mobility help overcome the obstacles of physical distance to social associations.

Physical propinquity exerts a pervasive influence on human relations. Its effects clearly illustrate the significance of the chances for social contacts for social associations (A-9), not merely for casual acquaintance but also for friendship and marriage. The consequences of chances or opportunities are often overlooked or oversimplified by constructing false dichotomies. Thus, the absence of friendships, with rare exceptions, between Angelenos and Bostonians might be interpreted by saying that people who are separated by more than 3,000 miles, as are the inhabitants of Los Angeles and Boston, cannot form friendships, but the small proportions of migrants who are no longer separated can, which accounts for the exceptions. This is not incorrect, though it is misleading, as the influence of very small physical distances on social associations reveals. Living a few hundred yards apart obviously does not make it impossible to form friendships, yet even smaller differences in physical distance influence the rate at which friendships are formed, as research has shown. Studies of housing communities disclose that increases of a few yards in the distance between residences reduce the likelihood of friendships (Merton 1948; Festinger, Schachter, and Back 1950), notably when the community is homogeneous (Gans 1967). Propinquity enhances the likelihood of marriage, too, in other cultures (Murdock 1949) as well as our own (Koller 1948; Sundal and McCormick 1951; Christensen 1958). The principle that propinquity governs the chances of social contacts and therefore the likelihood of associations can explain both the influences of very small physical distances and those of very large ones, which also make social associations only improbable and not impossible, as the exceptions show, and as would be true even if there were no exceptions owing to the very small probabilities.

The greater the physical propinquity between persons, the greater is the probability of associations between them (T-13). Propinquity increases the chances of fortuitous contacts among persons, which govern the likelihood of social associations (A-9). In addition, the theorem is implied by the axiom that associations among persons in proximate positions are more prevalent than those among persons in distant positions (A-1), if proximate is defined to include physical as well as social proximity. Propinquity need not be confined to place of residence. It can be alternatively defined on the basis of place of work, which also affects opportunities for social associations. The operational measures required for testing empirical hypotheses about the influences of propinquity and other aspects of spatial distributions on social associations are equivalent to those earlier adumbrated for measuring various aspects of status distributions (note 2, chapter 3), substituting physical for status distances.

The spatial distribution of people, which reflects the differences in propinquity among them, influences social life profoundly. It is in some ways an element of social structure and in others a condition that shapes it. The implications of spatial distributions for social associations essentially parallel those of other distributions of people among social positions, yet spatial distributions have certain distinctive features. This topic will be fully discussed in chapter 7. Attention now is restricted to one aspect of spatial distributions that has important implications for the influence of heterogeneity on intergroup relations.

The geographical segregation of groups or strata is a social manifestation of propinquity. It refers to the relationship between any parameter and the distribution of people among different places, that is, to the extent to which various groups or strata are located in different rather than in the same territories. Low segregation implies that most people live in proximity to members of other groups; high segregation implies that few do.[6] One can study the segregation of different groups among the communities in a society, or their segregation among the neighborhoods in a community, or their segregation in terms of where they work rather than where they live. The

6. A frequently used index of segregation is the index of dissimilarity (Duncan and Duncan 1955). It is based on the percentage distributions of groups among different places, summing one-half the absolute differences (or mean absolute differences). Thus, the criterion is not the actual physical distance between places but the extent to which different groups live in propinquity, that is, in the same areas.

analysis of segregation, however defined, focuses on the way propinquity and group differences interact in influencing social relations, not on the direct influences of people's propinquity on their relations independent of their group memberships.

Segregation of groups or strata among communities or among neighborhoods within them impedes social relations between their members (T-13.1). *The segregation of the groups delineated by a given nominal parameter among different places increases the preponderance of ingroup over intergroup associations* (T-13.11). *The segregation of social strata delineated by a given graduated parameter increases the inhibiting effect of status distance on social associations* (T-13.12). The three theorems are implied by T-13 directly and by A-9 indirectly: If propinquity promotes social associations (T-13) because it increases the chances of contacts on which associations depend (A-9), it follows that segregation, which entails low propinquity among groups or strata, reduces associations among them. Thus, segregation strengthens ingroup bonds at the cost of integrative intergroup relations in a community or society. Extensive intergroup relations cannot develop unless different groups are "integrated" in communities and neighborhoods, in the colloquial meaning of the word, that is, unless there is little spatial segregation. An illustrative empirical finding is that residential segregation of blacks and whites in California counties is inversely correlated with intermarriage between them (Heer 1966). The implication of T-13.11 that a reduction in a group's segregation from others attenuates ingroup bonds conforms to the finding of empirical studies that the residential dispersion of a kin group weakens kinship ties in modern society (Bott 1957), as well as in other cultures (Furer-Haimendorf 1956; Hopen 1958).

The spatial segregation of groups counters the positive influence of heterogeneity on intergroup relations (T-13.2). Segregation and heterogeneity have opposite consequences for the chances of social contacts between members of different groups and thus for the likelihood of associations between them (A-9). The overriding influence is not necessarily that of segregation. Heterogeneity curtails the negative influence of segregation on intergroup relations, just as segregation curtails the positive one of heterogeneity, particularly in contemporary society with widely available means of transportation. Thus, with the same amount of spatial segregation of two groups, the likelihood of intergroup contacts depends on how evenly the population is distributed between them (Erbe 1975), which means that it depends on the degree of heterogeneity (which is maximal for an even population distribution). Segregation of social strata also lessens their opportunities for forming social relations, but this reinforces the effect of inequality, whereas segregation of groups counters the effect of heterogeneity, because inequality and heterogeneity have opposite effects on social relations between persons in different positions (see T-7 and T-11). *The spatial segregation of social strata reinforces the negative effect of inequality on associations between persons in different strata* (T-13.3).

Not even the constraints of multiform heterogeneity on intergroup relations are immune from being diminished by the spatial segregation of groups. To be sure, several intersecting parameters make it quite unlikely that the groups delineated by all of them are highly segregated. But to the extent to which they are, their segregation does reduce the chances of contacts and consequently the rates of association among their members, weakening the positive influence of multiform heterogeneity on intergroup relations. Multiform heterogeneity must exist within communities, not merely in society at large, to have its full impact on intergroup relations. The higher the correlations of parameters, the more feasible it is for the consolidated group differences also to be substantially correlated with differences in location, that is, for the groups to be highly segregated. In this situation consolidation obliterates multiform heterogeneity, and its inhibiting effect on intergroup relations (T-12.11) is reinforced by segregation (T-13.1). A well-known example is the adverse effect of the segregation of poor blacks or poor immigrants in ghettos on the relations of these groups with others and their integration in society. *Segregation reinforces the negative effect of consolidated parameters on intergroup relations* (T-13.4).

The influences of the spatial distribution of people on their social relations are in principle the same as those of their other distributions among positions. Geographical location may be considered a parameter which affects social relations as other parameters do, except for having some characteristics of nominal and some of graduated parameters. People associate disproportionately with others in their own group, and they associate disproportionately with others in their own location. Status distance inhibits social associations, and so does physical distance. Segregation, which is defined by the correlation of location with one or more parameters, inhibits intergroup relations and counters the positive influence of heterogeneity on them. Correspondingly, consolidation, which is defined by the correlation of two or more parameters, inhibits intergroup relations and counters the positive constraints multiform heterogeneity would otherwise exert on them. Strong correlations of parameters with one another and with location may create such great barriers to intergroup relations that they transform a complex society into congeries of people connected only by the economic dependence of some on others.

Cosmopolitan Role Sets

The size of groups as well as their spatial distribution modifies the influences of intersecting parameters on intergroup relations. Multiform heterogeneity exerts greater constraints to associate with outsiders in small groups than in large ones. The distribution of workers among occupations and places of employment illustrates this. The many assembly-line workers in large factories can easily find associates in their occupational ingroups at their places of employment, but janitors and accountants in small factories cannot, because there are so few of them. The situation is the same for religious groups who live in various places. Protestants in large towns can have a large circle of friends all of whom are coreligionists and live in the same town, but Jews in small towns are too few to make this possible.

This conclusion is not contradicted by, nor does it contradict, the earlier one that many intersecting parameters exert compelling constraints to engage in intergroup relations. The constraints of multiform heterogeneity to establish *some* intergroup relations are compelling for all groups regardless of their size, because many intersecting parameters imply that all ingroup relations are simultaneously intergroup relations. No *particular* parameter is subject to these compelling constraints, though restrictions on intergroup relations in terms of any particular parameter entail more extensive intergroup relations in terms of others, so that the overall constraints on intergroup relations are inescapable. For small groups, intersecting parameters exert additional constraints to associate with outgroups, though not absolutely compelling ones for any particular parameter, because small size reduces the number of available ingroup associates. As the number of intersecting parameters increases, the size of the subgroups that are very small in terms of all of them decreases toward the limit of one person, at which point the constraints to engage in intergroup relations would be absolutely compelling. The inevitable intergroup relations at the limit indicate the increasing probability of intergroup relations when group size diminishes and moves toward the limit.

As group size in terms of one nominal parameter declines, the probability of intergroup relations in terms of other intersecting parameters increases (T-14). The smaller the size of a group, the greater are the chances that ingroup associates differ with respect to other social positions. Consequently, ingroup associations, which are prevalent (A-1.1), provide more opportunities for and thus increase the probabilities of intergroup relations in terms of *other* intersecting parameters in smaller than in larger groups (A-9). Moreover, the smaller the various groups delineated by two different intersecting parameters, the greater are the chances that fortuitous contacts involve persons who differ in one respect or both, which also increases opportunities for and probabilities of intergroup relations (A-9). Although the theorem refers to small size in terms of one parameter, it applies *a fortiori* to subgroups that are small in terms of several, and it applies to the probabilities of outgroup associations with respect to any of the parameters. For example, if there are few black professionals in a small city, the probabilities are great that they associate with whites, with nonprofessionals, and with persons in other cities.

Variations in group size exert two distinct influences on intergroup relations. A theorem formulated in chapter 2 stipulates that the probability of intergroup relations increases with decreasing group size (T-1.5). This follows from the proposition that in any dichotomy of groups the rate of intergroup associations of the smaller exceeds that of the larger group (T-1). Reference in these propositions is to group differences delineated by a single nominal parameter. The underlying principle, which makes T-1 true by definition (unless two groups have no contacts), is that the rates of association must be an inverse function of size because the same numerator (associations) is divided by a different denominator (size). In contrast, T-14 refers to the influence of size differences in terms of one parameter on the probabilities of intergroup relations in terms of others, for which this principle is clearly not applicable. Intersecting parameters are what account for the greater probability of small groups in one respect to have intergroup associates in other respects, in accordance with the implications of A-1.1 and A-9, as just indicated. If parameters intersect, the influence predicted in T-14 reinforces that in T-1.5 for subgroups that are small on several dimensions, which makes their probabilities of outgroup relations high, the more so the greater the multiform heterogeneity.

As a matter of fact, A-9 implies T-1.5, too. The smaller a group, the greater are the chances that fortuitous contacts of its members involve others who belong to different groups in terms of the same parameter. The resulting greater opportunities for establishing intergroup relations increase, according to A-9, the probability of intergroup relations of small groups over that of large ones, as predicated in T-1.5. Although T-1.5 and T-14 follow from the same axiom, their predictions are different: The former refers to the intergroup relations in terms of the same parameter that delineates the size differences under consideration, the latter to intergroup relations in terms of other parameters. These two distinct influences reinforce each other when parameters are intersecting, since small size in terms of either parameter promotes intergroup relations in terms of both. The assumption that people associate with persons in other groups as well as their own (A-0) is dispensable as a primitive proposition for the analysis of simple as well as complex social structures, since the theorems derived from it are deducible from A-9 and the definitions (and in complex structures, A-0 itself is derivable from A-1.1 and A-11).

An implication of T-1.5 and T-14 is that the members of small groups tend to have a greater variety of associates than those of large ones. For the smaller a group in terms of one parameter, the greater are the probabilities of intergroup associates in terms of all other parameters, this one (T-1.5) and any other (T-14). For example, members of small occupational groups not only are most likely to have associates in other occupations, they are also most likely to have associates that differ from them in ethnic background, religion, politics, inherited wealth, and indeed any attribute that is not more closely related to their occupational position than to others. Such a great variety of role relations is particularly probable for subgroups that are small in several respects, such as black professionals. It may be termed a cosmopolitan role set, borrowing two concepts of Merton's and joining them.

By *role set* Merton (1968, p. 423) refers to the "complement of role relationships which persons have by virtue of occupying a particular social status." The concept focuses on the different role relations of persons in a given social position, but not specifically on how extensive their associations and role involvements with outsiders are. Merton's (1968, pp. 447–53) concept of *cosmopolitan* does refer to the extent to which persons are involved in their role relations and orientations with the outside world rather than primarily their local community. By joining the two concepts, the meaning of cosmopolitanism is expanded to include role relations outside any group, not only outside the local community, and the concept of role set is specified to refer to extent of role involvement with many different outgroups. (A group's high rate of association with outgroups, the operational criterion of great role involvement with them, implies both more outgroup associations and associations with more different outgroups than does a low rate.) In short, the definition of cosmopolitan role set is that persons in a given social position have extensive role relations with others in many different social positions. A major condition that produces cosmopolitan role sets is the small number of incumbents of a social position or the small size of a group.

When parameters intersect, the decreasing size of a group increases the probability that its members have cosmopolitan role sets (T-14.1).[7] Cosmopolitan role sets would be expected to have a number of social and psychological consequences. Variations in a person's role set frequently create conflicts, role strains, and cross-pressures. But such a complex role set, as R. Coser terms it (1975, p. 243), "offers, at the same time as it makes incompatible demands, the structural opportunities . . . that help diminish the disorderly effects of contradictory expectations." She goes on to indicate (1975, pp. 246–51) how complex social relations further intellectual flexibility and comprehension, in particular. Small minorities of all kinds are most subject to such variable social experiences and their consequences, bad and good, according to T-14.1. Cosmopolitan role sets are expected to tend to make members of small minorities, compared to members of large groups, more insecure and anxious, less loyal and committed to their own groups, and less steadfast in their political and other allegiances owing to cross-pressures. But they are also expected to broaden the horizon of minority members and stimulate their intellectual curiosity; to reduce their ethnocentrism and increase their tolerance; to make them less rigid in politics and less resistant to change in their opinions, conduct, or surroundings. A cosmopoli-

7. Unless a small group is completely isolated, its rate of associations with larger groups in terms of the same parameter defining it must exceed their rates with its members; even when it is completely isolated, the probability of its intergroup associations in terms of *other* intersecting parameters exceeds that of the larger groups. For instance, the isolation of a small community increases the likelihood of associations across status lines more than that of a large community.

tan role set is a diverse social environment that gives persons a greater variety of social experiences, which has some disadvantageous and some advantageous sociopsychological consequences for them and for others. Not all these consequences are observable in all minorities, since other conditions may counteract them, such as the ideological commitment of a small sect or economic discrimination against an ethnic minority. Implications of T-14.1 are illustrated by the many Jews who have become atheists; the cosmopolitan tastes in art and food of elites; the success in intellectual fields of various ethnic minorities; and the tendency of members of such groups as Chinese, Indians, and Jews to become traders in those societies where they are minorities (Blalock 1967, pp. 79–84; Bonacich 1973), as successful trading depends on role relations with numerous groups.

Some implications of T-14.1 are quite unexpected and puzzling, however. For example, it implies that academics in universities are less cosmopolitan than persons in the same fields working for the government or in private industry, which many academics would dispute. But reference is not to intellectual sophistication or scope of knowledge; it is to the range of different associates and the breadth of social experiences it entails, which is probably narrower for academics (though not for business managers) in our ivory towers than for our colleagues in the outside world, where organizations are not composed mostly of scientists and scholars. T-14.1 also implies that people in a small town have more cosmopolitan role sets than those in a big metropolis, which appears to be a contradiction in terms, as a metropolis like New York is the prototype of cosmopolitanism. In some respects, like social class, people in small towns may actually have associates in a greater number of different positions than those in big cities, where the large numbers of persons in the various strata and groups lessen the restraints on inclinations to confine social intercourse to persons in proximate positions. Whether this is the case or not, inhabitants of small towns are predicated to have on the average more cosmopolitan role sets than those in large cities, provided that there are no differences in multiform heterogeneity between them.[8] Usually there are, of course; and multiform heterogeneity promotes cosmopolitan role sets.

Ceteris paribus, the more pronounced the multiform heterogeneity, the more prevalent are cosmopolitan role sets (T-14.2). Multiform heterogeneity enhances intergroup relations, because it entails both heterogeneity and intersecting parameters, either of which promote intergroup relations (T-11, T-12.1). T-14.2 is a corollary of the proposition that multiform heterogeneity enhances intergroup relations, since conditions that increase intergroup relations thereby expand cosmopolitan role sets, which are defined as extensive associations with a variety of outgroups. In other words, cosmopolitan

8. T-14.1 indicates that the influence of small group size on cosmopolitan role sets depends on intersecting parameters, which imply multiform heterogeneity.

role sets are from the perspective of various groups or communities what extensive intergroup relations are from the perspective of the encompassing society. The one does not produce the other, as the two are defined in the same terms. The great heterogeneity typical of big cities makes cosmopolitan role sets prevalent there, in accordance with T-14.2; but the larger components of most groups in big cities than in small towns have the opposite effect of reducing cosmopolitan role sets, in accordance with T-14.1. These are not two contradictory predictions that cannot be falsified, inasmuch as regression analysis can separate such opposite influences.

Compendium

A-9   Social associations depend on opportunities for social contacts.

A-10   As rare social practices in a group increase in frequency, group pressures that discourage them subside.

T-11   Increasing heterogeneity increases the probability of intergroup relations. (From A-9, or A-9, A-10.)

T-11.1   Ceteris paribus, the larger of two groups discriminates more than the smaller against associating with members of the other group. (From A-10, T-1.)

T-11.2   Increasing heterogeneity probably reduces the discrepancies in intergroup relations among groups. (From T-1.4.)

T-11.3   Increasing status diversity increases the probabilities of associations among persons whose status differs. (From A-9, or A-9, A-10.)

T-11.4   Increasing status diversity reduces the discrepancies in the rates of social association between strata. (From T-1.4.)

A-11   The influences of various parameters on social associations are partly additive, not entirely contingent on one another.

T-12   The lower the positive correlations between parameters, the more extensive are intergroup relations. (From A-1, A-11.)

T-12.1   Intersecting nominal parameters improve the integration of various groups by raising the rates of association between their members. (From A-1.1, A-11.)

T-12.11   Consolidated nominal parameters strengthen ingroup bonds and attenuate intergroup relations that integrate various groups. (From A-1.1, A-11.)

T-13   The greater the physical propinquity, the greater is the probability of social associations. (From A-9.)

T-13.1   Segregation of groups or strata among communities or among neighborhoods within them impedes social relations between their members. (From T-13; based on A-9.)

T-13.11 The segregation of the groups delineated by a given nominal parameter among different places increases the preponderance of ingroup relations. (From T-13; based on A-9.)

T-13.12 The segregation of social strata delineated by a given graduated parameter increases the inhibiting effect of status distance on social associations. (From T-13; based on A-9.)

T-13.2 The spatial segregation of groups counters the positive influence of heterogeneity on intergroup relations. (From A-9, T-13.)

T-13.3 The spatial segregation of social strata reinforces the negative effect of inequality on associations between persons in different strata. (From A-1.2, A-9.)

T-13.4 Segregation reinforces the negative effect of consolidated parameters on intergroup relations. (From T-12.11, T-13.1; based on A-1, A-11, A-9.)

T-14   As group size in terms of one nominal parameter declines, the probability of intergroup relations in terms of other intersecting parameters increases. (From A-1.1, A-9.)

T-14.1 The smaller the size of a group, the greater is the probability that its members have cosmopolitan role sets. (From T-1.5 and T-14; based on A-9.)

T-14.2 Ceteris paribus, the more pronounced the multiform heterogeneity, the more prevalent are cosmopolitan role sets. (From T-11, T-12.1; based on A-9, A-1, A-11.)

CHAPTER FIVE

Multiple Parameters

THE ANALYSIS OF MULTIPLE PARAMETERS, WHICH HAS BEEN INTRODUCED
in the preceding chapter, is carried further in this one. The earlier discussion
of intersecting and consolidated nominal parameters is complemented by
examining the intersection and consolidation among graduated and between
them and nominal parameters. The analysis is concerned with the implications of these various structural conditions, defined by the correlations of
parameters, for the differentiation among people; for their associations and
the integration of groups and strata; for social mobility; for interpersonal
conflicts; and for structural change.

Attempts to generalize about social life invariably involve simplifying
concrete historical reality by abstracting the influences of some elements
from it and taking those of other conditions as given. If the propositions are
properly formulated, they do not distort empirical reality, but they over-
simplify it by taking into account only selected conditions. Propositions
about multiple parameters simplify less than those about single parameters,
because they take into consideration not merely the influences of one parameter in isolation from other conditions but also how its influences are
modified by other structural conditions—its relationships with other parameters. However, the analysis of social differentiation and its consequences for
social processes remains on a very abstract level so long as concern is with
differentiation generally and specific forms of it are not distinguished. Formulating generalizations about social differentiation that apply to all its forms
is the objective here, but the distinctive significance of some specific forms of
differentiation is considered in later chapters.

Complex Structures

Structural parameters constitute a framework for comparative macrosociological inquiry. They are a conceptual framework that is imposed on empirical reality to abstract certain kinds of information from it. Comparative studies of societies, communities, or other collectivities are required to test the propositions that the structural conditions delineated by parameters have the stipulated consequences, since most of these conditions characterize the entire structure and not its components. The influences of inequality, heterogeneity, intersecting parameters, and consolidated parameters refers to variations observable only by comparing various social structures, though the influences of group size can be observed in research on a single one.

A society has a complex social structure if there are a great many different social positions, roles, and role relations. Numerous separate lines of differentiation of groups and strata make a social structure more complex. However, the number of parameters that are analytically distinguishable do not determine structural complexity. The same parameters, and hence the same number of them, must be used in describing every society to make meaningful comparisons.[1] Power and wealth are conceptually distinct, but if differences in the two virtually coincide in one society while being largely independent in another, these two parameters differentiate fewer social positions in the first than in the second society. If different ethnic groups also differ in religion, the two parameters delineate fewer subgroups than if they are cross-cutting. The criterion of structural complexity is not the number of parameters that can be analytically distinguished, but the degree of their independence, because the latter governs the number of different positions they delineate.

Intersecting parameters generate structural complexity; consolidated parameters limit it. To be sure, structural complexity also depends on the degree of differentiation that exists along the various lines—how great the heterogeneity of various kinds is, how much inequality in various forms occurs. However, the influence of the degree of intersection of parameters on overall differentiation is paramount. The polar extremes indicate this: Perfect correlations limit the total differentiation to that yielded by one parameter, whereas completely orthogonal parameters increase the differentiation resulting from one exponentially by the power of the number of parameters. The tremendous difference between these extremes reveals the strong impact substantial variations in the strength of correlations of parameters have on the number of socially differentiated positions, and thus on structural complexity.

1. Even a parameter that does not meet the criterion of one—affecting role relations—in one society or another must not be excluded in these comparisons.

The term *social position* needs to be reconceptualized for employment in the definition of structural complexity on the basis of the extent to which positions of all kinds have become differentiated. Originally the term referred to a position distinguished by a single parameter, such as Catholic or Protestant. But in the definition it refers to the specific position and role delineated by all parameters under consideration, such as Irish Catholic college graduate with a number of other social attributes. Structural complexity refers to the distribution of people among positions in this narrower sense, whereas heterogeneity and inequality refer to their distributions in terms of a single parameter. A complex social structure is characterized by both a multitude of social positions and extensive distribution of people among them, which implies great variations in roles and role relations.

The more parameters intersect, the greater the structural complexity (T-15). This is an analytic proposition, which is necessarily true given the definitions of terms, not a synthetic one, which relates independently defined terms. Yet such tautological propositions, as previously indicated, can have implications that are not entirely obvious, notably when contrasted or combined with other propositions that are not tautological. Structural complexity is nearly synonymous with structural differentiation, though not quite, because the form of differentiation alters its meaning. Paradoxically, intersecting parameters have opposite implications for the major forms of differentiation.

The more nominal parameters intersect, the greater the heterogeneity (T-15.1). Intersecting nominal parameters enhance heterogeneity by making it multiform, as discussed in the preceding chapter. When some kinds of group difference cut across other kinds, heterogeneity is multiplied as a multitude of subgroups is generated. The same principle applies to status diversity, which is heterogeneity in terms of status. When status differences in some respects cut across those in others, the multiplicity of status-defined positions increases. *The more graduated parameters intersect, the greater the status diversity* (T-15.2). Both of these theorems are entailed by the definitions of terms.

The case of inequality is different, however. The consolidation of inequalities clearly does not diminish them. If rich people also have much power and prestige and poor people have little, the inequality between them is not attenuated. On the contrary, it is intensified. The very opposite conditions mitigate inequalities: if inferior status of one kind is compensated by superior status of another, or at least if the poor are not also powerless and lacking in prestige. *The less graduated parameters intersect, the greater the inequality* (T-15.3). Whereas the foregoing illustrations make this apparent, the question arises as to how it is possible for intersecting parameters to have opposite implications for two types of differentiation that seem to be formally similar, if not identical. The reasons for the paradox are that the two types are not identical and that a distinctive characteristic of status differences is implicitly assumed in the above illustrations, an assumption on which T-15.3 depends.

A fundamental analytical distinction between nominal and graduated parameters is that nominal positions are unordered whereas graduated positions are ordered. Group memberships can only be the same or different. But status can differ in varying degrees and, moreover, in opposite ways. (Status diversity explicitly ignores this property of status.) The conception of status implies a direction as well as an order. If we do not know which end of a rank order is up, we do not speak of hierarchical status. There is a rough rank order between the political left and the political right, and between great religious piety and atheism, but we think of these as various positions and not as hierarchical status, because there are no higher and lower values, except from the perspective of the adherents of the various positions. High and low status, in contrast, is defined in universalistic, not in particularistic, terms, to use Parsons's (1951, pp. 62–63) well-known concepts. The powerless are in full agreement with the powerful as to which one is the superior position; the radicals and the reactionaries obviously do not agree on which of the two positions is superior. The poor surely know that they have less money and lower socioeconomic status than the rich; the atheists do not acknowledge that their position is inferior to that of the pious, though the pious think so. Status implies a universally recognized standard of valuation in a society, and often beyond, while group memberships are nominal positions precisely because, and only as long as, their valuation depends on the particular perspective of the group.

Status differences are differences in social resources of some kind which have general validity in social interaction as a currency that can be exchange for services or other resources. Inequality refers to the distribution of such a resource—an independent variate—among a population, whereas heterogeneity refers to the distribution of people among nominal positions, and there is no other variate that is, or can be, related to the frequency distribution of the population. The difference is reflected in the operational measures: that of heterogeneity rests on the percentage distribution of persons; that of inequality on the difference between the percentage distribution of persons and the percentage distribution of the resource or status attribute, which indicates mean status distance (average difference in resources) relative to mean status (average resources).[2] It is considered to be

2. The difference is evident in the computation formulae; that for heterogeneity is based on the fraction of the population (p_i) in various categories: Σp_i; that for the Gini index of inequality on the difference between the cumulative fraction of the population (p_j) and the cumulative fraction of the total status resource (s_j) in various categories: $2\Sigma(p_j - s_j)p_i$. This computation formula for the Gini index and the equivalent formula for it shown in note 5 of chapter 3 indicate the two equivalent meanings of inequality: the extent to which a large fraction of a resource is concentrated in a small fraction of the population, and the average distance in status relative to (twice) the average status.

axiomatic that *status differences are differences in comparable social resources of generally acknowledged validity in social exchange* (A-12).

This axiom in effect specifies the meaning of the concept of social status. Early in chapter 3 status was defined on the basis of variations in role relations by degree that reflect differences in status distance and thus, in the aggregate, a gradation of social positions. The distinction between nonhierarchical positions and hierarchical status can now be refined. Although nominal categories do not vary by degree, some social positions do without constituting hierarchical status, as exemplifed by more or less distant political positions and more or less distant relatives. For such social positions, role relations do vary by degree from the perspective of any particular position, depending on its social distance from others, because these nominal parameters contain one element of graduated parameters, though they lack another. They do entail a gradation, but the gradation does not have a direction that is independent of the perspectives of the various positions and that gives it a generally recognized apex and nadir. What supplies a direction and distinguishes vertical status from horizontally graded positions is that the criterion of position is the possession of a social resource that is generally valued.

The axiom that superior status entails superior social resources (A-12) implies the theorem that consolidated (little intersecting) graduated parameters enhance inequality (T-15.3), because largely coinciding differences in various resources increase the overall difference in resources. The socially useful resources underlying, by assumption, all forms of status furnish a common denominator for comparing and combining the significance of various forms of status differences, not merely by the investigator but by the participants themselves. Persons who are highly educated and affluent have greater social resources than those who are only highly educated or only affluent, and people take this into account in their role relations. Nominal positions have no such common denominator, whether or not social distances among them vary by degree. Highly correlated nominal parameters imply that people are concentrated in few positions, which decreases heterogeneity. In contrast, highly correlated graduated parameters imply that resources are concentrated in fewer positions, which increases inequality among their incumbents. Intersecting graduated parameters mitigate inequality, and negatively correlated ones actually diminish it, because in this case inferior status in some respects is compensated by superior status in others. But negative correlations between status differences rarely occur, as is also implied by the axiom.

Superior status in one respect helps to achieve superior status in another, because ample resources of one kind furnish the means for acquiring resources of another kind. A better education tends to raise income; wealth is a source of authority over employees; affluence enhances prestige; power facilitates acquiring wealth.[3] Thus, the assumption that status differences constitute differences in social resources (A-12) can explain the tendency of status consistency to develop, that is, of various aspects of status differences to be positively correlated. But what looks like perfect balance from the sociopsychological perspective—the consistency of various statuses of individuals—turns out to be an extreme imbalance from the structural perspective—all status privileges accrue to some and all status burdens are imposed on others. Although actual conditions are never that extreme, since various status dimensions are not perfectly correlated, they typically resemble this polar case more than its opposite, since various status dimensions tend to be correlated positively, not negatively. The consolidation of graduated parameters greatly magnifies inequalities by making them cumulative.

The strength of the correlations between nominal parameters and that between graduated parameters has parallel implications for structural complexity but opposite implications for horizontal and vertical differentiation, respectively, strange though it seems. Whereas low correlations of nominal parameters increase structural complexity by increasing heterogeneity, low correlations of graduated parameters increase structural complexity while *decreasing* inequality. For intersecting graduated parameters enhance status diversity (T-15.2), and thus structural complexity, by proliferating positions in ways that result in counterbalancing status differences which diminish inequalities.

The relationships between nominal and graduated parameters have not yet been considered. Strong correlations of a nominal with graduated parameters indicate great status differences among groups. If a nominal parameter that exhibits such strong correlations comprises many categories, it can be transformed into a new parameter, which may be called an ordinal parameter, by ranking the categories on the basis of the correlated status differences. For example, measures of occupational status have been constructed by ranking detailed occupations, which themselves are nominal categories, in terms of variations in their prestige (National Opinion Research Center 1947) or in the education and income of their incumbents (Duncan 1961). Much occupational heterogeneity may be accompanied by more or less occupational inequality, though both are defined by the occupational distribution, depending on the extent to which occupations differ in prestige, education, and income. Other measures of occupational status

3. A serious shortcoming of the functional theory of stratification (Davis and Moore 1945) is that it essentially ignores this influence of one status on another and assumes status differences to be determined by the need for various services and to constitute the incentives required to assure that the most important services are most readily furnished. These assumptions virtually imply that corporation executives, who are highly rewarded by their great power and prestige, should receive lower salaries than janitors, whereas in reality the great power they have enables them to assure that they do get higher salaries.

could be devised, for instance, an index of occupational authority could be based on the average scope of administrative authority in work organizations exercised by the incumbents of different occupations.

A caste system is distinguished from a class structure by the fact that an ascriptive nominal parameter exhibits a virtually perfect correlation with one graduated parameter or with several. A hierarchical ranking of groups has become institutionalized in a caste society, so that being born into a certain group determines a person's occupational status, prestige, and his or her status in other respects, with marriage and sociable intercourse between castes being prohibited. A defining characteristic of a class society is the absence of such ascriptive status differences. But this dichotomy over-simplifies matters; caste ingredients are found in class societies. When ascriptive group differences are strongly, albeit not perfectly, correlated with various status differences and intimate relations between these groups are greatly discouraged and very rare, albeit not completely absent, these groups may aptly be described as quasi castes. This describes the case of American blacks and whites—still today, despite some recent changes—who can properly be described as quasi castes in a class society.

Pronounced status differences among groups, even when they are short of these extremes, become character-defining properties of the groups and affect role relations accordingly. Although occupations are purely nominal categories, their substantial correlations with education, income, prestige, and authority have the result that people are oriented to occupational status when they think of or come in contact with physicians or grocery clerks or factory managers. Similarly, when most members of an ethnic group have little education, money, and power, this reflects on the entire group, and group membership itself becomes a sign of low status. Quasi castes are a polar case of this wider phenomenon. The consolidation of a nominal with graduated parameters tends to transform groups into hierarchical strata.

Implications for Social Processes

The consequences of structural parameters for processes of social association and mobility depend on their correlations. Intersecting parameters promote associations and mobility among groups and strata; consolidated parameters inhibit them. Cross-cutting lines of differentiation exert constraints to associate with persons whose position differs from one's own in one way or another. This is the case for intersecting vertical as well as intersecting horizontal lines of differentiation, although the two have opposite implications for the degree of differentiation, the one reducing inequality and the other enhancing heterogeneity. The general proposition that intersecting parameters further cross-cutting social associations (T-12), which has been discussed for nominal parameters (T-12.1, T-12.11) in chapter 4, applies to graduated parameters as well.

Intersecting graduated parameters integrate different strata by raising the rates of social associations among them (T-12.2). The intersection of graduated parameters implies that persons whose status is similar in one respect differ in status in other respects. Consequently, people's associations with others of proximate status (A-1.2) in terms of one parameter entail associations with persons whose status is not proximate in terms of other parameters, on the assumption that status proximity of one kind affects social associations also in the absence of status proximity of other kinds (A-11). This assumption does not require that millionaires and paupers who have the same education associate, only that people whose affluence differs are more likely to associate when they have the same education than when they do not. The theorem can be derived alternatively from A-12 and A-1.2: Low correlations of graduated parameters reduce the overall difference in status resources (A-12) that inhibits social associations (A-1.2). Negative correlations of graduated parameters promote social associations among different strata still more than low correlations, owing to the counterbalancing status differences. But negative correlations of graduated parameters are very rare, as we have seen. Indeed, low positive correlations are rare, too; graduated parameters tend to exhibit substantial positive correlations. The obverse theorem, which follows from the same assumptions, is therefore probably the relevant one in most situations. *Consolidated graduated parameters attenuate the rates of social associations among different strata and thus weaken their integration* (T-12.21).

The same principles apply to the relationships of nominal with graduated parameters. *The intersection of nominal by graduated parameters integrates groups and strata by raising the rates of social associations among them* (T-12.3). *The more consolidated are group differences with correlated status differences, the less frequent are integrative social relations among groups and strata* (T-12.31). Group differences and status differences that exert some independent influences (A-11) counteract each other's inhibiting effect on social associations (A-1) when their correlations are low but reinforce them when their correlations are high.

Thus, increasing status differences among groups depress both rates of association among groups, owing to the status differences, and among strata, owing to the group differences. For example, rates of intermarriage are higher between ethnic groups whose average socioeconomic status differs little than between those with great differences in socioeconomic status (Kennedy 1944). The associations among different hierarchical strata are correspondingly reduced by correlated group differences; for instance, the social relations between high and low socioeconomic strata are further attenuated when most poor people live in the central city and most more affluent ones in suburbs. Group differences in status consolidate group and status barriers to social intercourse.

Whether various group differences are highly correlated, or various status differences are, or group and status differences are, it inhibits social relations among persons whose social positions differ. The social distinctions implicit in consolidated parameters reinforce one another and widen social barriers, which constrains people to turn to their ingroups for social support, fortifies subgroup solidarities, and fragments society. Consolidated parameters counteract multiform differentiation and impede the social connections among groups and strata in society that integrate them into a community. If a viable society depends on these social connections, as seems plausible, the high correlations often observable among various status differences and between them and some group differences pose a threat to society's viability.

Status differences do cut across numerous group differences, of course, and the correlations of various status differences are evidently not perfect. Powerful persons may be Republicans or Democrats; wealthy persons may be in banking or in manufacturing; among the most educated are Catholics and Protestants; and not all people who have great power also have great wealth and are highly educated, though these three aspects of status are positively related. The extent to which a graduated parameter intersects with nominal or with other graduated parameters exerts more constraints on the social relations of the elite than on those of the more numerous lower strata. The small size of the elite in terms of any given graduated parameter increases the likelihood of associations with persons in different social positions not only in terms of this parameter, as previously noted (T-5), but also in terms of other parameters, in accordance with the influence exerted by small size in terms of a nominal parameter (T-14). The latter follows from the axioms that associations among elite members are prevalent (A-1.2) and that social associations depend on opportunities for social contacts (A-9): The smaller an elite's size, the greater are the chances that elite members differ with respect to those of their other social positions that are little related to elite status, which enhances the probabilities that the associations among the elite involve persons whose positions in terms of *other intersecting* parameters are different.

The smaller the size of an elite in terms of one graduated parameter, the greater are the probabilities that its members associate with persons whose positions differ from theirs in terms of other intersecting parameters (T-14.3). This theorem can explain a variety of research findings; for example, that leaders of gangs tend to associate more than followers do with members of other gangs (Whyte 1943); that community leaders are less likely than others to discriminate against minorities (Stouffer 1955); that persons in the highest occupational stratum are least likely to marry someone from the same neighborhood (Koller 1948; Sundal and McCormick 1951). Elites, like other small groups, are likely to have more diverse associates along various lines, in terms of the parameter defining their elite status as well as in terms other parameters intersecting it (T-14.3). Such diverse associates have been termed a cosmopolitan role set. However, the tendency of elite members to have cosmopolitan role sets depends on the extent to which the status-defining parameter intersects with other parameters and is diminished by the extent to which it is consolidated (positively correlated) with them. Status differences often exhibit substantial positive correlations, as noted. *The probability that the members of the elite have cosmopolitan role sets declines with increases in the positive correlations of the status-defining parameter with other parameters* (T-14.4).

The probability of extensive social relations among the elites defined by various parameters is greater than that among lower strata defined by them (T-14.31). If the members of the elite in terms of any graduated parameter are particularly likely to associate with persons in any position that differs from theirs in terms of other parameters (T-14.3), they are also particularly likely to associate with the members of another elite; the latter's corresponding likelihood to associate with them further increases the probability of extensive social relations; and the same is the case for the relations among all elites. Although T-14.3 depends on the proviso that the graduated parameters intersect, T-14.31 does not. For when the parameters do not intersect at all, the elites are identical, and the prevalent associations of the members of a single elite (A-1.2) obviate the need for the proviso. Society's small top strata in various spheres tend to have extensive social connections. A specific implication of the theorem is that the most powerful persons in different spheres—the economic, the political, the military—are likely to have close social relations and frequent communication which provide them with opportunities for common endeavors and concerted action. In short, the likelihood of the existence of a power elite (Mills 1956) can be predicated on purely formal grounds.[4]

Turning now to the influences of multiple parameters on processes of social mobility, these influences are in good part mediated by processes of social associations. If intersecting parameters increase rates of social associations among groups and strata (T-12), and if associates in other groups and strata encourage and facilitate mobility into them (PA-4), it follows that

4. An alternative derivation of T-14.31 resembles the grounds on which the existence of power elites is usually argued: If status differences entail differences in comparable resources (A-12), and if proximate positions promote associations (A-1.2), the proximity in resource position of various elites promotes association between their members. In short, different elites are unified by their common elite position. The specific point of the theory here is that the small size of elites invariably leads to extensive social connections among them. Mayhew and Levinger (1976a; see also Mayhew 1973) develop an interesting mathematical model which shows that the development of small elites is inevitable. This theory is not identical with but complemented by T-14.31, according to which these small elites become connected by extensive social ties.

intersecting parameters increase social mobility (T-16). Intersecting parameters imply that people have friends and relatives in other cities, other places of employment, other political parties, other occupations. Such social connections improve the chances of mobility. For example, shifts in political position are most frequent for persons whose associates have different political positions (Berelson, Lazarsfeld, and McPhee 1954, pp. 118–22); and shifts in jobs or occupations are often the result of communications from associates in different jobs or occupations (Granovetter 1974, pp. 48–50). The likelihood of moving to a new position is greatly diminished if one has no associates there. Consolidated parameters deprive people of agents that can facilitate social mobility and tend to confine them to their social origins, as people in earlier eras were and those in simple societies still are confined. *Consolidated nominal parameters restrict intergroup mobility* (T-16.1). *Consolidated graduated parameters restrict vertical mobility* (T-16.2).

Intersecting parameters exert additional influences on social mobility, which supplement those resulting from their influences on social associations, and which differ for nominal and graduated parameters. The axiom that ingroup associations are more prevalent than outgroup associations (A-1.2) implies that people are attracted to others in their own groups, whether or not they know them. When nominal parameters intersect, the attractive ingroup associates in terms of one parameter may stimulate mobility in terms of another. This is illustrated by Lieberson's (1972) findings that people tend to move to suburbs where others of similar ethnic and religious background live, just as migrants to a city tend to settle in neighborhoods where others from their place of origin already reside. For vertical mobility, however, being attracted to a higher position is not enough, since achieving it typically requires resources. In this case another mechanism is operative, which is implied by the axiom that status differences are differences in social resources (A-12). Intersecting graduated parameters indicate that some people who lack one kind of resource do have another which may enable them to acquire some of the first. Thus, high incomes enable persons without inherited wealth to accumulate some, and superior education enables persons in lower socioeconomic strata to move up to higher ones. Note that this process of mobility enhances status consistency and, in the terms used here, the consolidation of status differences, as it involves changes that increase the correlation between status dimensions. Yet consolidated parameters impede the processes of mobility implied by A-1.2 and A-12, as well as those mediated by associates in other groups or strata.

The degrees of intersection or consolidation of parameters constitute fundamental structural conditions that govern the social processes of association and mobility through which the various segments of a society are connected. Intersecting parameters further the integration of different groups and strata by exerting structural constraints that raise the rates of social association and mobility among them. No assumption about functional interdependence or common values has been made to account for the tendencies of persons in different social positions to associate with each other. Indeed, the sociopsychological assumption made is that people are predisposed to associate with others in similar rather than different positions (A-1). Although the assumption stipulates only proclivities for ingroup associations, tendencies to engage in intergroup associations can be derived from it in conjunction with analytic propositions defining properties of social structure. When many parameters are intersecting, intergroup relations of various kinds are frequent, notwithstanding ingroup preferences. But when parameters are strongly consolidated, intergroup relations are rare, even for persons who do not share a certain ingroup preference. For example, a strong preference for associating with academic colleagues leads to interethnic associations if ethnic background is largely unrelated to academic affiliation, but it inhibits interethnic associations if ethnic background and academic position are strongly correlated, even for individuals who have no ethnic bias. Variations in the structural conditions manifest in the correlations of parameters explain what influences given sociopsychological dispositions have on the social processes that integrate the segments of society.

Conflict and Integration

Not all social interaction is cordial, of course. Fights and quarrels also involve social interaction. Whereas such interpersonal conflicts may release built-up tensions and improve social relations in the long run, they cannot be said to improve social relations unless it can be shown that they result in more cordial social interaction at a later time. Abrasive social interaction itself, as long as it prevails and unless it brings these results in its aftermath, worsens social relations.

Social contacts between persons in different social positions—with different backgrounds and interests, different role attributes and expectations—often engender friction and conflict. Differences in opinions may lead to disputes and physical violence; differences in roles and interests may prompt one person to force another to do something against his or her will, as when the drill sergeant compels recruits to shine his boots, the boss compels employees to work late, the criminal forces his victims to hand over their money, or the police officer forces the suspect to put on handcuffs. Interpersonal conflict is defined as overt conflict between individuals involving direct interaction. It must be distinguished from four other types of conflict: (1) internal mental conflict, such as psychological strain or imbalance, a guilty conscience, role conflict; (2) conflict of interest, which may exist without finding expression in overt acts of conflict; (3) civil litigation, which is interpersonal conflict that has been institutionalized precisely to avert direct confrontation; (4) group conflict, which involves concerted action of two collectivities against each other. Group conflict will be discussed in chapter 9. Attention now centers on overt interpersonal conflict that entails direct contact.

The same structural conditions that make cordial intergroup relations more likely make interpersonal conflict between members of different groups more likely. For conditions that increase the probability of social contacts increase the likelihood of overt interpersonal conflict as well as that of harmonious social associations, since both depend on opportunities for social contacts. Strangely, therefore, the very conditions that foster the social integration of various groups and strata into a coherent social structure simultaneously precipitate frequent interpersonal conflicts among their members. Yet this is not so strange. Integrating diverse parts into a larger whole can be expected to entail some friction. When groups and strata remain far apart, there is less chance of friction in the form of interpersonal conflict among their members, but society is fragmented, and the great social distances are likely to be manifest in severe conflicts of interests which erupt intermittently in overt group or class conflicts. Comparatively frequent interpersonal conflict is the price of social integration in a diverse society.

In a recent paper, Mayhew and Levinger (1976b) develop a theoretical model along these lines. Three basic theorems of theirs (reworded) are: The expected number of social contacts increases at a multiplicative rate with size of place, that is, number of persons concentrated in a place; the expected number of contacts per person increases at a constant rate with size of place; the expected time per contact decreases at a declining rate with size of place. From the mathematical formulations of these theorems they (1976b, p. 96) derive the prediction that the frequency of social interaction of any kind—whether kisses or homicidal assaults, as they put it—"should initially increase at a multiplicative rate, but ultimately diminish to a relatively slow pace." They deal specifically with one form of interpersonal conflict, violent crimes against persons. Using other research as well as their own data, they indicate that the rates of these crimes increase with city size in the United States in accordance with the predicted logistic S-shaped curve. The large size and population density of a community increase contact opportunities and thus the probability of interpersonal conflict.

Although it seems reasonable to assume that the differences in background and interests among different social positions make interpersonal conflict more likely, no such assumption is required to arrive at the conclusion that social conditions that promote extensive intergroup relations also promote interpersonal conflict among groups. This conclusion follows from the definition of overt interpersonal conflict as involving direct interaction, inasmuch as conditions that increase the rates of social interaction among groups thereby increase the opportunities for and probabilities of overt interpersonal conflict. The only assumption required, which is virtually implicit in the definition, is that *overt interpersonal conflict depends on opportunities for social contacts* (PA-13). It is noteworthy that the assumption implies that interpersonal conflict is *less* likely between members of different groups than between persons in the same group, ceteris paribus, because the predominance of ingroup associations creates more opportunities for ingroup than intergroup conflict. Accordingly, interpersonal conflict would be expected to be particularly frequent in primary groups, and the frequent quarrels and fights in families and among friends make this not entirely implausible. Indeed, violent crimes against persons are most often committed by intimates (Morris and Blom-Copper 1964). However, the complex psychological factors that affect intimate relations make comparison between them and other relations questionable, which is the reason for the ceteris paribus. This problem does not exist—or at least is less acute—when the same type of social relation under different social conditions are compared.

Intersecting parameters increase the probability of interpersonal conflict between members of various groups and strata (T-17). *Multiform heterogeneity increases the probability of interpersonal conflict between members of different groups* (T-17.1). *Intersecting graduated parameters increase the probability of interpersonal conflict between members of different strata* (T-17.11). *The intersection of nominal by graduated parameters increases the probability of interpersonal conflict between members of different groups and strata* (T-17.12). All these theorems follow from T-12 and PA-13: that intersecting parameters increase the rates of associations among groups or strata or both, and thereby the probabilities of interpersonal conflict. Simple heterogeneity and status diversity in terms of a single parameter also make conflict between persons in different groups and strata more likely, since they, too, increase their social interaction (T-11, T-11.3).[5] This influence is illustrated by the empirical findings that the ethnic heterogeneity of American cities is positively related to crime rates (Angell 1974) and various kinds of overt conflicts between whites and blacks (Williams 1964, p. 119). In contrast, consolidated inequalities erect social barriers between various parts of society that reduce the likelihood of interpersonal conflict, owing to sheer lack of opportunity, but they by no means reduce the antagonism between the unequal groups with conflicting interests, nor the potential for overt collective conflict. A low incidence of interpersonal conflict in a diversified society is rarely a sign of pervasive concord; often as not it signifies suppressed discord.

5. Mayhew and Levinger (1976b) predict that city size increases conflict; the prediction here is that city heterogeneity does, particularly conflict between persons of different groups. Regression analysis can separate the influences of city size and heterogeneity to determine whether one, both, or neither of these predictions is correct.

Members of a minority experience dyadic conflict with the majority group more frequently than members of the majority do with that minority (T-17.2). The minority's higher rate of intergroup associations makes interpersonal conflict for its members more probable than for members of the majority, according to PA-13. But the theorem is implied as a deterministic, not merely probabilistic, proposition by T-1: Every dyadic conflict, like every other social association, involves one person in each group, which makes the frequency of such conflicts per person greater in the smaller group. The theorem does not apply to conflicts in which many majority members and only one or a few minority members participate, such as lynch mobs or pogroms, in most of which minority members are victimized. Except possibly as participants in such group aggression, majority members experience interpersonal conflict with the outgroup much less frequently than minority members. Thus, intergroup hostility plays an important part in the life of minorities while most members of the majority encounter little of it, quite independent of degree and direction of discrimination. American blacks and whites exhibit such a difference in intergroup experience. In South Africa, however, although blacks are much oppressed, they are less likely than whites to experience dyadic conflict with a member of the other race.

Members of an elite experience dyadic conflict with lower strata more frequently than lower strata do with members of the elite (T-17.3). The small size of the elite in terms of any graduated parameter implies this, in accordance with T-1. But the difference in the social position of an elite from that of a minority group alters the nature of interpersonal conflict and the experience it entails. It is plausible to assume that elite status is manifest in superordinate roles in social interaction (PA-6). People are typically reluctant to express antagonism against persons in superordinate positions, though they feel such antagonism. The tendency of lower strata to suppress negative reactions against the elite in social interaction makes it likely that most conflicts that occur in their interaction are initiated by the elite members, whose position does not impose the same restraints on their inclinations to contradict, criticize, or rebuke the other, only the much lesser restraint of noblesse oblige. Elite members experience more cross-class interpersonal conflict than other strata, owing to their small size, but typically as the instigators of these conflicts, owing to their superordinate status. Crimes such as holdups of affluent people are an exception, but the exception is more apparent than real. Although poor people instigate these conflicts, they do so with a resource—physical violence—in terms of which they are the superiors.

Whereas structural conditions that increase opportunities for social contacts increase the probabilities of both integrative social relations and interpersonal conflicts, this does not mean that the friendly associations and the conflicts occur between the same persons. It is more likely that these conditions lead to friendly intercourse between some persons and conflict between others. To be sure, frequent social interaction itself increases opportunities for conflict, but good interpersonal relations counteract the resulting greater probability of conflict, except perhaps in the most deep-rooted, and often ambivalent, human relations, like those in a family, as so dramatically portrayed by Eugene O'Neill in *Long Day's Journey into Night*. In any case, the theory implies that intergroup friendships and interpersonal conflicts between groups are positively correlated, because intersecting parameters increase intergroup contacts (T-12), which raises the probabilities of both friendly intergroup relations (A-9) and interpersonal conflict (PA-13). Such a correlation is implied even if all conflicts occur between strangers and none between friends, but in this case it would be entirely spurious, resulting from the influence of structural complexity (intersecting parameters) on different dyads, some who are friends and others who have conflict. Without making the explicit assumption that all interpersonal conflicts involve strangers or that all involve friends, neither of which is reasonable, one would expect some to involve either dyad, making the correlation partly spurious. The definition of strangers in this analysis is two persons who had no social relation prior to their conflict. (An alternative procedure is to divide social relations into those that are primarily friendly and those that are primarily antagonistic, which makes the friendship dyads and the conflict dyads by definition different ones. In this case, the premises imply a completely spurious positive correlation between the frequencies of these positive and negative intergroup relations in society, produced by variations in the structural complexity of societies.)

The extent of friendships and the extent of interpersonal conflicts between persons in different groups or strata are positively correlated (T-17.4). The positive correlation between the extent of friendships and the extent of interpersonal conflicts between persons in different groups or strata is considerably reduced when society's structural complexity (the degree to which parameters intersect) is controlled (T-17.5). In simple social structures the social barriers between tribes and clans minimize interpersonal conflict between their members, though not group conflict between them. Increasing structural complexity makes the integration of the diverse parts particularly dependent on positive relations between their members and simultaneously creates the conditions that foster these relations, yet these conditions also increase interpersonal conflicts between groups and strata. Complex structures make the dissimilar parts of large societies better integrated than are the similar parts of smaller societies with simpler structures. The price of this greater integration, which mitigates severe group conflict, is more frequent interpersonal conflict, not because intergroup relations involve more conflict than ingroup relations—indeed, even if they involve less—but because the same structural conditions that promote integrative relations also increase the probability of interpersonal conflict.

Structural Change

Processes of social association among groups and strata are the source of their social integration, and processes of social mobility are the source of most social change. Structural change is often preceded and accompanied by social conflict, and the nature of the conflicts in society affects the form as well as the specific content of social change. The rapid pace of change in complex social structures is the result of the influences of intersecting parameters on intergroup relations, conflict, and especially social mobility. The multiform differentiation in complex societies furthers change by attenuating ingroup bonds that restrict people's perspective, make different and new social situations threatening, and engender resistance to change. It creates overlapping groups that lead to various realignments in different conflicts and controversies about new policies (Coleman 1957), which reduces the likelihood that a single entrenched establishment with vested interests can repress forces of change. And the intersecting parameters stimulate social mobility by providing people with associates in different groups and strata.

Social mobility is the process through which social structures adjust to changing conditions by changing themselves. Whether new technological, economic, or other conditions create a need to change, the structural change nearly always depends on movements of people from some social positions to others. For example, conditions in the Industrial Revolution gave rise to more urbanized and industrialized social structures, and these changes were brought about by migration from rural to urban places and by occupational mobility from farm to industrial work. More recent advances in technology and productivity altered the occupational structure and expanded professional and technical occupations by opening channels of upward mobility into these occupations. Emergent value orientations also engender structural change by precipitating moves of people from their old groups to new ones. The Reformation changed the religious structure of societies because it prompted people to leave their religious group and move to another church. For a new ideology to change the political structure, it must induce supporters of the old parties to abandon their political positions and join the new social movement. Inplementing demands for the redistribution of wealth requires downward mobility of wealthy persons.

Not all structural change depends on social mobility, though most does, and even change that does not tends to have social mobility as its aftermath. Differential rates of fertility and of immigration from abroad alter society's structure in the absence of internal mobility. But the structural adjustments often required in consequence of these initial changes typically do involve social mobility, as exemplified by the pressures to move from farms to cities resulting from the high birth rates of farmers. Such adjustments *in* a social structure, which essentially restore it to an earlier state that exogeneous conditions have altered, have been distinguished from changes *of* the social structure itself (Parsons and Smelser 1956, pp. 247–49). The circulation of elites might illustrate changes in, though not of, a social structure; the concentration of wealth or power does not change, only the individuals who have it do. Generally, the degree of inequality or heterogeneity can only be changed by excess mobility in certain directions, not by motility—equal amounts of mobility in opposite directions—of which the circulation of elites is a special case. Does this indicate that excess mobility generates changes of the structure, and motility only changes in it? That depends on where the line between changes in and changes of a structure is drawn. Instead of relying on this dichotomy, several forms of structural changes are analytically distinguished in terms of the parameter scheme, to ascertain the significance for them of different patterns of social mobility and of structural complexity.

The following forms of structural change can be distinguished:

1. The distribution of the population among social positions may change without changes in the positions themselves, which alters the degree of inequality or of heterogeneity in terms of a single parameter, for example, income inequality or ethnic heterogeneity.
2. The number of positions delineated by a nominal parameter may change, which alters the degree of heterogeneity, for example, the division of labor.
3. The strength of the correlations of parameters may change, which alters the degree to which parameters are intersecting or consolidated, for example, the extent of multiform heterogeneity, the consolidation of status inequalities, or group differences in status.
4. The extent to which one form of differentiation is related to another may change, which is not the same as a change in the correlation of parameters; for example, the correlation of a society's inequality in education with its income inequality may decline, which must be distinguished from a decline in the correlation between an individual's education and income within a society.
5. New parameters may emerge or old ones disappear, which alters the parameter framework itself, for example, when thirteen colonies unite to establish one nation or when private property is abolished.

1. Changes in inequality in terms of a single graduated parameter can be conceptualized either as changes in the distribution of people among hierarchical positions or as changes in the distribution of a given social resource among people. The two are equivalent. Three conditions produce changes in inequality, as indicated in chapter 3: differences in net fertility among strata, differences in net immigration from abroad among them, and internal mobility. Thus, a major condition on which changes in inequality depend is excess vertical mobility in certain directions. Specifically, a rise in status of

lower or middle strata and a decline in status of highest strata diminish inequality, and status changes in opposite directions increase it. Equal amounts of mobility in both directions between two strata do not alter the degree of inequality. Heterogeneity is subject to parallel influences: Differences in net fertility and net immigration from abroad change the degree of heterogeneity in terms of a single parameter, as does excess social mobility from some groups to others, but equal amounts of mobility between two groups do not.

2. However, the degree of heterogeneity also changes when the number of positions (groups) delineated by a nominal parameter increases or decreases. (Since status is conceptualized as a continuous gradation, inequality cannot change in this way.) For example, new occupational specialties increase the division of labor; immigrants from a country not previously represented in a society increase ethnic heterogeneity; the assimilation of an ethnic group into the mainstream of society reduces ethnic heterogeneity; mergers of firms reduce the heterogeneity of economic markets. Most of these changes also depend on unidirectional mobility, including under it the intergenerational mobility involved in ethnic assimilation as well as moves of people from established to new groups, be they new religious sects, political parties, or occupational specialties. The only changes in number of groups that do not involve social mobility are administrative splits and mergers of organizations or their subunits—firms, government departments, unions, counties, election districts.

3. For parameters to become more intersecting or more consolidated requires that some people's social position in terms of one parameter changes, which necessarily alters this parameter's correlation with many others, specifically, with all other parameters that do not involve exactly parallel changes in social positions. Thus, high rates of migration from hometowns enhance multiform heterogeneity, since they attenuate the correlations not only between place of origin and place of residence but also between all attributes associated with birthplace and all those associated with current residence. When manual workers who were Republicans and managers who were Democrats switch to the other major party, whether in equal or in unequal numbers, it strengthens the correlation of occupation with party affiliation and the consolidation of these parameters. When some people's real income rises while that of others drops, income inequality may remain the same, but even when it does the relationships of socioeconomic origin and its correlates with income and its correlates become weaker, making these parameters more intersecting. Not only excess mobility in certain directions but also equal amounts of mobility in opposite directions change the extent to which parameters are correlated. Although the latter, motility, does not alter the degree of inequality or heterogeneity in terms of the given parameter, it does change the extent to which this parameter is intersecting or consolidated with others. Both motility and excess mobility

either increase or decrease the correlations of parameters. Given the importance of multiform heterogeneity and consolidated inequalities, motility must not be dismissed as entailing only changes in and not of the social structure.

4. The relationship between the extent of differentiation in one respect and that in another when societies are compared must be clearly distinguished from the relationship between differences in social positions in these two respects within societies. The latter refers to a correlation between two variables describing individuals—the correlation of parameters just discussed—for instance, the correlation between education and occupation in one society or all of them. The former refers to a correlation between two variables describing societies—specifically, the degree of differentiation in each society in two respects—for example, the correlation between educational inequality and occupational heterogeneity with societies as units of analysis. In other words, instead of correlating two social attributes of individuals, the two appropriate measures of dispersion are correlated for societies. The correlations of education and occupation within societies do not tell us how the degrees of variation in each are correlated for societies. The effects of conditions in societies on the relationships among various forms of differentiation depend on the specific forms under consideration. The same condition may affect the relationship of the division of labor with educational inequality differently from its relationship with the concentration of power. This topic is reserved for discussion in chapter 8. It suffices to state here that excess social mobility from some positions to others, since it affects population distributions, also changes the relationships between forms of differentiation.

5. The emergence of new parameters and the extinction of old ones are probably the rarest forms of structural change. The creation of new nations illustrates both forms: When several states establish a common federation, their former boundaries become parameters of the new society; when a province separates from the rest of a nation to establish a new one, the former internal parameter becomes an external boundary. The abolishment of slavery, of noble titles, and of private property are other illustrations of the obliteration of a structural parameter. A new religion—early Christianity, the Reformation—generates a new parameter. The last example entails social mobility, to join the new religious body; the others do not. A final illustration of the disappearance of a parameter is the assimilation of various nationality groups into a common nationality, as has happened for the older immigrant groups to the United States. This involves extensive intergenerational mobility and intergroup associations, partly through intermarriage, which reinforce each other.

All five general forms assumed by structural change often involve social mobility, though not every specific change depends on mobility. Whereas social mobility is not a necessary condition for changes in the social structure to occur, therefore, it is a sufficient condition for structural change. Social mobility invariably alters the extent to which parameters intersect or are consolidated, which is probably the most important structural change, because differences in intersection-consolidation have far-reaching implications for social life, as has already been indicated and will become increasingly apparent in subsequent chapters. Moreover, this important change in the degree of intersection or consolidation of parameters occurs not only, as some other changes do, as the result of excess mobility in one direction, but also as the result of equal number of moves in opposite directions, which do not alter the frequency distributions of people among positions. For motility, as such equal moves in opposite directions have been called, also changes the strength of the correlations of parameters and enhances, partly for this reason and partly for others, the flexibility of the social structure and its readiness to change. Herein lies the great significance of social motility for structural change.

The two patterns of social mobility—excess moves in certain directions and motility—tend to reinforce each other. Developments in the technological or political context of the social structure may engender social mobility in certain directions that adjust the social structure to the new conditions, such as improved methods of farming that reduce the need for farm workers or a minimum wage law that raises the income of the least skilled. This exogenously generated mobility stimulates further mobility—motility that is not required by and does not adjust to changing conditions—by weakening ingroup bonds and strengthening intergroup relations (T-4, T-4.7). Inmobility at high rates permeates select social circles with erstwhile strangers and undermines their exclusiveness. Outmobility at high rates disrupts the closed network of social relations that sets a group apart and keeps it together. As such loosening of ingroup ties raises the frequency of social mobility, the ingroup pressures discouraging it decline, in accordance with the assumption that growing acceptance of initially rare social practices reduces group pressures discouraging them (A-10). If divorce—a form of mobility between positions—becomes more frequent, it evokes less widespread social censure. Even downward mobility encounters less social disapproval when it is frequent, as exemplified by unemployment in a depression, which makes the experience less threatening, though of course not desirable. When increasing numbers of persons leave a community, ingroup pressures to remain there subside. Such weakening of ingroup bonds and the group pressures that maintain them makes the social structure more flexible and less resistant to further social mobility in order to effect structural changes when new conditions demand such adjustments.

High rates of social mobility promote structural change (T-18). *High rates of social motility promote structural change* (T-18.1). To summarize the reasoning: New developments stimulate social mobility in certain directions;

which weakens ingroup ties and increases intergroup relations (T-4.1); which stimulates additional mobility in both directions (T-4.7), that is, motility; which further weakens ingroup ties and ingroup pressures (A-10); which reduces resistance to mobility when it is required to effect structural change in response to new conditions; which speeds structural change. Social mobility, including motility, inevitably produces some structural change, owing to its altering the correlations of parameters, and it has repercussions, through the feedback processes outlined, that tend further to enhance social change, beyond that entailed by the initial mobility itself.

These reinforcing social processes of mobility and intergroup association that foster social change are rooted in the intersecting parameters of complex social structures. To be sure, the ultimate determinants of social change are technological, economic, political, and other developments, not the formal properties of social structures. These developments govern which forms of inequality decline and which increase, what forms of heterogeneity proliferate and what forms diminish, and whether as a result multiform differentiation is augmented or social differences along various lines become more consolidated. However, the characteristics of the social structure not only influence these developments but also determine how readily the structure itself responds to the pressures they generate, and hence the speed of structural change. If intersecting parameters promote mobility (T-16), and if mobility entails structural change (T-18), it follows that *intersecting parameters promote structural change* (T-18.2).

Consolidated parameters inhibit structural change (T-18.21). The consolidation of lines of differentiation makes social structures more rigid and resistant to change. When groups and strata intersect little, the infrequent associations and the low rates of mobility among them reinforce and sustain each other, and social disapproval of intruders who invade a group and of deserters who abandon their group strengthens social barriers. The minimal social connections among the various segments of society deprive it of readily available channels of social mobility to make the required structural adjustments when conditions change. Besides, consolidated status differences increase the chances that a united ruling elite with vested interests in the status quo can successfully block social change. The rigidity of consolidated structures is an impediment to gradual change, making it likely that the pressures of new developments to change are resisted until they build up and eventually erupt in a violent revolution.[6]

Although complex social structures change more readily than simple ones, owing to their intersecting parameters, one of the forms of change that is more likely to occur in them limits their structural complexity by making

---

6. The more consolidated status structure in France than in England in the early centuries of the Modern Age may well have bearing on the difference between the more gradual historical changes in England and the French Revolution (Moore 1966).

parameters less intersecting and more consolidated. The direction of most social change cannot be derived from an analysis of the formal attributes of social structures and social processes, because it depends on conditions exogeneous to the structure of positions itself, such as developments in the technology, the economy, and the polity. There is one exception, however: the influence of social mobility on the correlation of parameters. Whether mobility is likely to make parameters more intersecting or more consolidated is implied by the assumptions that have been made, as mentioned in passing earlier.

If ingroup associations are prevalent (A-1), and if associates in other groups increase rates of mobility to them (PA-4), it follows that people are most likely to move to those groups in terms of one parameter where there are many persons who belong to the same groups as they in terms of other parameters. For example, Catholics are most likely to move to neighborhoods where many Catholics live, and Protestants to those with many Protestants. Such tendencies increase the consolidation of parameters—in the illustration, the correlation of place of residence and religion. If status differences of various kinds entail comparable differences in social resources (A-12), moreover, it follows that the people who are most likely to rise in status in terms of one graduated parameter are those who have ample resources in terms of another, while those with scant resources of one kind are most likely to be downwardly mobile with respect to another status dimension. For example, the low-income young persons whose income is most likely to rise are the best-educated ones, and the rich people who are most likely to lose their wealth are those who have little power. These tendencies increase the consolidation of graduated parameters—in one illustration, the correlations of education and income, in the other, that of wealth and power. According to the theory, therefore, the most probable patterns of social mobility increase the consolidation of structural parameters and reduce multiform differentiation. *Ceteris paribus, social mobility increases the consolidation of parameters* (T-18.3).

This is an unexpected result of the theoretical analysis. Patterns of social mobility tend to reduce the very conditions that promote them—intersecting parameters. Complex social structures generate endogeneous processes of structural change, but one of these processes makes them less complex, which diminishes structural change. The most plausible interpretation of these self-generated processes is that they set limits to other social processes in complex structures that would otherwise reinforce each other without bounds, which, though not impossible, is very improbable. Thus, intersecting parameters promote both intergroup associations (T-12) and mobility (T-16), and increases in either increase the other (T-4, T-4.7), so that the mutually reinforcing influences would eventually obliterate the differences among groups or strata. This does happen, but very rarely. One reason that it occurs so infrequently is that processes of mobility tend to increase the correlation of parameters, which limits further mobility and thereby also further increases in intergroup associations. Similarly, the growth of structural complexity, resulting from a variety of exogeneous and endogeneous social forces, is kept within bounds by the counteracting social processes generated in complex structures that limit their complexity. But when such counteracting forces become predominant, they produce great structural consolidation and rigidity. The interplay of social processes that exert diverse and opposite influences on complex structures generates a dialectical pattern of social change.

Compendium

T-15   The more parameters intersect, the greater is the structural complexity. (From definitions only.)

T-15.1   The more nominal parameters intersect, the greater is the heterogeneity. (From definitions only.)

T-15.2   The more graduated parameters intersect, the greater is the status diversity. (From definitions only.)

A-12   Status differences are differences in comparable social resources of generally acknowledged validity in social exchange.

T-15.3   The less graduated parameters intersect, the greater is the inequality. (From A-12.)

T-12.2   Intersecting graduated parameters integrate different strata by raising the rates of social association among them. (From A-1.2, A-11; or from A-1.2, A-12.)

T-12.21 Consolidated graduated parameters attenuate the rates of social association among different strata and thus weaken their integration. (From A-3.2, A-11; or from A-1.2, A-12.)

T-12.3   The intersection of nominal by graduated parameters integrates groups and strata by raising the rates of social association among them. (From A-1, A-11.)

T-12.31 The more consolidated group differences with correlated status differences are, the less frequent are integrative social associations among groups and strata. (From A-1, A-11.)

T-14.3   The smaller the size of an elite in terms of one graduated parameter, the greater are the probabilities that its members associate with persons whose positions differ from theirs in terms of other intersecting parameters. (From A-1.2, A-9.)

T-14.4   The probability that the members of the elite have cosmopolitan role sets declines with increasing positive correlations of the status-defining parameter with other parameters. (From T-5, T-14.3; based on A-1.2, A-9.)

T-14.31 The probability of extensive social relations among elites defined by various parameters is greater than that among other strata defined by these parameters. (From T-14.3; based on A-1.2, A-9; or from A-1.2, A-12.)

T-16   Intersecting parameters increase social mobility. (From PA-4, T-12; based on A-1, A-12.)

T-16.1   Consolidated nominal parameters restrict intergroup mobility. (From PA-4, T-12; based on A-1, A-11.)

T-16.2   Consolidated graduated parameters restrict vertical mobility. (From PA-4, T-12; based on A-1, A-11.)

PA-13   Overt interpersonal conflict depends on opportunities for social contacts.

T-17   Intersecting parameters increase the probability of interpersonal conflict between members of various groups or strata. (From PA-13, T-12; based on A-1, A-11.)

T-17.1   Multiform heterogeneity increases the probability of interpersonal conflict between members of different groups. (From PA-13, T-12; based on A-1, A-11.)

T-17.11 Intersecting graduated parameters increase the probability of interpersonal conflict between members of different strata. (From PA-13, T-12; based on A-1, A-11.)

T-17.12 The intersection of nominal by graduated parameters increases the probability of interpersonal conflict between members of different groups and strata. (From PA-13, T-12; based on A-1, A-11.)

T-17.2   Members of a minority experience dyadic conflict with the majority group more frequently than members of the majority do with that minority. (From T-1.)

T-17.3   Members of an elite experience dyadic conflict with lower strata more frequently than lower strata do with members of the elite. (From T-1.)

T-17.4   The extent of friendships and the extent of interpersonal conflicts between persons in different groups and strata are positively correlated. (From A-9, PA-13, T-12; based on A-1, A-11.)

T-17.5   The positive correlation between extent of friendships and extent of interpersonal conflicts between persons in different groups or strata is considerably reduced when society's structural complexity (parameter intersection) is controlled. (From A-9, PA-13, T-12; based on A-1, A-11.)

T-18   High rates of social mobility promote structural change. (From definitions only.)

T-18.1   High rates of motility promote structural change. (From A-10.)

T-18.2   Intersecting parameters promote structural change. (From T-16, T-18; based on A-1, PA-4, A-11.)

T-18.21 Consolidated parameters inhibit structural change. (From T-16, T-18; based on A-1, PA-4, A-11.)

T-18.3   Ceteris paribus, social mobility increases the consolidation of parameters. (From A-1, PA-4, A-12.)

CHAPTER SIX

Substructures and Exchange

THE FIRST HALF OF THIS BOOK HAS PRESENTED THE BASIC THEORY OF structural differentiation and its implications for processes of integration. In this and the following three chapters the analysis is extended to deal with the significance of the substructures that compose a social structure. Having so far examined primarily social associations among different groups and strata, attention in this chapter is directed to the social relations within the small groups where most everyday life takes place and to the social processes in these substructures, after first distinguishing two kinds of connections between small groups and society. Most forms of differentiation in society, if not all, occur partly within substructures and partly among them; for example, society's division of labor is the result of the division of labor within and among communities, of that within and among work organizations; the implications of this difference will be traced in chapters 7 and 8. In these chapters and in chapter 9, concern is also with the distinctive significance of several specific forms of differentiation, such as the distribution of people among territories, the division of labor, and the concentration of power.

The components of social structures are themselves social structures. The macrostructure of society comprises social structures of various sorts, which in turn are composed of social structures, and this recurs until one arrives at the microstructures of small groups which consist of roles of individuals. There are two ways in which nominal parameters link the roles of individuals and the microstructures constituted by their role relations to the macrostructure of society: through a multiplicity of cross-cutting group affiliations, and through fusion with successively more encompassing group affiliations. After comparing these two principles of subdivision, attention turns to the social

127

relations and processes within substructures, notably the conditions that engender group cohesion and ingroup pressures, processes of social exchange, and the structural effects these processes generate in groups.

Concentric and Intersecting Circles

Individuals are related to their society by their group affiliations, which find expression in their social associations. Recurrent social interaction among group members establishes the networks of social relations that make groups distinctive, though interdependent, components of the larger social structure. At the same time, these regular face-to-face associations socialize individuals, furnish them social support, and make them integrated members of their groups and, through them, of their society. But how do ingroup associations, which create social barriers among groups, help integrate the members of different groups in society? One answer to this question has already been given: Intersecting parameters make ingroup associations in one respect intergroup associations in another, which establishes the social connections among groups that integrate them in society. This is not the only social mechanism, however, for overcoming group barriers and integrating diverse groups in society. Another is the incorporation of various groups into successively more encompassing ones and ultimately into the entire society.

From the perspective of the individual, his or her group affiliations assume either the form of intersecting circles—being young, black, female, and Catholic—or that of concentric circles—living in Gary, being a Hoosier, being an American; or, being a mason, a construction worker, a craftsman, a manual worker, a member of the labor force. In both cases the individual belongs to a number of different groups, and the groups are overlapping. But they are overlapping in different ways: in one instance as the result of cross-cutting boundaries; in the other as the result of successively wider boundaries. Simmel (1955, pp. 141–42, 151) emphasizes this difference and the significance of intersecting group affiliations for individuality:

> As the individual leaves his established position within *one* group, he comes to stand at a point at which many "intersect." The individual as a moral personality comes to be circumscribed in an entirely new way, but he also faces new problems. The security and lack of ambiguity in his former position gives way to uncertainty in the conditions of his life. . . . But it is also true that multiple group-affiliations can strengthen the individual and reinforce the integration of his personality. . . . The mere fact of multiple group affiliations enabled the person to achieve for himself an individualized situation in which the groups had to be oriented towards the individual. In the earlier situation the individual was wholly absorbed by, and remained oriented toward, the group.

Both concentric and intersecting group affiliations exist in all societies, but concentric circles are most significant in simple nonindustrial societies, and intersecting circles in complex modern ones. Evans-Pritchard's (1940) analysis of the social structure of the Nuer illustrates the importance of concentric circles for the differentiation of groups and their integration in Nuer society. The two major forms of differentiation are on the basis of kinship and of territorial-political affiliation. The broadest kinship group is a clan, whose members trace their descent to a common ancestor in the distant past. There are about twenty clans in Nuer society. Every clan branches into successively smaller lineages, whose members are united by increasingly recent common ancestors. The political structure reveals similar concentric circles. The smallest political units are villages, which have fifty to a few hundred inhabitants, and which compose successively larger tribal sections and, after four steps, the twelve major tribes of the Nuer.

The frequent feuds between lineages and wars between tribal sections or tribes disclose dramatically how successive subdivisions alternately divide and unite groups. The same two sections that have a long-standing feud, with recurrent wars, unite to fight in a war of their tribe against another tribe or of the Nuer against other people, which is evidently in principle no different from conflicts within and among modern nations. Although a person can belong to only one group on any given level, successive subdivision nevertheless implies that he or she belongs to that group at one time and does not belong to it at another, because such subdivision generates both fusion and fission of groups, as Evans-Pritchard (1940, pp. 136–37) calls it:

> A man is a member of a political group of any kind in virtue of his non-membership of other groups of the same kind. He sees them as groups and their members see him as a member of a group, and his relations with them are controlled by the structural distance between the groups concerned. But a man does not see himself as a member of that same group insofar as he is a member of a segment of it which stands outside of and is opposed to other segments of it. Hence a man can be a member of a group and yet not be a member of it. This is a fundamental principle of Nuer political structure. Thus a man is a member of his tribe in its relation to other tribes, but he is not a member of his tribe in the relation of his segment of it to other segments of the same kind. Likewise a man is a member of his tribal segment in its relation to other segments, but he is not a member of it in the relation of his village to other villages of the same segment. A characteristic of any political group is hence its invariable tendency towards fission and the opposition of its segments, and another characteristic is its tendency toward fusion with other groups of its own order in opposition to political segments larger than itself.

Concentric as well as intersecting lines of differentiation generate social connections that unite the very groups these lines divide. Concentric group barriers do so because the immediate affiliations of persons with smaller groups, which rest on frequent face-to-face associations, mediate affiliations with larger groups of which the smaller are constituent elements. Intersecting group barriers do so because ingroup associations in one respect entail intergroup associations in others. Successive subdivision of political-territorial units is important in industrial societies, as it is among the Nuer, but the kinship system does not constitute a form of successive subdivision that encompasses entire industrial societies, unlike the situation among the Nuer. Other nominal parameters with successive subdivisions in modern society are occupational position, religious denomination, and position in work organization.

A nominal parameter with successive subdivisions has one basic attribute of graduated parameters but not another. Successive subdivisions rank-order social distances among groups, though not the groups themselves. As previously mentioned, from the perspective of any particular group, others are more or less distant, without there being any socially agreed upon rank-order among the groups, that is, independent of any correlation of group differences with status differences. A Nuer village is closer to others in its tribal section than to those in other sections of its tribe, and its political as well as physical distance to villages in other tribes is still greater. Presbyterians are closer in their religion to Methodists than to Catholics. The administrative distance between two sections of one department in a firm is less than that between them and sections of other departments. For successive subdivisions to be socially relevant, they must influence role relations and social associations, as those in Nuer society apparently do. Some purely administrative subdivisions, such as those of American cities into census tracts, probably have no significance for people's social life, and are therefore not considered to constitute social subdivisions into groups. The definition of groups requires that differences in group membership are reflected in differences in role relations, which must apply to the subgroups distinguished by successive subdivision of a nominal parameter.

The prevalence of ingroup relations in subgroups probably exceeds that in the larger groups encompassing them delineated by the same nominal parameter (T-19). Prevalence is the ratio of actual divided by statistically expected frequencies of associations. The theorem is implied by A-1.1: If the prevalence of associations within subgroups exceeds that among them, it follows that the ratio of actual to expected associations within subgroups exceeds the ratio for the associations both within and among subgroups, and the latter indicates the prevalence of ingroup associations in the encompassing group. Although T-19 would be a deterministic proposition when only one encompassing group and its subgroups are compared, it is probabilistic when it involves all encompassing groups and their subgroups.[1] It applies to all levels of subgroups. Thus, professionals are expected to associate dispro-

---

1. The theorem is probabilistic if expected frequencies are defined on the basis of the entire population distribution. If separate statistical expectations are computed for every encompassing group, T-19 is deterministic for all comparisons, but also rather trivial.

portionately with other professionals, but not so much as physicians associate with other physicians, and the tendency of surgeons to associate with one another is expected to be still more pronounced. (Of course, other parameters modify this pattern; surgeons probably associate less with other surgeons in different cities than with internists in their hospital.) Evans-Pritchard (1940, pp. 137–38) observed such differences in ingroup relations and attachments among the Nuer:

> Tribal sentiment is weaker than the sentiment of one of its segments and the sentiment of a segment is weaker than the sentiment of a village which is part of it. . . . [And] it is also evident that the smaller the group the more contacts between its members, the more varied are these contacts, and the more they are co-operative.

Although the strength of social ties becomes attenuated with social distance, concentric circles connect people's narrower group affiliations directly to their affiliations with wider groups and with the entire society. Belonging to a village is what makes a Nuer a Nuer; being a Bostonian entails being an American; being baptized in a Methodist congregation makes a person a Protestant. Intersecting circles do not connect individuals directly to their society but to diverse other groups, which contributes to their being a more integrated member of a diverse society. Both concentric and intersecting lines of differentiation engender alternating fission and fusion of groups, in Evans-Pritchard's felicitous phrase, but the nature of the realignments is quite different, despite the fact that in both cases opponents in one conflict become allies in another. With regard to concentric circles, sometime opponents become allies against a third and larger opponent, and the core groups remain intact and united. When feuding villages fight together in a war against another tribe, the members of each village remain united and are together on the same side in both conflicts. With regard to intersecting circles, the entire population is reshuffled when different conflicts involve cross-cutting alignments, and there are no core groups that persist necessarily throughout all controversies. The adversaries in one conflict are lower and higher socioeconomic strata, in another women and men, in another hawks and doves, in another big cities and smaller towns, in another different regions, and no distinct social group remains together in all of them.

Concentric circles make the strong integration of individuals in particular ingroups the basic source of their integration in society and of enduring social support in conflicts, whereas intersecting circles make intergroup relations a major source of the integration of individuals in society at large and of social support in various conflicts. As intersecting lines of group affiliation increase with the growth of structural complexity, concentric lines lose their former significance, and one of them—extended kinship—degenerates. Kinship affiliation no longer integrates individuals in major segments of society and in society itself but instead fragments society into small clusters of close relatives surrounding nuclear families, which continue to be the main socializing agents of society and the mainstays of socioemotional sustenance of adults as well as children.

The extended kinship system is a fundamental element of the social structure of small societies, but it is not a structural parameter in large societies. This is unlikely to be fortuitous. The decline of extended kinship and the isolation of the nuclear family tend to be attributed to industrialization, particularly to the emphasis on achievement and universalism accompanying industrial developments, which contrasts with the emphasis on ascription and particularism intrinsic to kinship (Parsons 1951, pp. 178, 510; Theodorson 1953, pp. 481–82). The sheer size of society may also play a role in this decline, however.

Murdock's (1949, pp. 80–88) cross-cultural investigation indicates that rudimentary forms of differentiation occur when very small societies expand as the result of permanent settlement. Most nomadic bands are small and isolated, whereas most settled villages have established political ties and institutions that unite several of them, which implies that permanent settlement leads to federation that simultaneously expands society and gives it internal lines of differentiation. Another form of differentiation typically arises in these larger settled tribes: Class differences exist in most of them but in none of the nomadic bands, probably because permanent settlement creates opportunities for accumulating property (Lenski 1966, pp. 96–136). Numerous other anthropological studies have also observed that increasing differentiation of various kinds tends to accompany the population growth of societies (Oberg 1955; Kaut 1956) and that of kinship groups within them (Nadel 1946; Murphy 1956; Sahlins 1957).

The conjecture may be suggested that the growth of a structure of interrelated social positions depends not only on an increase in the number of different positions but also on a change in the nature of the dimensions that differentiate them. The grounds for this conjecture are that the number of social distinctions people are required to make in forming role relations must be limited; that differentiation reduces this number; and that some types of differentiation reduce it more than others, thereby contributing to further growth. Oberg (1955) offers an interpretation along these lines for his observation that the number of corporate descent groups into which society is differentiated increases with its increasing size: A large group makes it necessary for people to identify others and relate to them on the basis of general social categories, as there are too many persons to distinguish and remember all particular individuals. Simmel (1908, pp. 35–46) notes that a large society depends on such stereotyping, which accords with the results of psychological experiments that the number of individual objects that can be accurately discriminated is quite limited (see Hare 1976, p. 217). The general principle is explicated by Simon (1965, pp. 65–66) in an interesting paper on the basis of an analogy:

> There once were two watchmakers, named Hora and Tempus, who manufactured very fine watches. Both of them were highly regarded, and the phones

in their workshops rang frequently—new customers were constantly calling them. However, Hora prospered, while Tempus became poorer and poorer and finally lost his shop. What was the reason?

The watches the men made consisted of about 1,000 parts each. Tempus had so constructed his that if he had one part assembled and had to put it down—to answer the phone say—it immediately fell to pieces and had to be reassembled from the elements. The better the customers liked his watches, the more they phoned him, the more difficult it became for him to find enough uninterrupted time to finish a watch.

The watches that Hora made were no less complex than those of Tempus. But he had designed them so that he could put together subassemblies of about ten elements each. Ten of these subassemblies, again, could be put together in a larger subassembly; and a system of ten of the latter subassemblies constitutes the whole watch. Hence, when Hora had to put down a partly assembled watch in order to answer the phone, he lost only a small part of his work, and he assembled his watches in only a fraction of the manhours it took Tempus. . . .

Now if p is about .01—that is, there is one chance in a hundred that either watchmaker will be interrupted while adding any one part to an assembly— than a straightforward calculation shows that it will take Tempus, on the average, about four thousand times as long to assemble a watch as Hora

The conclusion Simon draws from his parable is that the evolution of a complex structure of interrelated elements takes much less time and is much more probable if the structure is what he calls hierarchical, that is, consists of interrelated substructures that in turn consist of substructures and only ultimately of substructures of simple elements. (Simon [1965, p. 65] explicitly notes that he uses the term *hierarchy* not in the conventional sense but extends it "to include systems in which there is no relation of subordination among subsystems.") He goes on to indicate that complex systems that do not have such a structure would be incomprehensible to us, given limited mental capacities that make it impossible to understand the interdependence of millions of unstructured elements. Should complex systems of that kind exist, therefore, they would escape our notice, so that the complex systems we know comprise series of substructures. Although Simon does not explicitly distinguish intersecting from successive subdivisions in this paper, his arguments for successive subdivisions apply *a fortiori* to intersecting ones, because intersection reduces the number of criteria required for classifying many elements and analyzing their interrelations even more than does successive subdivision.

Successive subdivisions enable people to establish appropriate role relations with a large number of others on the basis of relatively few criteria for making social distinctions. Individuals make fine distinctions, based on personality differences and not merely social attributes, among members of their intimate social circles, and less and less fine ones, largely based on social positions, in relation to others increasingly removed from them in terms of concentric circles. The Nuer make distinctions among individuals in their own village and among different villagers within their narrowest tribal section, but to a man outside their own tribe they probably relate simply on the basis of two criteria—that he does not belong to their tribe and that he is a Nuer. There are too many villages in all tribes to make distinctions among all of them, let alone among all individuals.

Intersecting parameters also enable people to establish relations with many others on the basis of few criteria, and they also entail treating others stereotypically on the basis of their social positions, except in the case of intimates. However, intersecting criteria of social discrimination (not used pejoratively) increase disciminating power. Even on first acquaintance people can relate to each other on the basis of a variety of social attributes— their sex, age, socioeconomic status, ethnic affiliation, and after a short conversation usually also their occupation, political affiliation, religion, and other attributes. Such narrow stereotypes based on numerous social attributes are hardly stereotypes any longer. Intersecting subdivisions increase the discriminating power of a given number of criteria much more than successive ones, because successive subdivision requires different criteria for each level and for each substructure. For example, if a country has two provinces, each with two counties, each with two towns, this successive subdivision requires seven dichotomous criteria (one for provinces, two for the counties in each, and four for the towns in each country) to yield the distinction among eight towns. But seven dichotomous intersecting criteria yield 128 (2^7) distinct subcategories.

The same number of criteria for making social distinctions permit people to establish a much greater variety of role relations if the criteria pertain to intersecting than if they pertain to successive subdivisions. Hence, intersecting parameters lead to more discriminating social interaction and less stereotypical treatment of persons one does not know well. These considerations also suggest, though this is sheer speculation, that the large size of a society requires that its social structure be mostly delineated by intersecting parameters, because of their greater power of discrimination, and that the significance of successive subdivision wanes with the increasing size of societies. If this is a valid conjecture, it implies that the erosion of extended kinship is the result, at least in part, of the sheer size of contemporary societies, not solely, and perhaps not primarily, of industrial and economic developments. It also implies that consolidated parameters have particularly deleterious consequences for social life and social integration in large contemporary societies.

Ingroup Relations

Small groups tend to have more extensive intergroup relations than large ones, both in terms of the nominal parameter that defines their size (T-1.5) and in terms of other intersecting parameters (T-14). The apparent inference is that small groups have less extensive ingroup relations than large ones, for the extent to which people can associate with others is not unlimited. To be sure, some persons spend much more of their time socializing and have many more associates than other persons, but there is no reason to assume that this is especially true for members of small groups. The high rates of intergroup associations of members of small groups would be expected to depress their rates of ingroup associations, which further implies that ingroup bonds and social cohesion, inasmuch as they rest on extensive social associations (Homans 1950), are weaker in small than in large groups.

This conclusion conflicts with much empirical evidence, however. Research indicates that ingroup bonds tend to be stronger the smaller groups are. Closeness and frequency of social associations are inversely related to group size (Fischer 1953), as are strength of affective ties and satisfaction (Coyle 1930; Trist and Bamforth 1951; Kinney 1953). Anthropologists indicate that lineage cohesiveness and size are inversely related (Lewis 1958, p. 125). Findings concerning nuclear families are similar. Members of small families seem to associate more with one another than those of large ones (Cancian 1964), and their social relations of all types are closer—those among siblings, those between them and parents (Hawkes, Burchinal, and Gardner 1958; Elder 1962), and those between spouses (Christensen and Philbrick 1952; Halpern 1956).

How can this contradiction be explained? One might question the assumption that high frequency of social interaction implies strong affective ties and strong group cohesion. The complex psychological forces that govern the intimate social bonds in families may not be accurately reflected in the frequency of social associations among members. The social cohesion of other primary groups may also depend on conditions other than sheer association frequency. Besides, the slight variations in size among primary groups, which are by definition small, may not be sufficient to capture the probabilistic predictions about variations in size made by T-1.5 and T-14. It is only probable that small groups have more extensive intergroup associations than large ones; and it is only probable that extensive intergroup relations restrict ingroup relations; and the product of these two probabilities may yield such a small probability that most empirical studies do not have large enough samples to observe the predicted differences. However, none of these ad hoc interpretations are satisfactory, and there is a simpler way to reconcile the contradiction.

The same frequency of ingroup associations per person creates a much denser network of ingroup associations in small than in large groups. If the average number of mutual ingroup friends is four in a group of five and also four in a group of ten, every possible mutual friendship pair in the small but less than one half of those in the large group are actually realized. To supply another illustration in which the rate of ingroup associations of the smaller group is lower than that of the larger, in accordance with the assumption that the high rate of intergroup associations of a small group reduce its rate of ingroup associations: The criterion of (nonexclusive) associate is mutual friend or spending more than a certain minimum of time per week together. The mean number of ingroup associates per person is five in the smaller group and ten in the larger. The small group has ten members, the large thirty. Therefore, each member of the small group has a close relation with more than one-half (five of nine) of the other members of his group, whereas each member of the large group has a close relation with only a little more than one-third (ten of twenty-nine) of the other members of his. Despite the lower rate (mean number) of ingroup associations in the smaller group, the density of ingroup associations is higher than in the larger group. The density of ingroup relations is indicated by the actual divided by the maximum number of possible relations, which is .55 in the small and .34 in the large group.

The density—of positive and nonexclusive—ingroup relations is considered to reflect the strength of ingroup bonds or group cohesion. The density of ingroup associates per group member is an inverse function of group size, and the number of intergroup associates per group member is also an inverse function of a group's relative size, which explains why small groups tend to have denser ingroup relations that make them more cohesive and simultaneously higher rates of intergroup relations than large groups. The density of ingroup associations is not the same as their rate, and neither is it the same as the preponderance of ingroup associations. The rate is the number of ingroup associations (counting each ingroup link twice) divided by number of egos, which is group size; the density is that rate divided by number of alters, that is, the number of associations (counting links twice) divided by the product of number of egos (size) and number of alters (size minus one); the preponderance of ingroup associations is their rate divided by the proportionate, not absolute, size of the group (the group's size divided by that of the total population).[2] In other words, the density of ingroup associations depends only on their rate and the group's own size, whereas the preponderance of ingroup associations depends on their rate and the size distribution of the entire population among groups. Both the preponderance and the density of ingroup associations in small groups are expected to exceed those in large ones, since the operational definition of the one is a linear transformation of that of the other for the same population. But the rate of ingroup

2. The formulae are: ingroup rate, a/n; ingroup density, $a/(n[n-1])$; ingroup preponderance, $(aN)/(n[n-1])$: where a is the total number of ingroup associations (counting every link twice, once for each participant), n the number of persons in the group, and N the total number of persons in the population. Thus, the preponderance of ingroup associations of a given group is their density times the number of persons in the total population. The measures of ingroup density and ingroup preponderance for the total population are obtained by summing the respective values in the formulae over all groups.

associations is not expected to be higher in small than in large groups unless special conditions engender greater ingroup pressures in small ones.

The probability is that small groups have denser networks of nonexclusive ingroup relations than large groups (T-19.1). The theorem follows from the definition. It is also implied by T-19: Many small groups are subgroups of others, while many large groups encompass others, and subgroups have more prevalent, and hence also denser, ingroup associations than encompassing groups. The theorem applies to number of nonexclusive associates of any kind and to amount of time spent with them in associations of any type, but it does not apply to exclusive associates. The reason is that the density of exclusive ingroup associations, like ingroup marriages, is identical with its rate, whereas the density of nonexclusive ingroup associations, like friendships, is the rate divided by the number of alters in the group. When all group members have an ingroup spouse, the rate of ingroup spouses per person is 1.00, which is the theoretical maximum. But the theoretical maximum for ingroup friendships is when every group member is a friend of every other one, which is a rate of ingroup friends per person far greater than 1.00, specifically, the number of group members minus one.[3] Actual friendships are much less likely to approach this maximum in large than in small groups, which increases the probability that ingroup associations are denser (actual rates are a larger fraction of the maximum) in small than in large groups. The difference between the operational criteria of density for exclusive and nonexclusive associations is not merely a technical difference of measurement but has substantive significance.

Since a person can have only one spouse at a time (in monogamous societies), only a few really close friends, but quite a number of more casual friends and still a greater number of acquaintances, the restrictions one kind of social associations imposes on another depend on the closeness of the relations under consideration. A person who is married to one person cannot be married to another, whereas a person with many acquaintances of one kind can also have many of another kind. A group's rates of ingroup and intergroup marriages do not impose the absolute limits on each other that marriage imposes on an individual, because variations in the proportion of unmarried persons make the rates of inmarried and intermarried not completely dependent on each other; but either rate surely imposes strong limits on the other. The general principle applies to group rates as well as to individuals: The closer a social relation is, the greater restraints do associations of one kind exert on associations of another kind. The criterion of closeness is degree of exclusiveness, ranging from marriage and mutual best friends to mere greeting acquaintances.

3. The formula for ingroup density of exclusive associations, like homogamy, is a/n, which is identical with the ingroup rate, that is, the fraction of group members whose spouse (or other exclusive associate) is a member of the ingroup, which cannot be greater than 1.00 or 100 percent.

The closer the social bond under consideration, the greater the probability is that the rate of ingroup and the rate of intergroup associations are inversely related (T-19.2). Extensive casual associations with other groups do not infringe much on ingroup relations,[4] but extensive intermarriage does, and conversely the prevalence of homogamy limits rates of intermarriage. The proposition implies that there is some conflict between strong ingroup bonds in subgroups and the social integration of the larger group encompassing them, which depends on strong intergroup relations among subgroups. The more people confine their intimate relations to their own subgroups, the less available are these strong bonds to knit the various subgroups into an integrated encompassing group. By the same token, when intimate relations among subgroups become as prevalent as those within them, subgroups lose their distinct identity. If Protestants are as likely to marry other Protestants outside as inside their own denomination, the social distinctions among these denominations are in the process of becoming obliterated, which may well also diminish the significance of the distinctive religious dogmas that the various denominations represent.

Strong bonds within subgroups and strong bonds among them that integrate them in their encompassing group are inversely related (T-19.3). For example, strong bonds in the nuclear family have been found to be inversely related to allegiance to the kinship lineage and clan (Hunter 1933; Benedict 1936; Wagner 1939) and to strong identification with the community (Talmon-Garber 1956). Strong family solidarity has also been reported to reduce social association with neighbors, friends, and relatives (Bott 1957; Gluckman 1959).

Increasing rates of intermarriage eventually threaten the survival of small groups (T-19.4). If outmarriage rates infringe on inmarriage rates (T-19.2), and if small groups have higher rates of intermarriage than large ones (T-1.5), it follows that a small group's survival as a distinct social unit, defined by an excess of ingroup over outgroup associations, is threatened before that of a large group is. The demise of a group is not necessarily tragic for its members. Full ethnic assimilation means that separate ethnic groups have failed to survive, often with beneficial consequences for their members, such as less discrimination against them. What makes group survival of great importance to its members is a distinctive ideology, for the survival of the valued ideology depends on that of the group. Ideology refers here to any value system that sets a group apart from the rest of society and that would therefore not endure were the group to become extinct, be it composed of religious, political, or other subcultural values. Small groups are most likely to be strongly committed to a pure ideology and intent on preserving it in its

---

4. The *proportions* of all associates who are ingroup and intergroup, respectively, are mathematical complements which are inversely related by definition, but this is not the case for the *rates* or mean numbers of ingroup and intergroup associates.

pristine form, as illustrated by the fervor of small religious and political sects, which contrasts with the compromising orientations in large churches (Troeltsch 1931) and political parties. Purges keep the ideology pure and simultaneously the group of adherents small. Ideologies that appeal to large groups are typically less pure and command less intense devotion, as Boulding (1962, pp. 281–82) points out, because the compromises on issues required to give an ideology wide appeal to large numbers with a variety of interests dilute the ideology and weaken commitment to it. Besides, the value system of the majority is by definition not one that sets a group apart from the rest of society.

In short, the ideological commitments that make the preservation of a group's separate identity of great importance are most likely in small groups, the very ones whose separate identity is most threatened by strong intergroup relations. Under these conditions, one would expect severe ingroup pressures that proscribe intermarriage and discourage assimilation to preserve the superior cultural tradition of the ingroup (Dozier 1951). Generally, discriminatory pressures against intergroup relations are most pronounced in large groups and directed against small ones (T-11.1), but small groups strongly committed to distinctive values constitute a special case that does not conform to this proposition. A new assumption is required to account for this special situation: *A small group's strong commitment to a distinctive ideology enhances ingroup pressures that discourage intergroup relations* (PA-14).

Small groups strongly committed to a distinctive ideology have less extensive intergroup relations than other small or large groups (T-19.5). Although ideological commitments often foster proselytizing, which involves social interaction with outsiders, very intensive social interaction among true believers compensates for these outgroup contacts and sustains firm ingroup ties. Strong value commitments make the intergroup relations of particular small groups very low, which requires that those of other small groups are especially high (T-1.71), since the average rate of intergroup relations of all small groups delineated by a parameter exceed the average of all large groups. The exclusiveness of a small group that discriminates against other groups in intergroup relations is likely to antagonize the other groups, and the distinctive ideology often also antagonizes them. As a result, other groups probably discriminate against such a group and are disinclined to associate with its members, which further reduces its intergroup relations. The discrimination by other groups against this group serves the same function of preserving its separate identity as does its own discrimination against them. One might even conjecture that a decline in discrimination by other groups against this one, unless accompanied by a weakening of its ideological commitment, would increase its discrimination against others, to fortify its distinct identity in the face of lesser external forces that helped sustain it. These ingroup and outgroup pressures imply another theorem: *Small groups strongly committed to a distinctive ideology have more extensive ingroup relations than other small or large groups* (T-19.6). The proposition applies to the rates, the density, and the preponderance of ingroup relations.

Social Exchange

Processes of social association can be conceptualized as processes of social exchange. Social interaction involves, in the words of Homans (1961, p. 13), "an exchange of activity, tangible or intangible, and more or less rewarding or costly, between at least two persons." Structural conditions channel these sociopsychological processes that govern the interpersonal relations of individuals. The focus of the theoretical analysis in this book is on the influences exerted by variations in social structure on the patterns of association among people, often in ways that change the structure itself. The dynamics of structural change is rooted in the diverse and sometimes contradictory effects various conditions in complex social structures have on social association and mobility, which generate structural changes in their own right and which condition the influences of exogenous developments on social structures. Processes of social exchange contribute to the dynamics of social change, because they interact with and modify the influences of structural conditions on patterns of social association, just as the structural conditions themselves interact with and modify the influences of exogeneous developments.

Mauss (1954, pp. 1, 3) has called attention to the significance and ubiquity of the exchange of gifts and services in simple societies:

> In theory such gifts are voluntary but in fact they are given and repaid under obligation.... Further, what they exchange is not exclusively goods and wealth, real and personal property, and things of economic value. They exchange rather courtesies, entertainments, ritual, military assistance, women, children, dances, and feasts; and fairs in which the market is but one element and the circulation of wealth but one part of a wide and enduring contact.

Such exchange processes characterize interpersonal relations in complex as well as simple societies, according to exchange theory. The underlying sociopsychological principle of social exchange can be succinctly put (Blau 1964, p. 89): "An individual who supplies rewarding services to another obligates him. To discharge this obligation, the second must furnish benefits to the first in turn." To elaborate (Blau 1974, p. 205):

> The conception of social interaction as an exchange process follows logically from the assumption that men seek to obtain rewards in their social associations. If a man is attracted to others because he expects associating

with them to be rewarding to himself, he will wish to associate with them in order to realize the anticipated rewards. Likewise, for them to engage in social interaction with him, they must also have an interest in doing so. But their interest in associating with him depends, according to the assumption, on their expectation that interacting with him will be rewarding to them. To implement his desire to associate with them, therefore, he must demonstrate to them that associating with him would benefit them. In brief, to reap the rewards expected from attractive potential associates, a man must impress them as a desirable associate by implicitly conveying the promise that social interaction with him will be rewarding for them too.

A person who derives benefits from associates is under obligation to reciprocate by supplying benefits to them in turn. People often go out of their way to do favors not only for friends but also for mere acquaintances and even for strangers, and they thereby create social obligations. The individual who fails to discharge his obligations and reciprocate in some form for benefits received robs others of incentives to continue to befriend him. Besides, such an individual is likely to be accused of ingratitude. This very accusation indicates that reciprocation for favors freely given is expected, and it serves as a social sanction to discourage men from forgetting their obligations. Gratitude, as Simmel noted, "establishes the bond of interaction, of the reciprocity of service and return service, even when they are not guaranteed by external coercion."

Both parties profit from the rewarding experiences they supply each other, and recurrent exchange of benefits cements the social bond between them. Social exchange may thus establish mutual bonds between peers, but it does not always do so; sometimes it creates a relation of superordination of one person over another. This happens when one person has something to offer which another needs, for example, help with his work, but the second has nothing the first needs to reciprocate for the help. The second person must choose one of four courses of action under these conditions: (1) force the first to help him; (2) get help from someone else; (3) do without help; and (4) reward the other by subordinating himself and complying with the other's wishes. If he cannot or will not choose any of the three other possibilities, his only alternative is subordination, which is a generic reward that gives the other interpersonal power, and which is likely, though not guaranteed, to induce her or him to supply help. A person who has benefits to offer that others need and for which they cannot reciprocate can attain power over them by making the supply of benefits contingent on their compliance. In short (Blau 1964, p. 8), "reciprocated benefactions create social bonds among peers, whereas unreciprocated ones produce differentiation of status."

The principles of social exchange indicate the sociopsychological processes underlying some of the assumptions that have been made and some connections between assumptions. A major form of social exchange consists of furnishing social approval and support for conformity with social expectations. If certain standards of conduct are widely accepted and expected in a group, it implies that people value them, and conformity with these valued expectations is rewarding and rewarded by social approval, while violations of the expectation are experienced as unrewarding and reacted to with social disapproval and ostracism. These exchange processes generate strong social pressures against social practices that deviate from generally prevailing ones, pressures that diminish as the deviant practices become more widely accepted and consequently more people approve and fewer disapprove of them, as has been assumed (A-10). Hence, intergroup relations that structural conditions make infrequent in certain groups are made still more infrequent by the exchange processes that generate these group pressures.

The axiom that superior status entails superior social resources (A-12) implies, in terms of exchange theory, that persons whose status is superior command compliance and assume superordinate roles in social associations, as has been assumed (PA-6). Hence, one could substitute the assumptions of exchange theory for this provisional assumption (PA-6) and derive the proposition it contains from exchange assumptions and A-12. The exchange principle that interpersonal power is a generic reward implies that subordination is unrewarding and consequently that social intercourse provides most intrinsic rewards for both parties when they have equal resources and neither is required to assume a subordinate role. The inhibiting influence of status distance on social relations assumed to exist (A-1.2) could be derived from these implications of exchange theory, at least with respect to intimate relations that are not prompted by instrumental considerations.

Exchange theory has another implication for intergroup relations which helps refine and supplement the earlier analysis of them. If status differences are differences in comparable social resources (A-12), exchange principles imply that two persons who differ on two status dimensions in opposite ways are more or less peers and are therefore more likely than those whose status differs in only one dimension to establish a sociable or intimate relation, which requires reciprocal exchange based on roughly equal resources. Indeed, such tendencies have become stereotypes: the marriage of the rich man and the lord's daughter, that of the learned man and the affluent bride, the dating of the football star and the prom queen. Great differences in wealth inhibit sociability, but poor, famous poets may well be invited to the homes of the wealthy. Merton (1941) employs such an exchange conception to explain patterns of intermarriage between blacks and whites.

Opposite status differences in terms of two parameters increase the probability of social relations between persons whose positions differ, although status differences generally decrease the probability of social relations, particularly intimate ones like marriage. Persons whose positions differ in terms of two nominal parameters are less likely to be intimate than those whose positions differ in terms of one. In contrast, persons whose positions differ in opposite directions in terms of two graduated parameters are more likely to be intimate than those whose positions differ in terms of one. This contrast corresponds to one noted earlier: Intersecting nominal parameters increase heterogeneity (T-15.1), whereas intersecting—and especially negatively correlated—graduated parameters decrease inequality (T-15.3).

Intergroup relations in terms of one nominal parameter are most probable for persons who belong to the same groups in terms of other nominal parameters (T-20). The theorem follows from A-1.1, that common group membership promotes associations, and A-11, that the influences of various parameters are somewhat independent. It is actually equivalent to T-12.1, that intersecting nominal parameters promote intergroup relations, except for a shift in focus to the persons involved in intergroup relations, for whom the proposition is probabilistic, although T-12.1 is deterministic for groups. *Status-distant associations in terms of one graduated parameter are most probable for persons whose status differs in the opposite direction in terms of other graduated parameters, ceteris paribus* (T-20.1). This theorem follows from A-12, that various status differences entail comparable differences in social resources for exchange, which implies that opposite status differences make overall status more proximate; A-1.2, that proximate status promotes social associations; and A-11, that the influences of various parameters are somewhat independent. Since position in a low-status group is a sign of low status and position in a high-status group a sign of high status, these assumptions have parallel implications for differences in group status.

When groups differ in status, owing to a nominal parameter's strong correlations with graduated parameters, intergroup relations are most probable for persons whose own status differs in the opposite direction from that of their group's status, ceteris paribus (T-20.2). *The stronger the correlation between a nominal and a graduated parameter, the greater is the probability that the personal status of intergroup associates differs in the opposite direction from their group status, ceteris paribus* (T-20.3). Both theorems are implied by A-1.2, A-11, and A-12, as is T-20.1, plus T-22.1, which is derived below, and which stipulates that a group's status reflects on that of its members. T-20.3 does not conflict, although it may seem to, with the previously formulated proposition that the correlation of a nominal with a graduated parameter inhibits intergroup relations (T-12.31). Such a correlation depresses the rate of intergroup relations, but those that do occur are most likely to involve persons whose own and group status differ in opposite directions. Data on black-white marriages appear essentially to conform to these expectations.

Intermarriages between whites and blacks are very rare, much rarer than other interracial marriages (Burma 1963), as expected on the basis of the very low status of blacks in various respects. The marriages between whites and blacks that do occur tend to involve disproportionate numbers of blacks with high status and disproportionate numbers of whites with low status (Wirth and Goldhamer 1944, pp. 289–96), in accordance with T-20.2 and Merton's (1941) prediction.[5] Since this pattern is only evident when the departures of actual frequencies from those statistically expected from the population distributions are examined, Merton's inexact term *frequent* seems to have misled some into thinking that the data fail to confirm his central hypothesis (Heer 1966, p. 266; see also Golden 1953, p. 182). However, table 13 in Wirth and Goldhamer (1944, p. 290) shows black intermarried grooms have higher status (59 percent above unskilled) than black men generally (40 percent), and their white brides have lower status (64 percent unskilled) than white women generally (16 percent); white intermarried grooms have lower status (41 percent unskilled) than white men generally (19 percent), though their black brides do not have higher status (23 percent above unskilled) than black women generally (38 percent). The reason for this last deviant case may well be that the status of a prospective bride depends more than the groom's on factors other than her occupation, such as her social origins, education, and looks, and this difference was still more pronounced half a century ago when these data were collected. In any case, only 9 percent of the intermarried individuals are white brides (40 of 552). Three of four comparisons involving more than 90 percent of the intermarried persons are in accord with theoretical expectations.

Structural Effects

Exchange processes in groups have structural effects that reinforce the influences of structural conditions on social associations. The consolidation of a nominal parameter with other parameters increases the preponderance of ingroup relations (T-12.11), and its intersection by other parameters increases the prevalence of intergroup relations (T-12.1). In other words, the weaker the correlations of a nominal with other parameters, the more widespread is the practice of associating with outsiders, simply as the result of structural conditions, that is, the positive influences of the intersecting parameters on intergroup relations in terms of the original parameter. But these differences also influence exchange processes in groups: When the practice of associating with outsiders becomes more widely accepted, it encounters less social disapproval, which reduces group pressures that discourage intergroup relations (A-10), and which consequently further increases their prevalence. For example, if the correlation between ethnic affiliation and education declines, the common interests of people with simi-

5. Merton also advances theoretical reasons for the greater likelihood of interracial marriages to involve a black man and a white woman. Not all specific predictions Merton derives from his theoretical analysis are confirmed by the Wirth-Goldhamer data, but the basic implications of the theory are.

lar education are expected to increase associations across ethnic lines, which is assumed to modify exchange processes and reduce group pressures that discourage interethnic associations, and thereby further to increase them. The implications of exchange processes and of the resulting group pressures, which have been incorporated into an axiom (A-10), are that the correlations of parameters have multiplicative effects on social associations. A-10 implies that a nominal parameter's consolidation with another parameter reduces, and that its intersection by another parameter increases, the rate of intergroup associations more than would the additive influences of the two parameters alone.

The pronounced intersection of parameters has a structural effect on the prevalence of intergroup relations, increasing them more than would the additive effects of the parameters alone (T-21). The theorem follows from the proposition that intersecting parameters increase intergroup relations (T-12) and the axiom that extensive intergroup relations reduce group pressures that discourage them (A-10). Since group boundaries make distinct group pressures most likely, these structural effects are expected to be most apparent for nominal parameters. Accordingly, two corollaries are: *The pronounced intersection of a nominal by other parameters has a structural effect on intergroup relations, increasing them more than would the additive effects of the parameters alone* (T-21.1). *The pronounced consolidation of a nominal with graduated parameters has a structural effect on the predominance of ingroup relations, increasing them more than would the additive effects of the parameters alone* (T-21.11). For example, status differences among ethnic groups have multiplicative effects inhibiting interethnic relations and enhancing ethnic ingroup relations. It must be noted, however, that a ceiling effect may counteract the structural effect predicated in T-21.11, and indeed even the additive effects on ingroup relations of the two parameters. If the predominance of ingroup relations in terms of each of two parameters is very high, the joint effect of two parameters cannot effect the expected increase, because this would require more than 100 percent ingroup associations, which is impossible.

What are the empirical predictions implied by these theorems? The general principle is that structural effects require empirical evidence that given conditions have multiplicative effects. If societies are arrayed by the degree to which ethnic differences are correlated with educational differences, for instance, T-12 predicts that the ratio of the actual frequency of interethnic associations to that expected on the basis of the population distribution is highest in those societies with the lowest correlations. In short, it predicts an inverse correlation *for* societies between this ratio, which indicates the prevalence of interethnic relations, and the correlation *within* each society between ethnic affiliation and education. Such a finding would corroborate T-12, not the structural effect stipulated in T-21. The latter requires estimating how much the influence of education on social associations would be expected, independent of other conditions, to modify the rate of interethnic associations. The prediction of T-21 is that the excess of actual frequencies of interethnic associations over these new statistical expectations is greatest in societies in which ethnic affiliation and education are least correlated, which indicates that low correlations between these parameters have a multiplicative effect on intergroup associations. Another implication of T-21 is that those nominal parameters within a society that are most highly correlated with graduated parameters have the strongest multiplicative effects inhibiting intergroup relations. Still another prediction is that an excess of actual over statistically expected rates of intergroup associations is greatest for those groups distinguished by a given nominal parameter that are most heterogeneous and internally differentiated in terms of other parameters.

In sum, the influences of structural conditions on the prevalence of intergroup relations are predicated to stimulate social processes that reinforce these influences, and empirical evidence of these reinforcing processes is that the combined effect of two (or more) structural conditions on intergroup relations is greater than that accountable for by their estimated independent effects. The prevalence of ingroup relations and that of intergroup relations are complementary: The more ingroup associations exceed statistical expectations, whether derived by one procedure or another, the more intergroup relations fall short of these expectations. If exchange processes magnify the influences of structural conditions, they increase the effect of consolidated parameters on ingroup and that of intersecting parameters on intergroup prevalence. In other words, they increase both the negative effects of highly correlated and the positive effects of weakly correlated parameters of intergroup associations. This implies that there must be a threshold at which exchange processes are balanced and switch from constituting group pressures that reinforce ingroup and discourage intergroup associations to generating sufficient social approval to encourage intergroup associations. This threshold is probably surrounded by a zone of indifference where there are no structural effects, which is taken into account by restricting the theorems to *pronounced* intersection or consolidation. Ascertaining these thresholds and zones of indifference for various parameters and communities would help clarify the ingroup pressures that maintain ethnocentrism and discrimination.

Exchange processes generate structural effects on the asymmetry in role relations between members of different groups, as well as on the extent of their intergroup relations, and these structural effects on superordination are what transform great group differences in average status into differences in the status of their entire memberships. When we say that WASPs have higher status than Jews, or blacks than whites, or aristocrats than commoners, we refer to prestige in the sense of Weber's (1946, p. 187) concept *Stand*, which is a much narrower concept than status, and which "is determined by a specific, positive or negative, social estimation of *honor.*" Although these differences in honorific standing are ultimately rooted in differences in social resources, the resources characteristic of the entire group membership govern the prestige standing of every member, regardless of his or her own, as Weber (1946, p. 187) indicates when he goes on to state: "Property as such is not always recognized as a status qualification, but in the long run it is, and with extraordinary regularity.... Both propertied and propertyless people can belong to the same status group, [however]." Social exchange may well be what translates the pronounced superiority of a group in resources into superior prestige standing that group membership as such bestows on individuals and that is socially expected to command deference. These social expectations are enforced by group pressures engendered in processes of social exchange.

When one group is greatly superior in average status and resources to another, owing to substantial correlations of a nominal with graduated parameters, most of its members are superordinate in their role relations with members of the other group, in accordance with the assumption that a person's superior status is manifest in superordination in role relations (PA-6). The prevalence of this social conduct implies that exchange processes give rise to group pressures that reinforce it and make it still more prevalent (in accordance with A-10). As most members of the superior group assume the superordinate role in their intergroup relations, this is the accepted social practice and becomes socially expected of all members, and conformity with this expectation is rewarded by social approval. Deviants in the superior group who do not assume a superordinate position in interaction with the other group encounter social disapproval, and more severe sanctions are often applied against members of the other group who fail to express the proper deference in intergroup relations. The social relations of whites and blacks in rural Mississippi are not the only illustration; in more subtle forms, these processes occur in all groups whose prestige differs. Social clues revealing group differences in status, independent of other individual status differences, are observable in the interaction between members of the old-established and of the newer professions, between men and women, between academics from major universities and those from small colleges.

The consolidation of a nominal with graduated parameters has a structural effect on superordination in intergroup relations, which is manifest in an influence of mean group status, independent of individual's own status, on superordination (T-22). Memberships in groups that differ substantially in average status bestow corresponding differences in status on individuals that affect superordination-subordination in their intergroup relations (T-22.1). T-22 follows from PA-6 and A-10, as indicated; T-22.1 is a corollary of T-22. Membership in a superior group exerts an independent influence on superordination, though not one that necessarily overshadows the influences of individual status differences. Whether it does depends partly on the extent of the various status differences and partly on the social situation in which the associations occur. Social associations in public, which are subject to social surveillance, are probably more influenced by group pressures and social expectations than associations in private, which are more likely to be largely governed by individual differences and personal considerations. This suggests that public social life is where group differences in status are most likely to be manifest in asymmetric role relations, in disregard of individual differences. It has frequently been commented upon that members of dominant groups tend to insist on deference in public from groups considered to be inferior, while they may have cordial peer relations with individuals in these groups in private.

Superordination in ingroup associations also depends on both the group's average status and the individual's own status, although in this case the reason is not that exchange processes and group pressures transform superior mean status of a group into superior status of all its members, which raises their likelihood of superordination. On the contrary, superior group status reduces the chances that a person with a given status has the superordinate position in ingroup relations. For the higher the average status of one's group, the lower is one's own relative to that of other group members. A person with an income of $20,000 belongs to the lower socioeconomic strata in Beverly Hills but to the upper ones on the Bowery. A policeman with a college degree is highly educated; a college faculty member with only a college degree has little formal education. The assumption that the person whose status is superior has the superordinate position in a role relation (PA-6) therefore implies: *The probability that a person with a given status has the superordinate role in ingroup associations declines with increasing mean status of the group* (T-22.2).

The stronger the correlations of a nominal with graduated parameters, the greater the probabilities are that, controlling their own status, members of high-status groups are superordinate in their intergroup but subordinate in their ingroup associations, and members of low-status groups are subordinate in their intergroup but superordinate in their ingroup associations (T-22.3). The theorem is a corollary of T-22.1 and T-22.2. When a baseball player moves from the minor to the major leagues, the higher prestige of his new team improves his own in baseball circles, but he was the star of his old team and is just a rookie in his new one. Equally bright students are superior to most fellow students when they go to a third-rate college but inferior to many when they go to a major university, while the difference in the renown of their alma mater has opposite consequences for their extramural social standing. The qualification in T-22.2 and T-22.3 that ego's status must be controlled is essential; otherwise the probability of superordination in ingroup relations is not generally less in high-status than in low-status groups but about the same in both.[6] Only if persons with the same status are compared, of whom there are necessarily unequal numbers in high-status and low-status groups, does the likelihood of superordination in ingroup relations decline with increasing group status. Generally, a person's own superior status increases his or her chances of superordination in ingroup as well as intergroup associations, but the additional effect of superior group status is to decrease these chances in ingroup while further increasing them in intergroup associations.

A variety of empirical studies have found that people's own characteristics and the average characteristics in their groups exert opposite influences on them, which corresponds to the pattern in T-22.2. Stouffer and colleagues (1949, pp. 250–54) report that noncommissioned officers were more satisfied than privates with the army's promotion system in World War II, but a large proportion of noncommissioned officers in an outfit reduced satisfaction with promotions. J. A. Davis (1966) finds that the abilities of college students are directly related to their expectations of going to graduate school, but the average student abilities in a college are inversely related to these expectations. Blau (1973, pp. 123–28) observes that the formal qualifications of faculty members reduce but the average qualifications at an academic institution raise faculty allegiance to the institution. What these findings have in common is that the independent variable is an aspect of social status: a soldier's rank, a student's academic ability, a faculty member's qualifications. Other variables that reveal such a reversal of influence are correlates of an aspect of status: Competitive office workers are more productive but the group with the higher average competition is less productive (Blau 1974, pp. 135–43), since competitive practices put a person into a more advantageous positions; faculty members primarily involved in teaching express more but those in academic institutions with high average teaching involvement express less commitment to their institution (Blau 1973), since teaching commands less social standing in academia than scholarly research.

Although status is typically measured in absolute terms, its influence is relative to the status of others, this being an inherent quality of social status, which is intrinsic to the meaning of the concept. A person's own absolute status and the average absolute status of her group are often observed to have opposite consequences for conduct, attitudes, and social relations, because what actually exerts an influence is relative status. The opposite consequences of ego's and alter's absolute status frequently reported simply reflect this influence of relative status or average status distance on social life.

The analysis of influences of social structure on patterns of conduct—

---

6. Within every group, the likelihood of superordination and subordination must be the same, just as it must be the same for the entire population, since every dyadic association involves either one superordinate and one subordinate role, or neither (if it is a peer relation).

specifically, processes of social association and mobility—is the central concern of this book. The concept of structural effects, originally introduced two decades ago (Blau 1957), does not refer to all effects of structural conditions on social patterns but to a certain type, namely, the influence on conduct exerted by the prevalence of an attribute in a group independent of any influence exerted by whether or not an individual has this attribute himself. A structural effect reflects the influence on ego's conduct of the social attributes of alters, not of her own attributes. For example, caseworkers in a welfare agency treated clients more considerately if they had an orientation toward service rather than eligibility procedures and also, independent of their own orientation, if they worked in groups most of whose other members had a service orientation. Such direct structural effects, when ego's and alters' attributes have parallel consequences for ego's conduct, have been distinguished from inverse structural effects, when alters' attributes have opposite consequences from ego's own for ego, as in the research findings cited above.

The sociopsychological processes mediating direct and inverse structural effects are fundamentally different, and so are the underlying structural constraints. Direct structural effects are the result of normative group pressures engendered by processes of social exchange, which are stimulated by certain structural conditions and reinforce their influences on social conduct. Inverse structural effects are the result of the significance of relative status, which is the joint product of the absolute status of ego and that of alters, and which influences social conduct in part directly and in part by stimulating comparison processes with different reference groups (Merton 1968) that influence it. An illustration of the latter is that the wider reputation of research-involved than of teaching-involved faculty members fosters an orientation to outside reference groups among the former and to inside ones among the latter, which produces the difference in institutional commitment noted above. Both kinds of structural effects are engendered by structural conditions, that is, the distributions of certain characteristics among group members. In the case of direct structural effects, however, the characteristics pertain to attitudes and practices, notably intergroup and ingroup associations, and the mediating factors are exchange processes and group pressures that reinforce the influence of prevailing attitudes and practices on conduct. In the case of inverse structural effects, by contrast, the characteristics are social resources (absolute status), and the mediating factor is relative status, which represents the structural constraints and sociopsychological influences on conduct exerted by the distributions of resources (status).

The concept of structural effects raises an interesting methodological issue. In American society the social standing of men is superior to that of women, and that of whites is superior to that of blacks. This is reflected in corresponding differences in power, income, and various other aspects of status. Now assume one finds that sex and race, with status controlled, exert influences on some conduct that are parallel to the influences exerted by status. Does this mean that the inherent superior status of males and of whites exerts an influence, or does it mean that the greater proportions of powerful and rich persons among men and among whites engender group pressures that exert a structural effect?[7] This question cannot be answered, because there is no way of analyzing nominal groups distinguished only by their labels. But it is the wrong question. What needs to be explained is why men and whites are socially superior, independent of their own social resources. One sort of explanation is that biological differences account for these social differences. The alternative explanation suggested here is that pronounced differences in social resources between groups give rise to social processes that transform great average differences in resources (status) between groups into categorical status differences rooted in group membership as such, independent of an individual's own resources. This is the direct structural effect noted in T-22.1, evidence for which requires that group differences in subordination persist if the various status correlates of group membership are controlled. When such structural effects generating major group differences in status have been institutionalized for centuries, the resulting quasi castes whose members are protected against status loss have become deeply entrenched and are difficult to dislodge, as the arduous struggles of blacks and women for equal rights demonstrate.

Compendium

T-19   The prevalence of ingroup relations in subgroups probably exceeds that in the larger groups encompassing them delineated by the same nominal parameter. (From A-1.1.)

T-19.1 The probability is that small groups have denser networks of ingroup relations than large groups. (From definitions; or from T-19, based on A-1.1.)

T-19.2 The closer the social bonds under consideration, the greater the probability is that the rate of ingroup and the rate of intergroup associations are inversely related. (From definitions only.)

T-19.3 Strong bonds within subgroups and strong bonds among them that integrate them in their encompassing group are inversely related. (From T-19.2.)

T-19.4 Increasing rates of intermarriage eventually threaten the survival of small groups. (From T-19.2, T-1.5.)

7. This basic methodological question may be underlying Hauser's (1970) objections to the conception of structural effects, although the explicit criticisms he makes are procedural, and these have been answered elsewhere (Barton 1970; Blau 1973, pp. 33–34, 110–11).

PA-14   A small group's strong commitment to a distinctive ideology enhances ingroup pressures that discourage intergroup relations.

T-19.5 Small groups strongly committed to a distinctive ideology have less extensive intergroup relations than other small or large groups. (From PA-14.)

T-19.6 Small groups strongly committed to a distinctive ideology have more extensive ingroup relations than other small or large groups. (From PA-14, T-19.2.)

T-20   Intergroup relations in terms of one nominal parameter are most probable for persons who belong to the same groups in terms of other nominal parameters. (From A-1.1, A-11.)

T-20.1 Ceteris paribus, status-distant associations in terms of one graduated parameter are most probable for persons whose status differs in the opposite direction in terms of other graduated parameters. (From A-1.2, A-11, A-12.)

T-20.2 Ceteris paribus, when groups differ in status, owing to a nominal parameter's strong correlation with graduated parameters, intergroup relations are most probable for persons whose own status differs in the opposite direction from that of their group status. (From A-1.2, A-11, A-12, T-22.1; based on PA-4, A-10.)

T-20.3 Ceteris paribus, the stronger the correlation between a nominal and a graduated parameter, the greater the probability is that the individual status of intergroup associates differs in the opposite direction from their group status. (From A-1.2, A-11, A-12, T-22.1; based on PA-4, A-10.)

T-21   The pronounced intersection of two parameters has a structural effect on intergroup relations, increasing them more than would the additive effects of the parameters alone. (From A-10, T-12; based on A-1, A-11.)

T-21.1 The pronounced intersection of a nominal by other parameters has a structural effect on intergroup relations, increasing them more than would the additive effects of the parameters alone (From A-10, T-12; based on A-1, A-11.)

T-21.11 The pronounced consolidation of a nominal with graduated parameters has a structural effect on the predominance of ingroup relations, increasing them more than would the additive effects of the two parameters alone. (From A-10, T-12; based on A-1, A-11.)

T-22   The consolidation of a nominal with graduated parameters has a structural effect on superordination in intergroup relations, which is manifest in an influence of mean group status, independent of individual's own status, on superordination. (From PA-6, A-10.)

T-22.1 Memberships in groups that differ substantially in mean status bestow corresponding differences in status on individuals that affect superordination-subordination in their intergroup relations (From T-22; based on PA-6, A-10.)

T-22.2   The probability that a person with a given status has the superordinate position in ingroup associations declines with increasing mean status of the group. (From PA-6.)

T-22.3   The stronger the correlation of a nominal with graduated parameters, the greater the probabilities are that, controlling own status, members of high-status groups are superordinate in their intergroup but subordinate in their ingroup associations, and members of low-status groups are subordinate in their intergroup but superordinate in their ingroup associations. (From T-22.1, T-22.2; based on PA-6, A-10.)

CHAPTER SEVEN

Ecological Structure

THE SUBJECT OF THIS CHAPTER IS THE SIGNIFICANCE FOR SOCIAL LIFE OF the spatial distribution of a society's population among different communities. The territorial distribution of people and its connections with their distributions among various social positions constitute the ecological structure. In other words, ecological structure refers to the relationships of a social structure to its territorial environment. Whereas current ecology encompasses the study of a great variety of environmental influences, ranging from those of natural resources and other species to those of pollution and noise, concern here is restricted to the influences of the distributions of people in physical space on the structures of differentiated positions and the processes of social association that develop among them.

After some reflections on the general implications of time and space for social life, consequences of community size and density for intergroup relations and interpersonal conflict are examined. Since social differences exist among communities and within them, the social differentiation in society—for example, society's division of labor—can be decomposed into that among and that within communities, and so can the influences society's differentiation exerts on social associations. Such an analysis comparing the significance of differentiation among and within communities is carried out, and it is then generalized to formulate propositions about differentiation among and within any substructures. These propositions, although themselves derived from others and thus not the most basic, may be considered to be the core of the theory.

Time and Space

Time and space permeate social life and the forms it assumes, because all social life occurs in time and in space. People establish and maintain social relations in processes of social interaction, which have a time dimension, and social distinctions among them are produced by and manifest in their differential social associations over time. Societies have institutions and traditions because organized patterns of social relations have become crystallized through many generations, and it is the passing of generations that provides the most elemental social experience of historical time. Changes in social structure, the conditions that produce them, and their repercussions must be traced through historical time, and the flexibility of a structure in adjusting to new conditions cannot be ascertained except by examining it over time.

The processes of social exchange underlying the associations of persons can be analyzed strictly in terms of the time investments involved, at least up to a point. Thus, the principle of reciprocity—favors create obligations—can be translated to mean that when one person has taken the time to do something for another, the other incurs a future time commitment to be used to benefit the first. A person who supplies unreciprocated benefits to others gains power over them and commands their compliance, which means that all their otherwise uncommitted time is at his disposal to be used as he wishes. Exercising power entails making demands on the time of others. The resources on which the power is based constitute frozen time, so to speak, that is, previous time investments to accumulate these resources. These previous time investments may have been made by the person who has the power, as in the case of knowledge, or by others, as in the case of inherited wealth. Pure sociability between peers involves no future obligations, since equal time investments bring equivalent returns. When two people greatly enjoy each other's company, time flies, which suggests that the psychological cost in time shrinks and is no longer measurable in chronological time. Conversely, boring company makes time go slowly and thus raises the psychological time cost beyond the time actually elapsed. However, it is probably preferable to define cost on the basis of objective, chronological time, and to attribute the difference in the psychologically experienced time to differences in the rewards obtained. Continuous time together eventually becomes less rewarding, while the cost in time and alternatives foregone increases, and the resulting changes in marginal profits are the reasons that people do not spend all their time together regardless of how much they enjoy each other's company.

The microtime in processes of social association (Lévi-Strauss 1963, pp. 282–83), which is counted in minutes and hours, is socially distinct from historical time, which is counted in years and centuries. The elemental units of historical time, preceding literacy and calendars, are generations, of living persons for shorter periods and of ancestors for longer ones. The Nuer again furnish a good illustration (Evans-Pritchard 1940, pp. 104–8, 193–202, 248–61). All the boys initiated into manhood during a number of successive years constitute an age-set, which has a name, and which remains a distinct group throughout the lives of these men. An age-set is a named cohort that moves through the age structure. The Nuer reckon historical time of a few decades in terms of age-sets, referring to past events by saying that they happened when the "That" or the "Dangunga" had been initiated. Longer time periods of scores of years or centuries are reckoned in terms of generations of ancestors. Hence, the structuring of historical time and the kinship structure are equivalent, since closer kin in narrower lineages trace their common descent to a more recent ancestor and distant kin in the clan to a very remote one. Historical time finds concrete expression in the social structure, and the social experience of having closer and more distant kin relations gives meaning to historical time and variations in it.

The saying that people without written records have no history is a half-truth. To be sure, historical records help preserve traditions and institutions and enable men and women to reflect on their past and analyze it. In the absence of written constitutions and records, rituals serve to perpetuate traditions and institutionalized principles of social organization. Although written records provide much more accurate knowledge of the past, they do not embody the past as fully in the social life of people as do rituals and a kinship structure that translates people's relations to the past into their current social relations. We have unquestionably more precise knowledge of our history than the Nuer have of theirs, are probably more aware intellectually of our past, and have perhaps a greater sense of history, but the past is not so much a living part of everyday existence for us as it is for the Nuer. One might even wonder whether historical records and understanding do not help shield society from the dead weight of its history and traditions and contribute to the rapid pace of social change in the modern world.

An emphasis on the importance of the time dimension for social life is not the same as an interest in historical analysis. On the one hand, social time encompasses more than historical analysis; it includes the microtime involved in the sociopsychological processes underlying structures of social associations as well as historical developments. On the other hand, historical analysis has two connotations, only one of which is relevant for theoretical generalizations about social structure. Historical analysis may refer to inquiries that take changes over time in societies into account, and it may alternatively refer to inquiries concerned with the unique constellation of social circumstances that characterize a particular historical period. It may seek to explain why revolutions generally occur, or it may seek to analyze the particular social conditions that led to the French Revolution. Of course, attempts to understand revolutions generally require some knowledge of the one in 1789, but the theoretical focus of the analysis is quite different. Macrosociological theory must take structural change into account, but it is emphatically not concerned with unique historical circumstances; on the contrary, it abstracts from these circumstances generic properties assumed to be independent of the historical period in which they were observed.

The time dimension penetrates social structures from two sides, as it were, being involved in the microprocesses that form structures of social associations and in the historical developments that alter the macrostructural forms. The theory presented here attempts to take this into account in recurrent references to processes of social association, processes of mobility, and structural change, such as increasing heterogeneity or decreasing inequality. The significance of social time is so interwoven with various aspects of social structures that it is not advantageous to single it out for separate analysis. The significance of physical space for social life can more easily be treated as a distinct topic, because it is manifest in the distribution of people among communities and neighborhoods. But spatial distributions and relations, too, are best analyzed within a broader theoretical framework in which their connections with other social distributions and relations are dissected and generic properties common to both can be discerned.

This is illustrated by changes in the conceptual framework of human ecology, which was perhaps the earliest theoretical scheme in sociology explicitly oriented to systematic research. Urban ecology was inspired by Park, and Hawley (1968) notes that it was initially defined narrowly by McKenzie (1925) as the study of the spatial and temporal relations of people as affected by their environment. The central concern of traditional ecological research in sociology was the urban environment—the various zones of a city and the changes in them produced by urban growth. Hawley (1950) broadened the conception of human ecology to encompass the study of the organization of social relations in communities generally, and Duncan (1959) broadened it further by defining it as the study of the interrelations of four components of the ecosystem—population, organization, environment, and technology. This conception of ecological theory makes it virtually synonymous with macrosociological theory, except that some special emphasis on spatial relations is preserved in practice, and cultural factors are not included, which is intentional, and which corresponds to the focus in this book on social structure rather than on culture.

The earliest developments of primitive structures of social differentiation already reflect the significance of the territorial distribution of people. Murdock's (1949) cross-cultural comparison cited in chapter 6 indicates that it is when nomadic bands settle permanently in villages that a political structure among them and internal class differences usually develop. Permanent settlement tends to lead to population growth, which stimulates further differentiation, as noted by other studies cited in chapter 6. Murdock (1949, pp. 314–21) concludes that six forms of social differentiation influence inti- mate relations, particularly sexual relations, in most societies, and all but two of these—age and sex—are related to people's territorial distribution. Inti- mate relations nearly everywhere are promoted by common membership in an ethnic group, a social class, a kin group (beyond the confines of kin relations excluded by incest taboos), and a political community, and prox- imity with respect to each of these group affiliations tends to be associated with physical proximity.

The spatial distribution of the population exerts much influence on social relations in modern societies as well as in simple ones. One reason is that physical distance greatly diminishes the opportunities for social contacts. To be sure, modern means of communication and transportation make it easier to maintain contacts with friends and relatives despite physical separation, but this merely reduces, it does not eliminate, the adverse effect of physical distance on the probability of social relations. Another reason for the perva- sive influence of people's spatial distribution on social life is that this distri- bution finds expression in several structural conditions that influence social associations. To distinguish these, it is first necessary to analyze the nature of spatial distributions.

The territorial distribution of people has one basic attribute of a nominal and one of a graduated parameter. It divides the population by place of residence into nominal categories, which have no rank-order, and which are distinguished only by their names, but it furnishes a rank-order of the physi- cal distances between people. From the perspective of any individuals, oth- ers live more or less far away, but these distances are different for people who themselves live in different places, and there is no rank-order of places from which the distances are derived, as there is for status distances defined by graduated parameters. Territorial distributions are in these respects equivalent to nominal parameters with successive subdivisions, which also rank social distances, do not rank groups, and constitute concentric circles from the perspective of individuals. Yet in two other respects spatial distri- butions differ from those yielded by nominal parameters with successive subdivisions. Physical distance is a natural ratio scale, not an ordinal rank- ing derived from the social relations among groups, and the territorial distri- bution is intrinsically continuous and does not generate distinct boundaries, whereas groups have distinct boundaries: A mechanical engineer is not an electrical engineer, and neither is a lawyer, nor are any of the three manual workers.

Although territories have no boundaries of their own and merge into one another, the places where people live become organized into political units and subunits, and their political borders thus supply territorial communities with boundaries. It appears that this unification of territorial and political subdivisions occurs in all societies, from the simplest to the most complex. Murdock (1949, pp. 84–86) discusses the political organization of villages as subunits of larger political structures, and Evans-Pritchard (1940, pp. 114–15, 139–50) deals at length with the complex territorial-political structure of the Nuer into tribes, successively narrower tribal sections, and villages, and he notes that villages are divided into hamlets and huts, but that these smallest territorial units are not political units. This corresponds exactly to the situation in modern nations, where the larger territorial divisions—states, provinces, towns—also constitute political units, and the smaller—neighborhoods, blocks—do not.

Several ways in which the spatial distribution of people influences social life can now be analytically distinguished. One is propinquity itself, which governs opportunities for social contacts. Another is that people live in different communities, which are both territorial and political units, and the characteristics of which affect social relations. Some aspects of the spatial distribution can be considered to be structural manifestations of propinquity. Thus, variations in the size and population density among communities determine the number of persons who live in physical proximity and hence the opportunities for social contacts with many, and often diverse, others. The extent to which different groups and strata are segregated within and among communities is another structural manifestation of propinquity which governs the probabilities of intergroup relations. Some influences of segregation on intergroup relations have been discussed in chapter 4; others will be analyzed in this chapter, after first examining the implications of size and density of place for social associations.

Urbanization and Communication

More than eighty years ago Durkheim (1933, pp. 256–63) emphasized that a large "volume" of people and their "material density" engender "dynamic density"; in other words, that the concentration of large numbers of persons in one place leads to high rates of social association. In a recent paper previously cited, Mayhew and Levinger (1976b) develop a mathematical model according to which the "density of social interaction" or frequency of social associations per person increases at a rapid rate with increasing city size. This principle is deducible from the assumption that social associations depend on opportunities for social contacts (A-9) and, more directly, from the proposition it implies that physical propinquity increases the probability of social associations (T-13). If physical distance impedes and proximity promotes opportunities for social communication and association, it follows that communication opportunities and association probabilities increase when the growing concentration of large numbers of people in one place decreases the average distance among them. In short, the frequency of social contacts increases with growing urbanization. Although the size of a place and its population density are not the same, of course, urbanization entails the concentration of large numbers of persons in a given place and thus increases in both, and no attempt is made to distinguish the influences of size and population density on social relations.

The probability of association with many different persons increases with the increasing size and population density of a community (T-23). Association with different persons refers necessarily to nonexclusive social relations, and it includes very brief and fleeting social contacts. Indeed, the theoretical model of Mayhew and Levinger (1976b) indicates that expected time per social contact decreases with increasing size of place and number of social contacts, which implies that people in large cities have many casual social contacts, though it is wrong to draw the inference from this that close relations are more superficial in big cities than in small towns. Urban persons are likely to spend more of their total time than rural persons associating with others, because they are surrounded by so many others, but they spend less time with each of their associates, except with their most intimate ones, because there are so many among whom they divide their time. Fleeting contacts with large numbers of persons have the result that people really do not know many of their acquaintances as individuals but think of and remember them in terms of social categories, to which Mayhew and Levinger attribute the greater anonymity of big cities.

Several more specific propositions follow from the theorem that physical propinquity raises the probability of social associations (T-13), jointly with the greater mean propinquity resulting from concentrations of persons: *The probability that people have wide circles of acquaintances increases with the increasing size of the community where they live* (T-23.11). *The probability that people have wide circles of acquaintances increases with the increasing size of the place where they work* (T-23.12). *The probability that people have wide circles of acquaintances increases with the increasing urbanization of society* (T-23.2). *The probability that people have wide circles of acquaintances increases with the increasing concentration of society's labor force in large work organizations* (T-23.3).

These propositions imply a fundamental change in social life that has occurred in this century in the United States and in other advanced industrial societies, a change that is still in progress in many industrial countries and that has not yet occurred in most developing countries. The majority of people in the United States at the beginning of this century lived and worked on farms, and this is still the case in many other countries. Today, the majority of Americans live in big cities or their suburbs and work in large organizations, and conditions in most countries reveal similar trends at various stages of development. Farmers and inhabitants of small towns have few associates, whom they know well. But people who live in a big metropolis and work in a large establishment tend to know many more persons much more casually. Europeans often accuse Americans of being superficial, having hardly any profound social relations, and calling persons friends whom they know only slightly; Americans frequently are disconcerted by the exclusiveness of Europeans, whose narrow social circles of lifelong friends and relatives outsiders cannot penetrate. There is some truth in these stereotypes, because social relations tend to become less exclusive and less deeply rooted with society's growing urbanization, the expansion of its work establishments, and its increasing heterogeneity. Of course, such changes in the nature of social relations that have been institutionalized for generations and centuries do not occur overnight, and they may occur more rapidly in a society of immigrants whose institutions and traditions are less firmly entrenched. In the long run, however, parallel developments in structural conditions can be expected to engender similar changes in the character of social relations.

Urbanization is a catalyst of social relations, which probably has a multiplier effect on the influences exerted by the conditions associated with it on social relations (T-23.4). The theorem is implied by T-23, with urbanization defined by the size and population density of communities: The influences on social relations of the conditions in the more urban places of a society are likely to have a predominant effect on the pattern of social relations, because the density of urban places makes social associations more likely and their large size means that many persons exhibit this pattern of associations. For example, if income inequality is more pronounced in big cities than in small towns, the influence of income on social associations in society is expected to be more pronounced than if income inequality and urbanization are inversely related. If big cities are more heterogeneous than small towns, this condition is likely to have a multiplier effect on the influence of heterogeneity on intergroup relations.

Big cities are typically more heterogeneous than small towns. The heterogeneity of the large metropolis is proverbial. The growth of cities depends on inmigration from rural areas and small towns, since the natural population increase is less in urban centers than in rural places and small towns. Inmigrants from diverse places make a community simultaneously larger, more densely populated, and more heterogeneous, at least with respect to place of origin and social background. But there are additional factors that make large cities heterogeneous in other respects. Big cities tend to have a more diverse economy and are less likely to be dominated by a single industry than small towns, Detroit being exceptional in this regard. Hence, the division of labor tends to be more pronounced in urban centers, which attracts people with a variety of skills, interests, and backgrounds. The anonymity of the metropolis attracts a variety of people, and so do the more extensive cultural activities found there. All of these conditions tend to contribute to the greater heterogeneity characteristic of big cities. Williams's (1964, p. 118) comparison of the ethnic composition in a national sample of 248 American cities shows that the proportions of foreign-born, of blacks, and of Jews increase with increasing city size, both in the North and in the South. These considerations and data justify the assumption that *a community's size and density are directly correlated with its heterogeneity* (PA-15).

The probability of intergroup relations increases with increasing size and density of the community (T-23.5). The theorem follows from PA-15, that size and density increase heterogeneity, and T-11, that heterogeneity increases the probability of intergroup relations. Thus, several studies report that interracial marriages are more prevalent in urban than in rural areas; specifically, disproportionate numbers of black-white (Wirth and Goldhamer 1944, pp. 281–84; Golden 1953, p. 180) and of Japanese-Caucasian couples (Strauss 1954; Schnepp and Yui 1955) have urban backgrounds. This proposition (T-23.5) and the one that urbanization is a catalyst of social relations (T-23.4) imply that *the probability of extensive intergroup relations in a society increases with its increasing urbanization* (T-23.6).

Two characteristics of complex industrial societies promote intergroup relations and thus integrative social connections among diverse groups. The first, as noted earlier, is the multiform heterogeneity of complex societies (T-12.1), and the second, as just indicated, is the urbanization of industrial societies (T-23.6), which increases the probability of intergroup relations by bringing various groups together in heterogeneous cities. But the same conditions also increase interpersonal conflict, because opportunities for social contact increase the likelihood of conflict (PA-13) as well as of cordial relations between persons (A-9). Accordingly, multiform heterogeneity increases the probability of interpersonal conflict among groups (T-17.1), and so does urbanization, as it also increases the likelihood of social contacts that constitute the occasions for interpersonal conflict. A general increase in conflict with increasing city size is implied by the mathematical model of Mayhew and Levinger (1976b), and an increase in conflict between persons from different groups with growing city size and density is implied by the proposition that size and density increase intergroup contacts (T-23.5) and the assumption that many contacts make interpersonal conflict more likely (PA-13). *The probability of interpersonal conflict between members of different groups increases with increasing size and density of the community* (T-23.7). This proposition and the one that urbanization is a catalyst of social relations (T-23.4) imply that *the probability of interpersonal conflict between members of different groups in a society increases with its increasing urbanization* (T-23.71).

In sum, urbanization shrinks the physical distances among members of a society and simultaneously concentrates diverse groups in large cities, which increases the opportunities for and probabilities of integrative intergroup relations, but which also increases the occasions for and probabilities of conflict between persons from different groups. To reiterate a point, interpersonal friction and conflict are the price of macrosocial integration in a diverse society. This would be the case even on the assumption that contacts between persons from different groups are no more likely to engender conflict than contacts between persons of the same group, because social conditions that increase the opportunities of persons to establish cordial relations also increase the occasions when persons can come into conflict. The frequent superficial contacts among strangers in big cities undoubtedly make conflict more likely than it is in places where people know most of their associates well and have little contact with strangers, but these fleeting contacts with strangers are the condition that increases the likelihood that erstwhile strangers from different groups come to know each other and sometimes become friends.

The axiom that social associations depend on opportunities for social contacts (A-9) implies that any reduction in the obstacles to contacts that are created by physical distance enhances the likelihood of social associations. Urbanization is not the only development that effects such a reduction; technical improvements in the means of communication and transportation are another. Urbanization furthers social associations by diminishing the average physical distance among people, and improvements in communication and transportation do so by making physical distance less of an impediment to social contacts. Carriages, streetcars, buses, and cars make it easy for people from different neighborhoods to get together; the postal system and the telephone enable them to maintain at least indirect contact with friends and relatives in distant towns and cities; and trains, cars, and planes make it possible to continue intermittent personal contacts with associates despite having become separated from them by long distances. These consequences of communication and transportation facilities permit people to sustain social relations already established over long distances, but they do not create opportunities for establishing new social relations. However, the availability of efficient means of transportation has other repercussions that do increase the chances of forming new social relations.

Widespread use of transportation facilities makes people more mobile and more likely to leave their neighborhood to live in more pleasant surroundings, and to migrate from their hometown to settle in other places where economic opportunities are better. Hence, ready access to efficient transportation tends first to increase the physical distances among many friends and relatives and then to make it easier for them to come together occasionally, notwithstanding their physical separation. Associates who live long distances apart naturally cannot sustain as frequent social intercourse as they had when they lived in close proximity. By putting more physical distance between persons with established social ties, extensive transportation facilities increase in two ways the chances that new social relations are formed. First, persons who are deprived most of the time of the company of their old associates are likely to turn to new associates nearby for regular companionship, taking advantage of the opportunities for social contacts proximity provides. Second, visits to friends and relatives in different communities bring people into contact with other persons there, which enhances the likelihood that members of different communities form new social relations. The extensive traveling on vacations and weekends encouraged by readily available means of transportation also brings people from different parts of a country together and supplies opportunities for them to associate.

Efficient means of transportation reduce the influence of physical propinquity on social associations (T-24). If associations depend on contact opportunities (A-11), and propinquity promotes associations by increasing contact opportunities (T-13), efficient means of transportation, by creating contact opportunities that are independent of propinquity, reduce the influence of propinquity on associations. This does not necessarily increase intergroup relations of various kinds. But it does attenuate the inhibiting effect of segregation on intergroup relations (T-13.11), and it does promote one form of intergroup relations, the one most directly impeded by physical distance. *The widespread use of efficient means of transportation improves the integration of different communities in society by raising the rates of social association among them* (T-24.1).

Large nations have existed in the past, but it is doubtful whether they constituted coherent societies in a meaningful sense, since there was so little connection among the various parts—the isolated villages and towns and provinces. Political nationhood alone does not create a unified society. Improvement in means of transportation and communication produce increasingly extensive social connections among communities, and thereby integrate them by transforming their relatively independent structures into components of the emergent structure of society.

Technological and industrial developments contribute to the macrosocial integration of society by improving channels of communication among its territorial and political subunits as well as by promoting urbanization, which concentrates diverse groups in the same locations and stimulates associations among their members. For these changes to occur, however, advances in technical knowledge must be complemented and implemented by efficient production methods that make the new technical facilities economical and widely available. Without the invention of the gasoline engine, automobiles could not have been produced, but without the large-scale production methods that made cars economical, they could not have had the great impact on American life they did have. Although it is technically possible to go to the moon, it is not economically feasible for many persons to make the trip. In short, the influences of technical progress on social life tend to be mediated by economic developments. This is a central thesis of Marx's, embodied in his analysis of the significance of productive relations for translating the impact of productive forces on society.

Economic conditions modify the influence of propinquity on social relations, because the widespread use of modern means of transportation and communication, and hence their effects on social life, depends on their cost.

For given costs, it depends on the resources available to incur them, which is made an assumption: *The availability of efficient means of transportation depends on financial resources* (PA-16). This assumption has several implications, jointly with the proposition (T-24) that efficient means of transportation reduce the influence of propinquity on social associations.

Ceteris paribus, the influence of physical propinquity on social relations in a society is inversely related to its wealth (T-24.2). In a rich society like ours, where most families have cars, physical propinquity is not so significant for social relations as in a poor society like India. The higher the gross national product per capita, the more people can afford efficient transportation, which makes their social relations less dependent on physical proximity. Even in a rich society, however, many persons are poor and do not have the means to travel. *The influence of physical propinquity on the social relations of individuals is inversely related to their income* (T-24.3). Thus, poor people are expected to associate more with neighbors than are rich ones. When incomes are very unevenly distributed many people are poor, though average incomes in the society may be comparatively high, which can modify, and possibly even nullify, the influence predicated in T-24.2. *Ceteris paribus, the influence of physical propinquity on social relations in a society is directly related to the degree of income inequality* (T-24.4).

Decomposition

Communities are component elements of a society, and they have their own social structures. The propositions advanced apply to the social structures of communities as well as those of entire societies.[1] For example, a religious group is predicted to have higher intergroup relations in those communities where it is a minority than in those where it constitutes the majority (T-1.5). Intergroup relations are predicated to be more prevalent in communities with pronounced multiform heterogeneity than in comparatively homogeneous ones (T-12.1). Status differences are expected to influence social relations less in communities where education, income, and power are weakly correlated than in those where they are strongly consolidated (T-12.21). Comparative studies of the communities in a society can be carried out, describing variations in their social structure, and testing the implications of the theory.

The structure of society comprises the structure of interrelations among and those within its substructures. Communities are not the only substruc-

---

1. Both the preceding and the following propositions apply to any local subunit; that is, communities may be defined more broadly than towns and cities to encompass entire metropolitan areas or more narrowly to refer to neighborhoods.

tures of societies, but they are particularly important ones, owing to the significance of the territorial distribution of people for their social relations, notwithstanding the mitigating influence of modern means of transportation on the significance of physical propinquity. For any form of differentiation, one can examine the extent of differentiation within and that among communities. Thus, one can analyze the extent of income inequality within various communities, and one can compare income differences among communities, including both how communities compare on the basis of average incomes and on the basis of internal variations in incomes. The degree of differentiation in the entire society can be decomposed into that within and that among communities. For instance, the division of labor in society can be decomposed into two parts, the amount of division of labor resulting from occupational differences within the various communities, and the amount resulting from the occupational differences among communities.

The influence of any form of differentiation in society on social associations can be correspondingly decomposed into the influence on social associations resulting from the differentiation within and that resulting from the differentiation among communities.[2] For example, the influence of society's ethnic heterogeneity on intergroup relations is the product of the influences the ethnic heterogeneity within communities and the influences ethnic differences among communities exert on intergroup relations. The effect of the correlation between parameters on the social relations in society can be also decomposed into two parts resulting from the concomitant variations of the parameters within and among communities, respectively. Thus, the effect of the correlation between race and income on social associations can be decomposed into the influence of the income differences between whites and blacks within various communities on their social relations and the additional influence resulting from the underrepresentation of blacks in the more affluent communities.

The problem posed now is *not* what influences various forms of differentiation within communities have on social associations. These influences have already been stipulated in the theorems advanced, which apply to the structure of communities as well as that of societies, as has just been mentioned. The question raised now is whether differentiation within its

2. The term *decomposition* is used generically to refer to decomposing the influence of a structural condition on social processes into those influences exerted by the conditions within substructures and that exerted by the relationships among them. In other words, the independent variables are partitioned to decompose their influences. The empirical procedure that would probably be used in most cases is analysis of variance or analysis of covariance rather than that used in path analysis to decompose a correlation coefficient into its various path coefficients. (But the within-group variance is of substantive interest, not merely a criterion to determine the statistical significance of the differences between groups.) I have throughout used the term *correlation* for any association between variables, whether the Pearsonian correlation coefficient or a nonparametric measure of association is most applicable, in order consistently to distinguish associations between variables from the social associations among people, which are often one of the variables.

communities or differentiation among them influences the social relations in society more, and this question is raised for various aspects of differentiation—heterogeneity, inequality, consolidation of differences. For example, heterogeneity tends to increase intergroup relations; does heterogeneity within or heterogeneity among communities increase them most? Inequality tends to reduce associations between different strata; does inequality within or inequality among communities reduce them most? Answers to these questions can be deduced from the propositions that have been advanced.

Concern, then, is with the analysis of a social structure in terms of its substructures, specifically, with the influences exerted on processes of social association by various aspects of differentiation within and among the substructures constituted by the communities in a society. Most social associations occur within communities, not among communities, owing to the strong influence of physical propinquity on social associations. One would therefore anticipate that (1) social associations are more strongly influenced by structural differences within communities than by structural differences among them. Thus, (2) great income differences among individuals and families within communities would be expected to depress the rates of associations between members of different economic strata more than do the differences in average incomes among communities. Similarly, one would expect that (3) income differences between whites and blacks within communities (the within-community correlations of race with income) inhibit the social associations between the two groups more than does the fact that more affluent communities contain disproportionately few blacks (the ecological correlation). Finally, since much heterogeneity increases and much inequality decreases the likelihood of social associations between persons in different social positions, one would anticipate that (4) the extent to which the two forms of differentiation occur within rather than among communities also has opposite consequences for these social associations.

Actually, all four of these plausible expectations are wrong. The opposite is the case with respect to every one of them: (1) Social differentiation within communities does not have as adverse an effect on social associations as do social differences among communities. Hence, (2) inequalities within communities inhibit social associations less than inequalities among communities. (3) The correlation of group differences with inequalities in society inhibits intergroup relations less if it results from the concomitant variation (correlations) within communities rather than that among communities (the ecological correlation). And although pronounced heterogeneity promotes and pronounced inequality inhibits associations between persons in different social positions, (4) whether either form of differentiation occurs primarily within or among communities exerts parallel, not opposite, influences on these associations.

Despite the fact that most social associations occur within communities, group and status barriers to social associations within communities inhibit them less than such barriers among communities. The apparent paradox results from the influences of the spatial distribution on social associations. Group and status barriers to social associations within communities are attenuated by the counteracting effect of physical propinquity, whereas group and status differences among communities constitute barriers to social associations that are reinforced by spatial segregation. This follows from the proposition that the segregation of groups and strata impedes social relations among their members (T-13.1). When group or status differences exist primarily *among* communities, this entails much spatial segregation among groups and strata, which reinforces the inhibiting effect of the social differences. In contrast, social differences that exist primarily *within* communities indicate that groups or strata are not physically separated but live in the same localities, which increases opportunities for social associations among their members. Among-community social differences are consolidated with and reinforced by physical distances, while within-community social differences intersect with the spatial distribution, and the intersection of parameters promotes associations between persons in different positions (T-12).

The more society's differentiation in terms of any parameter results from the differentiation within rather than among communities, the more probable are intergroup relations both in terms of this parameter and among different communities (T-25). The greater propinquity implied by within-community differences promotes associations between persons in different social positions (T-13), and the common social positions of persons in different communities promote associations among communities (A-1), on the assumption that parameters and the spatial distribution exert some independent influences (A-11). The more widely groups or strata are distributed among the various communities, the greater are the constraints on their members to associate with persons in different positions in their own communities and with persons in their own group or stratum in different communities. T-25 is the general formulation, and a number of corollaries are derived from the same three propositions (A-1, A-11, T-13). A still more general theorem (T-26) will be formulated in the next section of this chapter, under which all of the theorems about differences within and among communities can be subsumed.

The more society's heterogeneity in terms of a nominal parameter results from the heterogeneity within rather than that among communities, the more probable are intergroup relations both in terms of this parameter and among different communities (T-25.1). Heterogeneity promotes intergroup relations because it increases the chances that fortuitous encounters involve members of different groups, but primarily if the various groups live in the same locations. Chance encounters of physically segregated groups largely involve members of the same group, which diminishes the likelihood of intergroup associations. Moreover, the dispersal of group members entailed by greater within-community heterogeneity promotes social associations among different communities, because many ingroup relations involve persons from different communities. On the other hand, the concentration of various groups in different places entailed by greater among-community heterogeneity implies fewer social associations among different communities, because this situation obviates the need to cross community boundaries to maintain extensive ingroup relations. Heterogeneity that exists primarily within and not among communities fosters social associations both among the heterogeneous groups and among different communities, but the intervening social mechanisms that produce these two effects are not exactly the same. The probability of social associations among the parameter-delineated groups is increased by the greater statistical chances of social contacts between members of different groups, whereas the probability of social associations among different communities is increased by the greater constraints group dispersal exerts on crossing community boundaries to maintain ingroup relations. These constraints are greatest for small groups, and so are the probabilities that chance encounters within communities involve a person from another group.

The smaller the size of a group, the greater are the probabilities that much heterogeneity within rather than among communities increases its members' rates of association with persons in other groups and with those in different communities (T-25.11). Regardless of how great the religious heterogeneity of communities is, Protestants, as the majority group, have much opportunity to associate with other Protestants in their community. But a small minority, like Jews, are much constrained by the religious heterogeneity of communities to associate with Christians in their own communities and with Jews in other communities, particularly if the community in which they live is small. The size of the community affects these probabilities, just as the size of the group does. *The smaller the size of a community, the greater are the probabilities that much heterogeneity within rather than among communities increases its inhabitants' rates of association with persons in other communities and with those whose social position differs from their own* (T-25.12). Both of these propositions are essentially equivalent to the one previously formulated, that small size in terms of one parameter promotes intergroup relations in terms of this and other parameters (T-14.1), or rather, they are special cases of it applied to the territorial distribution among communities. For territorial distributions, despite some distinctive features, can be considered for most purposes as distributions among social positions, that is, as parameters.

The more society's inequality in terms of a graduated parameter results from the inequality within rather than that among communities, the more probable are social associations both among different strata and among different communities (T-25.2). If society's income inequality, for example, is largely the result of much inequality among and little within communities, it implies that socioeconomic strata are segregated in different places; if it is primarily the result of much inequality within and little among communities, it implies that differences in income intersect with difference in location. When status distance and physical distance more or less coincide, their inhibiting effects on social associations reinforce each other, but the more they intersect, the more their effects on social associations counteract each other, with propinquity's influence mitigating that of status distance and status proximity's mitigating that of physical distance. Although inequalities within communities inhibit social associations, they do not inhibit them so much as inequalities that are reinforced by residential segregation among strata. The segregation of groups or strata among different communities lessens the chances of social contacts between their members, and segregation consequently reinforces the negative effect of inequality on interstratum relations but counteracts the positive effect of heterogeneity on intergroup relations.

The constraints of within-community differentiation are greatest for the elite, owing to its small size, just as they are greatest for small groups generally. *The probabilities of the elite's association with persons in different strata and different communities are more increased than those of other strata by much inequality within and little among communities* (T-25.21). This is most likely for elites in small communities, which are especially small, but it also becomes increasingly likely for the elites in large communities the narrower the criterion for defining elite, since a narrower criterion circumscribes a smaller elite. T-25.21 implies that the top elites of various communities are most likely to have extensive social relations, which is a special case of the proposition that extensive social connections are likely among various small elites generally (T-14.31). The elites of different communities as well as other elites tend to be united into a dominant elite of society.

The more the consolidation of two parameters in society results from their concomitant variation within rather than that among communities, the greater are the probabilities of associations among members of different groups, different strata, and different communities (T-25.3). This complicated theorem derives from the same principles as the preceding ones. In brief, although the consolidation of parameters inhibits intergroup and interstratum associations, it inhibits them less when it is not further reinforced by segregation among different communities, and the absence of such reinforcement is implied by the concomitant variation of group and status differences within rather than among communities. When two social attributes of individuals are substantially correlated within communities but the two averages for communities are hardly correlated, it implies that great individual variations with respect to these correlated attributes exist within most communities, and that the persons who share these attributes are distributed among many communities. If these conditions exist (as they do when parameters are consolidated within but not among communities); and if physical proximity (T-13) and social proximity (A-1) exert independent influences (A-11) on social associations; it follows that associations among persons who differ in the two social attributes are promoted by their physical proximity in the same communities; and that social associations among communities are promoted by the social proximity of persons who share these attributes and live in different communities. The theorem can also be derived from the proposition that two intersecting parameters promote intergroup relations in terms of both (T-12), by considering the consolidated two parameters as a single parameter and the spatial distribution as the other intersecting parameter.

This theorem reveals the paradox in its most dramatic form: Consolidated social differences strongly inhibit social associations, and most social associations occur within communities, not among them; yet the stronger the consolidation of social differences within communities relative to that among communities, the smaller is their inhibiting influence on social associations, and the more they promote social associations among different communities as well. To repeat, this does not mean that consolidated status differences within communities do not discourage social associations, only that correlated status differences that are further consolidated by differences in location discourage them still more. For example, the correlation between education and income in society may result primarily from one of two conditions: (1) strong correlations of education and income within most communities, with unrelated small differences in average education and average income among communities; (2) most people with much education and high incomes live in some communities, and other communities differ similarly with regard to both education and income of inhabitants, but most communities are internally homogeneous, and the minor variations that exist in incomes and education are essentially uncorrelated.

The first case represents consolidation of education and income within communities, the second consolidation resulting from concomitant variations among communities. In the first situation, although the combined educational and income differences inhibit social associations substantially, this is mitigated by the physical propinquity of different strata, which promotes associations among their members within communities (particularly for the members of high strata in small communities); and the common interests of persons with similar education and income located in various places promote associations among different communities. In the second case, social associations among different strata are not encouraged by propinquity but discouraged by physical distance, and common educational and socioeconomic interests foster social associations largely within communities, whose inhabitants share these interests, and not among different communities, whose members tend to differ in these respects.

In sum, society's structural differentiation of all kinds promotes social relations among different groups, strata, and communities more, or inhibits them less, if it characterizes the internal conditions in communities than if it pertains to differences among communities. This is the case for heterogeneity, which itself increases the likelihood of intergroup relations, and for inequality, which itself decreases the likelihood of interstratum relations, and it is also the case for consolidated social differences. Differentiation among communities entails segregation of groups and strata, which depresses intergroup relations. Two aspects of the population's territorial distribution affect social relations in different ways. Whereas population density reinforces the influences of any condition correlated with it on intergroup relations, whether these influences are positive or negative, segregation—that is, differentiation among communities—inhibits intergroup relations, whatever the influences of community conditions on these relations. To be sure, much differentiation among communities tends to increase the homogeneity within them, as indicated by the second illustration above, which is likely to raise the prevalence of social associations within these communities and make them more cohesive than are more heterogeneous and differentiated communities, like the ones in the first illustration. But this prevalence of ingroup ties in homogeneous communities of a heterogeneous society is precisely what undermines macrosocial integration by attenuating intergroup relations—among communities, among other groups, and among strata. The integration of the various segments of a heterogeneous society depends on communities that are not very homogeneous, not highly cohesive, not largely self-contained in their social life.

Penetrating Differentiation

Society's ecological structure is rooted in the natural environment, and its importance is attributable to these roots. Geographical conditions and natural resources affect where people settle, what resources are available to them, and which settlements grow, though the influences of physical conditions are modified by the technology and organization people have developed to deal with their environment. The ecological structure may be said to mediate the influences of the physical environment on people's social relations. A basic principle governing the mediating process and responsible for the significance of the ecological structure is that opportunities for social associations depend on physical propinquity (T-13). This principle implies that the intergroup relations in society are profoundly affected by the spatial distribution, specifically, by the extent to which various groups and strata are dispersed among the same communities or segregated among different ones

(T-13.1). The preceding analysis of society's structure in terms of its sub-structures took advantage of the special significance of territorial distributions by defining substructures on the basis of territorial communities.

This analysis can be extended in two ways. First, several successive levels of substructure, instead of merely one, can be taken into consideration. Thus, a nation's differentiation can be decomposed into that within and that among its provinces, that within and that among towns, that within and that among neighborhoods. Second, the principles of substructural analysis can be generalized to apply to groups of any kind, not only territorial ones. The substructures of society's structure can be defined on the basis of any nominal parameter, and the total structural differentiation in terms of another parameter, or combination of parameters, can then be partitioned in order to decompose its influences on social associations into that of the internal differentiation of groups and that of the differentiation among groups. For example, the labor force can be divided on the basis of place of work, and society's division of labor can be decomposed into that within and that among work organizations, and further into that within and that among the divisions and the subdivisions of work organizations, in order to dissect the influences of these various aspects of the division of labor on social associations. Society's labor force can also be divided into major occupational groups, detailed occupations, and specialties within them to analyze income—or educational or other—differences within and among these successive levels of occupational substructures and discern the influences of these structural conditions on social relations. The three criteria substructures should meet for a general theoretical analysis of the penetration of differentiation into them are: having boundaries, being ordered, and having successive levels.

The conception of substructure implies that society is partitioned into subunits with more or less distinct boundaries. Since nominal parameters delineate groups with distinct boundaries, whereas graduated parameters do not, it is preferable to define substructures on the basis of a nominal parameter. This is not a hard and fast rule, however. Substantive considerations may prompt one to ignore it and to analyze the substructures of graduated strata, notwithstanding the arbitrary divisions made in classifying strata. Besides, the empirical status distribution may reveal discontinuities which make it possible to distinguish hierarchical strata that are not arbitrary. Still, nominal parameters are generally preferable to graduated ones for defining substructures.

However, the groups circumscribed by nominal parameters not only have distinct boundaries, which makes them suitable criteria of substructures, but also are unordered, which makes them unsuitable for theoretical analysis. To formulate theoretical generalizations requires analytical terms that comprise ordered categories, as pointed out in chapter 1. Hence, nominal subunits of society, such as communities or occupations, must be reconceptualized and transformed into ordered categories for purposes of theoretical analysis. One procedure for doing so is to classify them on the basis of analytical properties and examine the relationships between these properties, for instance, between community density and social contacts. Another procedure is to use the boundaries of nominal social categories, ignoring their substantive content and unique labels, as criteria of substructure to partition the relationships between other analytical properties of social structure into their relationships within and among substructures. Such a decomposition of the influences of differentiation on social relations within and among communities has been carried out in the preceding section.

The analysis is now extended to the significance for social life of the extent to which society's differentiation penetrates into its substructures, including not only territorial but also other substructures. There may be much ethnic heterogeneity in cities yet little in neighborhoods; great educational differences may exist within major occupational groups while there is little educational variation within occupational specialties. The decomposition question—how much of society's differentiation occurs among and how much within substructures—can be raised for successive levels of substructure, although only for nominal parameters with successive subdivisions (or possibly for graduated parameters). Although intersecting subdivisions are most distinctive of the complex structures of industrial societies, as suggested in chapter 6, there are important successive subdivisions in modern societies, notably territorial-political units, occupations, and work organizations, but also others, such as religion, unions, and large voluntary associations. In these cases the principle that differentiation can be partitioned into that among and that within substructures can be applied to several levels of substructure. For example, income differences can be compared among and within states, among and within counties, among and within towns, among and within neighborhoods.

The further society's differentiation penetrates into successive subunits of its structural components, the more it promotes the integration of groups and strata by increasing the social associations among their members (T-26). This is the most general theorem formulated about substructures. It follows from A-1, A-11, and T-12: Intersecting parameters promote social associations among different groups and strata (T-12), as proximity in terms of each fosters social associations (A-1), if their influences are, at least partly, independent (A-11); and further differentiation implies that otherwise consolidated social differences are intersecting. For example, if political affiliations differ much among states but little within them, party differences do not penetrate deeply into the territorial structure, and differences in politics and in location intersect only on the state level. If there are great differences in voting among communities but not within them, party differences penetrate more into the territorial structure and intersect with it on a further level. If there are great differences in voting among neighborhoods though not within them, political differences penetrate still further and intersect still more with differences in location, but still not so much as if there were also great political differences within neighborhoods. Another illustration: Income differences may be greater either among occupational groups or within them; either among detailed occupations or within them; either among narrow specialties or within them. For every comparison of levels, penetration of differentiation into substructures implies more differentiation within than among these substructures; more intersection of this form of differentiation with social positions in these substructures; and consequently greater constraints to engage in intergroup relations.

The more differentiation penetrates into the interstices of society, the more it contributes to intergroup relations. Although differentiation inhibits social relations, what appears like superficial differentiation inhibits it most, that is, differentiation that remains on the surface of other social differences and does not penetrate them. Whatever differences in education exist in society, they impede intergroup relations most if they largely coincide with differences among the major groups of society, because then they are reinforced by these group differences and in turn reinforce them. In contrast, were educational differences to exist mostly within, and not among, primary groups, the strong primary-group ties (T-19) would promote associations among persons whose education differs, and common education interests (A-1) would promote intergroup relations.

Differentiation within substructures, not among them, implies that the parameter defining the substructures and the parameter defining the differentiation intersect, whereas differentiation among substructures, not within them, implies that these two parameters are consolidated. Hence, the decomposition principles follow from the more general proposition that low correlations of parameters promote and high ones impeded intergroup relations (T-12). Specifically, T-12 entails T-25, that differentiation in society that exists largely within rather than among communities promotes intergroup and intercommunity relations, because differentiation within and not among communities means that such differentiation intersects with community affiliation. T-12 also implies T-26, that the deep penetration of differentiation into substructures promotes intergroup relations most, but here something additional is introduced. The new principle is that differentiation primarily within substructures on one level may constitute differentiation primarily among substructures in terms of the next level. Great socioeconomic differences within cities, involving internal differentiation and intersection, are often accompanied by comparatively small socioeconomic differences within neighborhoods, involving much differentiation among substructures and little intersection of status and location when this further level of subdivision is taken into consideration.

The criterion of penetrating differentiation is the narrowest subdivision for which the variation among individuals *within* substructures cannot be largely accounted for by the variation *among* substructures. For example, if a person's ethnic affiliation cannot be predicted within a certain margin of error from knowing in which community she lives, but can be from knowing in which neighborhood she lives, ethnic differentiation penetrates into communities but not into neighborhoods. The depth of penetration of income differences into the occupational structure is indicated by whether the individual incomes can be predicted, within specified limits, on the basis of information about people's major occupational group, or only from information about their detailed occupation, or only with data on their occupational specialty, or not even then.[3]

The further society's heterogeneity penetrates into successive subunits of its structural components, the more it promotes the integration of groups by increasing their intergroup relations (T-26.1). This theorem is a corollary of T-26, as are the others in the series formulated below. A well-known illustration is the ethnic heterogeneity of cities that does not penetrate into neighborhoods, which remain more or less homogeneous ethnically. This situation, notwithstanding the publicity given to backlash demonstrations, is predicted to increase social associations among ethnic groups not so much as ethnically mixed neighborhoods do, though more than ethnically segregated cities would. If blacks and whites work for the same companies, there is some opportunity for social interaction among them, though not much if they work in different departments. For heterogeneity to exert its full impact on enhancing intergroup relations, it must penetrate deeply into the substructures of society.

The homogeneity of wide social circles in a heterogeneous society attenuates intergroup relations and thus impedes macrosocial integration (T-26.11). The great width of homogeneous social circles implies that the existing heterogeneities do not penetrate them and that the parameters defining heterogeneity and the one circumscribing the social circles are highly correlated. If fraternal orders and clubs are ethnically homogeneous, the opportunities they provide for sociable companionship restrict social intercourse among different ethnic groups. Work organizations with educationally homogeneous employees, like plantations and universities, strengthen the barriers to social associations among different educational groups. The greater ease of sociable relations in homogeneous social circles tends to undermine the integration of groups in a heterogeneous society, the more so the wider the homogeneous social circles are.

The further society's inequality penetrates into successive subunits of its structural components, the more it promotes the integration of social strata and groups by increasing the social associations among their members (T-

<hr>

3. The criterion of penetrating differentiation can be based on predicting from subunit means either the total variation among individuals in society or their variation within subunits only. Variations among individuals are necessarily predicted better (or as well) from the means of narrower subunits than from those of broader subunits encompassing the narrower ones.

26.2). Although inequalities inhibit social relations, the deep penetration of inequalities into substructures minimizes this inhibition and even stimulates social relations among different strata, as well as among the substructures. Paradoxical as this may appear, it is evident by now that the counteracting influences of the affiliations in the substructures explain the paradox. The strong social ties in the nuclear family result in frequent social associations, despite great educational differences between parents and children, and even if there are also great ones between husband and wife, but great educational differences between distant cousins are likely to inhibit extensive social association. Penetrating inequalities imply inequalities within narrow subunits and virtual equality among them, that is, little difference in average social status among subunits. If all inequalities were to exist within the narrowest social circles—within work groups, within occupational specialties, within neighborhoods, within religious congregations—penetrating differentiation would be at a maximum, all these groups would be equal, and the strong social ties of their members would counteract the inhibiting influence of status differences on social associations, while the common interests of persons in similar status would promote intergroup relations. This is not possible, of course. The axiom that status distance inhibits social relations (A-1.2) implies that intimate primary groups rarely form among persons whose status differs much in several respects. The imaginary polar case is simply designed to show why and how the penetration of status inequalities counteracts their inhibiting effect on social associations. It is possible for people whose income differs to live in different cities, or in different neighborhoods of the same cities, or in the same neighborhoods, and whichever is the case will influence the likelihood of social associations among them.

The approximate equality of wide social circles in a society where inequality prevails inhibits social relations among groups and strata and thus impedes their integration (T-26.21). Given the existing inequalities, small status differences within groups imply large status differences among groups, which inhibit social associations among both the groups and the strata. The smaller the income differences within occupations, the greater are those among them, given the existing income differences in society, and these consolidated differences in occupational and socioeconomic interests greatly discourage social associations. If not only neighborhoods but entire suburbs of a metropolitan area are socioeconomically stratified, with each being composed largely of persons in the same socioeconomic stratum, the chances of social associations among different strata are much diminished.

The further the consolidation of parameters in a society penetrates into successive subunits of its structural components, the more it promotes the integration of groups and strata by increasing the rates of social association among their members (T-26.3). This paradox parallels that of T-26.2, and it is resolved in the same way. Consolidated parameters inhibit social associations among persons in different social positions, but they do so less, or even promote their associations, when counteracted by the close relations within narrow subgroups.

For instance, if the correlation between education and income can be largely accounted for by differences in occupation, the consolidation of education and income penetrates less into the occupational structure than if the correlation is not reduced much by controlling occupation. Penetrating consolidation implies that within most occupations the best educated have the highest incomes, but differences among occupations in average education and earnings are nearly uncorrelated. Under these conditions, common occupational interests encourage associations in unions and professional associations among persons whose education and income differ, and common educational and economic interests encourage associations among persons in different occupations. Less penetrating consolidation implies greater correlated differences in education and income *among,* and smaller uncorrelated differences in them *within,* occupations. Occupational differences more nearly coincide with educational and income differences in this situation, and this stronger consolidation of a third with two other parameters implies that the inhibiting effects of the first (occupation) and the other two (education and income) do now not counteract but reinforce each other, in accordance with the principle that consolidation inhibits intergroup relations of all kinds (T-12).[4]

The general principle is that the penetration of consolidated parameters into substructures reduces their consolidation with the parameter delineating the successive substructures, and this reduction in triple consolidation diminishes the inhibiting effect on social associations. To furnish one more example of this principle of penetrating differentiation: When the senior members of most clubs tend to have most prestige, without much correlation between average age and prestige among clubs (penetrating consolidation), the age-prestige differences inhibit social associations less, owing to the companionship within clubs, than when some clubs have older members with high prestige and others have younger members with low prestige (less penetrating consolidation), as differences in club membership combine with those in age and prestige to depress social intercourse. Moreover, associations between age mates and prestige peers produce more social connections among different clubs in the former situation than in the latter.

The intersection of parameters within broad social circles when these parameters are consolidated in society at large inhibits social relations among groups and strata and thus impedes their social integration (T-26.31). This is

4. Greater variation of two parameters within the narrow subunits of a third parameter than among these subunits, which entails deeper penetration, does not necessarily involve a stronger, or a weaker, correlation of the first two parameters themselves. Two parameters can be substantially correlated without covarying much within subunits, or without covarying much among subunits, though obviously not without either.

perhaps the most paradoxical theorem, inasmuch as intersecting parameters are the major structural condition that promotes integrative relations among groups and strata. But it is the complement of T-26.3, and rests on the same grounds. To illustrate: Fewer blacks than whites in American society are affluent (consolidation). If one assumes that income essentially determines where people live, the result would be that few blacks live in rich and many in poor areas, with no relationship between race and income within each area (internal intersection). This situation would inhibit social associations between blacks and whites, among socioeconomic strata, and among neighborhoods more than if the neighborhoods did not differ in proportion of blacks and average incomes, although this would inevitably mean—given society's racial income differences—a strong correlation between race and income within areas (internal consolidation or low intersection). Another example involves the sex differences in income in the country at large (consolidation). When the women's movement will be successful, men and women will earn the same in most or all occupations (internal intersection). But as long as women are disproportionately in lower-paid and men are disproportionately in high-paid occupations, the social relations at work between the sexes would not increase much. Indeed, they would increase less than if women were equally represented in most occupations though there were still income differences for the same work between them and men (internal low intersection), because in this situation the influence of common occupational positions would counterbalance rather than reinforce the influence of income differences. Intersecting parameters promote social relations, unless their intersection within subgroups occurs at the expense of their greater consolidation with subgroup differences.

The homogeneities and equalities within the subgroups of a heterogeneous society with substantial inequalities promotes a preponderance of ingroup relations, thereby furthering subgroup cohesion at the cost of greater fragmentation of society (T-26.4). This theorem subsumes T-26.11 and T-26.21 and simultaneously specifies that the stronger subgroup bonds are at the roots of the greater fragmentation of society. The prevalent ingroup relations in homogeneous and approximately equal social circles inhibit social associations not only among these social circles but also among persons whose positions differ in terms of the parameters defining the homogeneity and inequality within the social circles. Thus, ethnic homogeneity and income equality of work groups tends to discourage social associations among work groups, among ethnic groups, and among income strata. The broader the social groups are that preserve homogeneous peer relations by refusing social access to persons whose social position differs from theirs, the more fragmented society becomes.

Primary groups are typically homogeneous and exhibit little inequality. The significance of social proximity for social relations (A-1), particularly close and intimate ones, implies this. But the intersection of parameters makes it likely that even primary groups, notwithstanding their homogeneity and equality in many respects, are heterogeneous and unequal in some. Work groups are not completely homogeneous and not devoid of any status differences, friends do not have all social attributes in common, and neither do spouses. However, the generally low variability of social attributes within primary groups implies that most of the total correlations of parameters in society are the product of their concomitant variation (correlation) among rather than within primary groups, be they families, close friends, work groups, neighborhoods, or religious congregations. Hence, three basic attributes of primary groups impede intergroup relations—their homogeneity (T-26.1), their relative equality (T-26.2), and the low correlations of parameters within them (T-26.3). The resulting lesser intergroup relations are the cost of the greater ease of social intercourse among a small group of homogeneous peers.

The expansion of homogeneity from narrow to broad social circles is what particularly endangers the macrosocial integration of society. For the greatest obstacles to intergroup relations that integrate society result from the homogeneity of large groups, not that of small ones (T-26.11, T-26.21, T-26.31); the homogeneity of inner cities and suburbs, not that of individual households; the homogeneity of work organizations, not that of work groups; the homogeneity of occupations, not that of work teams or colleague friendship cliques. Comparatively great homogeneities and small inequalities in major segments of society produce consolidated status and group differences among them that impede their integration through social associations. But the social conditions in large segments of society, which are often formally organized, tend to be more amenable to being changed through formal social action, such as legislation, than the more intimate relations in the multitude of primary groups. Legislation that increases the heterogeneity and inequality within major components of society thereby reduces the consolidation of group and status differences. Antidiscrimination laws, if properly enforced, have these effects. Such legislation serves not only the interest of the particular groups that have been discriminated against but is also in the interest of society at large, as it averts its fragmentation and sustains its integration.

Compendium

T-23   The probability of associations with many different persons increases with the increasing size and population density of the community. (From T-13; based on A-9.)

T-23.11 The probability that people have wide circles of acquaintances increases with the increasing size of the community where they live. (From T-13; based on A-9.)

T-23.12 The probability that people have wide circles of acquaintances increases with the increasing size of the place where they work. (From T-13; based on A-9.)

T-23.2 The probability that people have wide circles of acquiantances increases with the increasing urbanization of society. (From T-13; based on A-9.)

T-23.3 The probability that people have wide circles of acquaintances increases with the increasing concentration of society's labor force in large work organizations. (From T-13; based on A-9.)

T-23.4 Urbanization is a catalyst of social associations, which probably has a multiplier effect on the influences exerted by the conditions associated with it on social relations. (From T-23; based on A-9.)

PA-15 A community's size and density are directly correlated with its heterogeneity.

T-23.5 The probability of intergroup relations increases with increasing size and density of the community. (From PA-15, T-11; based on A-9.)

T-23.6 The probability of extensive intergroup relations in a society increases with its urbanization. (From T-23.4, T-23.5; based on A-9, PA-15.)

T-23.7 The probability of interpersonal conflict between members of different groups increases with increasing size and density of the community. (From PA-13, T-23.5; based on A-9, PA-15.)

T-23.71 The probability of interpersonal conflicts between the groups in a society increases with increasing urbanization. (From T-23.4, T-23.7; based on A-9, PA-13, PA-15.)

T-24 Efficient means of transportation reduce the influence of propinquity on social associations. (From A-9, T-13.)

T-24.1 The widespread use of efficient means of transportation improves the integration of different communities in society by raising the rates of social association among them. (From A-9, T-13.)

PA-16 The availability of efficient means of transportation depends on financial resources.

T-24.2 Ceteris paribus, the influence of physical propinquity on the social relations in a society is inversely related to its wealth. (From PA-16, T-24; based on A-9.)

T-24.3 The influence of physical propinquity on the social relations of individuals is inversely related to their income. (From PA-16, T-24; based on A-9.)

T-24.4 Ceteris paribus, the influence of physical propinquity on the social relations in society is directly related to the degree of income inequality. (From PA-16, T-24; based on A-9.)

T-25   The more society's differentiation in terms of any parameter results from the differentiation within rather than that among communities, the more probable are intergroup relations both in terms of this parameter and among different communities. (From T-26; based on A-1, A-11.)

T-25.1   The more society's heterogeneity in terms of a nominal parameter results from the heterogeneity within rather than that among communities, the more probable are intergroup relations both in terms of this parameter and among different communities. (From T-26; based on A-1, A-11.)

T-25.11 The smaller the size of a group, the greater are the probabilities that much heterogeneity within and little among communities increase its members' rates of associations with persons in other groups and with those in different communities. (From T-26, T-14.1; based on A-1, A-11.)

T-25.12 The smaller the size of a community, the greater are the probabilities that much heterogeneity within and little among communities increase its inhabitants' rates of association with persons in other communities and with those whose social positions differ from their own. (From T-26, T-14.1; based on A-1, A-11.)

T-25.2   The more society's inequality in terms of a graduated parameter results from the inequality within rather than that among communities, the more probable are social associations both among different strata and among different communities. (From T-26; based on A-1, A-11.)

T-25.21 The probabilities of the elite's association with persons in different strata and different communities are more increased than those of other strata by much inequality within and little among communities. (From T-26, T-14.31; based on A-1, A-11.)

T-25.3   The more the consolidation of two parameters in society results from their concomitant variation within rather than among communities, the greater are the probabilities of associations among members of different groups, different strata, and different communities. (From T-26.3; based on A-1, A-11.)

T-26   The further society's differentiation penetrates into successive subunits of its structural components, the more it promotes the integration of groups and strata by raising the rates of association among their members. (From A-1, A-11, T-12.)

T-26.1   The further society's heterogeneity penetrates into successive subunits of its structural components, the more it promotes the integration of groups by increasing intergroup relations. (From T-26; based on A-1, A-11.)

T-26.11 The homogeneity of wide social circles in a heterogeneous society attenuates intergroup relations and thus impedes macrosocial integration. (From T-26.1; based on A-1, A-11.)

T-26.2   The further society's inequality penetrates into successive subunits of its structural components, the more it promotes the integration of social strata and groups by increasing the rates of association among their members. (From T-26; based on A-1, A-11.)

T-26.21   The approximate equality of wide social circles in a society where inequality prevails inhibits social relations among groups and strata and thus impedes their integration. (From T-26.2; based on A-1, A-11.)

T-26.3   The further the consolidation of parameters in a society penetrates into successive subunits of its structural components, the more it promotes the integration of groups and strata by increasing the rates of social association among their members. (From T-26; based on A-1, A-11.)

T-26.31   The intersection of parameters within broad social circles when these parameters are consolidated in society at large inhibits social relations among groups and strata and thus impedes their social integration. (From T-26.3; based on A-1, A-11.)

T-26.4   The homogeneities and equalities in the subgroups of a heterogeneous society with substantial inequalities promotes a preponderance of ingroup relations, thereby furthering subgroup cohesion at the cost of greater fragmentation of the society. (From T-26; based on A-1, A-11.)

CHAPTER EIGHT

Work Organization

THE DIVISION OF LABOR AND THE DISTRIBUTION OF POWER ARE TWO forms of social differentiation of great importance. Having examined social differentiation in general terms in most of this book, attention now turns to these two particular forms of crucial significance for social life. The organization of society's work through the division of labor is analyzed in this chapter, and power and its implications for conflict will be discussed in chapter 9.

How society's work is organized can be looked at from two perspectives: that of the occupations among which work is divided, and that of the organizations among which work is divided. Work organizations are all organizations, public and private, composed of members who are employed to perform work, as distinguished from voluntary associations, like unions or clubs, whose members are not employees, though they may have a small employed staff. One could speak of the division of labor among work organizations as well as that among occupations, but the term is usually reserved for the distribution of the labor force among occupations, and it is used in this restricted sense here. However, a central theme of the analysis is the significance of work organization for the division of society's labor among occupations.

The five main topics of this chapter are (1) the contrasting forms the division of labor assumes; (2) the conditions that further the division of labor's development; (3) a critical analysis of Durkheim's thesis that the functional interdependence generated by the division of labor is the source of the integration of modern society; (4) the influences the division of labor among and within work organizations exerts on social associations; and (5) the implications of the division of labor for various forms of inequality.

Forms of Division of Labor

The division of labor is a form of heterogeneity, but of a special sort. It is defined by a nominal parameter—occupation—which has successive subdivisions, and which is substantially correlated with several graduated parameters. Occupations differ in training and skills, perquisites and prestige, income and authority. On the basis of the status differences among them, occupations can be ranked, thereby creating a new parameter of occupational status. But the degree of status inequality so measured is distinct from the extent of the division of labor, which refers to the distribution of the labor force among many different occupations, ignoring the status differences among them. The operational criterion, as that of other forms of heterogeneity, is the statistical probability that two randomly chosen persons have different occupations. This probability, and thus the empirical measure of the division of labor, depends on how narrowly occupations are defined, and when the division of labor is advanced only detailed occupations furnish an accurate indication of the degree of division of labor.[1] (A simpler indicator of the internal division of labor in organizations is the number of occupational positions.)

The importance of space and time as dimensions of social life is illustrated by their implications for the division of labor. The spatial distribution of people is closely connected with the subdivision of work among them. "The division of labor varies in direct ratio with the volume and density of societies," according to a central thesis of Durkheim's (1933, p. 262). The concentration of many persons in one place increases opportunities for communication among them (as implied by T-23), and the distribution of tasks among different persons depends on such opportunities. Time, too, is intimately connected with the way tasks are distributed and the form assumed by the division of labor. Organizing work involves subdividing it, and tasks can be divided among people or among time periods or among both. These differences in organizing principles produce basic differences in the nature of the work and the form of the division of labor.

Complex jobs can be simplified by dissecting them into the various tasks they entail and organizing these tasks so that attention can concentrate on

---

1. The measure of division of labor is the index of heterogeneity: $\Sigma x_i^2/(\Sigma x_i)^2$, where x_i is the number of persons in an occupational category, and the sums are taken over all occupational categories. The division of labor in the United States increased steadily from .919 in 1900 to .990 in 1970, so measured, using detailed occupations (computed from data in U.S. Bureau of the Census 1960, pp. 75–78, and 1973, pp. 718–24). But if major occupational groups instead of detailed occupations are used as the categories, the increases in occupational heterogeneity are concealed after 1930; the values are .784 for 1900, .897 for 1930, and .869 for 1970. The reason is that some of the formerly small major occupational groups have started to expand beyond their proportional share of the labor force, notably "professional, technical, and kindred workers," and "clerical and kindred workers." Detailed occupations reflect the continuing increase in division of labor within these and other major occupational groups.

Among Persons

	Repetitive	Variable
Repetitive	1. All same routine	3. Routinized division of labor
Variable	2. All same craft	4. Specialized division of labor

Among Time Periods

FIGURE 4.   TASK VARIABILITY

one at a time. When an individual works alone, she simplifies a complex job by dividing it into parts and doing one at a time. This is what we do when we multiply two large figures, build a model airplane, or carry out an individual research project. But when several or many persons work on a complex job, it can be simplified in two ways, either by dividing tasks among different persons, or by dividing them among time periods of the same persons. The difference is in which of two dimensions—social space and time—tasks vary much and in which they do not. In one case different persons perform different tasks, but each performs the same repetitively throughout the day; in the other case different persons perform the same tasks, but the work of each is variable throughout the day.[2] If the overall job is quite simple it may not be divided in either dimension, and if it is very complex, it tends to be divided in both.

The cross-classification of task variability in two dimensions—among persons and among time periods—yields four prototypes of the organization of work (figure 4), which represent polar instances of empirical variations by degree in the two dimensions. Two of the four polar types involve no division of labor, and the other two indicate the two main forms of the division of labor:

1. If there is no variation in tasks either among persons or over time, all perform the same repetitive routines.
2. If tasks do not vary among persons but are variable over time, all persons perform the same diverse work, as illustrated by a crew of skilled workers in the same craft.

2. This conception of task repetition either among different workers or among different time periods is the result of discussions with Phelps K. Tracy.

3. If tasks vary among persons but each repeats the same over time, the division of labor is in the form of routinization, for instance, when skilled jobs are broken into simple routines on an assembly line.
4. If tasks vary both among persons and over time, the division of labor is in the form of specialized expertness; an illustration is the substitution of medical specialists for general practitioners.

The two major forms of division of labor are the subdivision of work into repetitive routines and its subdivision into expert specialties. Only the simplest kinds of jobs remain undivided and uniform both among persons and among time periods. A minimum of work complexity entails either jobs that are variable over time or a division of labor among persons into repetitive routines. Complex work often entails variability in both dimensions, a division of labor among diverse specialists each of whom performs diverse tasks. The division of labor in either form narrows the range of tasks of all or most jobs. However, when jobs are divided into repetitive routines, the training and skills needed to perform them are reduced, whereas when they are divided into fields of specialists, the narrower range of tasks permits greater expertness to be acquired and applied to the work, increasing the training and skills required to perform it. Specialists can perform tasks that would not be possible without the expertness attainable in a narrower field, as exemplified by theoretical high-energy nuclear physicists and brain surgeons. The division of labor among specialists narrows the range of tasks of individuals and thereby expands the range of tasks that can be accomplished in the society.

The two forms of the division of labor have opposite consequences for the competence needed to perform the work. Routinization lowers and specialization raises the training and skills required of the work force. But more thorough knowledge of complex responsibilities is necessary in order to organize them into simple routines than in order to perform them, and additional administrative proficiencies are necessary to coordinate the diverse routines. To build a car requires less engineering knowledge than to organize an automobile factory where cars can be built largely by workers with little skill, and the latter also requires administrative knowledge. The professional understanding and judgment of experts must be superseded by more precise knowledge of complex responsibilities before they can be organized into simple routines that can be carried out with little training and skills. This implies that the routinized form of the division of labor tends to be accompanied by great differences in training and skills, and quite likely also in income and authority, between a small staff of technical and administrative experts and a large complement of mostly unskilled and semiskilled workers.

The organization of complex responsibilities into simple routines reduces training time and labor cost. Hence, routinizing work is a means for increasing input-output efficiency and producing more with given manpower and economic resources. For example, by routinizing some of the work of physicians to enable nurses to perform it, expanded health services can be provided by the existing work force without a rise in cost. Whereas expert specialization gives rise to new accomplishments and thus improves the quality of the results that can be achieved, routinization enlarges the quantity of the results that can be achieved with given manpower resources. The division of labor in the form of routinization makes it possible to manufacture complex products with a largely untrained labor force, but it simultaneously wastes the actual as well as potential skills of workers by not taking advantage of them. The main impetus for the routinizing form of the division of labor is a concern with reducing labor cost and raising efficiency. Such a concern is characteristic of the managements of work organizations, whose decisions are governed by budgetary considerations, especially in profit-making enterprises but also in other work organizations, such as government agencies and hospitals. These economic pressures engender extensive routinization of work in large factories and offices.

The division of labor in work organizations that operate under budgetary restraints may give rise to a bifurcation of skills. Employing specialists is costly, and routinizing work reduces labor cost. Accordingly, advances in the division of labor in the form of routinizing more jobs reduce labor cost and thus free resources for hiring more specialists. These considerations suggest the hypothesis that the proportion of an organization's personnel with high skills and the proportion with low skills are positively correlated, as both increase with the advancing division of labor. Actually, this hypothesis of a bifurcation of skills was inferred from research findings on government agencies, which indicate that the proportion of routine clerical personnel is positively related to the division of labor and, independently, to the superior qualifications of the professional personnel (Blau and Schoenherr 1971, p. 218–19). The bifurcation hypothesis was lent some support by the finding from a study of universities and colleges that the academic division of labor is positively related to both superior qualifications of the faculty and a high proportion of clerical personnel (Blau 1973, pp. 71–72, 82–83).

However, recent research on 110 American factories fails to support the hypothesis that the division of labor engenders a bifurcation of skills.[3] A pronounced division of labor in these manufacturing establishments is posi-

3. The study is based on a sample of 110 New Jersey manufacturing establishments. For a brief description of research procedures, see Blau et al. (1976). The measure of division of labor used in earlier research on work organizations is the raw number of different occupational positions; but in this study of factories, both this raw number of positions and the measure of occupational heterogeneity were used, and the findings reported are those using the latter measure. Actually, the number of occupational positions, controlling size, exhibits similar relationships with other organizational characteristics as the measure of occupational heterogeneity. I acknowledge with thanks grant Soc-71-03617-A05 from the National Science Foundation, which supported this research.

tively correlated with the proportion of professionals (.39) and negatively with the proportion in the most routine manual jobs (−.22); these relationships persist when other conditions are controlled; and the correlation between the professional and the routine-manual component is negative (−.20), in contrast with the positive correlation predicted by the bifurcation hypothesis. But there is evidence of a bifurcation of skills within the white-collar sector of factories. The division of labor is positively correlated with both the proportion in professional (.40) and the proportion in routine clerical jobs (.52), and the proportionate size of these two personnel components—the most and the least trained among the white-collar workers—is positively correlated (.49), with the partial correlation when size (log.) and division of labor are controlled remaining positive (.36).

Although these data are cross-sectional and therefore do not demonstrate a causal sequence of variables, the inference derivable from them is that the causal sequence assumed in the original hypothesis of a bifurcation of skills should be reversed. The original hypothesis assumed that the savings in manpower cost effected by routinization supply the resources for employing costly specialists. This assumption implies that extensive routinization of manual jobs in factories, since it reduces labor cost, increases the employment of professional specialists; but the empirical evidence contradicts this implication. If the causal assumption is reversed, the findings in factories as well as the earlier ones can be explained. Costly specialists are a valuable manpower resource that must not be wasted by assigning to them routine duties that less trained and less costly personnel can perform. The more costly specialists are employed by an organization, the more less trained workers who can relieve costly specialists of routine work tend to be employed also. Clerks relieve professionals of routine duties, but unskilled manual workers do not. A bifurcation of skills appears to result from the influence many specialists in a work organization have on the employment of many persons who perform the routine duties that otherwise specialists would perform, not from the influence the savings realized by routinization have on the employment of specialists. This interpretation can explain why the bifurcation of skills in factories is confined to the white-collar sector, and it can also explain the earlier observations of bifurcation of skills, since these were made in empirical studies of white-collar organizations—government agencies and academic institutions.[4]

4. An alternative—or possibly complementary—interpretation suggested by Judith R. Blau explains the finding that the bifurcation of skills is confined to white-collar work on the basis of the difference in the power positions of white-collar and blue-collar specialists. It is in the interest of any group of specialists not to be robbed of their training investments and of the social utility of their expertise by a division of their jobs into simpler ones which can by performed by less trained personnel. The main threat does not come from completely unskilled positions (laborers or clerks) but from those with intermediate qualifications (semiskilled operatives for skilled workers and paraprofessional technicians for professionals). The more powerful positions professionals occupy have enabled them more successfully to resist the division of

The division of labor in large work organizations tends to result in large numbers of employees in relatively routine jobs and small numbers in jobs requiring specialized training and skills. This is how the subdivision of work effects savings in labor cost. The number of employees per position, as well as the total number, is typically larger for routine than for specialized work. In the manufacturing establishments studied, for instance, the average number of production workers per position is 5.3 and the average number of nonproduction workers per position is 2.1. Although the difference between production and nonproduction is not identical with that between routine and skilled work, since craftsmen in production are more skilled than clerks in nonproduction, three-quarters of the production workers are not skilled and only one-third of the nonproduction workers are clerks, so that the difference roughly indicates the greater subdivision of less routine work. One reason may be that minor differences in routine duties are less likely than those in specialized duties to be officially recognized and assigned distinct formal positions. Another reason undoubtedly is that the volume of various specific kinds of routine work is greater than that of specific kinds of specialized work.

When the division of labor remains predominantly in the form of routinization, it cannot become very advanced. Whereas the subdivision of work into simple routines entails an increase in the division of labor, as a single craft is replaced by several unskilled jobs with narrower duties, further increases in the division of labor depend on the expansion of specialized work that requires expert training and skills. Greater expertness tends to involve more specialized expertness. Since the volume of work in routine jobs is generally larger than that in specialized jobs, prevailing routinization implies an uneven distribution of persons among occupational positions, with many in more routine and few in more specialized ones. For this distribution to become less uneven requires that the more routine occupational groups contract and the more specialized ones expand. A reduction in routine work and an expansion of less routine work produce a more even distribution. Such a shift toward a less uneven occupational distribution increases the division of labor, by definition (unless accompanied by a considerable decline in number of occupations, which is unlikely). The division of labor in the United States has become more advanced in recent decades largely as the result of the growth of the smaller technical and professional occupations and the decline in size of the larger unskilled and semiskilled

labor, maintain their monopoly of knowledge and skills, and obstruct attempts of paraprofessionals to perform part of their work (Freidson 1970). But craftsmen, with less powerful positions than professionals in organizations and in society, were not able effectively to oppose the inroads of the division of labor into their sphere of competence, which was often divided into semiskilled as well as unskilled jobs. This difference in the power to prevent somewhat less skilled occupations from taking over part of one's own job can account for the bifurcation of skills in white-collar and its absence in blue-collar work.

occupations. In brief, whereas routinization is a form of division of labor, the most advanced division of labor entails a reduction in routinized work and a growth of specialized work.

Conditions for the Division of Labor

The evolution of the division of labor depends on a surplus of manpower resources. As long as the efforts of most people are needed to supply food and other means of subsistence, few can be spared for different work. A minimum of technological and economic development is essential to lift these restraints and free the time of substantial numbers for a variety of special pursuits. Early stages of the division of labor may have their roots in differences in resources and power, which enable some persons to reserve the less arduous tasks for themselves and force others to perform the harder labor. This conjecture is consistent with Udy's (1959) finding that a rudimentary division of labor—three or more different operations carried out concurrently—in nonindustrial societies is positively correlated with a status hierarchy of at least three levels. Although Udy's interpretation of the finding is that the need for coordinating the different tasks gives rise to a bureaucratic hierarchy, the alternative causal sequence suggested, that the status differences lead to the differentiation of jobs, is equally plausible. The dominant position of males in nearly all cultures is also likely to have some bearing on the division of labor by sex, which Murdock (1937) observed in all 224 tribes surveyed, and which typically assigns to men jobs that are more interesting (as well as farther from home), like hunting and fishing, and leaves to women the more tedious work, like grain grinding, water carrying, cooking, and gathering fuel and vegetables.

An advanced division of labor depends still more than early stages of its development on a surplus of manpower and resources, because it entails a growth of expert specialties that requires substantial investments. The lengthy training necessary to become a specialist makes it impossible for specialization to expand unless society can afford to relieve many young people from work for many years to undergo training, and to relieve numerous others from contributing directly to production in order to provide the training. Indeed, even routine jobs in comtemporary societies require some special skills, such as literacy and arithmetic, and thus quite a few years of schooling for everybody. Furnishing this education and training demands economic resources. Kuznets (1966, p. 190) notes that "modern economic growth has been accompanied by a substantial rise in the age of entry into the labor force."

Technological advances and industrial developments further the division of labor by raising labor productivity and thereby freeing manpower resources for specialized training and work. Besides, industrialization concentrates large numbers of people in cities and factories, which provides the opportunities for extensive communication that foster the division of labor, as Durkheim (1933) stresses. Cross-national data on fifty contemporary societies reveal that the degree of industrialization of a country, as indicated by the proportion of the labor force not in agriculture, is highly correlated with the division of labor (.85).[5] One might suspect that this very high correlation is partly produced by the fact that variations in agricultural work are less likely than those in industrial work to be reflected in distinct occupational categories recognized by a country's census. But any lesser subdivision of farming cannot affect the reported correlation, because the measure of division of labor is based on the distribution of the labor force among ten major occupational groups, only one of which is agriculture ("farmers, fishermen, hunters, loggers, and related occupations"). Industrialization results in the movement of growing numbers out of agriculture into numerous other major occupational groups and a great variety of detailed occupations within them, and it consequently greatly enhances the division of labor.

Large work organizations—factories, government bureaus, private offices—play an important part in the advancement of the division of labor. They are institutionalized mechanisms for organizing work on a large scale in the pursuit of given objectives. They bring large numbers of employees together, and their administrators have the responsibility and the authority to organize the work by subdividing it, and to provide explicit channels of communication that make extensive subdivision feasible. Large work organizations also have the resources to implement new technological knowledge by installing modern production equipment, which contributes to the industrialization on which advances in the division of labor depend. The stipulated objectives of organizations, such as a factory's product, a government agency's mission, or a corporation's profit, specify the nature of the output, supplying criteria for defining efficiency and creating budget constraints to minimize labor cost. An organization's division of labor is administratively enacted as a means to improve operations in terms of specified ends, in contrast with the division of labor in society at large, which is the emergent result of the actions of many people pursuing diverse ends. These conditions are likely to result in an extensive division of labor, particularly in the form of much routinization to reduce labor cost, unless substituting machines for routine workers can reduce labor cost still more.

To trace in summary fashion the intricate connections among social con-

5. The measure of division of labor is occupational heterogeneity, based on ten major occupational groups, computed from data in the *Yearbook of Labour Statistics* (1972). The problems encountered with measuring the division of labor on the basis of broad categories in the United States (see note 1 in this chapter) are unlikely to distort the international comparisons substantially, because most countries have only small proportions of their labor force in expanding occupations, and because the variation in the values of the measured division of labor is so great, ranging from .23 to .83. These results and others cited later have been obtained in a preliminary analysis of cross-national data carried out by Zeev Gorin and myself. The major source of these data is Taylor and Hudson (1971).

ditions that contribute to the development of the division of labor: Technological advances may well be essential for the development of the division of labor, because technical improvements in methods of work raise labor productivity and free manpower for diverse pursuits and for the training needed for specialized work. Of particular importance has been the technical progress in methods of agriculture throughout history—from digging sticks and hoes to harvesting combines and artificial fertilizers—which has furthered the division of labor by recurrently reducing the proportion of the population occupied with producing the basic necessities of life. As growing proportions of the labor force have moved from agricultural to industrial work, technological changes in industrial production have assumed increasing importance for the division of labor, which has magnified the significance of large work organizations. The managements of these organizations have the resources and interests to implement advances in technological knowledge by translating them into new methods of industrial production, as a means for improving efficiency by raising labor productivity. They also have the interest and authority to institute an extensive subdivision of work into simple routines, as another means for improving efficiency by lowering labor cost per output.

The consequent increasing routinization of work in industry contributes to the increasing mechanization of work. For the more routinized work has become, the easier it is to have it done by machines. Routinization creates the conditions that enable work organizations to mechanize and automate operations, and improvements in the methods of manufacturing machines reduce the cost of technical equipment and thus make it economically advantageous to mechanize and automate ever wider spheres of operations. As machines are substituted for more and more men and women performing routine jobs, growing proportions of the work force are engaged in skilled and specialized work. An example is the finding that automating operations in government offices reduces the proportion of personnel in routine clerical jobs (Blau and Schoenherr 1971, pp. 60–61, 83–94, 123–24). At the same time, the rising labor productivity resulting from technical improvements in industrial production makes it possible to shorten the working lives of people and extend their years of education and training, which furnishes the trained labor force without which the proportion in skilled and specialized occupations could not increase. Earlier industrial developments promoted large-scale routinization (as illustrated by mass-production methods), at least in part because when these developments occurred the labor force had little training and few industrial skills. These earlier advances in production methods, by raising labor productivity, helped to increase the schooling and training of the labor force, which combined with subsequent advances in production methods (as illustrated by chemical processing and automation) to diminish the proportion of workers in routine and unskilled and expand that in skilled and specialized jobs. Widespread routinization has been a

stage in the development of the division of labor, and its further development apparently reverses the trend and entails growing specialization.

Two plausible assumptions imply most of these influences on the division
of labor, though not all the complex interconnections among the developments that affect it: *The division of labor depends on opportunities for communication* (PA-17). *An advanced division of labor depends on substantial
training of the labor force* (PA-18).

*Opportunities for communication and association promote the division of
labor* (T-27). The theorem is entailed by PA-17 and used simply to link this
assumption to other theorems that can be derived from it. *Population density
increases the division of labor* (T-27.1). This theorem follows from T-23 and
T-27, that population density increases association opportunities and that
such opportunities further the division of labor. It is Durkheim's main thesis
of the causes of the division of labor. The concentration of large numbers of
persons promotes the division of labor, which therefore is more pronounced
in urban than in rural places. Durkheim's thesis has a corollary for societies,
which also follows from T-23 and T-27: *A society's increasing urbanization
increases its division of labor* (T-27.11). Both historical trends and cross-
national comparisons support this inference. The proportion of the American
population living in cities with more than 25,000 inhabitants has increased
from 31 to 45 percent between 1910 and 1970, and occupational differentiation has steadily increased during that period in the United States.[6] Cross-
national data reveal similarly that the proportion of a country's population
living in cities with more than 20,000 inhabitants and the division of labor are
substantially correlated (.64; based on 61 cases).

Conditions other than population concentrations that influence the
chances for communication and association also affect the development of the
division of labor, according to T-27. A society's linguistic heterogeneity inhibits communication among various parts of the population. Consequently,
linguistic heterogeneity impedes the development of the division of labor
(T-27.2). Cross-national data indicate the predicted negative correlation
between linguistic heterogeneity and division of labor (−.33; 56 cases).
However, Lieberson and Hansen (1974) conclude that the corresponding negative relationships between linguistic heterogeneity and economic development (GNP per capita and other indicators) is spurious, owing to the fact that
newer nations are both more heterogeneous linguistically and less developed
economically than older ones. This raises the question of whether the negative correlation between linguistic heterogeneity and division of labor is not
also the spurious result of differences in both between the developing newer
nations and the more industrialized older ones. But this does not seem to be
the case. Controlling a nation's age since independence does not reduce the

6. From .919 to .990; see note 1 in this chapter.

negative correlation between linguistic heterogeneity and division of labor, because age is entirely unrelated to divison of labor (.003; 63 cases).

The widespread use of efficient means of transportation promotes the development of the division of labor (T-27.3). The theorem follows from T-24.1, that efficient means of transportation promote social associations across physical distances, and T-27, that the division of labor depends on opportunities for association. Cross-national data indicate that a society's division of labor is positively correlated with the extent of railroad travel (passenger kilometers per square kilometer, .35; 40 cases) and with the proportion of the labor force in the transportation and communication industry (.74; 59 cases). Are these relationships the result of differences in economic development which find expression in differences in both transportation facilities and division of labor, or do extensive means of transportation influence the division of labor independent of differences in economic conditions? Economic conditions influence both transportation and the division of labor, and controlling economic differences reduces the correlations, but transportation facilities seem to influence the division of labor independent of economic differences, as indicated by the persisting partial correlations when gross national product per capita is controlled (for railroad travel, .27; for workers in transportation and communication, .64). Another implication of T-27 is that *improved efficiency in means of communication promotes the division of labor* (T-27.31).

Rising levels of education and skills promote an advanced division of labor (T-27.4). The theorem follows from PA-18, that an advanced division of labor depends on substantial training of the labor force. The level of education of the American population has increased dramatically since the beginning of this century, and so has the proportion of the labor force in the most highly skilled professional and technical occupations,[7] concomitant with the advances in the division of labor previously noted. These relationships cannot establish that a trained labor force affects advances in the division of labor, because other trends occurred at the same time, for example, economic growth. The cross-national data reveal the same relationships, and here it is possible to check whether they are spurious, owing to the influences of economic development. The correlation of the population's educational level and the division of labor in a society is .73 (64 cases), [8] and the partial correlation with economic conditions (GNP/cap.) controlled re-

7. The median years of school completed has increased from 8.2 at the beginning of this century to 12.6 in 1970. The first figure is estimated and the second computed from U.S. Bureau of the Census (1960, p. 215, and 1973, pp. 1623–24). The increase in "professional, technical, and kindred workers" has been more than threefold, from 4.3 to 14.5 percent, between 1900 and 1970 (U.S. Bureau of the Census 1960, p. 74, and 1973, p. 718).

8. The measure of education is the adjusted school enrollment ratio, the proportion of the estimated population 5–19 years of age who attend school (see Taylor and Hudson 1971, pp. 39–40).

mains .61. The correlation between proportion of the male labor force in professional or related occupations and the division of labor is .55 (65 cases), and the partial correlation with economic conditions controlled is .31. Although controlling additional conditions might reduce these correlations further, it seems unlikely that doing so would reduce the strong persisting relationship between education and the division of labor to close to zero. The findings indicate that superior levels of education and qualifications probably enhance the division of labor, in accordance with T-27.4.

Technological and economic developments greatly stimulate advances in the division of labor because they give rise to various conditions that promote these advances—urbanization, efficient means of transportation and communication, and the shortening of working lives that permit the lengthy schooling and training necessary to acquire specialized skills. Society's division of labor is positively correlated with its technological development, as indicated by energy consumption per capita (.51; 64 cases); its economic developments, as indicated by GNP per capita (.50; 65 cases); and, as already noted, especially with its industrial development, as indicated by the percent of the labor force not in agriculture (.85). It is noteworthy that the correlations of the division of labor with indicators of technological and economic developments, though substantial, are considerably lower than its correlations with industrial development and with the population's education (.73). This suggests that the influences of technological and economic developments on the division of labor are largely mediated by the spread of industrialization and by the rising levels of education they make possible.[9]

Large work organizations promote the division of labor in society (T-27.5). The theorem follows from T-27.1, that population density promotes the division of labor, since large work organizations concentrate many persons in one place. It is also implied by T-27, that the division of labor depends on opportunities for communication, since work organizations furnish formal channels of communication among employees. Moreover, large work organizations are instrumental in transforming advances in technological knowledge into expanding industrialization, which furthers the division of labor. When such roof organizations as corporations or government departments are very large, they tend to be composed of subsidiary organizations with different functions—plants, establishments, divisions, bureaus— and the roof organization's division of labor exists partly among and partly within the specialized subsidiaries. Research on subsidiary organizations shows that their size is strongly correlated with the number of occupational positions but not with the distribution of employees among these positions

9. The measure of industrialization (nonagricultural labor force) and education are so highly correlated (.80) that problems of multicollinearity make it inadvisable to estimate their separate effects on the division of labor. The simple correlations make it evident that the influence of industrialization is greater than that of education.

(Blau 1974, pp. 323–48; Rushing 1976, p. 686; Blau et al. 1976, p. 25). The reason for the lack of correlation between size and the more refined measure of internal division of labor probably is that the division of labor among specialized subsidiaries limits the occupational heterogeneity within them. Plants where only garments that have been cut elsewhere are sewn do not need designers and cutters.

Both the occupational differentiation among and that within organizations increase society's division of labor. The expansion of corporations and government agencies in this century may well have contributed to the concurrent increase in the division of labor. There are no cross-national data on organizations, but an indirect indication of large work organizations in a country is the proportion of its labor force in administrative, executive, and managerial occupations. The positive correlation of this proportion with the division of labor (.55; 65 cases) persists when GNP per capita is controlled (.35), which suggests that the prevalence of large work organizations in a country furthers its division of labor.

Interdependence Reconsidered

The division of labor in society is the basic cause of organic solidarity, according to Durkheim, which is the social solidarity characteristic of industrial societies. The mechanical solidarity characteristic of simple societies rests on the "beliefs and sentiments common to the average citizen of the same society...; one may call it the *collective* or *common conscience....* The part that it plays in the general integration of society evidently depends upon the greater or lesser extent of the social life which the common conscience embraces and regulates" (Durkheim 1933, pp. 79, 109). The division of labor restricts this source of social integration by making people's activities and beliefs less alike, but simultaneously engenders interdependence and thereby a new source of social integration (Durkheim 1933, p. 131):

> In effect, on the one hand, each one depends as much more strictly on society as labor is more divided; and, on the other, the activity of each is as much more personal as it is more specialized.... This solidarity resembles that which we observe among the higher animals. Each organ, in effect, has its special physiognomy, its autonomy. And, moreover, the unity of the organism is as great as the individuation of the parts is more marked. Because of this analogy, we propose to call the solidarity which is due to the division of labor, organic.

Much of Durkheim's theory has been incorporated in the assumptions and theorems presented about the division of labor. An important exception is the significance he attributes to functional interdependence for social integration (a term Durkheim [1933, p. 109] uses synonymously with solidarity and cohesion). The main causal assumptions of Durkheim's theory, schematically represented, are: volume of society—population density—frequent social interaction—division of labor—interdependence—organic solidarity. The assumption questioned is that the functional interdependence among different occupational groups is the intervening link between division of labor and social integration. Of course, if interdependence is considered to be the defining criterion of social integration, one cannot argue that the two are not related. But here social integration has been defined differently, on the basis of extent of social associations, and for societies as frequent direct associations among persons in different groups and strata. This criterion of social integration does not seem to be entirely foreign to Durkheim's analysis, and one might consider it to be implicit in his discussion, although interaction frequency enters his causal scheme explicitly at an earlier point. In any case, if social integration is not defined as interdependence but independently in terms of actual intergroup associations, it raises the questions of whether the division of labor promotes social integration and whether interdependence is the intervening variable that increases integrating social associations among the members of diverse groups.

The interdependence among occupational groups performing different functions naturally requires some social associations among some members of different occupations, but much less than is often implicitly assumed by envisaging everybody continually buying and selling things. The interdependence between migratory farm laborers and bank presidents—reflected in the first's car loan and the second's grapes—clearly does not engender face to face associations between them, and the same is true for much occupational differentiation and interdependence, though not for all, of course. There is no direct social contact between most persons performing different functions in complex society, despite their interdependence, because major functions are divided among organizations and their interdependence finds expression in transactions between organizations, not individuals. To be sure, business transactions of organizations involve face-to-face associations between persons, but not among most persons in the organizations. They entail direct social interaction primarily among managers who represent their organizations in negotiations with others, for instance, in a firm's negotiations with suppliers, government agencies, or unions. Thus, one type of role relation that entails face-to-face associations resulting from interdependence is that between managers who represent organizations in their business transactions. Two other role relations, which are more frequent, also involve direct associations rooted in occupational interdependence, namely, that between salesperson and customer, and that between supervisor and subordinate, including the employer-employee relation in relatively small firms.

Much of the economic interdependence resulting from occupational differentiation is unilateral dependence of some persons on others, as illustrated by employer-employee relations and by all relations between superiors and subordinates in work organizations. The underlying principle is that occupational differences are correlated with differences in status and social resources, which makes the persons in occupations with meager resources dependent on those in occupations with great resources. To be sure, the corporation president is dependent for his welfare on all his employees, but not on any single one of them, whereas the welfare of each of them depends on him, which makes him essentially independent of any one of them and each of them greatly dependent on him. Economic dependence on many is essentially independence, except when they engage in concerted action. (The best explanation of this is Knight's [1933] principle of insurance). Durkheim (1933, p. 129) at one point takes note of the one-sided character of people's social relations under conditions of much occupational differentiation, when he contrasts mechanical and organical solidarity in the following words: "The first binds the individual directly to society without any intermediary. In the second, he depends upon society, because he depends upon the parts of which it is composed." But this is a mere hint of imbalance in social relations which he does not pursue. Unilateral dependence implies differences in power, which are unlikely to engender the voluntary attachments connoted by the concepts of social integration and social solidarity.

The assertion that the functional interdependence resulting from the division of labor strengthens social integration implicitly assumes (unless integration is defined as synonymous with interdependence) that interdependence fortifies the social ties between persons who perform different functions, which is questionable on two grounds: Economic interdependence often involves no social contacts, and it often entails unilateral dependence and power differences that discourage rather than encourage social intercourse. Moreover, if integration in societies with little differentiation is explained by the assumption that *common* social attributes promote solidarity, integration in societies with much differentiation should not be explained by simply discarding this assumption and replacing it by its opposite, that the interdependence of persons with *different* social attributes promotes solidarity; this is essentially what Durkheim does. There is no need to make this switch, because the assumption that common social attributes promote and different ones impede integrative social relations (A-1) can explain integration in highly differentiated societies, too, specifically the contribution the division of labor makes to macrosocial integration and the conditions on which that contribution depends.[10] Indeed, the influence of the division of

10. The fact that occupational interdependence generates some social associations between different occupations raises the question of whether the assumption that associations are more prevalent among proximate than distant positions (A-1) is tenable for occupations. Three role relations were mentioned above as frequently involving social interaction engendered by the interdependence of different occupations: salesperson-customer, managers of different organi-

labor itself, independent of other conditions, on occupational integration is implied by the even simpler assumption that social associations depend on opportunities for social contacts (A-9).

The advancing division of labor increases the probability of social associations among different occupations that integrate them in society (T-28). No assumption about the integrative effect of interdependence is required for this theorem. It follows from the proposition that heterogeneity increases the probability of intergroup relations (T-11), owing to the increased chances of intergroup contacts (A-9), inasmuch as the division of labor is defined as a form of heterogeneity, the heterogeneity of occupational groups. As social associations among different occupational groups become more frequent with the growing division of labor, group pressures discouraging these intergroup relations subside (A-10), which further increases their frequency. Since the division of labor is nearly always most pronounced in large cities, the higher probability of social associations there also increases the likelihood of associations among different occupations. However, these influences of occupational heterogeneity are modified or counteracted by status differences among occupations, which inhibit social associations.

Ceteris paribus, inequality in occupational status depresses the social associations among different occupations and thus their integration (T-28.1). This theorem is a corollary of the principle that social associations are impeded by inequality (T-7), which rests on the assumption that status distance discourages social associations (A-1.2). Variations in division of labor or occupational heterogeneity—how widely distributed people are among different occupations—can be distinguished, both theoretically and empirically, from variations in occupational inequality—how great the differences in status among occupations are. The former enhances while the latter impedes integrative relations among occupations. The degree of occupational heterogeneity has no necessary implications for the degree of occupational inequality in most respects, but it does for the inequality in training and skills.

The two main forms of the division of labor have different consequences for vocational qualifications. The division of labor among simple routines

---

zations, and superior-subordinate in an organization. The last two have social positions in common—being a manager, and belonging to the same organization, respectively—and it is plausible to assume that the common social positions account for the frequency of their social interaction. Moreover, this frequency depends greatly on how much the social intercourse between managers, or between supervisor and subordinate, extends beyond the bare minimum instrumentally required by their business transactions, which in turn depends on their having other social positions, attributes, and interests in common. Salespersons and customers do not necessarily share social attributes, although unless they do share some their contacts tend to be very fleeting. In any case, despite their frequent social contacts with customers, salespersons undoubtedly associate more with fellow salesmen and saleswomen than with customers in any particular occupation, though not more than with all customers. In the light of these considerations, the assumption seems tenable that the influence of occupational interdependence on extent of social intercourse is outweighed by the influence of social proximity (A-1).

entails a modicum of occupational heterogeneity and great differences in training and skills between a few experts and many workers in routine jobs. In contrast, the division of labor among specialists entails more occupational heterogeneity and smaller average differences in training and skills. Early stages of the division of labor, predominantly in the form of routinization, have equivocal consequences for the social associations among occupational groups, since the greater heterogeneity encourages and the greater inequality in qualifications discourages them. As the division of labor advances further, however, occupational heterogeneity continues to increase while inequality in training and skills diminishes, both of which promote associations among different occupations. Hence, the propositions that the probability of intergroup relations is increased by heterogeneity (T-11) and decreased by inequality (T-7) imply the following theorems: *The more the division of labor is in the form of specialization rather than routinization, the greater is the probability that high rates of associations among different occupations integrate them* (T-28.2). *The relationship of the division of labor with high rates of social associations among occupations is nonmonotonic, becoming unequivocally positive only at advanced stages of the division of labor* (T-28.3).

The division of labor influences the integration of groups and strata generally, not only occupational ones, but its influence on them depends on its relationships to other forms of structural differentiation, on the correlations of the occupational parameter with other parameters. Only when parameters are consolidated does the assumption that common social attributes foster and different ones impede social associations (A-1) imply that relations between persons with different attributes are rare. When parameters are intersecting, this very assumption implies relatively frequent relations between persons with different attributes (T-12). Hence, the same assumption can explain extensive ingroup relations in small collectivities with consolidated homogeneities (mechanical solidarity) and extensive intergroup relations in large collectivities with intersecting heterogeneities (organic solidarity). The division of labor tends to cut across other group affiliations, particularly extended kinship groups. As the division of labor advances, differences in the daily work attenuate bonds of extended kinship, and common occupational pursuits and interests unite members of different families, communities, religions, and ethnic groups. However, occupational differences are usually correlated with differences in status—in education, income, prestige, and authority. Thus, the division of labor is a parameter that seems to intersect with other nominal parameters but to be consolidated with graduated parameters. If this conjecture is correct, the principle that intersecting parameters promote and consolidated ones impede integrative relations among different social positions (T-12) implies that the division of labor contributes to the integration of many nominal groups in society but has the opposite effect on the integration of hierarchical strata.

The more the division of labor intersects with other nominal parameters, the greater is the probability that intergroup relations strengthen society's integration (T-28.4). *The more the division of labor intersects with kinship lineages, the greater is the probability that weaker bonds of extended kinship strengthen society's integration* (T-28.41). *The more the division of labor is consolidated with graduated parameters, the greater is the probability that infrequent social associations among strata weaken society's integration* (T-28.42). Whether the contributions the division of labor makes to the integration of various segments in society outweigh the adverse effects of occupational inequalities on that integration depends on the extent of consolidated status differences among occupations. An advanced division of labor with much specialization lessens some occupational inequalities, as we have seen, but not others, as we shall see. Occupational status differences are not the same in all societies, and great ones are not inevitable.

Organizations and Occupations

The division of labor in society at large is the result of some division of labor within its various work organizations and some among them. It is particularly important to take this into consideration in modern societies, where so much of the total work is carried out in large organizations. The influences of the division of labor on intergroup relations can be decomposed into the influences of the occupational differences within and those of the differences among work organizations, in accordance with the procedure developed in chapter 7 for decomposing effects of social differentiation within and among communities, and within and among groups generally. The following discussion illustrates the principle of penetrating differentiation by partitioning the division of labor first among work organizations and then among the subunits within them. One could also reverse the procedure: Instead of examining the penetration of the division of labor into organizational substructures, one could use the division of labor as a criterion of successive substructures and analyze how other forms of differentiation penetrate into occupational substructures, as has been briefly exemplified on page 179.

The more of society's division of labor results from that within rather than from that among its work organizations, the more probable are extensive intergroup relations among occupations and among organizations (T-29). *The more the inequality in administrative authority in society results from that within rather than from that among work organizations, the more probable are extensive social associations among administrative strata and among different organizations* (T-29.1). Both theorems derive from T-26, that differentiation within subunits promotes intergroup and interstratum associations. Although the division of labor and status differences among occupations have opposite effects on associations among occupational strata (T-28, T-28.1), like heterogeneity and inequality generally, the fact that they occur within rather than among organizations has the same effect of promoting these associations. Regardless of how great are the status differences among occupations, therefore, much occupational differentiation within work organizations and little among them promotes integrative social relations among various economic segments of society. The tendency of the division of labor within work organizations to be pronounced promotes intergroup relations.

The size of work organizations exerts two countervailing influences on intergroup relations, however. It is in *large* work organizations where differentiation tends to be most pronounced, but it is in *small* ones where internal differentiation promotes intergroup relations most, because internal heterogeneity exerts most constraints on intergroup relations in small substructures (T-25.12), be they place of residence or place of work. Previous research has shown that an organization's size and its structural differentiation have several opposite effects on its characteristics—for examples, on the size of its administrative component (Blau and Schoenherr 1971, pp. 297–329)—and the present theory indicates that they also have opposite effects on intergroup relations outside the organization. The greater the occupational differentiation within an organization and the smaller its size, the greater is the probability that its members associate with persons in other occupations and with persons in other organizations. Indeed, the small size of an organization exerts special constraints on intergroup relations generally (T-14). The same principle applies to small occupational groups, and to high administrative ranks within an organization, owing to the few incumbents of high ranks.

Much division of labor within organizations increases the probabilities of intergroup and interstratum associations of small occupational groups most (T-29.2). *Much division of labor within organizations increases the probabilities of intergroup and interstratum associations of high administrative ranks most* (T-29.21). *The smaller an organization, the more its internal division of labor increases the probabilities of intergroup and interstratum associations* (T-29.22). T-29.2 is a special case of T-14.1, that members of small groups are most likely to have cosmopolitan role sets. The division of labor in universities, for example, makes cosmopolitan role sets more likely for archaeologists than for chemists, and more likely for janitors than for faculty members. This naturally does not mean that janitors are more widely read and erudite, only that they are expected to be less parochial in their friendships. T-29.21 is a special case of T-14.31 (as is T-25.21), the tendency for various elites to become socially connected and united in a power elite. For senior administrators of organizations, the likelihood of social connections among them to develop is reinforced by their responsibility for negotiating the transactions between organizations required by economic interdependence. T-29.21 also implies that organizational managers associate more extensively than nonsupervisory employees with persons who differ in administrative rank. As a matter of fact, the pyramidal structure of formal organizations makes it inevitable that rates of association with other ranks increase on the average with increasing rank.

The greater the consolidated inequalities among occupations within work organizations relative to the occupational inequalities among the work organizations in society, the more probable are extensive intergroup relations among occupations and among organizations (T-29.3). The theorem follows from T-26.3, that the consolidation of parameters within rather than among subunits promotes intergroup relations. It is also implied by T-25.3, substituting place of work for place of residence. The paradoxical nature of these premises is apparent in T-29.3. Consolidated inequalities inhibit social associations (T-12.21), in organizations as in all other social structures, yet T-29.3 appears to assert the opposite. Actually, it does not. Consolidated inequalities within organizations inhibit social associations *more than no consolidated inequalities within organizations,* but they inhibit social associations *less than consolidated inequalities among organizations.* For the latter inequalities imply that the correlated differences in occupation and in status are further consolidated by correlated differences in place of work, which inhibits social associations more than if the combined occupational and status differences intersect with place of work, which is implied by their being consolidated within rather than among organizations.

Compare two societies with roughly the same differences in education and income among occupations, that is, roughly the same occupational inequalities: In one, most organizations have employees with a wide range of occupations and education; the educational differences *within* organizations are *correlated* with income differences; but the small differences in average education and average income *among* organizations are *uncorrelated.* In the other, most organizations employ only college graduates or only high school graduates or only persons with lower educational levels; there are *corresponding differences* in average incomes *among* organizations; but income *differences within* organizations are *unrelated* to the minor differences in education. The first situation represents consolidation of occupational inequalities within, the second among, organizations. Persons whose occupational status differs are more likely to associate with one another when they work in the same place (first situation) than when they work in different places (second situation), and common occupational, educational, and economic interests are more likely to lead to associations among members of different organizations—in unions, professional associations, or informally—when most who share these interests work in different (first) than when they work in the same organizations (second). Hence, occupational inequalities within rather than among organizations make social associations among different occupations and organizations more likely, as predicated in T-29.3, paradoxical as it seems. This is the case whether occupational inequalities are defined by one graduated parameter or, as in the illustration, by two (or more) consolidated ones. Two correlated parameters—in the illustration, education and income—that are correlated with occupational differences inhibit social associations still more if they are also correlated with organizational differences.

The same principles apply to the comparison of the division of labor within the departments of an organization and among its departments, since the proposition concerning the consequences of differentiation within and among subunits for social associations (T-26) pertains to subunits of any kind. Gulick (in Gulick and Urwick 1937, pp. 15–25) draws a distinction between organizing responsibilities into departments on the basis of "process," or the nature of the work performed, and on the basis of "purpose," or the end-product being made. Organization by work process—accounting, typing, legal service—involves mostly division of labor among departments; organization by purpose—disbursing unemployment insurance, providing employment services, collecting taxes—involves much division of labor within departments. *The more of an organization's division of labor results from that within rather than from that among its departments, the more probable are extensive social relations among departments and among occupational positions* (T-30). *The more the occupational inequality in an organization results from that within rather than from that among its departments, the more probable are extensive relations among departments and among occupational positions* (T-30.1).

In short, heterogeneous departments promote instrumental and sociable relations that help integrate the diverse employees and parts of an organization into a cohesive social structure. Whatever technical advantages organization by process may have, it tends to fragment an organization, whereas organization by purpose involving more division of labor within departments tends to contribute to organization integration. Once more it is apparent that internal homogeneity, which probably contributes to subgroup solidarity, impedes the integration of the larger social collectivity. Internal inequality, like internal heterogeneity, is a centrifugal force within subgroups which directs their social life outward and thereby helps to avert the threat of fragmentation that strong ingroup bonds otherwise pose for the larger collectivity. Consolidated inequalities within departments also constitute such a centrifugal force, as implied by the proposition that consolidated parameters within subunits promote intergroup and interstratum associations (T-26.3). *The greater the consolidated inequalities among occupational positions within departments relative to those among the departments in an organization, the more probable are extensive social relations among positions and departments* (T-30.2).

An organization's hierarchy of authority constitutes consolidated inequalities among positions—correlated differences in authority over subordinates, control over organizational resources, income, perquisites, training. These differences exist within departments. Administrative ranks cross-cut the horizontal division into departments. According to T-30.2, this leads to communications among different ranks within departments, which are the official channels of communication, and to communications among different departments of persons in similar ranks, which are required for coordination (notwithstanding the stereotype that all coordination occurs through vertical channels), and which include most informal associations of administrators. Care must be taken not to misinterpret the implications of T-30.2 for hierarchical communication. It does not imply that hierarchical differences among positions make communication more likely, only that hierarchical differences among positions *within* departments make communication more likely than such differences *among* departments. Hierarchical authority itself, like status distance generally, inhibits social associations, in accordance with A-1.2, which is why obstacles to communication are observable in hierarchies of authority (Crozier 1964). Decentralization of authority reduces status distances, but it also decreases the frequency with which superiors review the work of subordinates (Jaques 1956), which may counteract the effect implied by A-1.2 on formal communications, though not on informal ones. *Decentralization of authority in an organization increases informal associations among different administrative ranks* (T-30.3).

The principle that the penetration of differentiation into successive subunits promotes intergroup relations (T-26) implies that the division of labor within departments promotes intergroup relations outside the organization as well as within it. Occupational heterogeneity, inequalities, and consolidated inequalities within departments of various organizations are centrifugal forces that foster associations with persons in other organizations who have similar occupational, educational, and economic interests. However, these occupational differences within departments must be accompanied by substantial occupational differences among departments for them to lead to extensive associations among members of different organizations rather than primarily of different departments within the same organizations. When people can readily find associates who share their social attributes and interests in neighboring departments, though not in their own, their proclivity to seek associates elsewhere is reduced. The social and physical proximity of departments implies this (A-1, T-13). Penetrating differentiation is a centrifugal force for social associations, but how soon that force is spent depends on the degree of differentiation in the wider circles surrounding the narrower ones.

Deep penetration of differentiation is undoubtedly infrequent. The degree of variation among individuals is greater in wider circles than in narrower ones, and average differences are also often, though not necessarily, greater among wider than narrower circles. Cities are more heterogeneous ethnically than neighborhoods. Socioeconomic differences among individuals are greater in religious denominations than in congregations. The division of labor is more pronounced in entire organizations than in their departments, and there is very little division of labor within the smaller subunits of departments. The homogeneity of diverse subunits has structural effects that reinforce the preponderance of ingroup relations and thereby impede the integration of the subunits. This is so whether the subunits are diverse departments of an organization that are internally homogeneous; diverse neighborhoods that are internally homogeneous; occupations with great socioeconomic differences among and small ones within them; or any other diverse internally homogeneous groups. The homogeneity of groups in a heterogeneous environment makes intergroup relations rare, which engenders exchange processes and group pressures that discourage intergroup relations further (A-10). Thus, the homogeneity of departments in organizations with a pronounced division of labor has multiplicative effects on the preponderance of ingroup relations. So does the occupational homogeneity of an entire organization. As a matter of fact, A-10 implies such structural effects for homogeneity of any kind of diverse groups of any kind. Specifically, they are implied by the proposition that consolidated parameters have structural effects augmenting ingroup relations (T-21.11), jointly with the assumption that ingroup relations are prevalent (A-1.1), since internal homogeneity of diverse groups entails the consolidation of the parameter delineating the groups with the one defining the homogeneity.

The homogeneity of diverse groups has a structural effect increasing the preponderance of ingroup relations (T-31). *The occupational homogeneity of a work organization, given the division of labor in society, has a structural effect increasing the social associations within the organization* (T-31.1). *The occupational homogeneity of departments in an organization with substantial division of labor has a structural effect increasing the social associations within departments* (T-31.2). The homogeneity of diverse groups strengthens ingroup bonds of social cohesion at the cost of the integration of the groups in the wider collectivity. By the same token, internal heterogeneity generates a centrifugal force that has structural effects promoting intergroup relations, as they are being less discouraged by group pressures the more prevalent they become, which weakens ingroup bonds but improves the integration among groups.

Division of Labor and Inequalities

An important theoretical advantage of focusing on specific forms of differentiation rather than on differentiation generally is that it raises the issue of how one form of differentiation is related to others, an issue that does not arise as long as differentiation is conceptualized generically and particular forms of it are not distinguished. The preceding discussion has indicated that social associations are influenced by the relationships of the division of labor with the distribution of the labor force among work organizations and with status inequalities, which poses the issue of how these various forms of differentiation are related to one another. Specifically, how is the division of labor related to other forms of heterogeneity and to various forms of status inequality?

Such relationships between forms of differentiation must be clearly distinguished from the relationships of the underlying parameters, as already mentioned in chapter 5. The latter refers to the correlation of two attributes of individuals within a society—for example, the correlation between the occupation of persons and their education. The former refers to the correlation of two forms of differentiation of societies—for example, the correlation between the division of labor of various societies and the extent of educational inequality in them. Although occupational differences among individuals are strongly correlated with differences in their education and with differences in their incomes, this does not tell us whether and how variations in the degree of occupational differentiation, or the division of labor, among societies are correlated with variations in the degree of educational inequality and of income inequality in these societies. Unless all individuals have the same occupation or the same income, which is an unrealistic polar extreme, the extent to which the division of labor and income inequalities are correlated for societies cannot be deduced from the extent to which occupation and income are correlated for individuals within societies.

Concern in macrosociological comparisons is with attributes of societies, not with attributes of individuals. But attributes of individuals are the component elements that, in combinations, constitute attributes of the structure of societies. Information on the occupations of individuals yields a measure of society's occupational heterogeneity or division of labor. Data on the income of individuals yields a measure of society's average income as well as one of its income inequality (the extra measure being indicative of the fact that ordered categories supply more information than unordered ones). The correlation between the occupation and education of individuals yields another measure describing a society, the extent to which education and occupation are consolidated rather than intersecting. Comparative studies analyze the interrelations of the attributes of societies, what consequences some characteristics of societies have for their other characteristics. For example, we have examined the implications that differences among societies in inequality, heterogeneity, and consolidation have for the existing patterns of social associations. Now we ask how variations among societies in the division of labor, one form of differentiation, are related to their variations in other forms of differentiation.

Some of the relationships of the division of labor with other forms of differentiation have already been noted, and others have been implicit in the analysis. Thus, the proposition was advanced that society's linguistic heterogeneity is inversely related to its division of labor (T-27.2). Implicit in the theorem that society's urbanization increases its division of labor (T-27.11) are two relationships of the division of labor with other forms of differentiation. T-27.11 implies that the division of labor is directly related to rural-urban heterogeneity, which increases with increasing urbanization, except for societies where the majority already lives in urban places, which are still relatively rare. It also implies that the division of labor is inversely related to the heterogeneity of the population's place of residence, since urbanization means that a large proportion of the population lives in comparatively few large communities. Similarly, the theorem that the large average size of work organizations is directly related to the division of labor (T-27.5) implies an inverse relationship of the division of labor with heterogeneity of place of employment.

The division of labor in society is inversely related to some forms of heterogeneity and directly to others, and it is probably also inversely related to some forms of inequality and directly to others. Its inverse relationship with inequalities in training and skills is implied by the distinction made between its two major forms, routinization and specialization. The subdivision of work mostly into simple routines reduces the average level of required training and skills and creates great differences between a few experts who organize the work of others and many workers in unskilled jobs. During these stages of industrialization, the skills of many farmers and craftsmen become socially useless as they move into routine jobs in mass production. But with further advances in industrialization, machines replace growing numbers of men and women in routine jobs, so that the division of human labor entails increasing proportions of specialists who require substantial training and skills to monitor, repair, and build the complex mechanical and automated equipment, and to supply various services (Blau et al. 1976). If the proportion of the labor force in the least skilled jobs declines and that in more skilled jobs expands, it follows that the average differences in skills and in the training needed to acquire them diminish.

At advanced stages of the division of labor, increases in it diminish inequalities in education and qualifications (T-32). The theorem follows from T-9.3, that upward mobility of lower strata reduces inequality, and the definition of an advanced division of labor, which entails decreasing proportions of the labor force in jobs requiring least education and qualifications.[11] The training of the labor force and the division of labor undoubtedly exert mutual influences on each other, which are assumed to involve the following causal

---

11. Changes in the division of labor redistribute the labor force independent of the effects of fertility and immigration, which are therefore ignored in T-32, although taken into account in T-9.3. But T-32 does depend on the assumption (A-5) that highly specialized experts are outnumbered by persons in more routine jobs.

processes: An advanced division of labor depends on substantial training of the labor force (PA-18). Rising levels of education and skills promote the development of an advanced division of labor (T-27.4), because they furnish the manpower resources necessary for this development. But the levels of training and skills of the labor force do not alone determine the degree of division of labor and are not monotonically related to it, since skills may go unutilized, as is the case for various acquired skills not in demand when the division of labor takes predominantly the form of routinization. The advanced division of labor creates a demand for more qualifications, providing incentives for obtaining them, and it diminishes inequalities in training and qualifications by shifting the distribution of the labor force from more to less routine jobs.

Empirical data lend some support to the prediction implied by T-32 that the most advanced forms of division of labor in contemporary societies are inversely related to inequalities in education and in occupational qualifications. The increases in the division of labor in the United States during this century have been accompanied by a substantial reducation in educational inequality, as observed in two analyses of census data using different procedures (B. Duncan 1968, p. 619; Jencks 1972, pp. 20–21). Data on the occupational distribution of American men in recent decades indicate that the inequality in occupational status, controlling age, has also declined between 1952 and 1972, as the most highly skilled professional and technical occupations have expanded.[12] Although the cross-national data needed to measure inequalities in education and in occupational skills are not available, rising levels of school attendance nearly always reflect declining educational inequality, and a large share of the labor force in professional and technical occupations tends to reflect lower inequality in occupational skills. Thus, the previously reported partial correlations of division of labor, controlling GNP per capita, with education (.61) and with the proportion in professional and related occupations (.31) make the inference probable that a country's division of labor is inversely related to inequalities in education and in occupational qualifications.

Since education and occupational qualifications affect income, one would expect the declining differences in them that have occurred with the advancing division of labor to be accompanied by a reduction in income inequality. Income inequality may have diminished in the United States in this century, but the evidence is inconclusive. Kuznets (1966, pp. 195–219) considers it to

---

12. Hauser et al. (1975) present the occupational distribution of American men by age and by year (1952, 1962, 1972) for twelve major occupational groups (p. 590), and they also report the occupational status scores for these occupational groups (p. 589). These data were used to compute Gini coefficients of inequality in occupational status for the three years presented, separately for the 35–44 and the 45–54 cohort. Inequality in occupational status declined (practically the same for the two cohorts) between 1952 and 1972, from .353 to .318 for the younger and from .351 to .321 for the older cohort.

have declined substantially, in other western countries as well as in the United States. But other investigators point out that income inequality in this country, thought it is lower now that it was at the beginning of this century, has declined largely in a single period, around World War II, not in the decades before or in the decades since (Miller 1966, esp. pp. 15–28).[13] In contrast, the division of labor has continued to increase steadily in recent decades, and inequalities in education and in occupational skills have declined. The fact that these historical trend lines are not parallel makes it questionable whether one can attribute the decline in income inequality to the increase in division of labor and to the concomitant declines in educational and occupational inequalities. The evidence from cross-national data is also equivocal. Sectorial income inequality is inversely correlated with the division of labor (−.46; 43 cases),[14] but the partial correlation when GNP per capita is controlled is only −.23, which is too small to place much confidence in it, particularly in view of the doubtful reliability of income data. The conservative conclusion is that the division of labor does not reduce income inequality, although there are limited indications that it is inversely related to income inequality.

Why have the reductions in educational and occupational inequalities, which apparently accompanied advances in the division of labor, not generated corresponding reductions in income inequality? For the decline in income inequality, even if one is willing to attribute it to these changes, was much less than that in inequality in education and qualifications (B. Duncan 1968, p. 618).[15] An answer to this question is suggested by Boudon (1973): The rising levels of education that diminish inequalities in education and qualifications also diminish the price qualified labor commands in the labor market. It is in the interest of every individual to acquire as much education as possible, since superior qualifications generally bring higher incomes. The resulting demand for more education is an important factor generating rising levels of education and thus a reduction in educational inequality when other conditions, notably increases in labor productivity and economic growth, permit the expansion of education. These social demands for educa-

13. Data for 1970 reveal little change in income inequality since 1960, the last year for which Miller presents data. The Gini coefficient for income inequality in 1970 (computed from Jencks 1972, p. 210) is .360, and Miller's (1966, p. 24) for 1960 is .369. Kuznets's argument that income inequality has declined in recent decades seems to be convincingly refuted by Miller (1966, pp. 20–26).

14. The data for income inequality among industrial sectors (from Taylor and Hudson 1971, pp. 82–83) are often used as proxy for the less widely available and probably less reliable data on income inequality among occupations. The correlation of the latter with the division of labor is −.40 (20 cases).

15. Cross-national data indicate a correlation of −.49 (51 cases) between level of school attendance and income inequality, which implies that a country's educational inequality and income inequality are positively related. But most of this relationship is the result of economic development; the partial correlation, controlling GNP per capita, is only −.19.

tion create an oversupply of qualified labor that depreciates its value in the labor market, inasmuch as the demand for qualified labor is governed largely by industrial conditions. Improvements in educational opportunities that reduce educational inequality do not give rise to similar improvements in occupational opportunities and similar reductions in income inequalities, because the availability of more qualified persons does not determine that these qualifications are actually utilized and has an adverse effect on the financial rewards qualifications command.

The basic assumption of Boudon's suggestive theory is that the utilization of qualified labor depends on the industrial demand for it and is relatively independent of the supply of it. Granting this assumption in the short run, it can be modified by assuming that the supply of qualified labor does influence its utilization and the demand for it in the long run (PA-18), as the training of the labor force is one of the conditions—albeit not the only one—that determines the way work is organized and the form of the division of labor. This assumption implies that diminishing inequalities in education and qualifications diminish income inequalities in the long run. The very fact that the oversupply of superior qualifications depreciates their market value implies that rising levels and declining inequalities in educational qualifications reduce the excess income superior education commands, and thus diminish income inequality. Boudon's theory explains why the income distribution does not readily change in response to changes in the distribution of education, which can account for the empirical findings that the historical changes in educational inequality and in income inequality are not closely parallel, although there seems to be some relationship between the two.

In sum, the long-term trends are that the advances in the division of labor that occur with technological and economic developments are accompanied by diminishing inequalities in education and in qualifications and probably, after some delay, also in income. Have inequalities in wealth and in power similarly declined with the advancing division of labor? A study of the distribution of wealth in the United States reports some "decline in inequality of wealth-holding from 1922 to 1953. The share of personal sector wealth of the top 1 percent of adults fell from 32 to 25 percent in this period" (Lampman 1962, p. 219). Whether this decline in the concentration of wealth is connected with advances in industrialization and the division of labor is a moot question.

But the concentration of power has undoubtedly increased in this century, and these changes, though there are no precise data to measure them, are connected with the organization of work. Two major forms of power in contemporary societies are the authority over employees and the control over the disposition of economic resources exercised by senior executives of work organizations. The expansion of work organizations has led to a growing concentration of these major forms of power. Increasing proportions of the labor force are employed by very large organizations, and increasing shares of the national assets are owned by them. Manufacturing provides a dramatic illustration: Firms with more than 1,000 employees increased their proportion of all employees in manufacturing from 15 to 33 percent between 1909 and 1967 (computed from U.S. Bureau of the Census 1917, p. 391, and 1971, pp. 2–5). And the 100 largest firms increased their share of all corporate assets in manufacturing from 35 to 48 percent between 1925 and 1967 (U.S. Cabinet Committee 1969, pp. 45, 92). These changes imply increasing concentration of power. Advances in the division of labor tend to be accompanied by decreases in various forms of inequality but by increases in inequality in power. Although the advancing division of labor does not generate the growing concentration of power, the two are likely to occur together, because the expansion of work organizations promotes both.

Compendium

PA-17   The division of labor depends on opportunities for communication.

PA-18   An advanced division of labor depends on substantial training of the labor force.

T-27   Opportunities for communication and association promote the division of labor. (From PA-17.)

T-27.1   Population density increases the division of labor. (From T-23, T-27; based on A-9, PA-17.)

T-27.11   A society's increasing urbanization increases its division of labor. (From T-23, T-27; based on A-9, PA-17.)

T-27.2   Linguistic heterogeneity impedes the development of the division of labor. (From T-27; based on PA-17.)

T-27.3   The widespread use of efficient means of transportation promotes the development of the division of labor. (From T-24.1, T-27; based on A-9, PA-17.)

T-27.31   Improved efficiency in means of communication promotes the division of labor. (From T-27; based on PA-17.)

T-27.4   Rising levels of education and qualifications promote an advanced division of labor. (From PA-18.)

T-27.5   Large work organizations promote the division of labor in society. (From T-27.1, or T-27; based on PA-17.)

T-28   The advancing division of labor increases the probability of social relations among different occupations that integrate them in society. (From T-11, A-10.)

T-28.1   Ceteris paribus, inequality in occupational status depresses the social associations among different occupations and thus their integration. (From T-7; based on A-1.2.)

T-28.2   The more the division of labor is in the form of specialization rather than routinization, the greater is the probability that high rates of associations among different occupations integrate them. (From T-7, T-11; based on A-1.2, A-9, A-10.)

T-28.3   The relationship of the division of labor with high rates of social associations among occupations is nonmonotonic, becoming unequivocally positive only at advanced stages of the division of labor. (From T-7, T-11; based on A-1.2, A-9, A-10.)

T-28.4   The more the division of labor intersects with other nominal parameters, the greater is the probability that intergroup relations strengthen society's integration. (From T-12; based on A-1, A-11.)

T-28.41 The more the division of labor intersects with kinship lineages, the greater is the probability that weaker bonds of extended kinship strengthen society's integration. (From T-12; based on A-1, A-11.)

T-28.42 The more the society's division of labor is consolidated with graduated parameters, the greater is the probability that infrequent social associations among strata weaken society's integration. (From T-12; based on A-1, A-11.)

T-29   The more of society's division of labor results from that within rather than from that among work organizations, the more probable are extensive social associations among occupational strata and among different organizations. (From T-26; based on A-1, A-11.)

T-29.1   The more the inequality in administrative authority in society results from that within rather than from that among work organizations, the more probable are extensive social associations among administrative strata and among different organizations. (From T-26; based on A-1, A-11.)

T-29.2   Much division of labor within organizations increases the probabilities of intergroup and interstratum associations of small occupational groups most. (From T-14.1; based on A-1, A-9.)

T-29.21 Much division of labor within organizations increases the probabilities of intergroup and interstratum associations of high administrative ranks most. (From T-14.31; based on A-1, A-9.)

T-29.22 The smaller an organization, the more its internal division of labor increases the probabilities of intergroup and interstratum associations. (From T-25.12; based on A-1, A-11.)

T-29.3   The greater the consolidated inequalities among occupations within work organizations relative to the occupational inequalities among the work organizations in society, the more probable are extensive intergroup relations among occupations and among organizations. (From T-26.3, or T-25.3; based on A-1, A-11.)

T-30   The more of an organization's division of labor results from that within rather than from that among departments, the more probable are extensive social relations among occupational positions and among departments. (From T-26; based on A-1, A-11.)

T-30.1   The more the occupational inequality in an organization results from that within rather than from that among its departments, the more probable are extensive social relations among occupational positions and among departments. (From T-26; based on A-1, A-11.)

T-30.2   The greater the consolidated inequalities among occupational positions within departments relative to those among the departments in an organization, the more probable are extensive social associations among positions and among departments. (From T-26.3; based on A-1, A-11.)

T-30.3   Decentralization of authority in an organization increases informal associations among administrative ranks. (From A-1.2.)

T-31   The homogeneity of diverse groups has a structural effect increasing the preponderance of ingroup relations. (From A-1, T-21; based on A-10.)

T-31.1   The occupation homogeneity of work organizations, given the division of labor in society, has a structural effect increasing the social associations within the organization. (From A-1, T-21; based on A-10.)

T-31.2   The occupational homogeneity of departments in an organization with substantial division of labor has a structural effect increasing the social associations within departments. (From A-1, T-21; based on A-10.)

T-32   At advanced stages of the division of labor, increases in it diminish inequalities in education and qualifications. (From T-9.3; based on A-5.)

CHAPTER NINE

Domination

Power "IS THUS BOTH AWFUL AND FRAGILE, AND CAN DOMINATE A CONTI-
nent, only in the end to be blown down by a whisper. To destroy it, nothing
more is required than to be indifferent to its threats, and to prefer other
goods to those which it promises. Nothing less, however, is required also." In
these few words, Tawney (1931, p. 230) was able to capture the gist of power,
and to indicate at the same time its compelling force and its elusiveness.

This penultimate chapter, preceding the synopsis of the theory in chapter 10, deals with power and its implications for social relations, with special
attention to its implications for group conflict. Hence, concern is with one
form of inequality, which is singled out owing to its generic significance. The
substantive importance of differences in power that enable some people to
dominate others is patent and needs no demonstration. Most forms of inequality are significant in some group contexts but not in others: Economic
differences are not relevant in every kind of group; differences in affection
are important in intimate relations but irrelevant for the relations among
societies. Not so for power, variations in which are of crucial importance for
all social relations, from those in dyads to those among large groups and
those among societies. By virtue of its pervasive significance, power is sometimes conceptualized as the single underlying status dimension in terms of
which all other social relations and positions are defined (Nadel 1957, pp.
109–15). Alternatively, power differences may be considered to be one kind
of, and analytically distinct from other, social differences (rather than a criterion for defining the others), for example, from differences in the closeness of
social relations, the wealth of persons, the prestige of positions. The latter
view is adopted here.

217

The practical importance of power directs attention to its policy implications. In most of this book the focus has been on constructing systematic theory in abstract terms, and the policy implications of the abstract principles have not been traced, except on a few occasions (for instance, in chapter 3). But it is hardly meaningful, or desirable, to deal with power without discussing its policy implications, which inevitably involves some value judgments. Hence, this chapter differs in emphasis and tone from others. After a conceptual analysis of power, there is less concern with formulating abstract theoretical propositions and more conjecture about policy implications, especially in the last section.

Facets of Power

Philosophers and social scientists have sought to understand power and have analyzed it ever since people began to contemplate the nature of society, which reflects the importance of power; yet we still do not fully comprehend power and there is little systematic research on it, which reflects its elusiveness. The manifestations of power are observable everywhere, and anything men and women value makes them subject to the power of others. But as soon as we put our finger on power and attempt to stipulate a criterion for defining it, often as not it escapes us, and we are left with a concept that leaves out many aspects of power or with a concept that does not refer to power itself but to a condition that produces it or to a consequence of it.

Thus, two statements often made in the conceptual analysis of power are that social power refers to power over people, not over nature, and that it is a property of the relations between people, not of people themselves (for example, Lasswell and Kaplan 1950, p. 75). Although both statements appear on the surface unexceptional, they are actually misleading, since they neglect importance aspects of social power if narrowly construed. Power over people is often exercised through power over nature, for example, by the destruction of crops or deforestation bombing in a war. Unless changing nature is a means for exercising power over people, it does not constitute social power, but to rely for the definition of power on the intention of people creates analytical problems that are best avoided. Hence, power over nature when it does affect the lives of people, intentionally or not, needs to be included under social power.

The difficulty with a definition of power as a property of social relations is even more serious, because power is often exercised indirectly, and great power typically is. The sergeant exercises power over privates in their social relations more frequently than does the general, who actually may not exercise power at all in his social interaction with privates but politely talk to them as if he were their peer, since his power over them is exercised indirectly through the chain of command. The monopoly power of a firm is not observable in social relations, nor is the power of a nation resting on its arsenal of hydrogen bombs. In abstract terms, to be sure, power pertains to the relations among people, groups, or nations, but unless this is derived from the analysis instead of being made an operational criterion of power, the most important forms of power elude the analysis. To deal with power relations does not necessitate defining power as a property of social relations, just as it is not necessary to define income as a property of social relations to analyze income inequalities, which is a relational concept. There are restricted aspects of power that constitute properties of social association and find expression in superordination and compliance in interpersonal relations. For most purposes, however, power, like any status, needs to be conceptualized as a social resource that is an attribute of social positions, and analytical procedures are used to bring out the relational properties of relative power and power differences. Unless power is defined as a property of positions and their incumbents, it is impossible to analyze inequalities in power and concentration of power.

Another problem is posed by the fact that great power increasingly obviates the need to implement its exercise through explicit sanctions or any other instrument of control. This problem pertains to the distinction between potential and actual power or, as it is sometimes called, having and exercising power (Lasswell and Kaplan 1950, p. 71; Dahl 1968, p. 412). A nation or person with limited power over others may actually have to use or threaten to use sanctions in order to control them; when power is greater, a communication directing others suffices to exercise it, without resort to sanctions; when it is still greater, power needs not even an express communication to control others, because their behavior is controlled by the anticipation of the benefits it will bring them to act in ways that make them the most reliable ally of a powerful nation or person. Dahl (1968, pp. 412–13) illustrates this process with the case of Senator R, who without any previous action from President C,

> votes *now* in a way he thinks will insure the president's favor *later* . . . [because he hopes] to receive a presidential appointment to a federal court. . . . If one holds that C cannot be a cause of R if C follows R in time, then no act of the incumbent president *need* be a cause of Senator R's favorable vote. Obviously this does not mean that Senator R's actions are "uncaused." The immediate determinant of his vote is his expectations. . . . [I]t appears, paradoxically, that it is not the president who controls the senator but the senator who controls the president—i.e., it is the senator who, by his loyal behavior, induces the president to appoint him to a federal court. . . . It is, then, not the king who controls the courtier but the courtier who controls the king.
>
> . . . The courtier does indeed exercise power over the king by successfully anticipating the reactions of the monarch and thereby gaining a duchy. But it was not this that we set out to explain. For it is the king who has, holds, or

possesses the capacity to confer the dukedom, and even though he does not *exercise* his power, he gains the willing compliance of the courtier.

... What is it, then, that distinguishes having power from exercising power? The distinction could hinge upon the presence or absence of a manifest intention. We could define the *exercise* of power in such a way as to require C to manifest an intention to act in some way in the future, his action to be contingent on R's behavior. By contrast, C might be said to *have* power when, though he does not manifest an intention, R imputes an intention to him and shapes his behavior to meet the imputed intention. ... Carried to the extreme, then, this kind of analysis could lead to the discovery of as many different power structures in a political system as there are individuals who impute different intentions to other individuals, groups, or strata in the system.

As Dahl indicates in the last sentence, this procedure transforms the study of power relations into the study of the perception of power relations, which confounds two different things. Whereas the perception of power— and hence also its misperception—influences power relations, it cannot be the only thing that influences them, and its influence cannot be analyzed without having an independent criterion of actual power relations. These difficulties have led investigators to analyze power and distinguish its types in terms of its sources—the resources that give people power over others. For example, the well-known typology of power by French and Raven (1959) is actually not a classification of power, as they indicate in the title of their paper, but of "The Bases of Social Power." The five types they distinguish are power based on rewards, on coercion, on the legitimate right to influence, on the other's identification with one, and on expert knowledge. As social psychologists, French and Raven confine their attention to the power exercised in interpersonal relations by one individual over another, explicitly excluding power over groups, and they stress the distinction between the potential power rooted in its base and the actual control of one person's behavior over another (1959, p. 151). Classifications of power on the basis of its source are also made by social scientists who are primarily concerned with the power exercised over an entire group or society such as Weber and Lasswell and Kaplan.

The dilemma of the analysis of power is that operational criteria of it fail to encompass all the subtle ways in which power influences people, often by altering the conditions of their existence without involving any social relations, and that concepts that include all kinds of power typically refer to the sources of power, not to power itself. Weber resolves this dilemma by treating power as the most general, abstract concept, which is not intended to be empirically measured, but which links the various sources of power to their effects on social action and conditions. Specifically, power is the unobserved theoretical term designed to explain the observable effects differences in major power resources have on the conditions of social life. Weber (1947, p. 152) defines power (*Macht*) as "the probability that an actor within a social relationship will be in a position to carry out his own will despite resistance, regardless of the basis on which this probability rests." This generic concept includes imposing one's will on a single associate in direct social interaction and imposing one's will on an entire collectivity, whether or not doing so involves direct social interaction. Weber himself essentially confined his interest to the latter, to the domination of a society or an organization by one person or a few. The only manifestation of power he analyzed in detail is *Herrschaft*, which refers strictly to the power exercised over a collectivity by a ruler or a ruling group. (Domination, the word used to translate *Herrschaft*, does not fully convey its meaning, since *Herrschaft* is absolutely restricted to power over a collectivity, while domination is not quite so restricted. One can speak of a husband's being dominated by his wife, but the German word cannot be used in speaking of interpersonal relations.)

Weber distinguishes forms of domination on the basis of their source, and he emphasizes (1968, p. 943) that two forms are of primary importance: "domination by virtue of a constellation of interests . . . and domination by virtue of authority." The former rests largely on superior economic resources that make it possible to influence people by controlling the conditions of their existence so that their self-interests constrain them to act in certain ways; the pure case is monopoly. Authority rests on social positions in which is vested the legitimate right of command, backed by sanctioning power and complemented by the duty to obey; the pure case in modern society is a bureaucratic hierarchy. Although Weber mentions in passing other sources of domination, such as vassalage and slavery, and although he devotes more attention to authority than to economic domination, the most distinctive feature of his analysis is his heuristic emphasis on the primary substantive significance of "two diametrically contrasting types" of domination, that resting on control over economic conditions and that resting on positions of authority.[1] Nadel (1957, pp. 114–15) makes a similar distinction between two major forms of power.

Lasswell and Kaplan (1950, p. 76) distinguish power from the broader concept of influence on the basis of the deterrent effect of negative sanctions:

> It is the threat of sanctions which differentiates power from influence in general. Power is a special case of exercising influence: it is the process of affecting policies of others with the help of (actual or threatened) severe deprivations for nonconformity with the policies intended.

Command over any resources that are valued by people bestows sanctioning power and hence is a base of power. Lasswell and Kaplan (1950) distinguish three quantitative dimensions of power: Its weight is the extent to which

---

1. Cohen, Hazelrigg, and Pope (1975) rightly point out that Parsons's (1937) interpretation of Weber's discussion of authority slights the importance of economic domination in Weber's theoretical scheme.

certain decisions are influenced; its scope is the number of different value spheres in which decisions are influenced, such as economic, political, and religious; and its domain is the number of persons whose conduct is controlled. They also distinguish eight values that can become the base of power, ranging from power itself and wealth to affection and enlightenment; cross-classification of the valued resources ego possesses and the values of alter thereby controlled yields sixty-four types of influence and power. Whereas this is a more systematic conceptual scheme of power than that of Weber, who never presents a comprehensive scheme of the various sources and forms of power, his has the advantage over theirs that it directs attention to the major forms of domination of a collectivity that must be taken into account in the study of the distribution of power in society. The serious limitation of their analysis is that they fail to distinguish between sources of power that are of primary significance in intimate personal relations, such as affection, and those that are relevant for the study of political power, which is their central concern.

A fundamental distinction is drawn among three facets of power, which cannot be analyzed in the same terms, and the confounding of which is responsible for much confusion in the analysis of power. The criterion of distinction is what power is an attribute of—whether it is a property of the social associations between persons, the social positions occupied by persons, or the collectivities composed of persons that may confront each other in a conflict. The generic definition of power—asserting one's will against resistance owing to available sanctions—applies to all three facets. But in the first case it characterizes the asymmetric social interaction in which one's will is imposed on another, which limits the power that can be so exercised to the scope of one's associates. In the second case it pertains to the power positions of persons that enable them to impose their will on others whether or not they have direct contact with them, and the greater the power is the more it involves indirect control that does not depend on social contacts. In the third case it refers to the property of a collectivity that empowers it to dominate another—a nation's domination of its colony, a majority's of an ethnic minority, a ruling elite's of a lower class.

The first facet of power is superordination, which is a property of the association between two persons, not a property of persons or their positions. It is a major asymmetric aspect of social associations, and it is defined by the differences in the frequencies with which one defers to the other and complies with the other's suggestions, requests, and directives. Variations in superordination can by analyzed in relation to variations in social positions or in social distances between positions, just as can variations in the frequency of social associations, or those in any other property of social associations, such as interpersonal conflict. Further problems can be analyzed, for instance, how group differences in average status have structural effects that tend to make superordination in intergroup relations independent of the individual's own status. What the concepts of superordination and compliance do not permit one to do is to examine the distribution of power in society, because these concepts ignore the indirect exercise of power, which is not relevant for the study of interpersonal relations, but the inclusion of which is indispensable for analyzing inequality of power and understanding patterns of domination in society.

The second facet is the power some persons have to control the decisions and actions of many others, which is a property of social positions and their incumbents, as are all social attributes; specifically, it is a social resource which defines status and status distance. It is independent of social associations, since it is mostly exercised indirectly. This is the type of power Weber singled out for attention, and it assumes various forms—facets are more abstract dimensions of power than its forms—as indicated by Weber's two basic forms of domination. An interesting feature of these two major types of Weber's is that they can be construed narrowly or broadly and have accordingly different implications. Interpreted as narrow categories, they center attention on the two most important forms of domination in modern society—economic control and administrative authority. Interpreted broadly, they can be considered an analytical distinction (rather than a typology) that encompasses all forms of power over large numbers. Power over large numbers must be exercised indirectly, either by controlling conditions in ways that force them to act in their own interests in accordance with one's will, or by having intermediaries—disciples, vassals, lieutenants—who spread one's pronouncements and enforce one's will. These are the two forms of domination Weber distinguishes. Even the ultimate power in the form of physical coercion can be conceptualized as imposing one's will on others by controlling conditions in ways that make it in their interest to obey.

A fundamental difference between Weber's two generic forms of domination is that the intervening mechanism that translates the ruler's will into the compliance of many subjects is nonhuman in one case and human in the other. When control over economic conditions or long-range missiles is used to force people to submit by making it in their interest to do so, the instruments through which power is exercised are impersonal conditions—jobs that are contingent on compliance, the destruction of cities threatened for failure to submit. But when commands of a ruler are transmitted and enforced by vassals or officials, the instruments through which power is exercised are human beings whose positions are organized in a chain of command. Human beings have a will of their own, which makes them less reliable instruments than are impersonal mechanisms, that is, nonhuman ones. The emphasis on impersonal authority and discipline is designed to make the human chain of command nearly as reliable an instrument of power as are genuinely impersonal mechanisms that are not composed of human beings. Another difference is that authority is confined to persons within a given jurisdiction—an army's soldiers, a firm's employees, a sect's converts, a country's citizens—whereas the power resting on control over impersonal conditions of interest to people has no such predefined limits. This does not mean that the power resting on control over objective conditions has no limits, however, for it hinges on the persisting interest of people in these conditions. The threat of excommunication is an important source of power, but only as long as people have an interest in remaining in the church. Even power over life and death does not bestow unlimited power, because people can choose death over submission, and sometimes do. The great significance of economic resources as a base of power is that they are of interest to all people because they are generalized means for a great variety of ends, whereas other valued sources of power, such as approval and affection, are of interest to narrower circles, though they may be of greater interest to them than money.

There are other differences between economic domination and executive authority, the two most prevalent specific forms that Weber's two generic forms of domination assume in contemporary societies. Administrative authority is by definition rooted in formal positions in organizations. Economic power is not, though empirically control over economic resources has become increasingly vested in executive positions in formal organizations and divorced from sheer ownership of wealth. Another difference is that the minimum is not the same for the two forms of power. Most people have no administrative authority, being on the bottom of organizational hierarchies, but most adults exercise a modicum of economic control, as consumer purchases exert some influence on economic conditions. However, the economic power exerted by the uncoordinated decisions of consumers is negligible compared with the great power corporation executives exercise in their decisions governing investments, production, and employment. A final difference is that the economic control of middle strata weakens that of the top stratum, but the administrative authority of middle managers does not weaken that of top managers; on the contrary, the authority of middle ranks over lower ones is the means through which top management exercises its authority. The authority of captains and sergeants over privates is what enforces the general's authority; what would diminish his authority is there lack of compliance with his commands, not their commanding the compliance of privates.

The third facet of power is the strength societies, or groups or classes within them, can muster in conflicts, which is a property of social collectivities. Groups can be ranked on the basis of the average power of their members, just as they can be ranked on the basis of average education or income, and so can entire societies. But this will not do as an indication of the difference in power of the collectivities, for several reasons. The most obvious is that the collectivity's strength depends on the total strength of its members, not their average strength. Five older and stronger boys are collectively not so strong as ten younger and weaker ones. Of course, this can readily be taken into account by ranking groups on the basis of total instead of average power. This would not furnish an adequate indication of differences in collective power either, however, because much of the strength of collectivities rests on powers that are not distributed among their members. The military power of a nation is not reflected in the power of its citizens. The power of a political machine is not the result of the average power of the members of the party. The firm commitments of supporters of a social movement to fight for the common cause do not increase their individual power but do enhance the movement's collective strength. A last and especially important reason for the difference between the power of a collectivity and the aggregate power of its members is that the strength a collectivity can mobilize depends in good part on how well it is organized.

Superordination in social associations has been briefly discussed in chapters 3 and 6. The next section deals with the distribution of power among social positions, the concentration of the two major forms of power, and their consolidation. The third facet of power is examined in the following section, including the implications of the power of various groups for group conflict.

Consolidated Powers

To analyze inequalities in power and the consolidation of various forms of power, power must be conceptualized as a property of social positions and their incumbents, since only such a concept of power makes it possible to speak of the distribution of power among people. This is the facet of power, as it is here called, with which Weber's conceptual analysis is concerned. In accordance with his emphasis, attention centers on the two forms of domination of special significance in modern societies, economic control and executive authority. Doing so admittedly leaves out of consideration the dominant positions of persons whose power rests on other grounds, such as legislators, union officials, judges, charismatic leaders, bishops, party bosses, as well as the extra power of generals, beyond their command authority, based on the force of arms. A complete analysis would also take the special character of these forms of power into account. In a study of international relations, for example, it is essential to deal with the power resting on the force of arms. Here concern is confined to the special character of the two forms of domination that are in all probability most prevalent within contemporary society.

A few comments are in order about the operational criteria for measuring these two forms of power in ways that permit ascertaining their distribution in a population, without attempting to go into the practical problems involved in their actual empirical measurement. A basic measure of executive authority is the number of employees under the jurisdiction of a given position in a work organization. For example, a general's authority score would be the number of soldiers under his command, a captain's the number in his company, and a private's zero; the authority of different ranks in private firms and government departments would be similarly defined. This measure can be standardized to make the total authority scores equal the number of employees, for both a particular organization and the entire society (minus top executives). A procedure for doing so, illustrated in table 3, is to divide the number of employees on each level by the number of superior ranks or levels above them (column 6), sum the results for all subordinates (column 7), and divide by number in rank to obtain the authority score per position (column 8). Instead of computing average scores for a rank, as in the table, separate scores for each person can be calculated to take into account variations in spans of control. The assumption implicit in these scores—the unadjusted as well as the adjusted ones—is that the authority over employees is equally divided among the various levels of their superiors. But this assumption can be altered. For instance, the extreme assumption that the authority of immediate supervisors is five times as great as that of superiors two or more levels removed yields the weighted authority scores in column 9.[2] Two further possible refinements are to weight or supplement the authority scores by indications of the degree to which authority is centralized and by its scope over various spheres of life, to take into consideration such differences as the more severe discipline army officers compared with factory managers have the authority to impose on subordinates. The scores are designed to be comparable across organizations and thus for all members of society.

A basic measure of economic power is the amount of financial resources at the disposal of a person at her discretion. For private individuals, their liquid assets govern their economic control. But for executives of organizations, the indicator of economic control is the amount of organizational resources they are authorized to allocate or invest at their discretion without consulting superiors (Jaques 1956). This means that the same financial assets that contribute to the economic power of a stockholder also contribute to that of an executive in the company in which the stocks are invested, since both can make decisions over the disposal of these assets, which is in accordance with the principle of Parsons's (1963) that invested resources create credit and enlarge the total resources and power available in the system. Although the practical problems of measuring the amount of financial assets over which an executive has discretion are not trivial, the operational criterion of economic control suggested is unambiguous. In Lasswell and Kaplan's (1950)

2. It does not seem plausible to assign more weight to the authority of middle managers than to that of the top executive. In any case, assigning them more weight over each subordinate would not alter the inequality measures much. The last row in table 3 shows that extreme weights do not alter the inequality measure much (.94 v. .98); it also shows that the first adjustment does not alter the measure at all (.98 v. .98), but this adjustment would affect the inequality measure for the entire society.

TABLE 3. PROCEDURE FOR COMPUTING AUTHORITY SCORES

(1) Level	(2) Number of Persons*	(3) Total Authority Score*	(4) Average Authority Score (3/2)	(5) Number of Levels Above	(6) Adjusted Number of Persons (2/5)	(7) Adjusted Total Authority Score**	(8) Average Adjusted Authority Score (7/2)	(9) Weighted Average Adjusted Authority Scores
1	1	3905	3905	—	—	840.42	840.42	860.42
2	5	3900	780	1	5	835.42	167.08	177.08
3	25	3875	155	2	12.5	822.92	32.92	39.58
4	125	3750	30	3	41.67	781.25	6.25	11.25
5	625	3125	5	4	156.25	625.00	1.00	5.00
6	3125	0	0	5	625.00	0	0	
TOTAL	3906					3905.01		
Gini Index			.98				.98	.94

*Sum of all values in column 2 below this row.

**Sum of all values in column 6 below this row.

227

terms, the basic criterion of authority is domain (number of persons), possibly supplemented by the weight and scope of authority, whereas the basic criterion of economic power is weight, which encompasses the domain of many persons and the scope of their activities that are affected by the weight of control over economic conditions.

The two major forms of power are highly concentrated, and other forms of power, like military power and legislative power, are undoubtedly still more highly concentrated. Inequality in power is very great, much greater than inequality in incomes or any other form of inequality. The hierarchical authority structure of formal organizations makes great concentration of administrative control in them inevitable. Thus, the Gini index of inequality for the authority scores in column 9 of table 3, though they rest on the assumption that immediate supervisors exercise much more authority than distant superiors, is .94, which is close to the theoretical maximum of 1.00, whereas a Gini coefficient of .50 for income inequality is high. As a matter of fact, the concentration of authority in organizations is necessarily very great whatever assumption one makes about the differences in authority among ranks, as long as one assumes that higher ranks have more authority and are less numerous than lower ones, an assumption entailed in the definition of a hierarchy of authority.[3] When resources are so highly concentrated, the Gini index of relative inequality loses meaning and fails to discriminate, as noted in chapter 3, and must be supplemented or replaced by the measure of absolute inequality or mean status distance (which is 9.5 for the unadjusted authority scores[4] in column 4 of table 3). Whereas relative inequality in authority is close to its theoretical maximum in virtually all work organizations, absolute inequality has no theoretical maximum and indicates the variation in the concentration of authority among organizations.

The larger an organization, the more its hierarchical structure concentrates authority, even when authority is much decentralized. The degree of decentralization in the form of delegation of responsibilities must be distinguished from, though it affects, the degree to which administrative control is, and continues to be, unequally distributed and thus concentrated. Actually, authority tends to be more decentralized in large than in small organizations (Blau and Schoenherr 1971, pp. 128–32; Blau 1973, pp. 172–73). Yet regardless of how small decentralization makes a superior's authority over subordinates, there remains some, and usually considerable, such authority

3. The pyramidal structure of organization implies that the majority of employees are nonsupervisory, with no authority, and empirical data confirm this. For example, in all employment security agencies of the United States (Blau and Schoenherr 1971), 79 percent of all employees are nonsupervisory (by happenstance, nearly the same percentage as in table 3 [80 percent], where it is the result of making the span of control for all positions on all levels five); in a sample of 110 New Jersey manufacturing establishments (Blau et al. 1976), the proportion of nonsupervisory employees is 89 percent. With such a large proportion with zero scores, the measure of inequality must be high, regardless of the scores assigned to various higher ranks. Thus, with 80 percent nonsupervisory employees, a Gini index computed for quintiles cannot be less than .80.

4. The adjusted scores cannot be used for computing absolute inequality.

vested in superordinate position. This authority, together with the very uneven frequency distribution among ranks, generates substantial concentration of authority, the more so the larger the organization is, owing to the large numbers of employees at the bottom of the hierarchy with no authority over others. Great concentration of administrative power is implicit in the pyramidal structure of large organizations, notwithstanding decentralization.

The growing size of work organizations in society implies increasing concentration of the power that rests on administrative authority. Mergers of firms make entrepreneurs who were previously not subject to the administrative authority of superiors subject to it, and they simultaneously expand the authority of the top executives of the conglomerates. Increasing numbers of men and women have come under the control of administrative authorities and lost their former independence as the result of the great decline in the proportion of self-employed in the labor force, which is estimated by Kuznets (1966, p. 187) to have been an average drop of "from over 35 to less than 20 percent" in various Western countries during this century. Moreover, the proportion of personnel in supervisory and managerial positions in organizations is inversely related to their size (Blau 1974, pp. 323–48), which implies that the increasing size of organizations enlarges the proportion of society's labor force in nonsupervisory positions without administrative authority, thereby increasing the inequality in administrative power.

The growth of organizations increases the inequality in economic power, too, because it concentrates economic resources in large organizations and gives their senior executives a dominating influence over economic conditions. The main thesis of Berle and Means (1932) is that large corporations have transferred much of the power earlier vested in the ownership of property to the senior executives of large corporations, and further growth of corporations and conglomerates has probably accelerated the process since they made their investigation nearly half a century ago. This thesis has evoked much controversy, and it has often been misinterpreted from opposite political perspectives. Conservatives have argued that the thesis shows that inherited wealth no longer plays an important role in modern society and that managerial qualifications and abilities determine who achieves dominant positions (Burnham 1941; Bell 1958). On the other hand, radicals have argued that the thesis is wrong because most top executives of large corporations are rich and because large stockholders have the power to fire them (Domhoff 1967; Zeitlin 1974). But the important change corporate ownership has produced is not in occupational opportunities. Top executives of large corporations are undoubtedly richer than most persons, and great wealth probably increases the chances of becoming such an executive. However, top executives of big corporations exercise much more power than can be attributed to their own wealth, because much of the power that was exercised by the owners of capital in precorporate periods is now exercised by the managers of corporations in which the descendants of independent entrepreneurs have invested their assets. One need not claim that stockholders have no power to assert that large corporate assets give senior executives much more economic power than their own wealth could command.

Large organizations consolidate major forms of power, since they concentrate both administrative and economic power in the hands of their top executives. Large government departments as well as large corporations have these consequences. Traditionally, the economic power of the third estate was divorced from the political power of the first, and through the nineteenth century the bureaucratic power of the state and the capitalist power of the rising middle class were largely distinct. But the difference between them has been much reduced by the expansion of both, as the large work force of private firms confronts them with problems of bureaucratic administration and the large budgets of government bureaus confront them with problems of business management. A government department's huge budget—that of the U.S. Department of Defense (1975) was $89 billion for 1975—concentrates tremendous economic power in its senior executives, and its many employees concentrate great authority in them, just as do a private firm's large assets and large work force. The continuing growth of organizations, which was previously commented upon, increasingly consolidates inequalities in power.

These conclusions can be formally derived from two assumptions. One is that *positions of authority over many employees in work organizations are the source of most authority in contemporary societies* (PA-19). It is assumed that administrative authority over employees outweighs in significance as a source of power other forms of authority, such as charismatic, traditional, and personal authority, as well as the authority of officials in voluntary associations. To be sure, some union leaders have more power than some executives of work organizations, and so do some religious leaders, but the assumption made is that most administrative power has its roots in positions of authority over many employees, including the president's position as the head of the executive agencies of the federal government. The other assumption is that *top positions in organizations with large financial resources are the basis of much control over economic resources in contemporary societies* (PA-20). The assumption is not that stockholders exercise no economic power, nor that consumers exercise none, only that much economic power is exercised by senior executives of large organizations.

As the number of employees in a work organization increases, authority in it becomes more concentrated (T-33). The theorem follows from T-9.2, that an increase in status of the highest stratum increases inequality, because an increase in number of employees raises the authority of top executives, defined by the number of employees under their jurisdiction, and concentration of authority is synonymous with inequality of authority.[5] The empiri-

5. T-9.2 rests on three assumptions, only two of which are required for T-33. The assumption that fertility is no less for lower than higher strata (PA-7) is obviously not needed for the

cally observed increase in the proportion of nonsupervisory personnel with increasing organizational size reinforces the predicated effect of size on the concentration of authority.

As the average number of employees of the work organizations in a society increases, the concentration of administrative power in the society becomes more pronounced (T-33.1). The theorem is implied by PA-19, that most administrative power is rooted in positions in work organizations, and T-33, that the large size of organizations concentrates administrative power. *As the average size of the financial resources of the work organizations in a society increases, the concentration of economic power in the society becomes more pronounced* (T-33.2). This theorem follows from PA-20, that top positions in wealthy organizations are the source of much economic power. Since some work organizations are labor-intensive and others capital-intensive, the number of their employees and their financial resources are not perfectly correlated. But the two tend to exhibit substantial correlations, particularly within industries, because employing a large number of persons requires large financial resources.[6] Given such a positive correlation, T-33.1 and T-33.2 imply: *The growing average size of the work organizations in a society increases the consolidation of administrative and economic powers* (T-33.3).

Not all forms of inequalities have become more consolidated, however. *The growing average size of the work organizations in a society reduces the consolidation of ownership of wealth and economic power* (T-33.4). The theorem follows from PA-20, that top positions in large organizations are the source of much economic power. It does not imply that ownership of wealth is not an important source of power, only that its significance as a power base independent of organizational position declines with the increasing size of organizations. T-33.4 contradicts a literal interpretation of Marx's thesis that ownership of the means of production continues to be the main source of power in societies where much wealth is concentrated in giant organizations, public and private. But inequalities in major forms of power have become

---

personnel of organizations. The assumption that immigration from outside into lower strata exceeds that into higher ones (PA-8) refers to appointments of outsiders to organizational positions on various levels. It is also assumed that an organization's authority structure is positively skewed (A-5).

6. The correlation of an organization's number of employees with measures of financial resources under its control varies from very strong to considerable, depending on the industry. For example, the correlation of number of employees (log.) is .95 (124 cases) with dollar volume of sales in department stores and .59 (1279 cases) with total assets in hospitals (Blau 1974, p. 325). It is .45 (36 cases) with total operating budget, but a high .84 (48 cases) with personnel budget, in manufacturing establishments (unpublished data from N.J. sample). A study of the country's largest firms, based on data from *Forbes* magazine, reports that the average correlation for sixteen industries between number of employees and financial assets of a company is .93 (512 cases), though it is less (no figure reported) for seven other industries (Broom and Cushing 1977, p. 162). A study of very small organizations—farmer cooperatives—similarly observes a correlation of .78 between number of employees and assets (153 cases; Evers, Bohlen, and Warren 1976, p. 335).

more consolidated with the growth of organizations, which conforms to Marx's prediction, and which has important implications for class differences in society.

An arbitrary division of people into hierarchical strata by some criterion of status does not constitute social classes, at least not in the sense in which the term has been used ever since Marx's influential writings by most authors critical of his analysis as well as those in agreement with it. Classes in the traditional sense refer to hierarchical groups with more or less distinct boundaries that demarcate common positions, conditions of life, and interests, as Dahrendorf (1959, p. 76) stresses, "not layers in a hierarchical system of strata differentiated by gradual distinctions." According to Marx, the major class boundary in modern capitalist society is defined by ownership of the means of production and lack thereof. One could interpret his discussion as being theoretically concerned with economic domination and using ownership simply as an empirical criterion of such domination, but Dahrendorf (1959, pp. 21–23) suggests that there are indications that ownership of private property is of intrinsic theoretical significance for Marx. In any case, corporate ownership has obliterated this clear boundary between the two broad social classes defined by ownership of means of production (Dahrendorf 1959, pp. 42–45), because stock ownership varies by degrees and does not divide people into a group of owners of property and another group who own only their labor.

However, the growing concentration and consolidation of administrative and economic powers has generated a new, fairly clear-cut class boundary between those who have no administrative authority and virtually no economic influence and those who have much power of both kinds, or at least some power of one kind or the other. This conception is similar to Dahrendorf's reformulation of Marx's theory in terms of authority relations, except that the broader concept of power relations is used (as it is by Collins 1975, pp. 62–73), and except for resting the concept of class boundaries on grounds different from his. The theoretical reason that Dahrendorf (1959, p. 170) substitutes authority for wealth as a criterion of class is that authority is necessarily dichotomous: "a clear line can at least in theory be drawn between those who participate in its exercise in given associations and those who are subject to the authoritative command of others." This is simply wrong; it confuses authority as a property of the interaction between two persons with authority as a property of social positions and their incumbents. Organizational hierarchies are clear evidence that the latter varies by degree, not dichotomously. Dahrendorf's dichotomous conception of authority forces him into tortuous arguments (1959, pp. 248–57, 289–301) to decide which ones of the many intermediate ranks in formal organizations belong to the ruling class by virtue of exercising authority, and which ones are subject to the authority of others. These arguments trying to transform a gradation into a dichotomy on philosophical grounds are exactly parallel to the Marxist ones Dahrendorf (1959, pp. 51–57) rejects—that ownership of the means of production is really still a dichotomy, notwithstanding the continuous empirical gradation.

There is no ruling class with a distinct boundary, though this does not mean that power is not highly concentrated and consolidated. Very few people are in dominant positions in which they exercise very great powers over the conditions in society and the life chances of all the people, but there is no boundary for drawing a clean line between those who do and those who do not belong to the ruling class. There is a distinct boundary, however, between those who have no administrative authority and those who have some or much. The growing size of organizations and concentration of authority enlarges the majority who have no authority. Most of that majority without administrative power also have practically no economic power, though all adults among them exercise a modicum of economic influence as consumers, and in a democracy a modicum of political influence through their vote as well.

The power structure of contemporary societies may be considered to comprise a lower class, a middle stratum, and an upper stratum, the different terms being designed to indicate the difference between a class delineated by a social boundary and a stratum arbitrarily divided from another. The lower class is composed of those who lack any administrative authority and whose other influences are confined to the minimum that is inherent in the rights of citizenship itself (Lenski 1966, pp. 82–84). They are virtually powerless, and they tend to be a growing majority. Since both administrative authority and economic power vary by degree, there is no clear line between those who exercise limited power and those in positions of dominant power, important as the difference between them is. Only in times of acute conflict between the powerless and the powerful does a line separating the ruling class emerge, because the alignments of middle strata in overt conflict draw that line.

Class boundaries weaken macrosocial integration by inhibiting social associations, which insulates the members of the lower class from the rest of society. *The concentration of power increases the insulation of the lower class from higher strata* (T-34). The theorem follows from T-7, that inequality increases the impact of status on social associations, which implies that increasing inequality enlarges the proportion of the lower class insulated from associations with higher strata. *The consolidation of different forms of power further increases the insulation of the lower class from higher strata* (T-34.1). If the concentration of power increases the insulation of the lower class (T-34), and if the consolidation of status differences reduce social associations among strata (T-12.21), consolidated powers further increase the insulation of the lower class. Moreover, the proposition that large organizational size promotes consolidation (T-33.3), and the proposition that consolidation promotes working-class insulation (T-34.1), jointly imply that large organizational size promotes such insulation: *The growing average size of the work organizations in a society increases the insulation of the lower class from dominant strata* (T-34.2). In sum, the growth of organizations, by concentrating and consolidating powers, widens the breach between the working class and the power elite. The working class is composed of individuals who have virtually no power, but this does not necessarily mean that the working class collectively has none.

Power and Conflict

All inequalities in resources imply a conflict of interest over the distribution of these resources on which status differences rest. Inequality in power does so particularly, because power, like wealth, is a generic resource for acquiring various other resources and privileges, which makes its possession of great advantage and interest. But a conflict of interest is not the same as overt conflict, and it may not lead to overt conflict, since it may remain suppressed, and since even when it finds expression it can do so in various forms, notably competition as well as overt conflict.

Simmel (1955, p. 58) distinguishes overt conflict from competition on the basis of whose hands hold the prize of the contest. In competition, in contrast to direct conflict, "the prize of the fight is not in the hands of either adversary. If one fights with somebody to obtain his money, wife, or fame, one uses quite other forms and techniques than if one *competes* with him as to who is to channel the public's money into his pockets, who is to win the woman's favor, who, by deed or word, is to make a greater name for himself." In other words, the question is whether a conflict of interest of two parties requires them to seek to obtain the prize in which both are interested from a third party or from each other. This is an important analytical criterion for distinguishing not only competition but also indirect conflict from direct confrontations. Direct collisions between two parties are avoided and transformed into indirect contests if the conflict at issue is decided by a third party, as in arbitration.

What are the various forms of overt conflict? To answer this question, one must first distinguish interpersonal conflict in the associations between individuals from conflict between collectivities, be they groups, classes, or societies, just as power as an attribute of interpersonal associations must be distinguished from power as an attribute characterizing collectivities.[7] In-

---

7. Three facets of power have been distinguished—as a property of associations, of positions of persons, and of groups—but only two facets of conflict are, because conflict refers to relations, not to positions of units being related, that is, either to interpersonal relations between individuals or to relations between groups.

terpersonal conflict, which frequently is a power struggle, takes primarily four forms: (1) verbal disputes; (2) physical fights; (3) the use of coercive sanctions or threatening their use to gain the upper hand in a conflict; (4) litigation, broadly defined to include calling the police as well as engaging in a lawsuit. The last is encompassed by Simmel's criterion that the prize is in the hands of a third party, although litigation is not a form of competition. Litigation averts the direct confrontations typical of overt conflict by relinquishing the right to decide the issue on one's own and putting the decision into the hands of a third party—a jury, judge, or peace officer. It is an institution for keeping serious overt conflict under control by substituting arbitration for direct confrontation.[8]

Conflict between collectivities—between groups or classes in society or between societies—also takes primarily four forms. Three of these are somewhat parallel to forms of interpersonal conflict, but the fourth is not. The first form of collective conflict is combat by the use of physical force, for example, war, revolution, insurrection, and lesser kinds of group violence, including police violence against strikers, demonstrators, or similar groups. The second form is employment of coercive sanctions in conflicts between groups, such as boycotts, strikes, intimidating or firing opponents, other economic sanctions, sabotage, pressure-group tactics. A third form of group conflict, which has been used increasingly in recent years, is litigation in behalf of a group, as illustrated by the lawsuits initiated by the NAACP to enforce desegregation, by class actions brought by other minorities, women, and environmentalists, and by court injunctions against strikers. Finally, the conflicts of groups and classes, and to some extent those of societies, take place in the political arena, involving elections, political parties and campaigns, and the transactions of parliaments and other legislative bodies.

Political as well as legal group conflict replaces direct confrontation by an indirect contest in which conflicts between parties are decided by requiring them to compete for a favorable decision of an outside agency, which is the anonymous voting public in the case of democratic elections. Various groups and classes must compete for having their interests represented by different political parties, and the parties must compete for a verdict from the voting public as to what political program representing which group interests will be implemented. The groups engaged in the contest are also voters, but democratic institutions constitute a screen, as it were, which separates the anonymous voting public from the groups on whose issues that public decides. The screen is most effective when most of the voting public is actually composed of persons who are outside the two groups in conflict on any particular issue. This implies that the screen is most effective if most controversies do not divide the entire society into opposing camps but leave many persons on the sidelines, functioning as more or less disinterested

8. Interpersonal conflict has been briefly discussed in chapter 5.

arbitrators when casting their votes, with different persons constituting the outsiders in different controversies. If a deep and enduring conflict of interest splits the society into the same two parts who confront each other on issue after issue, the screen becomes transparent, and voting is no longer a mechanism for having conflicts between two groups decided largely by disinterested outsiders. In this situation democratic elections are only a device for deciding conflicts between two adversaries by measuring their political strength, and though they thereby benefit society by obviating the need for violent confrontations, they are also less effective in preventing violence. In the heat of political battles, violent collisions, such as street fights, sometimes occur, and violent means, such as assassinations and political suppression, are sometimes used. Such resort to violence is most likely in the absence of a sizable third party not directly involved in the conflict and more interested in maintaining democratic processes than in the outcome of the conflict.

Democratic institutions are means for making collective decisions on issues in which various groups have great and conflicting interests, without the resort to violence that the strong conflict of interest would otherwise invite. The perseverance of democratic institutions requires that these means for arriving at decisions in important controversies become ends in themselves that are more important than the outcome of the controversies. Merton (1968, p. 253) has called the process by which means are transformed into ends in themselves *displacement of goals.* He uses the concept to explain bureaucratic red tape and inefficiency as the result of social pressures that make conformity with rules, originally designed to achieve certain ends, an end in itself. Democracy is a different manifestation of the process of displacement of goals, for although it is a means for achieving other collective ends, its survival depends on its becoming an end of overriding importance. But it is virtually impossible for groups to value democratic procedures beyond all other values and interests, beyond their religious convictions, their economic security, their very survival. When a group's interests are seriously threatened, fighting the threat tends to become an all-important end that justifies all means for its members, including resort to violence and disregard of democratic processes. Strong conflicts of interests imply that the advancement of the interests of some groups threatens those of others, which encourages recourse to any means to avert the threat, in disregard of democratic procedures.

The dilemma of democracy is that it depends on people's being more interested in maintaining democratic procedures than in attaining their political ends, but that no group can be expected to value democratic procedures beyond all its other interests. The dilemma is resolved if there are some groups in every conflict who are less interested in its outcome than in the endurance of democracy. This is the case if the serious conflicts do not involve most members of society on one side or the other but only some groups, while others have little interest in the outcome and can serve as protectors of democratic institutions against possible excesses of both adversaries, with different groups serving in this capacity in different controversies. But note what this implies: Democratic institutions are well suited for deciding issues that are not of importance to the majority of the population, and they are not well suited for resolving conflicts in which vital interests of most people are at stake.

Multiform heterogeneity engenders criss-crossing conflicts among many overlapping groups with diverse interests, which makes it likely that in any one conflict there are large numbers whose interests are not greatly involved and who can act as guardians of democratic procedures. Consolidated inequalities, however, engender conflicts about the distribution of resources and related issues that involve interests of great importance to most members of society, with largely the same persons on the opposite sides in most controversies. This is precisely the situation that puts democracy in jeopardy, since basic interests of most members of society that divide them along the same lines in repeated conflicts intensify hostilities and create pressures to disregard democratic procedures to achieve the important objectives. Theories of democracy that emphasize cross-cutting conflicts, such as Lipset's (1960), implicitly assume the existence of multiform heterogeneity and the absence of consolidated inequalities. However, modern societies are characterized not only by multiform heterogeneity but also by more or less pronounced consolidated inequalities. Of particular import is inequality in power, owing to the pervasive significance of power for social life.

Great inequality of power implies a strong conflict of interests between those who have much power and want to keep or enlarge it and those who have little power and are interested in acquiring some. Common interests may override these conflicting ones. Those with little or no power may obtain benefits from the exercise of power by others that outweigh their interest in improving their power position. For example, they may derive economic benefits from efficient management or political benefits from political leadership that make them uninterested in achieving a redistribution of power. Differences in power have two opposite implications for interests: They imply that some can coordinate activities for the benefit of all, and they imply that some enjoy advantages and privileges at the cost of others who do not. Only the latter is emphasized by Marx in his zero-sum conception of power, and only the former by Parsons, who rejects this zero-sum conception (see Dahrendorf 1959, p. 169). It seems highly dubitable that the disadvantageous consequences of being powerless are outweighed by the advantages accruing to the powerless from leadership, though ultimately this question should be decided on empirical grounds. Assuming that people with little power are interested in gaining more and those with much power are interested in not losing theirs, there is a conflict of interest between them.

A serious conflict of interest over the redistribution of power does not imply a great likelihood of overt conflict, however, because the very lack of power that makes groups interested in its redistribution also deprives them of sufficient resources to engage in conflict with those who have power and are interested in keeping it. Power is its own protection. To redress imbalances of power requires power. The concentration and consolidation of powers robs those with the greatest interest in changing the power structure of the resources to realize their interest. The powerful are not likely to give up their power without a struggle. Unless groups with little power can mobilize resources for this struggle, they have no chance of improving their power position. This seems to make the case of the lower class hopeless, since membership in it is defined by virtual lack of power. But the chances of the lower class to improve its power position, though slim, are not quite hopeless, because the power of a group is not identical with the power of its members.

A group can mobilize resources that differ from those available to its individual members, partly in kind and partly in degree that is so great that the quantitative difference becomes in effect a qualitative one. There is strength in numbers. The free time a poor person has does not affect his power; the meager income of a poor woman does not give her any meaningful economic power; the vote of a poor man does not give him any significant political power. Yet all of them, when pooled, become resources that contribute to the power of the group: the time devoted to organizing efforts; the dues collected for political campaigns; the buying practices organized for a boycott; the vote to put a candidate into office. For the power potential inherent in the large size of a group to be realized requires that their efforts be organized, coordinated, and pointed in the same direction.[9] A political organization for joint efforts is what converts the lack of effective resources of the individual members of a group or class into substantial common resources and collective strength for the power struggle.

Only a collectivity can be politically organized, which gives a group a power its members cannot have individually, whether the political organization (the term is used broadly) is a labor union, a pressure group, a faction within an established political party, or a separate party. Without being organized for joint efforts in the common interest, the potential power of a group is dissipated in diverse directions as individuals pursue their individual interests, which are not all alike. Differences in ethnic background, religion, and income entail some differences in interests among the lower class. Structural conditions determine whether the common interests of the

9. Empirical illustrations of the significance of the size of the weaker group for group conflict are the findings that the number of blacks in a city influence the probability of racial demonstrations (Spilerman 1971) and that the number of students at an academic institution influence the probability of student demonstrations (Scott and El-Assal 1969; Blau and Slaughter 1971).

lower class outweigh the divergent interests of its members and thus contribute to the chances of successful organizing efforts for the joint pursuit of class interests.

The consolidation of differences in power with other status and group differences makes the positions of people with practically no power—the lower class—also alike in other respects, which strengthens their common and minimizes their divergent interests. Powerless people who are equally poor and who belong to the same ethnic groups have much in common. On the other hand, differences in income among the lower class, the fact that many are unemployed while others have jobs, and variations in race or ethnic background generate divergent interests that can be, or appear to be, more pressing than the common interest in gaining the political power to effect some redistribution of resources. Thus, the substantial income differences among American workers who have in common positions at the bottom of hierarchies of administrative and economic power may well have bearing on the absence of a working-class party in the United States.[10] It is when differences in power are highly correlated with economic and social differences that conditions are most favorable for the development of an organized political movement among the weak that gives them collective strength.

Consolidated parameters and positions imply that little variation in life chances and interests among the weak and poor help unify them, in good part by fostering supportive and cooperative relations among them and restricting those between them and higher strata. Pronounced inequalities in power and resources create barriers to social associations (T-7, T-34). Consolidated graduated parameters aggravate inequalities (T-15.3) and, in effect, erect a class barrier that insulates most people with no significant power and meager resources from social intercourse with higher strata, thus strengthening ingroup relations in the lower class (T-12.21, T-34.1). The influence of insulation on uniting a group to organize collective action is illustrated by Kerr and Siegel's (1954) finding that workers who are isolated from the rest of the community are most likely to organize militant unions with high propensities to strike. Structural consolidation, moreover, reduces chances of social mobility (T-16.2), which deprives the underprivileged of much prospect for individual improvements, and it inhibits social change (T-18.21), which impedes adjustments to improve the conditions of the underprivileged

10. There is no empirical evidence to tell whether great differences in power raise or lower income inequality. Such evidence would have bearing on the issue of whether power is or is not zero-sum. If power differences raise income inequality, it would support the zero-sum thesis; if they lower it, it would support the non-zero-sum thesis that the benefits derived from power differences outweigh its disadvantages. But these two theses are so broad that they can hardly ever be clearly negated. Whatever the outcome of any one empirical test, power may also have other influences, so that supporters of either view can claim that the negative evidence is insufficient to warrant its rejection.

collectively. The consolidation of severe inequalities produces a revolutionary situation, when incentives to adopt a radical ideology are great for people who suffer from multiple deprivations, who are insulated from privileged strata, and who have little hope for improvements.

The adoption of a radical ideology by a group of the underprivileged generates new resources for organizing joint endeavors in the pursuit of the common ideals. A group's strong ideological commitments, which are regularly fortified by social approval, make its members greatly interested in advancing the common cause and willing to risk their jobs and even their lives for it. Such a radical movement that threatens to divest those with much power of all or some of it is naturally opposed by them with the great power at their command. The drastic sanctions frequently used to discourage participation in a radical movement require great sacrifices of men and women who nevertheless participate in it. Deep commitment to the common cause makes persons more interested in furthering it than in the benefits powerful opponents can withdraw, and thus relatively independent of their sanctioning power. In this way, joint commitment to an ideology creates new resources for organizing collective efforts and thereby endows the weak with collective strength.

Political positions tend to become polarized when developments have made conditions ripe for social change but the rigidities of a consolidated social structure have impeded it. As some become committed to a radical ideology of the left, others become committed to an extremist ideology of the right. Once a revolutionary movement intent on overthrowing the established power structure grows beyond a small vanguard, if not before, the dominant elite with vested interests in the existing social order will mobilize forces to combat this threat to their interests, sometimes by suppressing the radical party, sometimes by furnishing resources to support a counterrevolutionary party. The diametrically opposed interests and ideological commitments brook no compromise and invite resort to violence. Often as not, the violence is committed in defense of law and order by agents of the state against the radicals. When polarization makes incompatible political ends of overriding importance, democratic procedures are sacrificed in the struggle for political victory.

Democratic institutions are designed to forestall such polarization that is likely to spell their doom, by giving even the least powerful adults a vote that enables them to exercise collectively some political influence, and by providing a mechanism for gradual and orderly social change and adjustment. But when historical conditions change, the democratic institutions themselves are in need of adjustments lest they can no longer serve these functions.[11]

11. The danger signs indicating this need are apparent enough in a nation where an increasing proportion of the electorate, a much larger proportion than in other democracies, do not find the political alternatives available to them of sufficient interest to exercise the right to vote.

The differentiated structure of modern society and the higher levels of education call for more extensive participation in democratic processes than voting in occasional elections. Voting on various issues would take more advantage of cross-cutting allegiances than two-party elections. The superior knowledge and qualifications of an educated population should be taken advantage of in a complex democracy by providing opportunities for democratic participation in the management of the organizations where people work and of the other institutions in which they have a stake—their churches, their unions, their schools.

Probably the most important structural change since the American Constitution was adopted has been the rise of huge organizations to dominant positions. Large organizations are essential for industrialized society and, indeed, for large-scale democracy, and their productivity contributes to the high standard of living enjoyed by Americans and people in other advanced industrial societies. Yet the tremendous powers concentrated in these organizations and their executives are incompatible with democracy in the long run, and we have not learned how to adjust our democratic institutions to control that power. This is the challenge confronting us: to find ways to curb the power of organizations in the face of their powerful opposition, without destroying in the process the organizations, which we need, or democracy itself, which we cherish.

Compendium

PA-19 Positions of authority over many employees are the source of most authority in contemporary societies.

PA-20 Top positions in organizations with large financial resources are the basis of much control over economic resources in contemporary societies.

T-33 As the number of employees in a work organization increases, authority in it becomes more concentrated. (From T-9.2; based on A-5, PA-8.)

T-33.1 As the average number of employees of the work organizations in a society increases, the concentration of administrative power in the society becomes more pronounced. (From PA-19, T-33; based on A-5, PA-8.)

T-33.2 As the average size of the financial resources of the work organizations in a society increases, the concentration of economic power in the society becomes more pronounced. (From PA-20.)

T-33.3 The growing average size of the work organizations in a society increases the consolidation of administrative and economic powers. (From T-33.1, T-33.2; based on PA-8, PA-19, PA-20.)

T-33.4 The growing average size of the work organizations in a society reduces the consolidation of ownership of wealth and economic power. (From PA-20.)

T-34   The concentration of power increases the insulation of the lower class from higher strata. (From T-7; based on A-1.2.)

T-34.1 The consolidation of different forms of power increases the insulation of the lower class from higher strata. (From T-12.21, T-34; based on A-1.2, A-11; or on A-1.2, A-12.)

T-34.2 The growing average size of the work organizations in a society increases the insulation of the lower class from dominant strata. (From T-33.3, T-34.1; based on A-1.2, PA-8, A-11, PA-19, PA-20; or on A-1.2, PA-8, A-12, PA-19, PA-20.)

CHAPTER TEN

Synopsis of Theory

THIS FINAL CHAPTER PRESENTS THE BODY OF THE FORMAL THEORY IN concise form. First a few comments are made on the metatheoretical assumptions implicit in the theoretical approach adopted. In the rest of the chapter all theorems are briefly derived. This review of the skeleton of the theory does not include any elaborations that give the skeleton flesh and blood by indicating the significance of the theorems that make them meaningful. Theorems deducible from the same premises are presented together as far as possible, so that their ordering differs somewhat from that in which they originally appeared in the book. The propositions are grouped into four sections: differences in size, frequency distributions, nexus of parameters, and differentiation within substructures.

Theoretical Framework

There is a variety of approaches to theorizing in sociology and in the other social sciences. Assuming that sociology is a nomothetic discipline concerned with general principles, not an idiographic one concerned with unique circumstances, one difference is whether the objective of the theorist is to elaborate an analytic conceptual scheme or to advance a system of synthetic propositions some of which are empirically testable (Merton 1968, pp. 139–55). Another issue is whether the theory is designed to explain empirical findings by the fact that they fit into a meaningful pattern of interrelations (Kaplan 1964, p. 333)—Weber's *Verstehen*—or by the mere

243

fact that they are logically implied by more general propositions (Braithwaite 1953, pp. 342–50). If the latter, formal paradigm of theorizing is accepted, the procedure for building the theory may be either inductive, starting with empirical findings and subsuming them under generalizations from which they are deducible, or deductive, starting with definitions and general assumptions and deducing from them empirically testable propositions. The approach in this book has been to employ deductive procedures in building a formal body of logically related propositions,[1] and whereas not all of them constitute a single system derived from the same premises, all subsets of propositions derive from a specific conception of social structure in which the theory is rooted.

Social structure is an abstraction, of course, not an object that can be observed directly. What a theory of social structure comprises and explains, therefore, depends on the conception of social structure adopted, which abstracts certain aspects of empirical reality and ignores others. But Lévi-Strauss (1963, p. 279) goes too far when he says, as already quoted in chapter 1, that "social structure has nothing to do with empirical reality but with models built after it." The logically related propositions that compose a theoretical model or "structure" are not the same as the empirically related elements that compose the social structure and that the theory is designed to explain. The theoretical scheme must not confound the conceptually abstracted yet still observable relations of elements with the propositions advanced to explain them, lest the theoretical propositions be not falsifiable. Indeed, in his own work Lévi-Strauss (1969) develops a system of theorems to account for the independently observable structures of kinship relations in various societies, which seems to contradict his expressed view that a social structure is a theoretical model rather than an aspect of empirical reality to which the model refers. It is true, however, that the theorist's concepts of the interrelated elements that constitute the social structure determine which parts of reality are visible as well as the nature of his theory. Very different theories of social structure are constructed depending on how its interrelated elements are conceptualized, for example, whether they are functionally interdependent institutions or communication networks among individuals, culturally integrated value orientations or conflicts of economic interests between classes.

The theory presented is grounded in a quantitative conception of social structure.[2] The elements of social structure are the various social positions people occupy, which find expression in role relations among persons in

1. The conception of theorizing is based on Braithwaite's (1953) and Popper's (1959); see also Nagel (1961, pp. 29–46) and Hempel and Oppenheim (1948). The differences and controversies among these philosophers of science do not directly affect the approach in this book.

2. Lévi-Strauss (1963, pp. 293–96) notes the importance of quantitative properties of social structure. But his own theories, particularly his later theories about myths, focus on culture rather than on social structure defined in quantitative terms.

proximate positions that differ from those between persons in distant positions; the interrelations of elements are the associations among persons in different positions. Attention centers on the quantitative properties of social structure, notably the number of persons who belong to different groups and occupy different positions; the frequency distributions among positions; the frequencies of social associations; the degree to which variations in positions defined by different parameters are correlated; the extent to which the differentiation in terms of one parameter occurs within the substructures in terms of another parameter. This quantitative conception of social structure is inspired by Simmel. It does not encompass everything important in social life, nor does the theory resting on it. It is a primitive theory confined to the rudimentary properties of social structure. In particular, it ignores cultural differences, and another theory is required to deal with them. There is room for several theoretical paradigms in sociology at this early stage of its scientific development, as Merton (1975) stresses in a recent paper. But social structure is not culture, and the study of its quantitative dimensions—which constitute its core and distinguish it from culture—has been long neglected by sociologists, including most mathematical sociologists, two exceptions being Harrison C. White and Bruce H. Mayhew.

Theories also differ with respect to the substantive significance of their primitive assumptions. In some theories the primitive assumptions are brilliant insights that make the theory important; Darwin's theory is an illustration; so is Freud's. In other theories the primitive assumptions are givens, which are not original ideas but so obvious that they can be taken for granted, and the contribution of the theory rests on the new knowledge derived from the systematic analysis of the implications of combinations of simple assumptions and definitions. Much of economic theory, based on the assumptions of rationality and maximizing utilities, illustrates this type (the marginal principle, however, exemplifies a brilliant insight). The theory presented is of this second type, in which the primitive assumptions are not of great substantive import.

The substantive focus is on drawing the implications of the quantitative properties of social structure for social life. It is on the conclusions about social associations that are deducible from analytic propositions defining structural properties, directly or in combination with certain simple assumptions. Some of these assumptions rest essentially on psychological principles—for instance, the axiom that people prefer associates with whom they share social attributes (A-1)—just as some of the assumptions of economic theory do—for instance, that people maximize their own utility. This does not mean that the theorems can ultimately be explained in psychological terms (just as economic theory cannot be), because the sociopsychological premises must be combined with premises referring to structural properties to yield the conclusions. The structural premises cannot possibly be derived from psychological antecedents, since they are fundamentally arithmetic principles. When some simple arithmetic and some simple psychological propositions are applied jointly to properties of collectivities, a sociological theory comprising propositions about social structure *sui generis* is generated.

The theory is sociological in the specific sense that it explains patterns of social relations in terms of properties of social structure, not in terms of the assumptions made, whether or not these are derivable from psychological principles. The nature of the logical formulations employed makes the explanations structural. In a typical formulation, the major premise stipulates variations in structural properties, and the minor premise stipulates tendencies of people that are assumed to be invariant. The theorem about variations in social relations deduced from these premises is explained by the structural variations contained in the major premise, not by the invariant tendencies contained in the minor premise, because invariant conditions cannot account for variations in other conditions. For example, the major premise refers to variations in the extent to which structural parameters intersect, and the minor premise refers to the tendency of people to prefer ingroup to outgroup relations, which is assumed to be given and variations in which are not considered. The theorem implied by these premises (T-12) explains why intergroup relations are more or less prevalent, notwithstanding preferences for ingroup relations, in terms of structural conditions—the implications of variations in the intersection of parameters for social relations. To explore the implications of structural properties in a variety of substantive contexts, a considerable number of assumptions have been introduced (twenty), but most of them are used for deriving merely a few theorems. Only four axioms serve as premises for many theorems (A-1, A-9, A-10, A-11). In any case, the unity and distinctive character of the theory are rooted in the quantitative properties in terms of which social structure is defined, not in the assumptions. For the theorems have in common that they derive from primitive propositions at least one of which is analytic and defines one of several related quantitative properties of social structure.

Braithwaite (1953, p. 76) stresses the importance of abstract theoretical concepts that are not directly observable and have meaning only as elements of a theoretical system in which they imply propositions with terms that are directly observable: "A theory which it is hoped may be expanded in the future to explain more generalizations than it was originally designed to explain must allow more freedom to its theoretical terms than would be given them were they to be logical constructions out of observable entities." The endeavor here has been the opposite: to define most theoretical terms used precisely on the basis of operational criteria. The justification is that at this stage of development in sociological theorizing the main problem to be confronted is to have terms that are sufficiently precise to be employable in a deductive theory. Only when this problem has been overcome is the time ripe for advancing to theorizing with abstract terms that are not explicitly defined, as exemplified by the more abstract nature of Einstein's than Newton's concepts. Until then, abstract terms that are not explicitly operational must be used sparingly in systematic theories.

The generic terms used in theoretical generalizations are inherently abstract, even when defined by precise criteria, as Braithwaite (1953, pp. 85–87) notes. Although *group size* is a term that is precisely defined, for instance, universal propositions about the implications of size differences in all groups are not amenable to direct observation, as only some groups, not all possible ones, can be empirically observed. In this sense, most of the theoretical concepts employed are abstract. A few of the broadest concepts used are also abstract in the other sense of being defined only indirectly, not by explicit operational criteria, notably the concept of social structure itself and the overall characteristics of a social structure. A social structure has been defined as a multidimensional space of social positions among which a population is distributed; its complexity has been defined as the great number of different positions and the wide distribution of people among them. But these are not operational criteria that can be used to devise a measure of structure or a measure of complexity. The overall complexity and differentiation of a social structure must be inferred from the empirically observable specific degrees of differentiation and the correlations of the various parameters. Correspondingly, the overall degree of structural integration must be inferred from the directly observable patterns of social association with respect to various parameters.

Whereas the content of the theory is the quantitative dimension of social life, the form in which the theorems have been stated is qualitative. Only qualitative relationships have been indicated—if X increases, Y decreases—without attempting to specify the exact function that quantitative relationship assumes—how much Y changes with a given change in X. The reason is that deterministic qualitative propositions can often be formulated when quantitative ones cannot be (see Boudon 1973, pp. 199–201), because unknown other conditions influence the quantitative function but do not affect the qualitative comparison. Not all the theorems derived are deterministic, but some are.

Three types of theorems can be distinguished on the basis of the nature of the connection between terms. First, deterministic theorems stipulate an invariant relationship for every case regardless of any other conditions; for example, the rate of intergroup associations between two groups is higher for the smaller of the two (T-1). Second, probabilistic theorems stipulate that a relationship occurs in the majority of cases, though not in every one, regardless of other conditions; for example, the rate of outgroup associations probably increases with decreasing group size (T-1.5). Third, ceteris paribus theorems stipulate an influence of one condition on another that may be modified or suppressed by other conditions; for example, ceteris paribus, parameters that delineate ascribed positions are more salient than other parameters (T-4.3). But a distinction must be made between ceteris paribus propositions for which the other influences are unknown and those for which they are known, because in the latter case several ceteris paribus propositions can be combined into a deterministic set of propositions.[3] Many deterministic theorems are analytic propositions, which are true by definition or entailed by the terms of their premises, but this makes them no less significant in a deductive system of propositions in which the conclusions are synthetic propositions referring to relationships between independently defined terms. Deterministic propositions, including analytic ones, are of special importance as early links in chains of deductions, since conclusions derived in several steps from probabilistic and ceteris paribus propositions become increasingly tenuous.

The following synopsis of the theory presents all theorems with a brief reference to the premises from which they are deduced. It is organized to indicate the various theorems that follow from the same premises, but assumptions and theorems that have numerous implications in various combinations, such as A-1, A-9, and T-12, must be reintroduced at several points, since not all deductions can be traced simultaneously. To distinguish the derivation of a theorem from its possible later use as a premise, its number is set in boldface type at the place where it is derived in this summary. A sketchy overview of some of the implications the theorems have for one another is shown in figure 5. Not included in the figure are assumptions, definitions, and the implications of a theorem for others in its own set (a set being the theorems with the same digit to the left of the point). Thus, only the implications of a theorem in one set (usually the first one in the set) for theorems in another set are presented in the figure. It is evident that T-1 and T-12, both of which are deterministic propositions, have the widest range of implications. Definitions of major terms are provided in appendix A, and all assumptions are listed in appendix B. A separate index for assumptions and theorems, by number, is supplied.

Differences in Size

The rate of social associations of a group is the number of symmetric dyadic associations, however defined, of its members with a given set of persons (others in own group, those in another group, those in all other

---

3. It is not always simple to decide whether a theorem should be formulated in one or the other of these ways. For example, the proposition that the small size of a group in terms of one parameter tends to promote intergroup relations in terms of other parameters (T-14) is deterministic for a large number of parameters and substantial size differences; probabilistic for size differences with respect to some parameters; but requires a ceteris paribus if two specific parameters are singled out for attention. In this case the theorem has been formulated as probabilistic, on the assumption that the wording indicates that reference is not to two particular parameters.

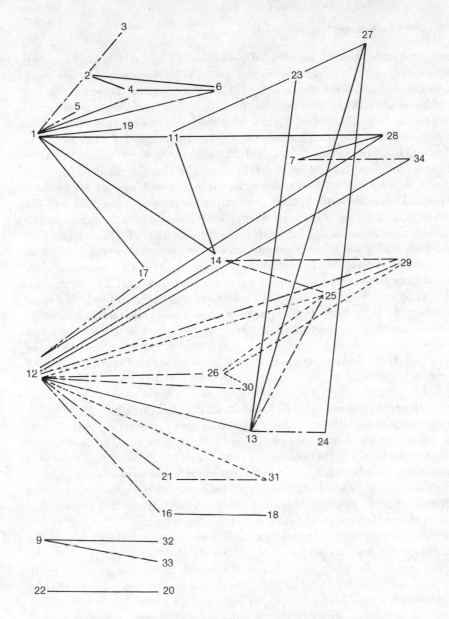

NUMBERS INDICATE SETS OF THEOREM

  _.._ Antecedent (left number) implies all consequences in set (right number)
  ____ Antecedent (left number) implies some consequences in set (right number)
  ...... Antecedent (left number) is alternative premise for all consequences
      (right number)
  ___ Antecedent (left number) is alternative premise for some consequences
      (right number)

FIGURE 5. CHAINS OF IMPLICATIONS: THEOREMS

groups) divided by the number of group members. It follows from this definition that the rate of intergroup associations between two groups is higher for the smaller of the two (**T-1**). This deterministic theorem, which is essentially an analytic proposition entailed by the definition, is pregnant with implications. It implies, jointly with three criteria of symmetric dyadic association, that the proportion who are intermarried (**T-1.11**), the mean number of intergroup associates (**T-1.12**), and the average amount of time spent in intergroup associations (**T-1.13**) are higher for the smaller of any two groups. It implies that every numerical minority—as well as all of them combined provided that they constitute less than one-half of the population—has more extensive intergroup relations with members of the majority than the majority has with minority members (**T-1.2**); specifically, that the minority has a larger proportion who are intermarried (**T-1.21**), that its members average more intergroup associates (**T-1.22**), and that they spend more time per person in intergroup associations (**T-1.23**). It also implies, inasmuch as people's scope of associations is not unlimited, that most members of a large majority have no close associate in small minority groups (**T-1.3**). It further implies that the greater the difference in size between two groups, the greater is the discrepancy in intergroup associations between them (**T-1.4**), because this discrepancy is an inverse function of the ratio of group size.

If for any two groups the smaller must have a higher rate of intergroup associations, as predicated by T-1, it follows that the probable rate of intergroup associations (with any other or all other groups) increases with declining group size for all groups delineated by a given nominal parameter (**T-1.5**). This probabilistic theorem is restricted to the groups distinguished by a given parameter, because extent of intergroup relations is also influenced by differences in the salience of parameters, for example, the greater salience of race than of white ethnic background for social intercourse. T-1 also implies that for close relations, of which no individual can have many, the probability of insulation from intergroup relations is less in the smaller than the larger of the groups delineated by a nominal parameter (**T-1.8**).

It is possible for a larger proportion of minority than majority members to be insulated from any social associations between the two, but only when other minority members have particularly many intergroup associates, because the average number of intergroup associates must be higher for the minority, according to T-1 and, specifically, T-1.22. The implication is that if a minority has a larger proportion of members than the majority who are insulated from intergroup contacts, the variation in number of intergroup associates within the minority must exceed that within the majority (**T-1.6**). This principle applies to the subgroups as well as individuals within a minority and hence to the several specific minorities that together constitute a broader minority group, for instance, the various nationality groups that compose the foreign-stock minority in the United States. T-1.6 therefore implies: If some minorities are more insulated from the majority than the majority is from them, other minorities have particularly extensive intergroup relations with the majority (**T-1.7**). A corollary, which is also deducible from T-1.2, is: If some minorities have lower rates of intergroup relations with the majority than the majority has with them, other minorities have particularly high rates of intergroup relations with the majority (**T-1.71**).

The salience of a parameter is the strength of its influence on social associations, as indicated by the preponderance of ingroup over intergroup relations. Changes in salience entail changes in the *number* of intergroup associations, but the resulting changes in *rates* of intergroup associations depend on the relative size of two groups, for the same reason that the rates themselves do, namely, that size is the denominator in ratios with a common numerator. T-1 applies to changes in the common numerator as well as to the original numerator, and thus implies that changes in a parameter's salience change a minority's rate of intergroup associations with the majority more than the majority's (**T-2**). It also implies probabilistic theorems about variations in group size, specifying the direction of change: Reductions in a nominal parameter's salience probably increase the rates of intergroup associations of small groups more than those of large ones (**T-2.11**). Intensified salience of a parameter probably decreases the rates of intergroup associations of small groups more than those of large ones (**T-2.12**).

Discrimination by a majority against a minority in social intercourse is one of the factors, though not the only one, that determines the amount of social association between the two groups, which reflects the parameter's salience. T-2 implies that such discrimination has paradoxical consequences for the rates of intergroup relations. *Ceteris paribus* (*hereafter abbreviated CP*), the more a majority discriminates in social intercourse against a minority, the smaller the discrepancy between the majority's lower and the minority's higher rate of intergroup associations (**T-3**). CP, as a majority's discrimination in social intercourse against a minority subsides, the discrepancy between the majority's lower and the minority's higher rate of intergroup associations becomes greater (**T-3.1**). Jointly with the proposition that insulation from close intergroup relations is inversely related to group size (T-1.8), T-2 implies that reduced discrimination by a majority against a minority enlarges the difference between the majority's higher and the minority's lower proportion of members who are insulated from close intergroup contacts, CP (**T-3.2**). Strange as it seems, a decline in discrimination by the majority against a minority increases the difference in the proportion of members of the two groups who have the social experience of participating in intergroup life.

The principle embodied in T-1 that the rates of intergroup associations of two groups are an inverse function of their size applies to arbitrary categories of persons as well as groups with natural boundaries, provided that there are any social associations between them. For any division of status above the median, consequently, the higher stratum has a higher rate of associations with the lower than the lower has with the higher (T-5). If an elite is defined as a small top stratum of the population in terms of any status criterion, T-1, specifically T-1.3, implies that most people are insulated from social contacts with the elite (T-5.1). It is reasonable to assume that status distributions are positively skewed, with frequencies increasing with decreasing status except for the lowest strata (A-5). Two implications of this assumption and T-1 are: CP, except for the lowest strata, the probability of association with status-distant persons increases with increasing status (T-5.2). Except for the lowest strata, the probable discrepancy in the rates of associations of two strata with each other increases with increasing status distance between them (T-5.3). Size differences among strata alone have these consequences, without taking into account any direct influence of status differences on social associations, and these influences of status itself are the reason that T-5.2 must be qualified by ceteris paribus (as demonstrated in chapter 3). On the assumption that status distance inhibits social associations (A-1.2), this influence of status and that of size differences (A-5, T-1) combine to make it probable that the rates of association of higher with lower strata decline less with increasing status distance than do the rates of lower with higher strata (T-5.4).

In a skewed status distribution (A-5), the size differences among strata imply (T-1) that, except for the lowest strata, the probability of people's associating with others below them is greater than their probability of associating with others above them (T-5.5). The reason is that a hierarchical structure makes it hardly feasible for most people to associate more with higher than lower strata, because this would require inconceivably high rates of associations of the small number of persons in the highest strata. If one assumes that superior status is manifest in superordinate roles in social associations (PA-6), T-5.5 implies that all people except those in the lowest strata are probably the superordinate in most of their nonpeer social associations (T-5.6). This is only possible because the members of the lowest strata must assume the subordinate role in most of their nonpeer associations, inasmuch as the total number of superordinate and subordinate roles in dyadic associations must be the same.

The influence of size differences is not confined to friendly interpersonal relations but extends to interpersonal conflict. Every overt dyadic conflict, whoever instigates it, involves two persons, just as every dyadic social association does. Accordingly, T-1 implies: Members of a minority experience dyadic conflict with the majority group more frequently than members of the majority do with that minority (T-17.2). Members of an elite experience dyadic conflict with lower strata more frequently than members of lower strata do with the elite (T-17.3).

The extent of ingroup as well as that of intergroup relations depends on a group's size. The density of ingroup relations, which may be considered an index of group cohesion, is defined as the actual number of ingroup associates per group member divided by the maximum possible (which is the number of group members minus one). Hence, the density of ingroup relations is an inverse function of group size, which implies a high probability that small groups have denser networks of ingroup relations than large ones (T-19.1). Both density of ingroup and rate of intergroup relations are an inverse function of group size, which explains why small groups tend to have both denser ingroup and more extensive intergroup relations than large ones. Moreover, the assumption that social associations are more prevalent among persons in proximate than those in distant social positions (A-1) implies that subgroups have higher rates and denser networks of ingroup relations than the larger groups they compose (T-19), which further increases the likelihood that small groups, many of which are subgroups of larger ones, have denser ingroup relations than large ones.

The scope of people's associates is not unlimited, particularly for close associates. The maximum number of associates a person can have is only one for current spouse and only a few for good friends, but a large number for casual acquaintance. The existing associations of group members limit the chances of other associations much more for close than for superficial relations. The stricter limits close relations impose on alternative relations imply that the closer the social bond under consideration, the greater is the probability that the rate of ingroup and the rate of intergroup relations are inversely correlated (T-19.2). This theorem in turn implies that close bonds within subgroups and close bonds among them that integrate them in the encompassing group are probably inversely correlated (T-19.3). There is some conflict between strong ingroup bonds and strong intergroup relations that integrate subgroups in an encompassing group and the society. To be sure, small groups tend to have denser networks of ingroup as well as more extensive intergroup relations, which mitigates this conflict. But this is the case only for nonexclusive associates, not for exclusive ones, like spouses, for which the conflict is severe. Homogamy limits rates of intermarriage, and increasing rates of intermarriage infringe more and more on ingroup marriages. T-19.2, together with the greater probability of high intermarriage rates of small groups (T-1.11, T-1.5), implies that increasing rates of intermarriage eventually threaten the survival of small groups (T-19.4). Assimilation entails lack of survival of a group, which is not necessarily disadvantageous for its members. But firm commitment to a distinctive ideology makes the preservation of a group's separate identity of great importance to its members. The assumption that small groups firmly committed to a distinctive ideology exert strong ingroup pressures to protect the group's survival (PA-14) implies, especially in combination with T-19.2, that such small groups have, CP, less extensive intergroup (T-19.5) and more extensive ingroup relations (T-19.6) than other small or large groups. Ideological small sects constitute an exception to the general principle that small groups tend to have high rates of intergroup relations (T-1.5), and their low rates further increase the likelihood of high rates of intergroup relations of other small groups (T-1.71).

Social mobility also influences intergroup relations, in part by altering the relative size of groups, and in part independent of any change in their size. The principle that size is inversely related to intergroup associations (T-1) implies that net outmobility increases and net inmobility decreases rates of intergroup associations, CP (T-4.6), and it implies that net upward mobility increases the rates of interstratum associations of the origin and decreases those of the terminal strata, CP (T-6.3). Changes in size alone account for these influences, and the theorems need to be qualified by ceteris paribus because other factors also affect associations, including other influences of mobility.

The theorems about the direct influences of social mobility on intergroup relations depend on two assumptions: Proximity of social positions promotes social associations (A-1), and established role relations resist disruption (PA-2). It follows from these two propositions that social mobility promotes intergroup relations, CP (T-4), because mobile persons have associates in their former group as well as in their present one. High rates of mobility have further repercussions, inasmuch as it is plausible to assume that strangers who have a common associate often become associates themselves (PA-3), which implies that mobile persons tend to bring together their associates in their former and in their present groups. It therefore follows from T-4 and PA-3 that high rates of mobility between two groups increase the rates of association between their nonmobile as well as their mobile members, CP (T-4.1). Applying this theorem to vertical mobility, two corollaries are: CP, high rates of vertical mobility between two strata increase the rates of association between their nonmobile as well as mobile members (T-6); CP, increasing vertical mobility in a society reduces the inhibiting effect of status on social associations (T-6.1).

Since the operational criterion of salience is a parameter's inhibiting effect on social association, another corollary of T-4.1 is that increasing rates of mobility reduce a parameter's salience, CP (T-4.2). This theorem, jointly with the definition of ascription, implies that parameters that delineate ascribed positions are more salient than other parameters, CP (T-4.3); and it implies that increasing rates of vertical mobility reduce the salience of status for social intercourse, CP (T-6.11). However, the consequences of changing rates of mobility for intergroup relations are contingent on group size, even when mobility is equal in both directions—termed motility—and thus does not affect group size, because changes in salience affect the rates of social associations of small groups more than those of large ones (T-2). Accordingly, three inferences of T-4.2 and T-2 are: CP, an increase in motility between a minority and a majority increases the minority's rate of intergroup associations more than the majority's (T-4.4); CP, an increase in motility among groups probably increases the rates of intergroup associations of small groups more than those of large ones (**T-4.5**); CP, rapid circulation of the elite increases the social contacts of elite members with others much more than the social contacts of others with the elite (**T-6.2**). All theorems in this chain of deduction have been qualified by ceteris paribus, since salience and thus associations may be subject to other influences, but the reinforcing assumptions (PA-2 and PA-3) make the theorems highly probable. Finally, intergroup relations have feedback effects on social mobility, on the assumption that associates in other groups or strata encourage and facilitate mobility there (PA-4). This assumption implies that high rates of intergroup associations increase rates of social mobility, CP (**T-4.7**), and that a parameter's pronounced salience inhibits social mobility, CP (**T-4.71**).

Frequency Distributions

The distributions of a population among social positions define structural differentiation. The two main forms of differentiation are heterogeneity, which refers to people's distribution among groups with boundaries delineated by a nominal parameter, and inequality, which refers to people's distribution in terms of a status continuum delineated by a graduated parameter. Heterogeneity is defined as the probability that two randomly chosen persons do not belong to the same group. Inequality is defined as mean status distance relative to mean status. Status diversity, which is the equivalent of heterogeneity for positions delineated by a graduated parameter, is defined as the probability that two randomly chosen persons do not have the same status or do not belong to the same equidistant status interval.

Changes in inequality are completely determined by three conditions: (1) differences among strata in net fertility—birth rates minus death rates; (2) differences among strata in net immigration—immigration from outside minus emigration; (3) internal mobility. Any change in status—for example, in income or in power—is included in the concept of mobility. The lower strata are those below median status; the distinction between the highest and middle strata depends on the degree of inequality (see note 8 in chapter 3). The axiom that the status distribution is positively skewed (A-5) implies the following theorems: CP, if the net fertility of lower strata exceeds that of other strata, inequality increases (**T-8**). CP, if the net immigration into lower strata exceeds that into other strata, inequality increases (**T-8.1**). CP, downward mobility of lower or middle strata increases inequality (**T-9.1**). CP, upward mobility of the highest strata increases inequality (**T-9.2**).[4] Although these four theorems have been qualified by ceteris paribus, the entire set is

4. T-9.1 and T-9.2 are somewhat differently formulated in chapter 3, using assumptions about fertility and immigration instead of ceteris paribus.

deterministic, since the only other conditions that influence inequality and require the ceteris paribus are those specified in the three other theorems. A caveat is necessary, however: Opposite rates of mobility of specific strata must not be averaged for use as terms in the theorems, because status changes of extreme strata influence inequality more than those of less extreme ones.

Corresponding theorems can be derived from A-5 about reductions in inequality: CP, upward mobility of lower or middle strata diminishes inequality (T-9.3). CP, downward mobility of the highest strata diminishes inequality (T-9.4). Empirical data justify not only the assumption that status distributions are positively skewed (A-5) but also two other assumptions: that the rates of net fertility of lower strata are no less than those of other strata (PA-7), and that in developed countries, like the United States, rates of net immigration into lower strata are no less than those into other strata (PA-8). Under these assumptions, differences in fertility and immigration can only increase inequality, not decrease it, and thus cannot counteract patterns of mobility that also increase it, which makes it possible to combine T-9.1 and T-9.2 into a deterministic theorem, omitting the ceteris paribus: If lower or middle strata are downwardly or highest strata upwardly mobile, without any of them moving in opposite directions, inequality increases. Another inference derivable from these three assumptions is that for inequality to diminish it is necessary that some lower or middle strata experience upward mobility or some highest strata experience downward mobility (T-9).

Changes in status diversity are also completely determined by the three conditions that determine changes in inequality, though not in the same ways. The assumption that the status structure is positively skewed (A-5) implies that there is less status diversity among lower strata and that the lower strata contribute less to the total status diversity than the higher strata, from which the following propositions can be deduced: CP, if the net fertility of lower strata exceeds that of higher strata, status diversity declines (T-10). CP, if the net immigration into lower strata exceeds that into higher strata, status diversity declines (T-10.1). CP, downward mobility from higher toward modal status reduces status diversity (T-10.2). CP, upward mobility from lower toward modal status reduces status diversity (T-10.3).[5] CP, upward mobility from modal status increases status diversity (T-10.4). CP, downward mobility from modal status increases status diversity (T-10.5).

The assumption that status distance inhibits social associations (A-1.2) implies, given the definition of inequality in terms of mean status distance, that reductions in inequality diminish the impact of status on social associations, CP (T-7). It also implies that decentralization of authority in organizations, since it reduces differences in authority, promotes informal relations

5. T-10.1 and T-10.2 were somewhat differently formulated in chapter 3, using assumptions about fertility and immigration.

among administrative ranks, CP (T-30.3). An inference of T-7 is that the concentration of power, which entails great inequality and a highly skewed distribution, insulates most of the large class of persons who have virtually no power from higher strata, CP (T-34).

Heterogeneity creates barriers to social intercourse (as implies by A-1.1, that social associations are less prevalent among than within groups), but much heterogeneity weakens these barriers. This paradoxical conclusion is deducible from the highly plausible—indeed, practically tautological—axiom that social associations depend on opportunities for social contacts (A-9). For this axiom implies that increasing heterogeneity, which by definition entails greater chances that fortuitous contacts involve persons of different groups, increases the probability of intergroup associations (T-11). It also implies that increasing status diversity, which is correspondingly defined, increases the probability of associations among persons whose status differs (T-11.3). On the assumption that widespread social practices meet less social disapproval that discourages them (A-10), the initial increases in intergroup relations resulting from increased heterogeneity, owing to greater opportunities, are reinforced by the lesser ingroup disapproval intergroup associations encounter as they become more widely accepted. According to A-10 and T-1, the intergroup relations between two groups tend to encounter more disapproval in the larger group, where they are less widespread, which implies that the larger of two groups discriminates more than the smaller against associating with the other group, CP (T-11.1). An exception to this proposition, which reveals the need for the ceteris paribus, is the previously mentioned tendency of ideological sects to exert strong ingroup pressures that discriminate against intergroup associations (T-19.5). The theorem that the discrepancies in rates of intergroup associations are an inverse function of size differences (T-1.4) has two implications: Increasing heterogeneity, which usually reduces size differences, probably reduces discrepancies in intergroup relations among groups (T-11.2). Increasing status diversity, which always reduces size differences, reduces discrepancies in rates of associations among strata (T-11.4). In short, heterogeneity and status diversity, two forms of differentiation, lessen the differences in intergroup involvement.

If social associations depend on opportunities for contacts (A-9), physical propinquity increases the probability of social associations (T-13), since propinquity increases the chances of contacts. A number of inferences derive from this theorem: The probability of association with many different persons increases with increasing size and population density of a place (T-23). The probability that people have wide circles of acquaintances increases with the increasing size and population density of the community where they live (T-23.11); with the increasing size of the place where they work (T-23.12); with the increasing urbanization of society (T-23.2); and with the increasing concentration of the labor force in large work organizations (T-23.3). Moreover, T-23 implies that urbanization is a catalyst of social relations, which probably has a multiplier effect on the influences exerted by the conditions characteristic of urban places on social relations (**T-23.4**).

Large cities attract diverse people from many places, which warrants the assumption—supported by empirical data—that community size and density are positively correlated with heterogeneity (PA-15). Given this assumption, the theorem that heterogeneity promotes intergroup relations (T-11) implies that the probability of intergroup associations increases with increasing size and density of a community (**T-23.5**). This theorem, jointly with the principle that urbanization is a catalyst of social relations (T-23.4), implies that the probability of intergroup relations in a society increases with increasing urbanization (**T-23.6**). It also implies, jointly with the assumption that overt interpersonal conflict depends on opportunities for contact (PA-13), that the probability of overt interpersonal conflict between members of different groups increases with increasing size and density of a community (**23.7**). This in turn implies, jointly with T-23.4, that the probability of interpersonal conflict between members of different groups increases with the increasing urbanization of society (**T-23.71**).

Urbanization promotes conflict of various kinds, just as it promotes a more intense, varied, and stimulating social life, owing to the greater opportunities for both interpersonal conflict and diverse social relations. The nostalgic image of the peaceful coexistence of different groups in the past, when they lived in rustic communities, is a mirage. Small tribes living in different communities are recurrently at war, and what little peace there is among them results from their ingroup prejudices that keep them apart. A rustic life entails less friction than an urban life, but it also entails less contact among diverse people, more intolerance, and less civilization, which is a high price to pay for reduced friction.

The simple axiom that social associations depend on opportunities for contact (A-9) has many implications. It implies that propinquity increases the probability of social associations (T-13), as already noted. In combination with this proposition (T-13), it (A-9) further implies that efficient means of transportation, which enhance contact opportunities across social distances, reduce the influence of propinquity on social associations, CP (**T-24**); and that such transportation improves the integration of different communities in society by increasing the social associations among distant places, CP (**T-24.1**). But people's use of efficient transportation may be assumed to depend on financial resources (PA-18). Three inferences of this assumption and T-24 are: CP, the influence of physical propinquity on social associations is inversely related to society's wealth (**T-24.2**); CP, it is inversely related to an individual's income (**T-24.3**); CP, it is directly related to the degree of income inequality in society (**T-24.4**).

The division of labor is a form of heterogeneity of special importance. A corollary of the theorem that heterogeneity raises the probability of intergroup relations (T-11) is that an advanced division of labor promotes social associations among different occupations, CP (T-28). The ceteris paribus refers to the fact that occupational differences are nearly always correlated with various status differences, which have the opposite effect, according to the theorem that status inequality depresses social associations (T-7): CP, inequality in occupational status depresses the social associations among occupations (T-28.1). The more advanced the division of labor, the more it divides work, not into simple routines performed by large numbers with little training and skill, but into many specialities each performed by relatively few persons with much training and skill. Two inferences can be derived from this property of the division of labor in combination with T-11 and T-7: The extent to which the division of labor is in the form of expert specialization rather than routinization increases the social associations among different occupations, CP (T-28.2). The relationship between the division of labor and the prevalence of social associations among different occupations is nonmonotonic, being most positive at advanced stages of the division of labor (T-28.3).

The assumption that the division of labor depends on opportunities for communication (PA-17) entails the theorem that opportunities for communication and association promote the division of labor, CP (T-27). Several inferences can be derived from this theorem. It implies, jointly with the principle that the concentration of many persons in one place fosters social associations (T-23), that a community's size and density increases the division of labor, CP (T-27.1); and that society's urbanization does, CP (T-27.11). It implies that linguistic heterogeneity impedes the development of the division of labor, CP (T-27.2); and that improvements in means of communication promote it, CP (T-27.31). T-27 also implies, jointly with the proposition that transportation facilities increase social associations among different places (T-24.1), that efficient means of transportation further the development of the division of labor, CP (T-27.3). Moreover, T-27.1 implies that large work organizations promote the division of labor in society, CP (T-27.5). In other words, the average size of a society's work organizations and its division of labor are positively correlated. Inasmuch as the most advanced division of labor involves a shift from much routine work to more work by expert specialists, the assumption seems justified that an advanced division of labor depends on substantial training of the labor force (PA-18). This assumption entails the theorem that rising levels of education and qualifications lead to the development of an advanced division of labor, CP (T-27.4). Many factors affect the progress of the division of labor, quite possibly more than have been specified, which requires the propositions to be qualified by ceteris paribus.

An advanced division of labor depends on a trained labor force, and it transforms the training of the labor force into economically utilized and socially significant occupational skills. The training and skills of the labor force do not directly determine the degree of division of labor, however, because supply of training and skills is not identical with demand for them, and they may go unutilized, as is the case for craft skills at stages when the division of labor takes predominantly the form of routinization. The advanced division of labor takes advantage of people's skill potential by requiring specialized qualifications for more and more work, and it thus creates incentives for many to acquire substantial vocational education. Accordingly, an inference of the proposition that upward mobility of lower strata reduces inequality (T-9.3) is that advanced stages of the division of labor diminish inequalities in education and occupational qualifications, CP (T-32). There is a complex interdependence between the division of labor and the training of the labor force, since demand for and supply of qualified labor mutually influence each other. Economic theory would lead one to expect that the diminished inequalities in amount of training accompanying an advanced division of labor will diminish income inequalities in the long run.

Whereas an advanced division of labor tends to diminish some inequalities in society, it is likely to be positively correlated with inequality in power, not because an advanced division of labor itself intensifies the concentration of power, but because large organizations promote the development of both. If administrative authority is defined by the number of persons under a manager's jurisdiction, the authority of top executives increases with the increasing size of organizations. Hence, the theorem that increasing status of the highest stratum increases inequality (T-9.2) implies that authority becomes more concentrated with the increasing size of a work organization (T-33). This theorem implies, on the assumption that authority over employees is the source of most administrative power in contemporary society (PA-19), that the expanding size of the work organizations in a society engenders growing concentration of administrative power, CP (T-33.1). Top executives of an organization exercise authority over the allocation of its economic resources as well as over its employees. Two inferences can be derived from the assumption that top positions in organizations with large assets are the source of much control over economic resources in contemporary society (PA-20): The expanding size of the work organizations in a society engenders growing concentration of economic power, CP (T-33.2). The expanding size of the work organizations in a society reduces the correlation of ownership of wealth and economic power, CP (T-33.4). However, T-33.1 and T-33.2 imply that the expanding size of the work organizations in a society increases the correlation of administrative and economic power, CP (T-33.3). In short, giant organizations concentrate and consolidate two major forms of power in the hands of few men.

Nexus of Parameters

The most important attribute of society's structure is its being delineated by multiple lines of differentiation. This has not yet been taken into consideration in the review of the theory, which has so far been confined to social differentiation in terms of a single parameter (except for the brief references just made to correlations of power). A society has a complex structure if people are widely distributed among a multitude of different social positions, which depends partly on the degree of differentiation in terms of each parameter and primarily on the nexus of parameters, the degree to which numerous parameters are intersecting rather than consolidated. The operational criterion of intersecting parameters is the converse of the positive correlation between them (that is, a low positive or a negative correlation). Structural complexity is defined by the number of different social positions and the wide distribution of the population among them; but this number cannot be directly observed, nor can the distribution of people among positions many of which they occupy simultaneously. These, and therefore structural complexity, must be inferred from the degrees of differentiation in various respects and, particularly, the extent to which parameters intersect.

This conception of social structure entails the following analytic propositions: The more parameters intersect, the greater the structural complexity (T-15). The more nominal parameters intersect, the greater the multiform heterogeneity (T-15.1). The more graduated parameters intersect, the greater the overall status diversity (T-15.2). However, the case is different for inequalities. Whereas consolidated *group* differences—for example, a strong correlation between religion and ethnic background—reduce the overall heterogeneity in society, consolidated *status* differences—for example, a strong correlation of income and power—do not reduce overall inequality; on the contrary, they intensify it. The reason is that status dimensions are socially recognized and valued rank-orders which make various statuses comparable and combinable, so that being both poor and uneducated is socially treated as being lower in status than being affluent and uneducated. The assumption is made that status differences are differences in comparable social resources of generally acknowledged validity in social exchange (A 12). This assumption implies that the more graduated parameters are consolidated, the greater the overall inequality (T-15.3).

Intersecting parameters promote intergroup relations, and consolidated parameters impede them. This is the case whether the form of differentiation of the parameters themselves promotes intergroup relations, as heterogeneity does, or impedes them, as inequality does; and it is the case whether both parameters refer to distributions among social positions or one of them refers to the spatial distribution of people among different places. If a social distribution of people is highly correlated with their spatial distribution, it means that the various groups or strata are geographically segregated and live largely in different cities or neighborhoods. Segregation is a social manifestation of physical propinquity; when segregation is low, most people live in proximity to other groups or strata; when it is high, few do.

Several implications concerning segregation follow from the theorem that physical propinquity increases the probability of social associations (T-13), which in turn derives from the assumption that social associations depend on opportunities for contact (A-9): The spatial segregation of groups or strata reduces the probability of social associations between their members (T-13.1). The spatial segregation of the groups delineated by a nominal parameter increases the probable preponderance of ingroup over intergroup relations (T-13.11). The spatial segregation of social strata delineated by a graduated parameter decreases the probability of social associations between persons whose status differs (T-13.12). The spatial segregation of groups counters the positive influence of heterogeneity on intergroup relations (T-13.2). The spatial segregation of social strata reinforces the negative influence of inequality on social associations among different strata (T-13.3).

These theorems are a special case of the general principle that substantial positive correlations of parameters inhibit social associations. Geographical segregation means that a parameter pertaining to the social distribution of people is correlated with their spatial distribution, which has essentially the same significance for social life as the correlations of two social distributions. Physical distance undoubtedly inhibits social associations more than do many forms of social distance, though surely not more than all. The influences of social and physical proximity on social relations are equivalent, whatever the differences in degree of influence. Spatial distributions can be treated as parameters, and the above theorems about segregation can be subsumed under the following ones about correlated parameters, the extent to which parameters are consolidated or intersect.

Intersecting parameters exert compelling constraints to engage in intergroup relations, provided that a considerable number intersect substantially, because people's ingroup relations in one respect are intergroup relations in others when numerous parameters intersect. In contrast, consolidated parameters widen the barriers among groups and strata, as one form of social distance is reinforced by others. There must be a threshold in the strength of the positive correlation of parameters at which they switch from being intersecting and furthering intergroup relations to being consolidated and hindering them. The constraints of multiple parameters, depending on their correlation, are deducible from two assumptions: Social associations are more prevalent among persons in proximate than those in distant social positions (A-1); the influences of various parameters on social associations are partly additive (A-11). The latter assumption implies that social associations are more prevalent among persons who share two than those who share only one of these two social positions (though not necessarily more than among persons who share a different social position which may be more salient), and it is required to make inferences about the influences of two or three parameters, though not if many intersecting parameters are under consideration.[6]

6. Many intersecting parameters exert compelling constraints on intergroup relations, which obviates the need for A-11. For the same reason, A-11 was not used above for deriving the

The basic theorems about implications of the correlations of parameters are deducible from these two assumptions: The lower the positive correlations of parameters, the more extensive are intergroup relations (T-12). Intersecting nominal parameters increase intergroup relations which integrate various groups (T-12.1). Consolidated nominal parameters strengthen ingroup bonds and weaken intergroup relations (T-12.11). Intersecting graduated parameters increase social associations among different strata which integrate them (T-12.2). Consolidated graduated parameters attenuate social relations among different strata (T-12.21). The intersection of nominal by graduated parameters increases social associations among groups and strata which integrate them (T-12.3). The consolidation of group differences and status differences attenuates social relations among groups and strata (T-12.31). Both the influences of multiple intersection and those of multiple consolidation are cumulative. Thus, an implication of T-13.1 and T-12.11 is that segregation reinforces the negative effect of consolidated parameters on intergroup relations, CP (T-13.4).

A great many inferences are deducible from T-12, in combination with various definitions and other propositions. It implies: The intersection of the division of labor with group differences promotes integrative intergroup relations, CP (T-28.4). The intersection of the division of labor with kinship lineages weakens bonds of extended kinship, CP (T-28.41). The consolidation of the division of labor with differences in occupational status attenuates integrative relations among occupational groups and strata, CP (T-28.42). Jointly with the proposition that the concentration of power insulates the lower class from higher strata (T-34), it (specifically T-12.21) implies that consolidated powers further insulate the lower class from social intercourse with higher strata, CP (T-34.1). The latter, jointly with the proposition that the expanding size of organizations consolidates powers (T-33.3), implies that the growing average size of organizations increases the insulation of the lower class from dominant strata, CP (T-34.2).

Intersecting parameters enhance not only integrative relations but also interpersonal conflict among groups and strata. This follows from the assumption that overt interpersonal conflict depends on opportunities for social contact (PA-13) and the theorem that intersecting parameters promote social contacts among different groups and strata (T-12). The implications of these two propositions are: Intersecting parameters increase the probability of interpersonal conflict between members of various groups and strata (T-17). Multiform heterogeneity increases the probability of interpersonal conflict among groups (T-17.1). Intersecting graduated parameters increase the

theorems about segregation (T-13.1 to T-13.3). Although not any physical distance inhibits social intercourse more than some salient forms of social distance, sufficient physical distance exerts compelling restraints on chances of social association (A-9, T-13), obviating the need for the assumption that its influence is partly independent of that of other parameters. If one rejects this argument, the theorems about segregation require this assumption (A-11).

probability of interpersonal conflict among different strata (T-17.11). The intersection of nominal by graduated parameters increases the probability of interpersonal conflict among groups and strata (T-17.12). Moreover, if intersecting parameters increase the chances of intergroup contacts (T-12) on which both friendly associations (A-9) and interpersonal conflict (PA-13) depend, it follows that the extent of friendships and the extent of interpersonal conflict among groups and strata are positively correlated, CP (T-17.4); and that this positive correlation is much reduced if degree of parameter intersection is controlled, CP (T-17.5). Integrative relations among groups and strata cannot develop without opportunities for social contact, but these also increase the chances of interpersonal conflict among their members. There is a misleading positive correlation between extent of intergroup relations and conflict between group members, which is largely—and perhaps entirely—spurious, resulting from the effects of the same structural conditions on the probabilities of both friendly relations and interpersonal conflict.

The structural constraints exerted by intersecting parameters on intergroup relations depend on a group's size. They are greater for smaller than for larger groups, because the smaller a group is, the greater is the likelihood that ingroup associates in terms of one parameter have different social positions in terms of intersecting parameters. If ingroup associations are prevalent (A-1); and if small size increases the chances that ingroup associations in terms of one parameter involve intergroup contacts in terms of intersecting parameters; and if social associations depend on opportunities for contact (A-9); it follows that the smaller the size of a group in terms of one nominal parameter, the greater is the probability that its members have extensive intergroup relations in terms of intersecting parameters (T-14). By the same token, the smaller the size of an elite in terms of one graduated parameter, the greater is the probability that its members associate with persons whose positions differ from theirs in terms of other parameters (T-14.3). An implication of the last proposition is that there is a high probability of extensive social relations among various elites defined by different graduated parameters (T-14.31). This theorem can explain the tendency of various elites in society to become integrated into one dominant elite.

A person who has associates in many different groups may be characterized as having a cosmopolitan role set. Since the small size of a group enhances the probabilities of all kinds of intergroup relations, in terms of this parameter (T-1.5) as well as intersecting ones (T-14), the probability of cosmopolitan role sets increases with decreasing group size when parameters intersect (T-14.1). Whereas the small size of an elite makes cosmopolitan role sets likely (in accordance with T-5 and T-14.3), elite status in one respect is often correlated with status and group differences in others, and such consolidation of parameters reduces the probability that elite members have cosmopolitan role sets (T-14.4). Generally, the prevalence of cosmopolitan role sets in society depends on low correlations of structural parameters, because intersecting parameters in complex social structures promote inter-group relations, which entail a greater variety of role relations. Thus, an implication of the theorems that intergroup relations are promoted by heterogeneity (T-11) and by intersecting nominal parameters (T-12.1) is that multiform heterogeneity makes cosmopolitan role sets more prevalent, CP (T-14.2).

Structural conditions, defined by the distributions of people and the nexus of parameters, often generate social processes that reinforce the initial effects of these conditions on role relations. Processes of social exchange tend to reward conduct that conforms to widely accepted and expected group practices with social approval, while violations of these expectations are reacted to with disapproval. Such social processes have structural effects on social relations, that is, multiplier effects of the influences directly attribut-able to the structural conditions themselves. Structural effects on intergroup relations can be inferred from the theorem that intersecting parameters increase intergroup relations (T-12) and the axiom that group pressures that discourage social practices subside as these practices become more wide-spread (A-10). Three inferences are: CP, the pronounced intersection of parameters has a structural effect on the prevalence of intergroup relations, increasing them more than would the additive effects of the parameters alone (T-21). CP, the pronounced intersection of a nominal by other parame-ters has a structural effect on the prevalence of intergroup relations, increas-ing them more than would the additive effects of the parameters alone (T-21.1). CP, the pronounced consolidation of a nominal with graduated parameters has a structural effect on the predominance of ingroup relations, increasing them more than would the additive effects of the parameters alone (T-21.11).

Strong correlations of a nominal with graduated parameters have struc-tural effects not only on the prevalence of ingroup associations but also on superordination in intergroup relations. Such strong correlations mean that one group is greatly superior in average status and resources to another, or that some groups are greatly superior to others. In this situation, most members of the first group (or groups) have the superordinate role in their relations with most members of the second, according to the assumption that superior status is manifest in superordination in role relations (PA-6). As superordination on the part of one group and subordination on the part of the other are the prevailing social practices, group pressures arise that enforce them, in accordance with the assumption that social pressures discourage deviations from widely accepted social practices (A-10). Once superordina-tion and subordination are socially expected and enforced as an inherent right of the members of one group and an inherent obligation of the mem-bers of another, group membership itself is transformed into ranked status, in the sense of Weber's *Stand*. Hence, the inferences of the two assumptions are: CP, the pronounced consolidation of a nominal with graduated parameters has a structural effect on superordination in intergroup relations, which is manifest in an influence of mean group status, independent of individual's own status, on superordination (**T-22**). CP, membership in groups that differ greatly in average status bestow corresponding status differences on individuals that affect superordination-subordination in their intergroup relations (**T-22.1**).

The group's average status affects superordination in *ingroup* relations in the opposite way, because the higher the status of one's group, the lower is likely to be one's own status relative to that of other members. PA-6 implies that the probability that a person with a given status has the superordinate role in ingroup relations declines with increasing mean status of the group (**T-22.2**). A further inference of this theorem and T-22.1 is: CP, strong correlations of a nominal with graduated parameters make it likely that persons with a given status are superordinate in intergroup and subordinate in ingroup relations if they belong to high-status groups, and that they are subordinate in intergroup and superordinate in ingroup relations if they belong to low-status groups (**T-22.3**). Thus, the average socioeconomic status of WASPs is higher than that of Chicanos, which makes WASPs superordinate in intergroup relations, but WASPs with median status are inferior to most WASPs, while Chicanos with the same median status are superior to most Chicanos.

One can look at intergroup relations from the perspective of the participants and ask what persons are most likely to be involved in them. A corollary of the theorem that intersecting nominal parameters promote intergroup relations (T-12.1) is that intergroup relations in terms of one nominal parameter are most probable for persons who belong to the same groups in terms of other nominal parameters (**T-20**). This theorem follows from the same two assumptions as T-12.1: that common or proximate social positions promote social associations (A-1) and that the influences of various parameters on social associations are partly additive (A-11). For graduated parameters, however, the case is different. The assumption that various status differences are differences in comparable social resources (A-12) implies that opposite status differences make overall status more proximate. The inference of A-12, jointly with A-1 and A-11, is that status-distant associations in terms of one graduated parameter are most probable for persons whose status differs in the opposite direction in terms of other graduated parameters, CP (**T-20.1**). Together with T-22.1, that a group's status reflects on the status of its members, these three assumptions yield two other inferences: CP, when groups differ substantially in status, intergroup relations are most probable for persons whose own status differs in the opposite direction from their group status (**T-20.2**). CP, the stronger the correlations between nominal and graduated parameters, the greater is the tendency for the personal status of intergroup associates to differ in the opposite direction from their group status (**T-20.3**).

Social mobility, too, is influenced by the nexus of parameters. This can be deduced from T-12, that the correlation of parameters governs the extent of social associations among groups and strata, and PA-4, that associates in other groups and strata encourage and facilitate mobility there. Consequently, intersecting parameters increase social mobility (**T-16**); consolidated nominal parameters restrict intergroup mobility (**T-16.1**); and consolidated graduated parameters restrict vertical mobility (**T-16.2**). Intersecting parameters exert additional influences on social mobility which reinforce those predicated in these theorems on the basis of PA-4. An inference of the assumption that ingroup associations are more prevalent than outgroup associations (A-1.1) is that people are attracted to members of their own groups even when they do not know them. Intersecting nominal parameters imply that many people who belong to different groups in terms of one parameter share group memberships in terms of others, and these attractive, as yet unknown, potential ingroup associates along intersecting lines are likely to stimulate intergroup mobility, as exemplified by people who move to neighborhoods where others share their ethnic background. For vertical mobility, the assumption that supplements the influence of PA-4 is A-12, that status differences are differences in social resources. Intersecting graduated parameters imply, given this assumption, that people lacking some resources have others which facilitate their acquiring the first—that is, social mobility—as illustrated by persons who use their wealth to improve their power position or who use their power to enhance their wealth.

Processes of social mobility implement structural change and adjustment in response to the pressures of new developments, and these processes of change are rooted in intersecting parameters. Structural change occurs when the distribution of people among social positions or when the relationship between parameters is altered, which implies that social mobility engenders structural change (**T-18**). To be sure, only excess mobility in certain directions changes the degree of inequality or heterogeneity in terms of a given parameter. Motility—equal amounts of mobility in opposite directions—does not, but it nevertheless contributes to structural change, both directly and indirectly. Since people do not move with respect to all their positions simultaneously, motility alters the relationship between parameters, which implies that motility engenders structural change (**T-18.1**). Moreover, motility makes the social structure more flexible and less resistant to change, because it expands intergroup associations (T-4.1), which in turn facilitate subsequent social mobility (T-4.7) when the pressure of new conditions require such mobility to effect structural adjustments. A complex structure stimulates these social processes that speed change and adjustment. The theorem that intersecting parameters increase social mobility (T-16) and T-18 imply that intersecting parameters increase the probability of structural change (**T-18.2**) and that consolidated parameters decrease this probability (**T-18.21**).

Whereas a complex structure changes more readily than one with consolidated parameters, some of the changes its intersecting parameters promote tend to make these parameters less intersecting and more consolidated. If ingroup associations are prevalent (A-1.1); and if associates in other groups increase rates of mobility there (PA-4); it follows that people are most likely to move to those groups in terms of one parameter where there are many persons who belong to the same groups as they in terms of other parameters; and this implies that social mobility increases the consolidation of nominal parameters, CP (T-18.3). Moreover, if status differences are differences in comparable resources (A-12), it follows that those persons are most likely to rise in status in terms of one parameter who have ample resources in terms of others, which correspondingly implies that social mobility increases the consolidation of graduated parameters, CP (T-18.31).[7] Various conditions in complex social structures further enhance their complexity, but it appears that this growth of complexity is kept within bounds by countervailing social processes that foster consolidation and thereby lessen structural complexity.

Differentiation within Substructures

The components of a complex social structure are themselves social structures, which are interrelated. A complex social structure is comprised of the multidimensional space of social positions and role relations within and among its substructures. It is possible to go beyond the analysis of various forms of differentiation, their connections, and the implications of these forms and their connections for social associations and integration, by taking into consideration substructures. Any form of differentiation can be partitioned into the differentiation existing within and that among the major substructures of a society, for instance, its communities or its work organizations. The influence of society's differentiation on social associations can then be decomposed into that exerted by the differentiation within substructures and that resulting from the differentiation among them.

Since physical propinquity strongly influences social associations (T-13), most social associations occur within rather than among communities. One would therefore expect that social relations are more adversely affected by barriers that exist within communities than by such barriers among communities; for instance, that social associations are more inhibited by the income inequalities within communities than by the difference in average incomes among communities. Actually, the opposite is the case. Society's inequalities inhibit social relations less if they exist primarily within than if they exist largely among communities, and the same is true for all forms of differentiation in regard to all kinds of substructures. The reason is that the

---

7. T-18.3 and T-18.31 were combined in one theorem in chapter 5.

adverse effect of inequality on social intercourse is counteracted by physical propinquity for status differences within communities. Generally, differentiation within substructures means that the parameter delineating the differentiation and the one circumscribing the substructures are intersecting, which promotes intergroup relations, whereas differentiation among substructures means that they are consolidated, which inhibits them.

The principle from which the theorems about differentiation within substructures can be deduced is that intersecting parameters promote intergroup relations (T-12). Alternatively, they can be directly derived from the primitive assumptions from which T-12 is deduced. The issue is not what influences differentiation in communities or in organizations has on social relations—these influences are specified by the theorems about differentiation—but what influences on social relations are exerted by the fact that society's existing differentiation occurs primarily within rather than among its communities or organizations or other substructures. The basic theorem for communities is: The more society's differentiation in terms of any parameter results from that within rather than among communities, the more probable are intergroup relations both in terms of this parameter and among communities (**T-25**). Differentiation within communities entails intersection, whereas that among them entails consolidation, of the parameter with people's spatial distribution. Consequently, T-25 is implied by T-12, that intersecting parameters promote intergroup relations in terms of both parameters. It is also implied by the axiom that social associations are more prevalent for proximate positions (A-1) and the assumption that the influences of parameters are partly additive (A-11), because the physical proximity of different groups in the same communities promotes associations among them and the proximate social positions of persons in different communities promote associations among communities. Since A-1 has not been used to refer to physical proximity, however, it is preferable to add another premise to this derivation, T-13, that physical propinquity promotes social associations, which implies that differentiation within rather than among communities promotes intergroup relations.

T-25 has numerous corollaries, which are deducible from the same premises: The more society's heterogeneity in terms of a nominal parameter results from that within rather than among communities, the more probable are intergroup relations both in terms of this parameter and among communities (**T-25.1**); the smaller the size of a group under this condition, the greater are the probabilities of intergroup and intercommunity relations (**T-25.11**); CP, the small size of a community under this condition promotes intergroup and intercommunity relations (**T-25.12**).[8] The more society's inequality in terms of a graduated parameter results from the inequality within

8. T-25.11 and T-25.12 are also implied by T-14.1, the probability that members of small groups have cosmopolitan role sets when parameters intersect. But the heterogeneity of large cities exerts a counteracting influence on intergroup relations, according to PA-15, which is the reason for the ceteris paribus in T-25.12.

rather than that among communities, the more probable are social associations both among different strata and among different communities (T-25.2); the smaller an elite under this condition, the more probable are its associations with other strata and with elites in different communities (T-25.21).[9] The more the consolidation of two parameters in society results from their concomitant variation within rather than that among communities, the greater are the probabilities of associations among members of different groups, strata, and communities (T-25.3).

It is paradoxical that inequalities and even consolidated inequalities, which greatly inhibit social associations, promote social associations of all kinds when they occur primarily within communities where most social associations take place. The paradox is explained by the reinforcing effect of segregation. When rich powerful persons and poor powerless people live in the same communities, associations between them are not so unlikely, owing to propinquity, as when they live in different communities, owing to segregation; the former situation where different strata are not segregated also makes associations among communities more likely, owing to the greater dispersal of persons with the same consolidated status and interests among different communities.

The division of labor in society can be partitioned into that within work organizations and that among them. The effects on social relations of the internal division of labor, which means that organizations and occupations intersect, can be correspondingly deduced either from the axioms that social associations are more prevalent for proximate positions (A-1) and that the influences of parameters are partly additive (A-11), or from the theorem that intersecting parameters promote social associations (T-12): The more society's division of labor results from that within rather than that among work organizations, the more probable are intergroup relations among occupations and among organizations (T-29). The more the inequality in administrative authority in society results from that within rather than that among organizations, the more probable are social associations among administrative strata and among organizations (T-29.1). Pronounced differentiation within organizations increases the probabilities of intergroup associations of various kinds with the decreasing size of an occupational group (T-29.2); with increasing administrative rank (T-29.21); and with the decreasing size of the organization, CP (T-29.22).[10] The greater the consolidated inequalities among occupations within work organizations relative to these occupational inequalities

9. T-25.21 is also implied by T-14.3, the probability that elite members have cosmopolitan role sets when parameters intersect.

10. T-29.2 is also implied by T-14.1, the probability that members of small groups have cosmopolitan role sets when parameters intersect. T-29.21 is also implied by T-14.3, the probability that elite members have cosmopolitan role sets when parameters intersect. T-29.22 is also implied by T-25.12, that the small size of a place promotes intergroup relations when there is much heterogeneity within substructures.

among the organizations in society, the more probable are social associations among occupational strata and among organizations (T-29.3).

The same premises have implications for the influences on social relations of the division of labor within the departments of a work organization relative to that among its departments: The more an organization's division of labor results from that within rather than that among its departments, the more probable are social relations among departments as well as occupations (T-30). The more of the inequality in an organization's administrative authority exists within rather than among its departments, the more probable are social relations among departments as well as administrative ranks (T-30.1). The greater the consolidated inequalities among occupational positions within departments relative to those among the departments of an organization, the more probable are social relations among departments as well as occupational strata (T-30.2). In short, the social integration of the various parts of a work organization is furthered by much internal division of labor in its subunits, that is, by an organization of responsibilities on the basis of major purpose rather than specialized work process, in Gulick's (1937) terms.

The general principle is that differentiation of any kind among substructures of any kind promotes integrative social relations among both the substructures and the differentiated social positions. The complementary principle is that the homogeneity of diverse subunits attenuates intergroup relations and accentuates ingroup relations, and processes of social exchange tend to have structural effects reinforcing these tendencies. Such multiplier effects are implied by the axiom that ingroup relations are prevalent (A-1.1) and the theorem that consolidated parameters have structural effects that reinforce the prevalence of ingroup relations (T-21), inasmuch as internal homogeneity of diverse groups entails consolidation: CP, the homogeneity of diverse groups has a structural effect increasing the preponderance of ingroup associations more than additively (T-31). CP, the occupational homogeneity of work organizations, given society's division of labor, has a structural effect increasing the prevalence of social relations within the organizations more than additively (T-31.1). CP, the occupational homogeneity of departments in organizations with substantial division of labor has a structural effect increasing the prevalence of intradepartmental social relations more than additively (T-31.2).

The penetration of social differentiation into substructures exerts a centrifugal social force on social relations that integrates the substructures in the larger social structure. Although inequality hinders and heterogeneity furthers intergroup relations, they both further them if they penetrate into substructures, and so does the penetration of consolidated social differences. The heterogeneity of society is often superficial, confined to large places and groups without penetrating into smaller ones, which minimizes and possibly suppresses the impact of heterogeneity on intergroup relations. The pronounced inequalities in society tend to be accompanied by much smaller inequalities in various social circles, which maximizes the adverse effects of inequalities on social relations among different strata. The lesser variabilities in narrower social circles imply that the correlations of parameters are in large part the result of their concomitant variations among rather than within substructures, and this failure of consolidated social differences to penetrate into substructures maximizes their adverse effects on intergroup relations.

General theorems about penetrating differentiation into substructures are deducible from the premises from which the propositions about the division of labor within organizations and within their subunits are derived, since the implications of these premises pertain generically to substructures of any kind. Indeed, the general theorems below subsume and imply the less general ones about differentiation within communities (T-25 series), organizations (T-29 series), and organizational subunits (T-30 series). Differentiation primarily within substructures on one level—for example, within cities—may constitute differentiation primarily among substructures on the next level—for example, among neighborhoods. If this is taken into consideration, the general inferences of A-1 and A-11, or of T-12, are:

The penetration of society's differentiation into its successive substructures increases the probability of social associations that integrate both the substructures and the differentiated social positions (T-26). The probability of social associations that integrate the differentiated social positions as well as the substructures increases with the increasing penetration of society's heterogeneity into its substructures (T-26.1); with the increasing penetration of society's inequality into its substructures (T-26.2); and with the increasing penetration of the consolidation of parameters in society into its substructures (T-26.3). Corollaries of the last three theorems are: CP, the homogeneity of wide social circles in a heterogeneous society impedes macrosocial integration (26.11). CP, the approximate equality of wide social circles in a society where inequality prevails impedes macrosocial integration (T-26.21). CP, the intersection of parameters within wide social circles when these parameters are consolidated in society at large impedes macrosocial integration (T-26.31). What accounts for the last paradoxical proposition is that the correlation of two parameters is in this case reinforced by their correlations with a third, the one delineating the social circles. Finally, T-26.11 and T-26.21 can be subsumed under one theorem, which is deducible from T-26 or directly from the premises: CP, the internal homogeneity and relative equality of diverse and unequal groups promote ingroup bonds that fragment society (T-26.4).

Small social circles tend to be much more homogeneous and much less unequal than the broader groups that encompass them. But it is possible for substantial heterogeneity and inequality to prevail within narrow substructures. The more the existing heterogeneities and inequalities penetrate into the typically little differentiated narrow substructures of society, the greater their centrifugal force integrating the various segments of society.

Epilogue

The endeavor in this book has been to construct a systematic theory of social structure. I have attempted to explain the patterns of social associations between people in terms of the changing structures of social positions among which people are distributed in communities and societies. The explanations have taken the form of indicating that variations in the way people's dyadic relations become structured can be deduced from analytic propositions referring to the quantitative properties of structures of social positions, jointly with synthetic propositions that are either primitive assumptions about given tendencies or theorems previously derived.

The foundation of the theory is a quantitative conception of social structure, which is viewed as a multidimensional space of social positions among which people are distributed. The positions are distinguished by differences in role relations and social associations, and they are more or less integrated by the actual associations between persons who occupy different positions. The coordinates of the multidimensional space of positions are called structural parameters, which designate specific forms of differentiation, such as income or race, and the extent of differentiation in any one respect is indicated by the population distribution in terms of the parameter. A fundamental assumption underlying the theory is that the structure of differentiated positions exerts much influence on patterns of social relations and particularly on the frequency of intergroup relations that integrate various segments of society.

The central thesis is that extensive intergroup relations depend on the degree to which structural parameters intersect, as indicated by their low correlations, and are inhibited by consolidated status and group differences, which are reflected in strong positive correlations of parameters. Even if one assumes that people invariably prefer to associate with members of their ingroups rather than with outsiders, intersecting parameters, by making ingroup associates in one respect outsiders in others, exert structural constraints to maintain intergroup relations, which is likely to modify ingroup preferences in the long run. In contrast, even if one assumes that people have only a few ingroup preferences and none concerning other social differences, consolidated parameters also impede intergroup relations with respect to the other social differences. An implication of intersecting parameters is that various forms of differentiation, of inequality and heterogeneity, penetrate into the substructures of society. Penetrating differentiation is a centrifugal force that promotes social relations with outsiders.

Variations in structural conditions among societies largely govern the variations in intergroup relations among them, and these variations have undoubtedly profound consequences for the experiences and orientations of individuals, for the integration of society, and for its political institutions. Pluralistic theories of democracy, which emphasize its viability, implicitly assume the existence of intersecting parameters, and Marxist theories of democratic capitalism, which emphasize its lack of viability, implicitly assume the existence of consolidated parameters. The contradictory conclusions of these theories are not surprising given their opposite assumptions; but the assumptions are not made explicit. Making them explicit reveals that the theoretical inferences of the two theories, though not the practical implications drawn from them, are largely parallel, inasmuch as both implicitly infer that the viability of democratic institutions depends on strongly intersecting parameters and is endangered by strongly consolidated ones. And that may well be correct.

Definitions of
Major Terms

Associations The extent or rate of social associations of a group is their number of symmetric dyadic associations, however defined, with a given set of persons (own group, other group, all other groups) divided by the number of group members. Three major kinds are percent married, mean number of associates, and mean amount of time spent in associations.

Close Bond The closeness of a social bond is defined by its approximation to an exclusive bond, of which a person can have only one at a time like spouse or mutual best friend.

Concentration The concentration of a social resource is equivalent to the degree of inequality in its distribution.[1]

Cohesion Ingroup cohesion is the density of (nonexclusive) ingroup associations.[2]

Complexity Structural complexity is a theoretical term referring to the number of positions in a multidimensional space and the distribution of people among them, which is inferred from the degree of intersection of parameters and the degrees of differentiation in various respects.

1. The empirical measure for inequality or concentration is the Gini index:

$$\frac{2\Sigma s_i p_i \, (p_{b_i} - p_{a_i})}{2\Sigma s_i p_i}$$

where p_i is mean status in category i; p_i the fractions of the population in category i; p_{b_i} and p_{a_i} the fractions of the population whose status is below and above that category, respectively; and the sum is taken over all i's.

2. The empirical measure of density of ingroup relations or ingroup cohesion is: $a/(n[n-1])$, where a is the number of ingroup associations (counting every link twice) and n the number of group members.

Consolidation   The consolidation of parameters is the strength of their positive correlation.

Cosmopolitan Role Set   It is defined by a person's having role relations with others in a large number of different social positions.

Density   The density of ingroup relations is the average number of ingroup associates per person divided by the theoretical maximum.[3] It must naturally be distinguished from population density, which is the number of persons per area.

Differentiation   Structural differentiation refers to the distribution of people among social positions, either in terms of a specific parameter or, as a theoretical concept, in terms of all parameters. Its main forms are heterogeneity, inequality, and status diversity. As a theoretical term, it is essentially equivalent to structural complexity.

Discrepancy   The discrepancy in the intergroup associations of two groups is the difference in their rates of association with each other.

Discrimination   It is the tendency of one group to restrict social intercourse with another.

Diversity   Status diversity refers to the great number of different statuses among which a population is distributed. It is the graduated-parameter equivalent of heterogeneity. Its minimum is when all persons occupy the same status; its maximum when every person occupies a different status.[4]

Division of Labor   It is equivalent to occupational heterogeneity.[5]

Elite   The top stratum on any status dimension who constitute a small fraction of the population—usually much less than 1 percent.

Fertility   Net fertility is birth rate minus death rate.

Graduated   A graduated parameter is a status criterion underlying the hierarchical distinctions people make in their role relations.

Group   Groups are broadly defined as all nominal categories of persons who share a social position (social attribute) that influences their role relations. Groups are parts of a society (or other larger collectivity). They have boundaries and no rank-order.

Heterogeneity   It is the distribution of the population among many groups, defined by the probability that two randomly chosen persons do not belong to the same group.[6]

High Stratum   High or higher strata are all persons above median status.

Highest Stratum   The highest strata depend on the existing degree of inequality, being a smaller proportion of the population the greater the inequality. They are the strata whose downward mobility reduces inequality, whereas all other strata's upward mobility reduces it (see note 8, chapter 3).

---

3. See note 2.

4. The empirical measure of heterogeneity, status diversity, or division of labor is: $1 - p_i^2$, where p_i is the fraction of the population in category i and the sum is taken over all i's.

5. See note 4.

6. See note 4.

Immigration   Net immigration is the percent of a group or stratum who have entered it from outside the system during a given period minus the percent who have left it for outside.

Inequality   It is the average difference in relative standing, specifically, the mean status distance in a population divided by twice the mean status, for any criterion of status.[7]

Insulation   The proportion of members of a group or stratum who have no social contact with other groups or strata.

Integration   Macrosocial integration refers to the extensive social associations among different groups and strata, either in terms of a specific parameter of, as a theoretical concept, in terms of all parameters. For specific parameters, it is defined by the ratio of observed intergroup associations to those theoretically expected on the assumption of independence.

Intersection   The degree to which parameters are intersecting is the inverse of their positive correlation. Maximum intersection for nominal parameters is when they are orthogonal; for graduated parameters, when they exhibit a correlation of minus one.

Low Stratum   The low or lower strata are all persons below median status.

Lowest Stratum   The lowest strata are those below modal status in a smoothed frequency distribution.

Middle Stratum   The middle strata are all persons whose status is above median and who do not meet the criterion of highest strata.

Mobility   Social mobility refers to any change of status of the members of a stratum or group relative to the rest of the population. Excess mobility in a given direction can be distinguished from motility.

Motility   Mobility of equal numbers between groups or strata in both directions, which leaves the distribution among positions unaltered.

Nominal   A nominal parameter is a criterion of group membership underlying social distinctions people make in their role relations.

Parameter   Structural parameters are all characteristics that distinguish people and that are reflected in their role relations. They are the coordinates in the multidimensional space of social positions that are implicit in the social distinctions people make in their social associations.

Penetrating Differentiation   It is the degree to which differentiation exists within successive subunits of a social structure.

Position   A social position is any attribute of people implicit in the social distinctions they make in their social associations, that is, any attribute that influences people's role relations. A position is either a status or a group membership defined by a single parameter; more abstractly, it is the combination of statuses and group memberships defined by multiple parameters.

Predominance   The predominance of ingroup relations is the extent to which the observed ingroup associations exceed those theoretically ex-

7. See note 1.

pected on the assumption of independence. It is the complement of prevalence of intergroup relations.

Prevalence The prevalence of intergroup, or of ingroup, relations is the ratio of the observed associations to those theoretically expected on the assumption of independence. Prevalence of intergroup relations is equivalent to macrosocial integration.

Propinquity Physical propinquity is the small distance in space between persons, strata, or groups.

Proximity Proximity is the opposite of social distance, including ingroup versus outgroup, small status distance, and physical propinquity.

Routinization The division of labor mostly into simple routines is manifest in occupational heterogeneity accompanied by low levels of training and skills.

Salience A parameter's salience is indicated by the predominance of ingroup relations, the extent to which observed ingroup associations exceed those theoretically expected on the assumptions of independence.

Segregation Spatial segregation of groups or strata refers to the extent to which they live (or work) in different territories and thus to the average physical distance between their members.

Specialization The division of labor into expert specialties is manifest in occupational heterogeneity accompanied by high levels of training and skills.

Status Social status is a characteristic of people that rank-orders them and affects their role relations in accordance with this ordering. Absolute status refers to the variate itself or the quantity of the social resource it entails, such as dollar income, years of education, amount of power; proportionate status refers to position in the variate's percentile distribution, such as wealthiest decile; relative status refers to some persons' hierarchical position and resources relative to those of others, for example, how much of the total wealth is concentrated in the richest decile. Status distance is the difference in absolute status between persons, strata, or groups.

Stratum Social strata are any arbitrary divisions of the population on the basis of a status criterion. Equidistant strata are defined in terms of equal absolute status intervals, not equal population percentages.

Structure Social structure is a theoretical term defined as the multidimensional space of social positions among which a population is distributed and which reflect and affect people's role relations and social associations.

Substructure A complex structure's substructures are the components into which it is divided by a nominal parameter to analyze social relations and differentiation within and among these substructures.

Successive Subdivision A nominal parameter that divides the population into broad categories and then into narrower categories is said to involve successive subdivision.

Urbanization A place's urbanization is defined by its size and population density; a society's is defined by the proportion of the population living in large and densely populated places.

Work Organization   It is an organization all or nearly all of whose members are employed to perform work, as distinguished from a voluntary association.

APPENDIX B

List of Assumptions

A-1   Social associations are more prevalent among persons in proximate than between those in distant social positions.

A-1.1 Ingroup associations are more prevalent than outgroup associations.

A-1.2 The prevalence of associations declines with increasing status distance.

PA-2   Established role relations are resistant to disruption.

PA-3   Strangers who have a common associate become associates themselves more often than strangers who do not.

PA-4   Associates in other groups and strata encourage and facilitate mobility there.

A-5   The status distribution is positively skewed so that the mean is above the median and the single mode is below it.

PA-6   Superior status is manifest in superordinate roles in social associations.

PA-7   The rates of net fertility of lower strata are no less than those of higher strata.

PA-8   The rates of net immigration from outside the social structure into lower strata are no less than those into higher strata.

A-9   Social associations depend on opportunities for social contacts.

A-10   As rare social practices in a group increase in frequency, group pressures that discourage them subside.

A-11   The influences of various parameters on social associations are partly additive, not entirely contingent on one another.

A-12   Status differences are differences in comparable social resources of generally acknowledged validity in social exchange.

PA-13 Overt interpersonal conflict depends on opportunities for social contacts.

PA-14 A small group's strong commitment to a distinctive ideology enhances ingroup pressures that discourage intergroup relations.

PA-15 A community's size and density are directly correlated with its heterogeneity.

PA-16 The availability of efficient means of transportation depends on financial resources.

PA-17 The division of labor depends on opportunities for communication.

PA-18 An advanced division of labor depends on substantial training of the labor force.

PA-19 Positions of authority over many employees are the source of most authority in contemporary societies.

PA-20 Top positions in organizations with large financial resources are the source of much control over economic resources in contemporary

References

ALKER, HAYWARD R., JR., and BRUCE M. RUSSETT. 1966. "Indices for Comparing Inequality." In *Comparing Nations*, edited by Richard L. Merritt and Stein Rokkan, pp. 349–72. New Haven: Yale University Press.

ANDERSON, GALLATIN. 1957. "Il Comparaggio: The Italian God-Parenthood Complex." *Southwest Journal of Anthropology* 13: 32–53.

ANGELL, ROBERT COOLEY. 1951. "The Moral Integration of American Cities." *American Journal of Sociology* 57 (July, pt. 2).

———. 1974. "The Moral Integration of American Cities, II." *American Journal of Sociology* 80 (November): 607–29.

ARDENER, E. W. 1954. "The Kinship Terminology of a Group of Southern Ibo." *Africa* 24: 85–99.

BARNES, JOHN A. 1949. "Measures of Divorce Frequency in Simple Societies." *Journal of the Royal Anthropological Institute* 79: 37–62.

———. 1954. "Class and Committees in a Norwegian Island Parish." *Human Relations* 7: 39–58.

———. 1957. "Land Rights and Kinship in Two Bremnes Hamlets." *Journal of the Royal Anthropological Institute* 87: 31–56.

BARNETT, LARRY D. 1962. "Research in Interreligious Dating and Marriage." *Marriage and Family Living* 24 (May): 191–94.

BARRON, MILTON L. 1951. "Research on Intermarriage: A Survey of Accomplishments and Prospects." *American Journal of Sociology* 57: 249–55.

BARTON, ALLEN H. 1970. Critique of Hauser's "Context and Consex." *American Journal of Sociology* 76: 515–17.

BEALER, ROBERT C., FERN K. WILLITS, and GERALD W. BENDER. 1963. "Religious Exogamy: A Study of Social Distance." *Sociology and Social Research* 48: 69–79.

BELL, DANIEL. 1958. "The Power Elite—Reconsidered." *American Journal of Sociology* 64 (November): 238–50.

BENEDICT, RUTH. 1936. "Marital Property Rights in Bilateral Society." *American Anthropologist* 38: 368–73.

BERELSON, BERNARD R., PAUL F. LAZARSFELD, and WILLIAM N. MCPHEE. 1954. *Voting*. Chicago: University of Chicago Press.

BERELSON, BERNARD R., and GARY A. STEINER. 1964. *Human Behavior: An Inventory of Scientific Findings*. New York: Harcourt Brace Jovanovich.

BERLE, ADOLF A., JR., and GARDINER C. MEANS. 1932. *The Modern Corporation and Private Property*. New York: Macmillan.

BLALOCK, HUBERT. 1967. *Toward a Theory of Minority Group Relations*. New York: Wiley.

BLAU, PETER M. 1957. "Formal Organization: Dimensions of Analysis." *American Journal of Sociology* 63: 58–59.

————. 1964. *Exchange and Power in Social Life*. New York: Wiley.

————. 1973. *The Organization of Academic Work*. New York: Wiley.

————. 1974. *On the Nature of Organizations*. New York: Wiley.

BLAU, PETER M., and OTIS DUDLEY DUNCAN. 1967. *The American Occupational Structure*. New York: Wiley.

BLAU, PETER M., and ELLEN L. SLAUGHTER. 1971 "Institutional Conditions and Student Demonstrations." *Social Problems* 18: 475–87.

BLAU, PETER M., and RICHARD A. SCHOENHERR. 1971. *The Structure of Organizations*. New York: Basic Books.

BLAU, PETER M., CECILIA MCHUGH FALBE, WILLIAM MCKINLEY, and PHELPS K. TRACY. 1976. "Technology and Organization in Manufacturing." *Administrative Science Quarterly* 21 (March): 20–40.

BLUMER, HERBERT. 1954. "What Is Wrong with Social Theory?" *American Sociological Review* 19: 3–10.

BONACICH, EDNA. 1973. "A Theory of Middleman Minorities." *American Sociological Review* 38: 583–94.

BOTT, ELIZABETH. 1957. *Family and Social Network*. London: Tavistock.

BOUDON, RAYMOND. 1971. *The Uses of Structuralism*. London: Heinemann.

————. 1973. *Education, Opportunity, and Social Inequality: Changing Prospects in Western Society*. New York: Wiley.

BOULDING, KENNETH E. 1962. *Conflict and Defense*. New York: Harper.

BRAITHWAITE, RICHARD B. 1953. *Scientific Explanation: A Study of the Function of Theory, Probability and Law in Science*. Based upon the Tarner Lectures, 1946. Cambridge: At the University Press.

BROOM, LEONARD, and ROBERT G. CUSHING. 1977. "A Modest Test of an Immodest Theory: The Functional Theory of Stratification." *American Sociological Review* 42: 157–69.

BURGESS, ERNEST W., and HARVEY LOCKE. 1953. *The Family*. 2d ed. New York: American Book Co.

BURMA, JOHN H. 1963. "Interethnic Marriage in Los Angeles, 1948–1959." *Social Forces* 42: 156–65.

BURNHAM, JAMES. 1941. *The Managerial Revolution.* New York: John Day.

CANCIAN, FRANCESCA M. 1964. "Interaction Patterns in Zinacanteco Families." *American Sociological Review* 29 (August): 540–50.

CENTERS, RICHARD. 1949. "Marital Selection and Occupational Strata." *American Journal of Sociology* 54: 530–35.

CHAMPERNOWNE, D. G. 1973. *The Distribution of Income between Persons.* Cambridge: At the University Press.

CHRISTENSEN, HAROLD T. 1958. *Marriage Analysis.* 2d ed. New York: Ronald.

CHRISTENSEN, HAROLD T., and ROBERT E. PHILBRICK. 1952. "Family Size as a Factor in the Marital Adjustments of College Couples." *American Sociological Review* 17: 306–12.

COHEN, JERE, LAWRENCE E. HAZELRIGG, and WHITNEY POPE. 1975. "De-Parsonizing Weber: A Critique of Parsons' Interpretation of Weber's Sociology." *American Sociological Review* 40 (April): 229–41.

COLEMAN, JAMES S. 1957. *Community Conflict.* New York: Free Press.

COLLINS, RANDALL. 1975. *Conflict Sociology: Toward an Explanatory Science.* New York: Academic Press

COOLEY, CHARLES H. 1902. *Human Nature and the Social Order.* New York: Scribner.

COSER, ROSE LAUB. 1975. "The Complexity of Roles as a Seedbed of Individual Autonomy." In *The Idea of Social Structure: Papers in Honor of Robert K. Merton,* edited by Lewis A. Coser, pp. 237–64. New York: Harcourt Brace Jovanovich.

COYLE, GRACE L. 1930. *Social Process in Organized Groups.* New York: R. R. Smith.

CROZIER, MICHEL. 1964. *The Bureaucratic Phenomenon.* Chicago: University of Chicago Press.

DAHL, ROBERT A. 1968. "Power." In *International Encyclopedia of the Social Sciences,* edited by David L. Sills, vol. 12, pp. 405–15. New York: Macmillan and Free Press.

DAHRENDORF, RALF. 1959. *Class and Class Conflict in Industrial Society.* Stanford: Stanford University Press.

DAVIS, JAMES A. 1966. "The Campus as a Frog Pond." *American Journal of Sociology* 72: 17–31.

DAVIS, KINGSLEY. 1941. "Intermarriage in Caste Societies." *American Anthropologist* 43: 376–95.

DAVIS, KINGSLEY, and WILBERT E. MOORE. 1945. "Some Principles of Stratification." *American Sociological Review* 10: 242–49.

DOMHOFF, G. WILLIAM. 1967. *Who Rules America?* Englewood Cliffs, N.J.: Prentice-Hall.

DOZIER, B. 1951. "Resistance to Acculturation and Assimilation in an Indian Pueblo." *American Anthropologist* 53: 56–66.

DUNCAN, BEVERLY. 1968. "Trends in Output and Distributions of Schooling." In *Indicators of Social Change,* edited by Eleanor B. Sheldon and Wilbert E. Moore, pp. 601–70. New York: Russell Sage.

DUNCAN, OTIS DUDLEY. 1959. "Human Ecology and Population Studies." In *The Study of Population: An Inventory and Appraisal,* edited by Robert M. Hauser and Otis Dudley Duncan, pp. 678–716. Chicago: University of Chicago Press.

———. 1961. "A Socioeconomic Index for All Occupations." In *Occupations and Social Status,* edited by Albert J. Reiss, pp. 109–38. New York: Free Press.

DUNCAN, OTIS DUDLEY, and BEVERLY DUNCAN. 1955. "A Methodological Analysis of Segregation Indexes." *American Sociological Review* 20: 210–17.

DURKHEIM, EMILE. 1933. *The Division of Labor in Society.* Translated by George Simpson. New York: Free Press.

ELDER, GLEN M. 1962. *Adolescent Achievement and Mobility Aspirations.* Chapel Hill: Institute for Research in Social Sciences, University of North Carolina.

ERBE, BRIGITTE MACH. 1975. "Race and Socioeconomic Segregation." *American Sociological Review* 40: 801–12.

EVANS-PRITCHARD, E. E. 1940. *The Nuer: A Description of the Modes of Livelihood and Political Institutions of a Nilotic People.* London: Oxford University Press, Clarendon Press.

EVERS, FREDERICK T., JOE M. BOHLEN, and RICHARD D. WARREN. 1976. "The Relationships of Selected Size and Structure Indicators in Economic Organizations." *Administrative Science Quarterly* 21: 326–42.

FAUNCE, D., and J. A. BEEGLE. 1948. "Cleavages in a Relatively Homogeneous Group of Rural Youth: An Experiment in the Use of Sociometry in Attaining and Measuring Integration." *Sociometry* 11: 207–16.

FESTINGER, LEON, STANLEY SCHACHTER, and KURT W. BACK. 1950. *Social Pressures in Informal Groups: A Study of Human Factors in Housing.* New York: Harper.

FISCHER, P. H. 1953. "An Analysis of the Primary Group." *Sociometry* 16: 272–76.

FORTES, MEYER. 1945. *The Dynamics of Clanship among the Tallensi.* London: Oxford University Press.

FREIDSON, ELIOT. 1970. *Professional Dominance.* New York: Atherton.

FRENCH, JOHN R. P., and BERTRAM RAVEN. 1959. "The Bases of Social Power." In *Studies in Social Power,* edited by Dorwin Cartwright, pp. 150–67. Ann Arbor: Institute for Social Research, University of Michigan.

FURER-HAIMENDORF, CHRISTOPH VON. 1956. "Elements of Newar Social Structure." *Journal of the Royal Anthropological Institute* 86: 15–38.

GANS, HERBERT J. 1967. *The Levittowners: Ways of Life and Politics in a New Suburban Community.* New York: Pantheon.

———. 1973. *More Equality.* New York: Pantheon.

GLICK, PAUL C. 1960. "Intermarriage and Fertility Patterns among Persons in Major Religious Groups." *Eugenics Quarterly* 7 (March): 31–38.

GLUCKMAN, MAX. 1959. *Custom and Conflict in Africa.* New York: Free Press.

GOLDEN, JOSEPH. 1953. "Characteristics of the Negro-White Intermarried in Philadelphia." *American Sociological Review* 18: 177–83.

GOODE, WILLIAM J. 1964. *The Family*. Englewood Cliffs, N.J.: Prentice-Hall.

GOODNOW, R. E., and R. TAGIURI. 1952. "Religious Ethnocentrism and Its Recognition among Adolescent Boys." *Journal of Abnormal Social Psychology* 47: 316–20.

GOULDNER, ALVIN W. 1970. *The Coming Crisis of Western Sociology*. New York: Basic Books.

GRANOVETTER, MARK S. 1973. "The Strength of Weak Ties." *American Journal of Sociology* 78: 1360–80.

———. 1974. *Getting a Job*. Cambridge: Harvard University Press.

GULICK, LUTHER, and L. URWICK, eds. 1937. *Papers on the Science of Administration*. New York: Institute of Public Administration.

HALPERN, JOEL. 1956. *A Serbian Village*. New York: Columbia University Press.

HARE, A. PAUL. 1976. *Handbook of Small Group Research*. 2d ed. New York: Free Press.

HARARY, FRANK, R. Z. NORMAN, and DORWIN CARTWRIGHT. 1965. *Structural Models: An Introduction to the Theory of Directed Graphs*. New York: Wiley.

HAUSER, ROBERT M. 1970. "Context and Consex: A Cautionary Tale." *American Journal of Sociology* 75: 645–64.

HAUSER, ROBERT M., PETER J. DICKINSON, HARRY P. TRAVIS, and JOHN N. KOFFEL. 1975. "Structural Changes in Occupational Mobility among Men in the United States." *American Sociological Review* 40 (October): 585–98.

HAWKES, GLENN R., LEE BURCHINAL, and BRUCE GARDNER. 1958. "Size of Family and Adjustments of Children." *Marriage and Family Living* 20: 65–68.

HAWLEY, AMOS H. 1950. *Human Ecology: A Theory of Community Structure*. New York: Ronald.

———. 1968. "Human Ecology." In *International Encyclopedia of the Social Sciences*, edited by David L. Sills, vol. 4, pp. 328–37. New York: Macmillan and Free Press.

HEER, DAVID M. 1966. "Negro-White Marriage in the United States." *Journal of Marriage and the Family* 28 (August): 262–73.

HEMPEL, CARL G., and PAUL OPPENHEIM. 1948. "The Logic of Explanation." *Philosophy of Science* 15: 135–75.

HOLLINGSHEAD, AUGUST B. 1949. *Elmtown's Youth*. New York: Wiley.

———. 1950. "Cultural Factors in the Selection of Marriage Mates." *American Sociological Review* 15 (October): 619–27.

HOMANS, GEORGE CASPAR. 1950. *The Human Group*. New York: Harcourt Brace Jovanovich.

———. 1961. *Social Behavior: Its Elementary Forms*. New York: Harcourt Brace Jovanovich.

HOPEN, C. EDWARD. 1958. *The Pastoral Fulbe Family in Gwandu*. London: Oxford University Press.

HUNTER, MONICA. 1933. "The Effect of Contact with Europeans on the Status of Pondo Women." *Africa* 6: 259–76.

JAQUES, ELLIOTT. 1956. *The Measurement of Responsibility*. Cambridge: Harvard University Press.

JENCKS, CHRISTOPHER. 1972. *Inequality.* New York: Basic Books.

KAPLAN, ABRAHAM. 1964. *The Conduct of Inquiry.* San Francisco: Chandler.

KAUT, CHARLES R. 1956. "Western Apache Clan and Phratry Organization." *American Anthropologist* 58: 140–46.

KENNEDY, RUBY JO REEVES. 1944. "Single or Triple Melting-Pot? Intermarriage Trends in New Haven, 1870–1940." *American Journal of Sociology* 49: 331–39.

KERR, CLARK, and ABRAHAM SIEGEL. 1954. "The Interindustry Propensity to Strike: An International Comparison." In *Industrial Conflict,* edited by Arthur Kornhauser et al., pp. 189–212. New York: McGraw-Hill.

KINNEY, ELVA E. 1953. "A Study of Peer Group Social Acceptability at the Fifth-grade Level in a Public School." *Journal of Educational Research* 47: 57–64.

KNIGHT, FRANK H. 1933. *Risk, Uncertainty and Profit.* 2d ed. Boston: Houghton Mifflin.

KOLLER, MARVIN R. 1948. "Residential Propinquity of White Mates at Marriage in Relation to Age and Occupation of Males, Columbus, Ohio, 1938 and 1946." *American Sociological Review* 13: 613–16.

KORTE, CHARLES, and STANLEY MILGRAM. 1970. "Acquaintance Networks between Racial Groups: Application of the Small World Method." *Journal of Personality and Social Psychology* 15: 101–8.

KRAVIS, IRVING B. 1973. "A World of Unequal Incomes." In *Income Inequality,* edited by Sidney Weintraub, pp. 61–80. Special issue of the *Annals of the American Academy of Political and Social Science.* Philadelphia.

KUZNETS, SIMON. 1966. *Modern Economic Growth: Rate Structure and Spread.* Studies in Comparative Economics. New Haven: Yale University Press.

LAMPMAN, ROBERT J. 1962. *The Share of Top Wealth-Holders in National Wealth, 1922–56.* A Study by the National Bureau of Economic Research. Princeton: Princeton University Press.

LASSWELL, HAROLD D., and ABRAHAM KAPLAN. 1950. *Power and Society: A Framework for Political Inquiry.* Yale Law School Studies, vol. 2. New Haven: Yale University Press.

LAUMANN, EDWARD O. 1973. *Bonds of Pluralism: The Form and Substance of Urban Social Networks.* New York: Wiley.

LAZERWITZ, BERNARD. 1961. "Some Factors Associated with Variations in Church Attendance." *Social Forces* 39: 301–9.

LENSKI, GERHARD. 1966. *Power and Privilege: A Theory of Social Stratification.* New York: McGraw-Hill.

LESSA, WILLIAM A. 1950. "Ultihi and the Outer Native World." *American Anthropologist* 52: 27–52.

LÉVI-STRAUSS, CLAUDE. 1963. *Structural Anthropology.* Translated by Claire Jacobson and Brooke Grundfest Schoepf. New York: Basic Books.

———. 1969. *Elementary Structures of Kinship.* Translated by Rodney Needham, James H. Bell, and John R. von Sturmer. Boston: Beacon.

LEWIN, KURT. 1948. *Resolving Social Conflicts.* New York: Harper.

LEWIS, OSCAR. 1958. *Village Life in Northern India.* Urbana: University of Illinois Press.

LIEBERSON, STANLEY. 1972. "Suburbs and Ethnic Residential Patterns." *American Journal of Sociology* 67: 673–81.

LIEBERSON, STANLEY, and LYNN K. HANSEN. 1974. "National Development, Mother Tongue Diversity, and the Comparative Study of Nations." *American Sociological Review* 39 (August): 523–41.

LIPSET, SEYMOUR MARTIN. 1960. *Political Man.* Garden City, N.Y.: Doubleday.

LIPSET, SEYMOUR MARTIN, and REINHARD BENDIX. 1959. *Social Mobility in Industrial Society.* Berkeley and Los Angeles: University of California Press.

LITTLE, KENNETH L. 1957. "The Role of Voluntary Association in West African Urbanization." *American Anthropologist* 59: 579–96.

LOCKE, HARVEY J., GEORGES SABAGH, and MARY MARGARET THOMES. 1957. "Interfaith Marriages." *Social Problems* 4 (April): 329–35.

LOEB, EDWIN M. 1933. "Patrilineal and Matrilineal Organization in Sumatra: The Batak and the Minangkabau." *American Anthropologist* 35: 16–50.

MAISONNEUVE, JEAN. 1966. *Psycho-sociologie des affinités.* Paris: Presses Universitaires de France.

MAUSS, MARCEL. 1954. *The Gift.* New York: Free Press.

MAYER, ADRIAN C. 1953–54. "Fiji Indians Kin-Group: An Aspect of Change in an Immigrant Society." *Oceania* 24: 161–71.

MAYHEW, BRUCE H. 1973. "System Size and Ruling Elites." *American Sociological Review* 38 (August): 468–75.

MAYHEW, BRUCE H., and ROGER L. LEVINGER. 1976a. "On the Emergence of Oligarchy in Human Interaction." *American Journal of Sociology* 81 (March): 1017–49.

———. 1976b. "Size and Density of Interaction in Human Aggregates." *American Journal of Sociology* 82: 86–110.

MCCLELLAND, DAVID C. 1961. *The Achieving Society.* New York: Van Nostrand.

MCKENZIE, RODERICK D. 1925. "The Ecological Approach to the Study of the Human Community." In *The City,* by Robert E. Park, Ernest W. Burgess, and Roderick D. McKenzie, pp. 63–79. Chicago: University of Chicago Press.

MERCIER, PAUL. 1951. "The Social Role of Circumcision among the Besorube." *American Anthropologist* 53: 326–37.

MERTON, ROBERT K. 1941. "Intermarriage and the Social Structure: Fact and Theory." *Psychiatry* 4: 361–74.

———. 1948. "The Social Psychology of Housing." In *Current Trends in Social Psychology,* edited by Wayne Dennis et al., pp. 163–217. Pittsburgh: University of Pittsburgh Press.

———. 1968. *Social Theory and Social Structure.* New York: Free Press.

———. 1972. "Insiders and Outsiders." *American Journal of Sociology* 78: 9–47.

———. 1975. "Structural Analysis in Sociology." In *Approaches to the Study of Social Structure,* edited by Peter M. Blau. New York: Free Press.

MERTON, ROBERT K., PATRICIA S. WEST, and MARIE JAHODA. 1951. "Patterns of Social Life: Explorations in the Sociology and the Social Psychology of Housing." Paper prepared for the Bureau of Applied Social Research.

MILLER, HERMAN P. 1966. *Income Distribution in the United States.* A 1960 Census Monograph. Washington: Government Printing Office.

MILLS, C. WRIGHT. 1956. *The Power Elite.* New York: Oxford University Press.

MITCHELL, J. CLYDE. 1969. "The Concept and Use of Social Networks." In *Social Networks in Urban Situations,* edited by J. Clyde Mitchell, pp. 1–50. Manchester: Manchester University Press.

MOORE, BARRINGTON, JR. 1966. *Social Origins of Dictatorship and Democracy.* Boston: Beacon.

MORRIS, T. P., and L. BLOM-COPPER. 1964. *A Calendar of Murder.* London: M. Joseph.

MURDOCK, GEORGE P. 1937. "Comparative Data on the Division of Labor by Sex." *Social Forces* 15: 551–53.

———. 1949. *Social Structure.* New York: Macmillan.

MURPHY, ROBERT F. 1956. "Matrilocality and Patrilineality in Mundurucu Society." *American Anthropologist* 58: 414–34.

NADEL, S. F. 1946. "Land Tenure on the Eritrean Plateau." *Africa* 16: 1–22.

———. 1957. *The Theory of Social Structure.* New York: Free Press.

NAGEL, ERNEST. 1961. *The Structure of Science.* New York: Harcourt Brace Jovanovich.

NATIONAL OPINION RESEARCH CENTER. 1947. "Jobs and Occupations: A Popular Evaluation." *Opinion News* 9: 3–13.

NEWCOMB, THEODORE M. 1961. *The Acquaintance Process.* New York: Holt, Rinehart & Winston.

OBERG, KALERVO. 1955. "Types of Social Structure among the Lowland Tribes of South and Central America." *American Anthropologist* 57: 472–87.

PARSONS, TALCOTT. 1937. *The Structure of Social Action.* New York: McGraw-Hill.

———. 1951. *The Social System.* New York: Free Press.

———. 1963. "On the Concept of Political Power." *Proceedings of the American Philosophical Society* 107 (June): 232–62.

PARSONS, TALCOTT, and NEIL J. SMELSER. 1956. *Economy and Society: A Study in the Integration of Economic and Social Theory.* New York: Free Press.

PARTEN, MILDRED B. 1933. "Social Play among Preschool Children." *Journal of Abnormal and Social Psychology* 28: 136–47.

PEARSON, KARL. 1907. "Reply to Certain Criticisms of Mr. G. U. Yule." *Biometrika* 5: 470–76.

POPPER, KARL R. 1959. *The Logic of Scientific Discovery.* New York: Basic Books.

PORTES, ALEJANDRO, and KENNETH L. WILSON. 1976. "Black-White Differences in Educational Attainment." *American Sociological Review* 41: 414–31.

PRZEWORSKI, ADAM, and HENRY TEUNE. 1970. *The Logic of Comparative Inquiry.* New York: Wiley-Interscience.

RADCLIFFE-BROWN, A. R. 1940. "On Social Structure." *Journal of the Royal Anthropological Institute* 70: 1–12.

RAINWATER, LEE. 1974. *What Money Buys: Inequality and the Social Meanings of Income.* New York: Basic Books.

RUSHING, WILLIAM A. 1976. "Profit and Nonprofit Orientations and the Differentiations-Coordination Hypothesis for Organizations." *American Sociological Review* 41: 676–91.

SAHLINS, MARSHALL D. 1957. "Land Use and the Extended Family in Moala, Fiji." *American Anthropologist* 59: 449–62.

SCHAPERA, I. 1946. "Some Features in the Social Organization of the Tloka (Bechuanaland Protectorate)." *Southwest Journal of Anthropology* 2: 16–47.

SCHNEPP, G. J., and A. M. YUI. 1955. "Cultural and Marital Adjustment of Japanese War Brides." *American Journal of Sociology* 61: 48–50.

SCOTT, J., and M. EL-ASSAL. 1969. "Multiversity, University Size, University Quality, and Student Protest: An Empirical Study." *American Sociological Review* 34: 702–9.

SEEMAN, MELVIN. 1956. "Intellectual Perspective and Adjustment to Minority Status." *Social Problems* 3 (January): 142–53.

SIMMEL, GEORG. 1908. *Soziologie*. Leipzig: Duncker & Humblot.

————. 1950. *The Sociology of Georg Simmel*. Translated, edited, and with an introduction by Kurt H. Wolff. New York: Free Press.

————. 1955. *Conflict and the Web of Group Affiliations*. New York: Free Press.

SIMON, HERBERT A. 1065. "The Architecture of Complexity." In *General Systems: Yearbook of the Society for General Systems Research*, edited by Ludwig von Bertalanffy and Anatol Rapoport, vol. 10, pp. 63–76. Bedford, Mass.

SMITH, M. 1944. "Some Factors in the Friendship Selections of High School Students." *Sociometry* 7: 303–10.

SPILERMAN, SEYMOUR. 1971. "The Causes of Racial Disturbances: Tests of an Explanation." *American Sociological Review* 36: 427–42.

STINCHCOMBE, ARTHUR. 1975. "Social Structure and Politics." In *Handbook of Political Science*, edited by Nelson W. Polsby and Fred I. Greenstein, vol. 3, pp. 557–662. Reading, Mass.: Addison-Wesley.

STOUFFER, SAMUEL. 1955. *Communism, Conformity, and Civil Liberties: A Cross-Section of the Nation Speaks Its Mind*. Garden City, N.Y.: Doubleday.

STOUFFER, SAMUEL, EDWARD A. SUCHMAN, LELAND C. DEVINNEY, SHIRLEY A. STAR, and ROBIN M. WILLIAMS, JR. 1949. *The American Soldier*, vol. 1, *Adjustment during Army Life*. Princeton: Princeton University Press.

STRAUSS, ANSELM L. 1954. "Strain and Harmony in American-Japanese War-Bride Marriages." *Marriage and Family Living* 16: 99–106.

SUNDAL, A. PHILIP, and THOMAS C. McCORMICK. 1951. "Age at Marriage and Mate Selection: Madison, Wisconsin, 1937–1943." *American Sociological Review* 16: 37–48.

TALMON-GARBER, Y. 1956. "The Family in Collective Settlements." In *Transactions of the Third World Congress of Sociology*, vol. 4, *Changes in the Family*, pp. 116–26. London: International Sociological Association.

TAWNEY, R. H. 1931. *Equality*. New York: Harcourt Brace Jovanovich.

TAYLOR, CHARLES L., and MICHAEL C. HUDSON. 1971. *World Handbook of Political and Social Indicators*. Ann Arbor, Mich.: Inter-University Consortium for Political Research.

THEODORSON, G. A. 1953. "Acceptance of Industrialization and Its Attendant Consequences for the Social Patterns of Non-Western Societies." *American Sociological Review* 18 (October): 477–84.

THOMAS, JOHN L. 1951. "The Factor of Religion in the Selection of Marriage Mates." *American Sociological Review* 16: 487–91.

TRAVERS, JEFFREY, and STANLEY MILGRAM. 1969. "Experimental Study of the Small World Problem." *Sociometry* 32 (December): 425–43.

TRIST, E. L., and K. W. BAMFORTH. 1951. "Some Social and Psychological Consequences of the Longwall Method of Coal-Getting." *Human Relations* 4: 3–38.

TROELTSCH, ERNST. 1931. *The Social Teaching of the Christian Churches*. New York: Macmillan.

UDY, STANLEY H., JR. 1959. "The Structure of Authority in Non-Industrial Production Organizations." *American Journal of Sociology* 64: 582–84.

U.S. BUREAU OF THE CENSUS. 1917. *Abstract of the Census of Manufacturers*. Washington: Government Printing Office.

———. 1960. *Historical Statistics of the United States, Colonial Times to 1957*. Washington: Government Printing Office.

———. 1971. *Census of Manufacturers, 1967*, vol. 1, *Summary and Subject Statistics*. Washington: Government Printing Office.

———. 1973. *Statistical Abstract of the United States, 1973*. 94th ed. Washington: U.S. Department of Commerce.

U.S. CABINET COMMITTEE ON PRICE STABILITY. 1969. *Studies by the Staff (January)*. Washington: Government Printing Office.

U.S. DEPARTMENT OF DEFENSE. 1975. *Annual Defense Department Report: FY 1976 and FY 1977*. Washington: Government Printing Office.

VEBLEN, THORSTEIN B. 1919. "The Intellectual Pre-eminence of Jews in Modern Europe." *Political Science Quarterly* 34: 33–42.

WAGNER, GUNTHER. 1939. "The Changing Family among the Bantu Kavirondo." *Africa* 12 (supp.).

WARNER, W. LLOYD, and PAUL S. LUNT. 1941. *The Social Life of a Modern Community*. New Haven: Yale University Press.

WEBER, MAX. 1946. *From Max Weber: Essays in Sociology*. Translated and edited by Hans H. Gerth and C. Wright Mills. New York: Oxford University Press.

———. 1947. *The Theory of Social and Economic Organization*. Translated by A. M. Henderson and Talcott Parsons; edited with an introduction by Talcott Parsons. New York: Oxford University Press.

———. 1968. *Economy and Society*. 4th ed. 3 vols. Translated by E. Fischoff et al.; edited by Guenther Roth and Claus Wittich. Totowa, N.J.: Bedminster.

WHITE, HARRISON C., SCOTT A. BOORMAN, and RONALD L. BREIGER. 1976. "Social Structure from Multiple Networks, I: Blockmodels of Roles and Positions." *American Journal of Sociology* 81 (January): 730–80.

WHYTE, WILLIAM F. 1943. *Street Corner Society: The Social Structure of an Italian Slum*. Chicago: University of Chicago Press.

WILLIAMS, ROBIN M., JR. 1964. *Strangers Next Door: Ethnic Relations in American Communities.* Englewood Cliffs, N.J.: Prentice-Hall.

WILLITS, FERN K., ROBERT C. BEALER, and GERALD W. BENDER. 1963. "Interreligious Marriage among Pennsylvania Rural Youth." *Marriage and Family Living* 25 (November): 433–38.

WINCH, ROBERT F. 1958. *Mate Selection: A Study of Complementary Needs.* New York: Harper.

WIRTH, LOUIS, and HERBERT GOLDHAMER. 1944. "Negro-White Intermarriage in Recent Times." In *Characteristics of the American Negro*, edited by Otto Klineberg, pp. 276–300.

YASUDA, SABURO. 1964. "A Methodological Inquiry into Social Mobility." *American Sociological Review* 29: 16–23.

Yearbook of Labour Statistics. 1972. Geneva: International Labor Office.

YINGER, J. MILTON. 1968. "A Research Note on Interfaith Marriage Statistics." *Journal for the Scientific Study of Religion* 7: 97–103.

ZEITLIN, MAURICE. 1974. "Corporate Ownership and Control: The Large Corporation and the Capitalist Class." *American Journal of Sociology* 79: 1073–1119.

Index of Names

Alker, H. R., 58, 58n
Anderson, G., 88
Angell, R. C., 88, 114
Ardener, E. W., 25

Back, K. W., 90
Bamforth, K. W., 135
Barnes, J. A., 2, 25, 88
Barnett, L. D., 24
Barron, M. L., 24, 88
Barton, A. H., 151n
Bealer, R. C., 20, 25, 37
Beegle, J. A., 37
Bell, D., 229
Bender, G. W., 20, 25, 37
Bendix, R., 40
Benedict, R., 138
Berelson, B. R., 24n, 111
Berle, A. A., 229
Blalock, H., 97
Blau, J. R., 190n
Blau, P. M., 14, 32, 37, 64, 65, 140–41,
    149, 151n, 189, 189n, 194, 204, 210,
    226, 228n, 229, 231n, 238n
Blom-Cooper, L., 114
Blumer, H., 12

Bohlen, J. M., 231n
Bonacich, E., 97
Bott, E., 92, 138
Boudon, R., 2n, 212, 213, 247
Boulding, K. E., 139
Braithwaite, R. B., 12, 13n, 14, 244,
    244n, 246, 247
Broom, L., 231n
Burchinal, L., 135
Burgess, E. W., 41
Burma, J. H., 20, 24–25, 88, 143
Burnham, J., 229

Cancian, F. M., 135
Centers, R., 37, 49
Champernowne, D. G., 64n
Christensen, H. T., 91, 135
Cohen, J., 221n
Coleman, J. S., 117
Collins, R., 232
Cooley, C. H., 11
Coser, R. L., 96
Coyle, G. I., 135
Crozier, M., 207
Cushing, R. G., 231n

295

Index of Subjects

Abstraction, 1–2, 12–16, 62, 63, 101, 158, 209, 218, 220, 244, 246–47
Administrative
  hierarchy, 51–52, 205, 206–7
  power, 221, 223–24, 225–34, 239, 241, 260
Age, 4, 8, 37, 47, 73, 159, 179
Ascription, 39, 41, 44, 70, 107, 132, 254
Assets: *see* Wealth
Assimilation, 35–36, 39, 41, 119, 120, 138–39, 253
Association time, 20–22, 24, 27–28, 33, 34, 42, 47, 48*n*–49*n*, 135, 137, 156, 161, 250
Assumptions, 281–82; *see also* the following index of assumptions and theorems
Authority, 8, 52, 59, 193, 194, 203, 204, 206–7, 213, 215, 221, 223–24, 225–34, 241, 260, 270, 271
Automation, 194

Balance theory, 38
Barriers, social, 10–11, 29, 79, 87, 93, 116, 128–30, 168–69, 239, 257, 268
Bifurcation of skills, 189–90

Blacks, 20–21, 22–23, 25–26, 32, 79, 92, 114, 115, 142–44, 150–51, 162–63, 180
Bond: *see* Close relations; Ingroup relations; Intimate; Subgroup cohesion
Boundaries, 7, 16, 46, 145, 159, 174, 175, 232–33, 251, 255

Capitalism, 68–69, 229–32, 274
Caste, 107
Catholics, 24–25, 26, 37, 79, 123, 130
Centrifugal force, 206, 207, 271–73
Ceteris paribus proposition, 38*n*, 39, 65, 247–48, 255–56
Change
  conditions of, 40–41, 117–24, 125, 140
  in heterogeneity, 78–83
  historical, 156–58, 186*n*, 192–95, 239–40
  in inequality, 60–73, 255–56
  resistance to, 96, 117, 121–22, 267
  in salience, 33–36, 39–40, 43, 251
  in size, 40, 54–55, 70, 132–34, 229, 231–34, 241–42, 254
Class, 3, 18, 37, 48, 50, 71–73, 107, 132, 158–59, 232–34, 242, 257

Index of Assumptions
and Theorems

Boldface numbers indicate the page on which the
assumption is introduced or is initially derived.